THE DREYFUS AFFAIR

Art, Truth, and Justice

Edited by

Norman L. Kleeblatt

UNIVERSITY OF CALIFORNIA PRESS

Berkeley · *Los Angeles* · *London*

The Dreyfus Affair: Art, Truth, and Justice has been published on the occasion of the opening of the exhibition organized by the Jewish Museum, New York. The exhibition dates are September 13, 1987–January 15, 1988. Exhibition staff: Norman L. Kleeblatt, Curator; Phillip Dennis Cate, Consulting Curator for Graphic Arts; Anita Friedman, Senior Research Associate; Irene Z. Schenck, Research Associate; Stephen Brown, Exhibition Coordinator.

University of California Press
Berkeley and Los Angeles, California

University of California Press, Ltd.
London, England

Copyright © 1987 by The Regents of the University of California

Library of Congress Cataloging-in-Publication Data

The Dreyfus affair.

Catalog of a loan exhibition held at the Jewish Museum.
Bibliography: p.
1. Dreyfus, Alfred, 1859–1935—Exhibitions. 2. France—Politics and government—1870–1940—Exhibitions. 3. Antisemitism—France—History—19th century—Exhibitions. 4. Treason—France—History—19th century—Exhibitions. 5. France—Intellectual life—19th century—Exhibitions. 6. Artists—France—Political activity—History—19th century—Exhibitions. 7. Authors, French—Political activity—History—19th century—Exhibitions. I. Kleeblatt, Norman L. II. Jewish Museum (New York, N.Y.)
DC354.D88   1987   944.06   87–16241
ISBN 0–520–05939–5 (alk. paper)

Printed in the United States of America

1 2 3 4 5 6 7 8 9

Contents

Chronology of the Dreyfus Affair

COMPILED BY ANITA FRIEDMAN

1893

JANUARY 1   Dreyfus begins probationary term with the General Staff of the Army. Rotates through the bureaus of the Ministry of War.

13   Henry returns to the Statistical Section (a division of the General Staff concerned with intelligence and espionage).

1894

JUNE 24   Sadi Carnot, President of the Republic, assassinated by an anarchist.

JULY 20   Esterhazy approaches Schwarzkoppen at the German Embassy to offer his services.

AUGUST 15   Esterhazy delivers revised Artillery mobilization plans and receives payment from Schwarzkoppen.

MID TO LATE SEPTEMBER   Documents intercepted at the German Embassy sent to Henry.

27   The bordereau arrives at the offices of the Statistical Section.

OCTOBER 6   Dreyfus falls under suspicion as author of the bordereau.

13   Experts fail to agree if handwriting on bordereau is Dreyfus's.

Mercier orders Dreyfus to the Ministry of War the following Monday on a pretext.

14   War Office develops plans for Dreyfus's arrest and imprisonment.

15   Dreyfus accused of high treason and arrested.

29   *La Libre Parole* announces the arrest of an officer accused of espionage.

31   *Le Soir* identifies arrested officer as Dreyfus.

NOVEMBER 14–29   D'Ormescheville conducts investigation of charges.

DECEMBER 3   D'Ormescheville submits report asserting the likelihood of Dreyfus's guilt.

4   Court-martial ordered; Dreyfus allowed to write to his wife for the first time.

19–22   Dreyfus's first court-martial; held in closed session. Sentenced to perpetual deportation and military degradation.

31   Petition for appeal rejected. Du Paty de Clam attempts to obtain a confession.

1895

JANUARY 5   Degradation of Dreyfus in the courtyard of the Ecole Militaire.

17   Félix Faure elected President of France.

FEBRUARY 22   Dreyfus departs France for French Guiana.

APRIL 13   Dreyfus placed in solitary confinement on Devil's Island.

JULY 1   Picquart named head of the Statistical Section.

1896

MID-MARCH   Picquart receives a document (the petit bleu) revealing Esterhazy as a German spy.

LATE AUGUST   Picquart establishes Esterhazy as the author of the bordereau.

SEPTEMBER 6–OCTOBER 20   After a false report of his escape, Dreyfus shackled to his bed every night.

SEPTEMBER 14   *L'Eclair* publishes a detailed article revealing that a secret file had been given to the judges at Dreyfus's court-martial.

18   Lucie Dreyfus petitions the Chamber of Deputies demanding justice.

Henry begins to tamper with documents in order to construct evidence against Dreyfus and later to discredit Picquart.

OCTOBER 27   Gonse and de Boisdeffre order Picquart away from Paris on a contrived mission.

NOVEMBER 6   Bernard Lazare launches the revisionist campaign with the publication, in Brussels, of *A Judicial Error: The Truth about the Dreyfus Case.*

10   *Le Matin* publishes a photograph of the bordereau.

1897

FEBRUARY   With secret subsidies from the duc d'Orleans, a royalist pretender, Jules Guérin organizes the Ligue Antisémitique Français.

EARLY APRIL   Picquart prepares a statement to be opened in the event of his death.

MARCH 4 Picquart-Henry duel.

APRIL 2 Zola verdict annulled and sent for remand.

MAY 8, 22 National elections. Most politicians remain silent on the Dreyfus Affair.

JULY 7 Cavaignac, Minister of War, reads forged Henry documents to the Chamber of Deputies as proof of Dreyfus's guilt.

9 Picquart attacks Cavaignac's evidence in a letter to the Prime Minister.

12 Esterhazy arrested and charged with swindling his nephew and sending forged telegrams to Picquart.

13 Picquart arrested on charge of divulging secret military documents.

18–19 Zola convicted again; flees to England.

AUGUST 5 Grand Jury of the Court of Appeal finds against Picquart in his civilian charge against du Paty for complicity with Esterhazy in forging telegrams.

12 Grand Jury dismisses forgery charge brought against Esterhazy and his mistress by Picquart.

13 Henry's forgery of a principal document discovered.

27 Esterhazy discharged from army for "habitual misconduct."

30–31 Henry confined after confessing to forgeries and commits suicide. General de Boisdeffre resigns.

SEPTEMBER 1 Esterhazy flees.

3 Cavaignac resigns. Madame Dreyfus again appeals to the Chamber of Deputies.

25 Poet-activist Paul Déroulède revives the Ligue des Patriots as an anti-Dreyfusard organization.

26 Cabinet sends Lucie's request for an appeal to the criminal chamber of the Court of Appeal.

DECEMBER 8 Picquart, accused of forgery and violation of the espionage law, wins a High Court ruling that effectively transfers his case to a civilian court.

DECEMBER 17, 1898– *La Libre Parole* solicits contributions to finance Madame Henry's suit
JANUARY 15, 1899 against Joseph Reinach (*le monument Henry*). Reinach had accused Henry of being Esterhazy's accomplice. Over 25,000 contributions were received.

31 Anti-Dreyfusard intellectuals found the Ligue de la Patrie Française.

1899

FEBRUARY 10 The Chamber of Deputies passes the law requiring that the decision on revision be rendered by the united chambers of the Court of Appeal.

16 Félix Faure dies and is succeeded two days later by Emile Loubet.

23 Followers of Déroulède and Guérin fail to induce troops in President Faure's funeral procession to stage a coup.

MAY 29 Combined chambers of the Court of Appeal begin to hear Dreyfus's appeal for a new court-martial.

JUNE 1	Du Paty de Clam arrested.
3	Court of Appeal revokes the verdict of 1894 and orders Dreyfus to another court-martial in Rennes.
	Esterhazy, interviewed in *Le Matin,* confesses to authorship of bordereau but states he was under orders known to the Secretary of War and the Army Chief of Staff.
4	Protesting the decision of the Court of Appeal, a royalist assaults President Loubet at the Auteil races. Other royalists and anti-Semitic demonstrators battle with the police.
5	Zola returns from England.
9	Dreyfus sails for France. Picquart freed.
11	One hundred thousand leftists stage a peaceful counter-demonstration at Longchamps. Police attack the crowd.
22	Waldeck-Rousseau forms a new government termed by the opposing nationalists "the Dreyfus Ministry."
AUGUST 7–SEPTEMBER 9	Court-martial in Rennes. Dreyfus found guilty with extenuating circumstances and sentenced to ten years.
AUGUST 11–SEPTEMBER 20	Guérin barricades himself in his headquarters on the rue de Chabrol after an aborted royalist coup planned to coincide with General Mercier's testimony in Rennes.
19	Dreyfus accepts a pardon. Scheurer-Kestner dies.
21	Minister of War Galliffet issues order: "The incident is over."
NOVEMBER 17	Waldeck-Rousseau proposes general amnesty bill for all but Dreyfus, who is left free to pursue a revision of the Rennes verdict.

1900

JANUARY 22	Dissolution of the Assumptionist order.
APRIL 14	Paris World's Fair opens.
MAY 22	Chamber of Deputies opposes any government attempts to reopen the case.
28	Minister of War Galliffet resigns. He is succeeded by General André.
DECEMBER 24	Chamber of Deputies version of Amnesty Law covering all criminal acts and lawsuits arising out of the Affair is passed by the Senate.

1901

JULY 1	Law of Associations passed; establishes a method for dissolving religious orders.

1902

JUNE 19 André pushes for reform of the army; the Senate begins debate on proposal to reduce national military service from three to two years.

27 One hundred twenty Church schools closed.

SEPTEMBER 29 Zola dies of accidental asphyxiation at home.

1903

APRIL 6–7 Jaurès seizes opportunity in the Chamber to propose reconsideration of the Rennes verdict.
André begins War Office investigation of all documents.

NOVEMBER 26 Dreyfus petitions for retrial based on findings of the André inquiry.

1904

MARCH 5 Criminal Chamber agrees to review Rennes verdict.

JULY 7 All teaching by religious orders banned.

NOVEMBER 15 General André resigns in scandal over promotions.

28 Criminal Chamber refers Dreyfus case to combined chambers of the Court of Appeal.

1905

APRIL 21 Two-year service bill passed.

JULY 3 Parliament passes law separating church and state.

1906

JULY 12 Court of Appeal annuls Rennes verdict without remand.

13 Parliament votes to reinstate Dreyfus as a captain and Picquart as a brigadier general.

21 Dreyfus receives the cross of Knight of the Legion of Honor in a courtyard of the Ecole Militaire.

OCTOBER 25 Clemenceau becomes Prime Minister; appoints Picquart Minister of War.

1908

JUNE 4 Zola's ashes are transferred to the Pantheon. Gregori fires two shots at Dreyfus, slightly wounding him in the arm.

BERTILLON

BOISDEFFRE

CLEMENCEAU

DEMANGE

Annotated List of Characters

COMPILED BY ELIZABETH CATS

BARRÈS, MAURICE (1862–1923)
Anti-Dreyfusard. Man of letters. Boulangist deputy for Nancy from 1889 to 1893. Worked for *La Patrie*; attended Rennes trial for *Le Journal*. In 1898, he became one of the founders and leaders of the Ligue de la Patrié Française (League of the French Fatherland), formed in opposition to the League of the Rights of Man.

BASTIAN, MARIE-CAUDRON
Agent for Statistical Section; employed in the German Embassy. Her overt job as a charwoman enabled her to search the garbage bags and hand over scraps of paper and fragments.

BERTILLON, ALPHONSE (1853–1914)
Chief of the Identification Department of the Judicial Police. Testified at 1894 trial and at Rennes that the bordereau was in Dreyfus's handwriting.

BILLOT, GENERAL JEAN-BAPTISTE (1828–1907)
Life Senator; minister of war, 1882–1883, 1896–1898. He had taken a big part in reconstructing the French Army in 1875. Sent Picquart away from the War Office and later ordered his arrest. He remained convinced of Dreyfus's guilt.

BLUM, LÉON (1872–1950)
Dreyfusard writer. He became associated with the Socialist Jean Jaurès during the Dreyfus Affair and assisted Labori in preparing for Zola's trial. In 1936 he became France's first Jewish and Socialist premier.

BOISDEFFRE, GENERAL RAOUL FRANÇOIS CHARLES LE MOUTON DE (1839–1919)
Army chief of staff from 1893 to 1898. He remained convinced that "Dreyfus's guilt has always been a certainty." At Zola's trial, in order to avoid producing a false document, he maintained that war with Germany was at stake. He was stunned at the confession of Colonel Henry and resigned from the army in 1898.

BOULANGER, GENERAL GEORGES (1837–1891)
Minister of War 1886–1887. In 1889 he tried unsuccessfully to seize the reins of government. Bredin writes of him: "He was a man who seemed to unite all of France's malcontents." After his defeat he fled to Brussels and in 1890 dissolved the Comité National Boulangistre. In 1891 he shot himself at the grave of his mistress.

CASIMIR-PÉRIER, JEAN (1847–1907)
Prime Minister in 1893, then President of the Republic, 1894–1895.

CAVAIGNAC, GODEFROY (1853–1905)
Anti-Dreyfusard; member of a famous Republican family. Minister of War 1895–1896; 1898. After investigating the documents in the secret file on Dreyfus, he ordered Henry's arrest. Though convinced that discovery of forgeries would make no difference vis-à-vis Dreyfus's guilt, he resigned from the War Office in 1898.

CLEMENCEAU, GEORGES (1841–1929)
Dreyfusard leader, later Minister of Interior, then Prime Minister in 1906; Formed a "victory cabinet" in 1917 and was one of the main figures at the Peace of Versailles. During the Dreyfus Affair, as political editor of *L'Aurore,* he wrote scathing articles protesting Dreyfus's innocence. He came up with the title of Zola's article "J'Accuse." Like many other Dreyfusards, he was incensed over the amnesty verdict at Rennes.

D'ORMESCHEVILLE, MAJOR BEXON
Conducted pretrial investigation; judge advocate of the first court-martial.

DRUMONT

ESTERHAZY

HENRY

MME. HENRY

DEMANGE, EDGAR (1841–1925)

Lawyer for Alfred Dreyfus at 1894 Court Martial. Represented Mathieu Dreyfus at Esterhazy trial. During the Rennes trial served as defense counsel together with Labori. Among Dreyfus's supporters, the two men represented opposing factions regarding defense strategies.

DÉROULÈDE, PAUL (1846–1914)

Anti-Dreyfusard poet; Boulangist Deputy; leader of the Ligue des Patriotes, which attempted an unsuccessful coup at Félix Faure's funeral. He had planned massive demonstrations before the Rennes trial, but was arrested the night before. After Dreyfus's pardon he was condemned to ten years in exile.

DREYFUS, CAPTAIN ALFRED (1859–1935)

After eight years of service as an officer in the artillery and the cavalry, Alfred Dreyfus was admitted to the Ecole de Guerre, graduating ninth in a class of eighty-one. In 1894, Captain Dreyfus was a probationer on the General Staff when he was accused of passing military secrets to the Germans. Convicted of treason, he was sent to Devil's Island. A second court-martial in 1899 convicted him again, but he accepted a pardon with the proviso that he could continue his attempts to prove his innocence. His wife Lucie (1869–1945) and his brother Mathieu (1857–1930) organized his defense and later initiated the movement for revision. He was finally rehabilitated in 1906.

DRUMONT, ÉDOUARD (1844–1917)

Anti-Semitic leader. In 1886 he wrote *La France Juive,* in which he attacked Jewish finance and described medieval anti-Semitic legends. In 1892 he launched the journal *La Libre Parole* in which he attacked Jews in the army and later the Dreyfusards until Dreyfus's reinstatement in 1906.

DU PATY DE CLAM, MAJOR MERCIER, MARQUIS (1853–1916)

General Staff officer. In 1894, after Dreyfus's arrest, he was the first to declare that the bordereau was in Dreyfus's hand, and testified against him at the trial. In 1897 he became personal assistant to General Gonse, who, together with Colonel Henry, involved him in intrigues with Esterhazy. As the intermediary of the General Staff, du Paty de Clam met with Esterhazy in Montsouris Park, and assured him of his safety if he obeyed orders from the military.

ESTERHAZY, MARIE-CHARLES-FERDINAND WALSIN- (1847–1923)

Infantry officer; grandson of illegitimate member of French branch of Austro-Hungarian Esterhazys. He married into aristocracy, and spent his whole life gambling, amassing debts, and running after women. In 1894 he approached German attaché Schwarzkoppen and began to spy for him. He was the author of the bordereau for which Dreyfus was convicted. When suspicion began to be focused on him, Colonel Henry de-

cided that Esterhazy should be warned of his forthcoming arrest, and arranged the secret meeting in Montsouris Park with Gribelin and du Paty de Clam, who assured him of the support of the General Staff. In order to save himself from a court-martial, Esterhazy invented a veiled lady and claimed she had sent him a photograph of a document given to her by Picquart. Esterhazy was acquitted. After hearing of Colonel Henry's confession and suicide, he fled to England, where he remained until his death.

FAURE, FRANÇOIS FÉLIX (1841–1899)

Anti-Dreyfusard. President of the Republic 1895–1899.

FORZINETTI, MAJOR FERDINAND

Governor of Cherche-Midi prison; a Dreyfusard who insisted on humane treatment of the captain during his imprisonment there.

GALLIFFET, GENERAL GASTON, MARQUIS DE (1830–1909)

An ardent Republican; Minister of War from 1899 to 1900. After Dreyfus's pardon at the Rennes trial, he sent a manifesto to the army and to the newspapers declaring "the incident is closed" and prepared the way for an amnesty to be given to all officers involved.

LABORI   LAZARE   MÉLINE   MERCIER

GONSE, GENERAL CHARLES-ARTHUR (1838–1917)

Deputy Chief of Staff; leading anti-Dreyfusard among army officers; life long friend of General de Boisdeffre. He gave evidence at 1894 trial that the bordereau was in Dreyfus's writing, and though informed by Picquart of the petit bleu and other evidence, he refused to believe it. He involved du Paty de Clam in communicating to Esterhazy that he would be defended by the Army. After Colonel Henry's confession, Gonse was replaced and put on half pay.

GRIBELIN, FELIX

Archivist in Statistical Section; took part in meeting at Montsouris Park (with Esterhazy), disguised wearing dark blue spectacles.

HANOTAUX, GABRIEL (1853–1944)

Historian and statesman; member of the French Academy; Minister of Foreign Affairs 1894–1895, 1895–1898. Transmitted to the government German and Italian denials of relationships with Dreyfus.

HENRY, MAJOR HUBERT-JOSEPH (1847–1898)

Member of the Statistical Section, later Head of Intelligence Bureau. Testified at first trial that Dreyfus was a traitor. Began to tamper with documents from 1896 on and forged among other documents the *faux Henry*. He entangled de Boisdeffre, Gonse, du Paty de Clam further and further in his lies and forgeries. After confessing to Cavaignac in 1898, he committed suicide in Cherche-Midi.

JAURÈS, JEAN (1859–1914)

Historian, statesman and Socialist deputy, he led his party to support a review of the Dreyfus case.

JOUAUST, COLONEL ALBERT

Presiding Judge at the court-martial at Rennes, 1899.

LABORI, FERNAND (1860–1917)

Distinguished criminal lawyer, known for his flamboyant manner. He defended Zola (1898) as well as Dreyfus at the Rennes trial. Owing to the disagreement with Demange and conflict over defense policies, he was asked indirectly by Mathieu Dreyfus and Joseph Reinach to forego his closing statement.

LAUTH, CAPTAIN JULES

Member of Statistical Section. Associate of Henry in anti-Dreyfus campaign.

LAZARE, BERNARD (1865–1903)

French writer; one of Dreyfus's earliest supporters. He published several books to demonstrate his innocence, for example, *Une Erreur judiciaire; la vérité sur l'affaire Dreyfus* (1896) and *Comment on condemne un innocent* (1898). He took part in the Second Zionist Congress in 1898, but had a falling out with Herzl shortly thereafter.

LEBLOIS, LOUIS (1854–1927)

Lawyer and friend of Picquart; Dreyfusard.

LOUBET, EMILE (1838–1929)

President of the French Republic from 1899 to 1906. Dreyfusard; favored revision; pardoned Dreyfus.

MAURRAS, CHARLES

Royalist writer; anti-Dreyfusard.

MÉLINE, FÉLIX-JULES (1838–1925)

Anti-Dreyfusard, Premier from 1896 to 1898. In 1897, at the opening session at the Palais Bourbon, he made the famous remark: "Il n'y a pas d'Affaire Dreyfus!" ("There is no Dreyfus Affair!"). A moderate republican, he did not wish to provoke the army.

PICQUART   REINACH   ROCHEFORT   SCHEURER-KESTNER

MERCIER, GENERAL AUGUSTE (1833–1921)

Responsible for the arrest of Dreyfus in 1894. He remained an accomplice in the injustices done to Dreyfus. At the Zola trial (1898) he said that in 1894 he had proof of Dreyfus's guilt, which if produced in open court would have led to a war with Germany.

PICQUART, LIEUTENANT-COLONEL, MARIE-GEORGES (1854–1914)

Born in Alsace. After attending the *École Superieure de Guerre,* he joined the War Office. He was present at the court-martial of Dreyfus in 1894 and later became Head of the Statistical Section. In 1896 he came into the possession of fragments of a letter known as *le petit bleu* addressed to Major Esterhazy. Later he discovered that the writing of the *bordereau* was in Esterhazy's handwriting. Convinced that Dreyfus was innocent, he went to his superior officers who were unwilling to re-open the Dreyfus case. Picquart discussed his findings with his lawyer Leblois, who brought it to the attention of Scheurer-Kestner. Picquart was sent to prison and dismissed from the army. He was reinstated in 1906.

PANIZZARDI, COLONEL ALESSANDRO

Italian Military Attache in Paris; close personal friend of Colonel von Schwarzkoppen, with whom he shared a knowledge of Secret Service reports.

REINACH, JOSEPH (1856–1921)

Dreyfusard leader; historian and writer. Nephew of Baron de Reinach of Panama Scandal notoriety. He had served on the staff of General de Galliffet and was an excellent officer as well as a staunch Republican. Author of *L'Histoire de L'Affaire Dreyfus* in seven volumes. This work is considered the definitive work on the political and journalistic aspects of the Affair.

ROCHEFORT-LUÇAY, HENRI-VICTOR, COMTE DE (1830–1913)

Journalist; politician. A former Communard who had been exiled, Rochefort returned after the amnesty of 1880 to found the anti-establishment newspaper *L'Intransigeant.* He fled again after the fall of Boulanger, remaining in London until 1895. The most popular Nationalist leader, he united Socialist principles with anti-Semitism. During the Affair, Rochefort's paper attacked individual Dreyfusards with such vehemence that Reinach brought suit against him and won.

SANDHERR, COLONEL JEAN-CONRAD (1846–1897)

Head of Statistical Section when Dreyfus was arrested in 1894. Passionate anti-Semite.

SAUSSIER, GENERAL FÉLIX-GASTON (1828–1905)

As Military Governor of Paris, he recommended against pursuing the investigation of Dreyfus, but was finally forced to order the court-martial.

SCHEURER-KESTNER, AUGUSTE (1833–1899)

Dreyfusard; Life Senator; vice president of the senate. Born in Alsace. From early 1897, he began to suspect that Dreyfus was innocent and worked toward the revision of the 1894 verdict until his death.

SCHWARZKOPPEN, COLONEL MAXIMILIEN VON (1850–1917)

Military attache in the German Embassy in Paris. Together with the Italian military attache Panizzardi he conducted espionage operations. He employed Esterhazy as a spy from 1894 to 1896. He denied repeatedly that he had any dealings with Dreyfus.

TRARIEUX, LUDOVIC (1849–1904)

Dreyfusard leader; lawyer; Minister of Justice in 1895. Founder and first President of the League of the Rights of Man. In December 1897 he informed the Senate of the judicial errors committed during his ministry, but to no avail.

ZOLA

WALDECK-ROUSSEAU, RENÉ (1846–1904)
Belated Dreyfusard; Premier from 1898 to 1900.

ZOLA, ÉMILE (1840–1902)
Well-known French novelist and champion of Alfred Dreyfus. In a twenty-volume cycle of novels (about the family Rougon-Macquart), Zola depicted French life and society during the Second Empire. These novels were followed by great popular successes, such as *L'Assommoir* (1878), *Nana* (1880) and *La Débâcle* (1892). After he became convinced that Dreyfus was innocent, he wrote a series of articles, that were published in *Le Figaro* (1897). His involvement reached a climax in the publication of his article "J'Accuse" in *L'Aurore* on January 13, 1898. For this, he was tried and found guilty of libel, but the verdict was overturned by the Court of Appeal. During a second trial in Versailles he fled for England to avoid his sentence. The Dreyfusards had failed in their attempt to have the case tried on all the issues raised in "J'Accuse." In 1899, when he heard that there would be a retrial for Dreyfus he returned to Paris. He died in 1902 of asphyxiation. Dreyfus attended the public funeral.

ZURLINDEN, GENERAL ÉMILE (1840–1929)
Minister of War (1898). As military governor of Paris, he ordered the court-martial of Picquart.

Lenders to the Exhibition

Ackland Art Museum, The University of North Carolina

Allen Memorial Art Museum, Oberlin College

Ben Apfelbaum, New Rochelle

Archer M. Huntington Art Gallery, University of Texas at Austin

Archives Nationales, Paris

Artine Artinian Collection, Palm Beach

The Art Institute of Chicago

The Ashmolean Museum, Oxford

The Leo Baeck Institute, New York

The Baltimore Museum of Art

Bibliothèque Nationale, Paris

Mr. and Mrs. Bertram H. Bloch, Berkeley, California

The Boston Public Library, Print Department

Mr. and Mrs. Ronald Bouscher, Amsterdam

The Brooklyn Museum

Iris and B. Gerald Cantor, New York

Centre de Documentation Juive et Contemporaine, Paris

Bernard and Josephine Chaus, New York

The Denver Art Museum

The Dreyfus Family, Paris

Galerie Paul Vallotton S.A., Lausanne

Sibylle Gaudry, Paris

Henriette Guy-Loé, Sucy-en-Brie and Geneviève Noufflard, Paris

The Houghton Library, Harvard University

L'Illustration, Courtesy Eric Baschet

The Israel Museum, Jerusalem

The Jewish Museum, New York

Jewish National and University Library, Jerusalem

Jewish Theological Seminary, New York

Josefowitz Collection, Lausanne

Victor Klagsbald, Paris

Mairie de Gerardmer

Madeleine Malthête-Méliès and the heirs of Georges Méliès

J. Robert Maguire, Shoreham, Vermont

The Metropolitan Museum of Art, New York

List of Donors

Major funding for this exhibition and catalogue has been provided by the National Endowment for the Humanities, a Federal agency. Additional funding has been received from the following:

Benefactors

The Florence J. Gould Foundation
Wachtell, Lipton, Rosen & Katz

Patrons

Bengal Graphics
Gloria and Barry H. Garfinkel
Alan C. Greenberg Foundation, Inc.
Oscar & Regina Gruss Charitable &
    Educational Foundation
The Lucius N. Littauer Foundation
The Reed Foundation

Sponsors

Lillian and Jack N. Berkman
Donald G. Drapkin
Alvin H. Einbender
Fried, Frank, Harris, Shriver, Jacobson
    Fund, Inc.

Sondra and Charles Gilman, Jr.
    Foundation
Golenbock and Barell
Carol and Gershon Kekst
Jules Kroll Foundation
Lowey, Dannenberg & Knapp
Philip Morris Companies
Geri and Lester Pollack
Revlon Foundation
Ridgefield Foundation
Sunny and Abe Rosenberg Foundation,
    Inc.
The Edmond de Rothschild Foundation
Michael Scharf
Shereff, Friedman, Hoffman &
    Goodman
Skadden, Arps, Slate, Meagher & Flom
Warner Communications, Inc.
Weil, Gotshal & Manges
James D. Zirin

Dreyfus Exhibition Sponsors
Committee

Barry H. Garfinkel, Co-Chairman
Bernard W. Nussbaum, Co-Chairman
Floyd Abrams
Jack N. Berkman
Kenneth J. Bialkin
Steven Brill
Donald J. Cohn
Donald G. Drapkin
Alvin H. Einbender
Paul H. Epstein
James Finkelstein
Peter Fishbein
Joseph H. Flom
Hon. Marvin E. Frankel
David A. Garfinkel
Judith Goldstein
Milton S. Gould
Alan C. Greenberg
Harold Grunfeld
Milton Handler
Alvin K. Hellerstein
Helene L. Kaplan
Gershon Kekst
Victor A. Kovner
Jules Kroll
Herbert Kronish

Steven J. Kumble
Jerome Lipper
Stephen Lowey
Edward H. Meyer
Ira Millstein
Martin D. Payson
Lester Pollack
Richard Ravitch
Dean Norman Redlich
Carole Rifkind
Ernest Rubenstein
Herbert Rubin
Michael Scharf
Victoria Schonfeld
Irving S. Shapiro
Leon Silverman
Jerold Solovy
Howard Squadron
Sidney H. Stein
Milton Strom
Richard Tofel
Raymond S. Troubh
Michael Varet
Melvyn I. Weiss
William Zabel
James D. Zirin

Foreword

EUGEN WEBER

On 31 October 1894 the Havas News Agency announced the arrest of an officer "suspected of having handed the enemy confidential documents of little importance." The following day, the chief anti-Semitic rag of Paris, *La Libre Parole,* announced that the officer in question was Captain Dreyfus, a Jew of Alsatian origin. Tried and found guilty in December, Dreyfus would be condemned to deportation for life, and shipped to Devil's Island in February 1895. Critics of his sentence pointed out that death sentences could be meted out for desertion, or even for mere insubordination. In response, the minister of war introduced a bill making treason punishable by death.

Almost two years after these events, a trickle of articles and pamphlets brought to the public an inkling of the Dreyfus family's unwillingness to accept Alfred Dreyfus's guilt. By the autumn of 1897, the trickle had become a flood, and the campaign for revision of an allegedly improper (hence unjust) verdict was rocking the political establishment. Revisionists and antirevisionists clashed in the press, in parliament and, soon, in the streets. In November 1897, there was enough about the case in the press that Camille Pissarro, the painter, could send his son Lucien a large batch of newspapers dealing with the case. On 13 January 1898, Emile Zola published his open letter to the president of the Republic, denouncing the authors of the injustice committed in 1894 and the maneuvers designed to conceal and perpetuate the miscar-riage of justice. Georges Clemenceau, editor of *L'Aurore,* on whose front page the letter appeared, contributed a title: "J'Accuse." That day, Pissarro, busy painting the Place du Palais-Royal from the window of a room in the Hotel du Louvre, heard his fellow Impressionist, Armand Guillaumin, say that if Dreyfus had been shot at once people would have been spared all this commotion. "Everyone at Durand-Ruel agrees, except the doorman."[1]

The commotion was serious. Demonstrations, duels, brawls shook Paris and many provincial cities. In Roanne, nowadays best known for the restaurant of the Frères Troisgros, the Jeunesses Socialistes (Young Socialists) attacked "the government and Jewry," while the Catholic vicar denounced the Jewish and Masonic plot initiated by Lord Palmerston (unfortunately long dead by then), and ended a vitriolic sermon by crying "Down with Zola! Down with the Jews!"[2] Revisionism and antirevisionism divided friends and even families: Degas, as Linda Nochlin tells us, broke with the Halévys; the real-life Prince de Chimay broke with his family, as the fictional Duc de Guermantes did with his. The more or less anarchist, more or less socialist bohemian habitués of the Chat Noir and other Montmartre cabarets split; Dreyfus supporters on one side, opponents on the other. Social life became a minefield. Or a bore. In March 1898, Manet's pretty niece, Julie, noted in her diary that a mid-Lent party had fizzled because the principal guests, Monsieur

Mallarmé and Monsieur Renoir, talked endlessly about the Affair—"really, we have enough of this business."[3]

Julie Manet was out of luck. A cascade of ministerial resignations, government crises, *coups de théâtre,* and sudden turns of fortune kept the public on its toes and the papers in special editions until June 1899, when France's highest court of appeals, the Cour de Cassation, ordered a retrial, which took place at Rennes, in Brittany, during August and September. When this new court-martial found Dreyfus guilty once more, though with extenuating circumstances, the "shameful verdict" that everyone (who was anyone) awaited with bated breath was posted outside the Casino at Evian, "to the great joy of the entire Casino staff." Marcel Proust, taking the waters at Evian that year, found the young poet Anna de Noailles sobbing as though her heart would break, crying out between sobs: "How could they do such a thing?"[4] Proust was more philosophical: The verdict, he predicted, would be quashed. And it was. Dreyfus was pardoned; then, within a few years, rehabilitated by the Cour de Cassation; reintegrated in the army; and decorated with the Legion of Honor.

Throughout all this, as ever, at least in France, judicial proceedings had been as much affected by political pressures as politics had been by judicial transactions. Benjamin Martin's account of the legal shenanigans shows how little, then as now, the administration of justice had to do with justice, how readily the law swayed to the breath of political majorities. Martin concludes that for both sides—as happens in so many moral contests—ends, in the event, would justify the means.

Means were dirtier and more violent even than today. The clash of principles degenerated into the sort of brawl that follows a good wake. The tone of debate was inconceivably virulent: scurrilous, personal, and mostly directed below the belt. Not all Catholics were anti-Dreyfusards; but these were the years when the Church conceived its opponents as literally commanded by the Devil. Catholic or not, most of those who joined the fray saw their opponents as satanic. Past revolutions had taught the French to hate their neighbors or, at least, suspect them. The Dreyfus revolution confirmed the belief that one's neighbors were evil to boot.

Dreyfus lived on until 1935. But the Dreyfus Affair had entered history or, as the narrator of Proust's *Remembrance of Things Past* would have it, prehistory; becoming part of the far-off days before World War I, which, Susan Suleiman argues below, cast its overwhelming shadow on everything that went before.

And yet, after nearly a century, the Affair is still with us. Witness this exhibition, the third on the subject since 1973. Witness the Affair's many bequests to us: the entry of intellectuals into the political fray; the crystallization of modern anti-Semitism; the complementary invention of Zionism; finally, in France, the shaping of new political configurations in which fresh national divisions joined those that a century of revolutions had produced. It was the Affair that, within a few contentious years, precipitated the separation of Church and State. It was the Affair that turned the presence of Jews in France into a Jewish Question: a convenient pretext for endless acrimony and debate.[5] It was the Affair that allied anti-Semitism clearly with the Right; and persuaded the Left—especially socialists, hitherto much given to offensive rhetoric on the subject—that anti-Jewish expressions are bad form. It was, indeed, the Affair that launched anti-Semitism on its amazingly successful twentieth century career; and also suggested the special affinity of Jews for social justice. As Paula Hyman shows, Jewish Emancipation stemmed from the French Revolution. Michael Burns's moving description of Dreyfus's family background indicates how a despised, oppressed social group found the way to success and self-respect, and learned to identify these with France, and personal and family honor with the honor of France. But there was more. Popular lore had linked the Jews with money power and with the newfangled privileges of wealth. It took the Affair for the Jewish community to align itself with the cause of equality as it had with the cause of opportunity.

Some Jews had associated themselves with the Left before the 1890s, yet the popular stereotype placed them on the side of the oppressors. Henceforth, whatever the popular image said, more and more Jews would sense that freedom from the inequities that oppressed them went naturally with freedom from inequities oppressing others. Such notions gave their foes one more stick with which to beat them. But the new alliance, or the new preference, generally held firm.

Why should a banal spy story, even one converted into a miscarriage of justice, produce such resonance?

The first explanation bears on the state of France in the 1890s—a country that, for one hundred years, had known no generation without a revolution or a coup d'état, and that still teetered on the brink of both when Dreyfus went to trial in 1894 as in 1899. Scandal after scandal had shaken the Republic, and tarnished the prestige of its leaders. The political class lived in fear of a coup: even Pissarro saw one in the offing.[6] The summer and autumn of 1898 would see colonial conflict with Britain over who should control the sources of the Nile. The Fashoda crisis was so serious that Paul Valéry, then working at the Ministry of War, predicted a war with England soon.[7] A secretary of the president of the Republic, looking back, described the structure of the State (and of the war ministry in particular) as unstable and precarious.[8] No wonder that the enemies of the Republic should seize on the business of Dreyfus as an opportunity to discredit the regime, and perhaps to topple it.

But why should anti-Semitism furnish their battle cry? In 1892, a work on anti-Semitism in France had concluded there was nothing to it: "This crisis of socialism—for anti-Semitism is a socialist malady—will not last."[9] Michael Marrus indicates why the prediction was wrong: Anti-Semitism was deeper and more pervasive than a mere passing fever. Its roots tapped Christian beliefs that survived the waning of Christianity; in popular resentment of new money powers perceived as more oppressive, because less familiar than the feudal regime of old; in frictions created by foreign immigration at a time of serious economic depression; and in animosity toward a social group identified by accent and by provenance with the German enemy to the east.

Marrus mentions a diocesan bulletin depicting France invaded by a Jewish race. We must not make too much of the term "race." At that time, people used it loosely to describe groupings of family, profession, psychological type, and the like, not just to designate an ethnic group. Jews used it too. Linda Nochlin quotes Ludovic Halévy, Offenbach's librettist, describing himself as being

"of the Jewish race." Yet it was true that late nineteenth-century France, prey to demographic decline, was figuratively speaking invaded by many "races." None was more evidently alien, in that day, than the Jews; none more concentrated in Paris, where national papers were written and national politics waged.

Explanations of anti-Semitism come from as many directions as do rationalizations of anti-Semitism. None seems to me as forceful as the fact that history and cultural tradition made Jews the resident aliens par excellence. In a country obsessed by the ideal of cultural unity, the Jewish community, as Paula Hyman shows, was caught in a bind between patriotic assimilation (of which the Dreyfus family provides one example among many) and persistent particularism, irrigated by immigration and confirmed by traditional stereotypes.

Linda Nochlin reminds us that these stereotypes were so strong that even Jews could not escape them, and artists like Pissarro reproduced them in their works as a matter of course. Jew-haters had a rich treasury of images from which to draw: Not only of the Jew as traitor or exploiter; but, more subtly, of the Jew as Other—obstinately alien, solitary, stiff, reticent, isolated, apart, conspiring with fellow Jews against the gentiles in whose midst they lived.

Such problems and prejudices, however, could have continued as a nagging but politically insignificant irritation, had they not been crystallized by the press. The 1880s and 1890s would see the rise of a popular press in France, with mass-circulation newspapers vying with each other for whatever news would catch attention—exaggerating it, if need be inventing it. The Dreyfus spy case had been a nine-day wonder. The Dreyfus Affair provided richer pastures, its every twist and turn a pretext for special editions and for higher sales.[10] It was the anti-Semitic press that pushed hesitant military officials into prosecuting and convicting Dreyfus on flimsy evidence. It was in the press that the advocates of revision made their case. It was a press hungry for sensational fare to serve up to its public that launched the tales of Jewish, clerical, military, or foreign plots and counterplots, which turned a mere court case into an Affair and endowed it with moral and historical dimensions. Without the press there would have been no Dreyfus Affair. Without the press Dreyfus would not have been vindicated. We may regard the scandal of Dreyfus as the first great triumph of the Fourth Estate.

There was, of course, no Jewish plot to save Dreyfus, as there were no anti-Jewish masses leagued against him. When the chips were down, the foes of Dreyfus called on profound reserves of prejudice and resentment, his friends on more tenuous traditions that associated France with humanity and justice. Michael Burns has recently demonstrated that even these were minority concerns.[11] The "real people" of France, to whom both sides liked to refer, cared little about Dreyfus and less about miscarriages of justice that did not affect them personally. But some more thoughtful folk did care, and they constructed a myth and then maintained a memory that still, to this day, evokes the possibility of justice fair and square.

Notes

1. Camille Pissarro, *Letters to his Son Lucien,* ed. John Rewald (New York: Appel, 1972), 314, 318.
2. Marcel Gouinet, *Histoire de Roanne et de sa région* (Roanne, 1977) II, 276.
3. Julie Manet, *Journal 1893–1899,* (Paris: C. Klincksieck, 1979), 156.
4. Marcel Proust, *Selected Letters 1880–1903,* ed. Philip Kolb (New York: Doubleday, 1983), 197.
5. The subject catalog of the Bibliothèque Nationale devotes 46 pages to Jews during the period 1882–1894, one full volume and a third of another for the period 1894–1925. The number of works listed under *Israël* and *Israélites* also rises significantly during the second period.
6. Pissarro, *Letters,* 320.
7. Manet, *Journal,* 211.
8. Charles Braibant, *Félix Faure à l'Elysée* (Paris: Hachette, 1963), 59.
9. Mermeix, *Les Antisémites en France* (Paris, 1892), 90.
10. On September 9, 1899, after the Rennes court-martial "recondemns Dreyfus," a Paris lawyer noted in his diary that his servant had to wait in line for ten minutes to get a newspaper. Henri Dabot, *Calendriers d'un bourgeois du Quartier Latin, 1888–1900* (Péronne, 1905).
11. Michael Burns, *Rural Society and French Politics* (Princeton: Princeton University Press, 1984).

Director's Preface

The Dreyfus Affair was an extraordinary event that took place during twelve years at the turn of the nineteenth century. Involving the accusation, conviction, retrial, and final rehabilitation of Alfred Dreyfus, a Jew and captain in the French army, the human drama of the Affair and the social and political issues at its core still resonate nearly one hundred years later.

The subject of the Dreyfus Affair is a complicated one, and in the exhibition, we have presented the history of the events constituting the Affair, and done so within the larger context of French Jewish history and important issues in French social history of the period. Additionally, we have hoped to raise the many moral, sociological, and ethical questions about the Affair that seem relevant in the light of contemporary attitudes and politics.

In many ways this project epitomizes the goals of the Jewish Museum's programming during the 1980s. It makes use of fine arts and popular artifacts and it uses a particular historic event to address aspects of art history as well as broad humanist themes. We have presented paintings done at the time of the Affair to show the concern of individual artists in the moral drama of Alfred Dreyfus. We have included some of the enormous outpouring of popular imagery to show the pervasiveness of mass media in shaping public opinion. On the surface, the Affair was as immediate as the latest newspaper or broadside. On a more fundamental level—more evident in the fine arts—there were basic social and ethical issues at stake: the responsibility of the press, the power of the individual versus the state, the role of the artist and intellectual in society, and the insidious nature of anti-Semitism.

Norman Kleeblatt, Curator of Fine Arts at the Museum, conceived this exhibition and publication. His vision, imagination, energy, and enormous commitment have fueled this project since its earliest days. Other staff, board members, special friends of the museum, scholars, lenders, and funders have been essential to the realization of a very ambitious goal. The National Endowment for the Humanities provided major funding for both planning and implementation of the project. Attorneys Barry Garfinkel and Bernard Nussbaum headed a special fund-raising committee. Assistant Director for Public Affairs Rosemarie Garipoli supervised all the fund-raising and public relations efforts. We are grateful to the many generous funders, listed on page xxii, who believed in the project and made contributions, and to the lenders to the exhibition, listed on page xx, who have been most generous in their willingness to participate by sending works from both private and public collections.

Educational programming has been a major component of this project, and Judith Siegel, Director of Education, and Jean Bloch Rosensaft, Assistant Director of Education, have created imaginative programming for children and adults. Virtually every department of the Museum worked on *The Dreyfus Affair: Art, Truth, and Justice,* and the staff of the Fine Arts Department, Stephen Brown, Anita Friedman, and Irene Z. Schenck deserve particular thanks. On behalf of the Jewish Museum, I express my deepest gratitude to everyone who gave time, cooperated with the Museum, and provided encouragement.

Joan H. Rosenbaum
Director, The Jewish Museum

Acknowledgments

This book and the exhibition it documents began more than ten years ago when I was first becoming acquainted with the Jewish Museum's collection. I had discovered an uncatalogued poster from the *Musée des Horreurs* series, titled "Dreyfus est un traitre." Aesthetically it both shocked and tantalized me, but ideologically its diatribe was devastating. The image became indelible in my mind. Could such vicious, anti-Semitic material ever be displayed? If so, how? And what would this product of the darker side of human nature tell anyone about the man Dreyfus, or the Affair associated with his name which became the enormously complex scandal that rocked French society for an entire decade? Or for that matter, what could this type of work—which is never discussed in references to late nineteenth-century posters—add to our knowledge of that popular medium?

Many thoughtful people helped shape my particular vision of the Dreyfus Affair and the exhibition. In acknowledging those involved in this project, I do so chronologically, giving a short history of the exhibition's evolution.

My challenge was to express visually a complicated subject that dealt at once with ethical issues, politics, art, popular culture, and anti-Semitism. In both exhibition and catalogue, I have tried to examine the history of the Dreyfus Affair in particular and the period of the 1890s in general by cutting a swath across art and illustration, popular and high culture. This approach may at times be somewhat jarring, but it reveals an overall picture of fin-de-siècle society, its aspirations and prejudices, more than either an art exhibition or a history exhibition would reveal by itself.

My work has been shaped no doubt by the Jewish Museum's mission to offer exhibition programs not only of art and archaeology but also ethnography, history, and culture. My thinking is also firmly grounded in the worldview of the 1980s. This era has seen numerous efforts to re-examine the cultural products of past eras, particularly those of the nineteenth century. Only twenty years ago this material and this approach would not have been considered viable. I admit also to having been influenced by such recent monumental and multifaceted exhibitions as *Dream and Reality: Vienna 1870–1930* as it was conceived and mounted by Hans Hollein in Vienna in 1985.

My first professional discussions about this material came about when I met Dennis Cate, Director of the Jane Voorhees Zimmerli Art Museum, who was most enthusiastic about the Dreyfus material and knew much that could be added to such an exhibition. Dennis in turn introduced me to Herbert and Ruth Schimmel, important collectors of Toulouse-Lautrec's works and documents of the period. Their knowledge, personal holdings, and enthusiasm added greatly to our original discussions. With Dennis Cate's knowledge of the print media of the period, we came up with a proposal to do a small exhibition at the Jewish Museum on printmakers and the Dreyfus Affair which would perhaps include some ephemera. The idea was appealing to both of us and appeared to serve the field of print scholarship.

When I proposed this idea to the exhibition committee of the Museum's Board of Trustees, I was asked to expand the concept to reflect the seriousness and importance of the subject. Thus I owe my most important thanks to the vision of this group, chaired by Stuart Silver, which saw the potential for what I hope will be recognized as significant and useful work.

During the spring of 1982 I delved into some of the literature on the Dreyfus Affair. Anita Friedman, Senior Research Associate and Irene Z. Schenck, Research Associate in my department, aided in this effort and became as fascinated as I with the breadth and possibilities of the subject. To them I owe an enormous debt of gratitude for their research and for their continued dedication and involvement with almost every aspect of both exhibition and publication. Anita and Irene wrote the plate captions and the section descriptions for the checklist, attended to details of the catalogue, and contributed texts and labels for the exhibition proper. Anita Friedman also prepared a concise chronology and handled aspects of foreign research and grant applications. For their efforts, sustaining support, and friendship I thank them both wholeheartedly. Although Stephen Brown joined this staff at a fairly late moment in the exhibition and catalogue process, his nine months on the project have proved invaluable. He has undertaken the heavily detailed task of endless correspondence, telephone calls, and the various complex checklists that had to be prepared for both internal and external use. He has helped conceive and almost single-handedly supervised the preparation of the video production. He has also assisted in the development of the educational pamphlet, and has compiled the bibliography. I have also benefited much from my numerous critical conversations with him concerning the scope and ramifications of the exhibition.

A planning grant approved by the National Endowment for the Humanities created the structural backbone for both exhibit and book. Preparation of this planning grant drew significantly on contributions of Virginia Strull, then Director of Development at the Museum. She challenged my opinions and helped me to flesh out a well-reasoned project. Scott Spector and Julie Zeftel also deserve mention for their assistance with this proposal. I also thank Elizabeth Cats for her assistance with certain research aspects of that project. She has continued to be tremendously supportive throughout the exhibition period and is to be thanked especially for her compilation of the brief biographies in the Annotated List of Characters of the Affair.

The highly positive reception of our application at the offices of the NEH did much to spur us on. During both planning and implementation phases we benefited from the ideas, input, and encouragement of Victor Sorrel, Peter Patrikis, Gabriel Weisberg, and Marcia Semmel of that agency.

This publication could not have been possible without the serious commitment of seven scholars who contributed original essays, frequently adding new research findings to their respective fields. They have also aided greatly at different points in the project to my thinking about the exhibit and especially from the all-day seminar that was held with them during the planning period. I am deeply indebted and grateful to Michael Burns, Dennis Cate (once again), Paula Hyman, Michael Marrus, Benjamin Martin, Linda Nochlin, Susan Suleiman, and not least to Eugen Weber for his fusion of these informative papers into a Foreword.

Stanley Holwitz of the University of California Press became enamored with the concept of this book from the moment we had our first short conversation about it in my office. His enthusiasm and that of the Editorial Committee of the University Press helped to create and shape this volume. To Steve Renick, Director of Design of that institution, I owe particular thanks for his interest in the project and for his appreciation of the significance of the visual material. His sensitive handling of the design adds significantly to the aesthetic result and also to the usefulness of the book. Shirley Warren is to be commended for her skillful coordination of all phases of this publication. I thank these three for their hard work, professionalism, and not least, good humor. To Genise Schnitman, who gave careful attention to the editing of the individual essays and to Shawn Woodyard who edited the checklist, go my deep appreciation.

During preparation of the implementation grant, and throughout her tenure at the Museum, Joan Diamond, then Assistant Director of Development, shared tremendous enthusiasm for the project and offered thoughtful contributions to my ideas about the exhibition. Rosemarie Garipoli, Director of Public Information, along with Joan Diamond and later Barbara Perlov at the Museum must be complimented for their success in undertaking the huge fund-raising campaign to support production of the exhibition and the book. To Barry Garfinkel and Bernard Nussbaum, the two attorneys who headed our Dreyfus committee, I am extremely grateful both for their confidence in this project and in me.

The exhibition designer Lynne Breslin and I practically began our respective design and curatorial careers together, and we have jointly worked on numerous exhibitions. Each experience has been a wonderful merging of sensibilities and mutual understanding of perceptions and conceptions. I cannot thank her and Shauna Mosseri, her associate, enough for their fine three-dimensional expression of my vision. The public's understanding of the exhibition will be greatly enhanced by their installation.

Because I insisted on showing only original materials, be it art or ephemera, I depended a great deal on the insight, confidence, and generosity of curators, scholars, and librarians both in the United States and abroad. From France, I owe a particular debt of gratitude to Geneviève Monnier at the Elysée Palace, whose interest in the project, introduction to key personnel, and access to information did much to expedite matters for me. At the Bibliothèque Nationale, Laure Beaumont and Françoise Jestaz made numerous suggestions and provided assistance on many levels. Bernard de Montgolfier and Dominique Morel at the Musée Carnavalet did much to facilitate my numerous visits and the many loans from their institution. Hervé Joubeaux provided similar selfless assistance at the Musée de Bretagne in Rennes. For the assistance of the many others in French institutions, I am enormously grateful though I cannot possibly enumerate individually all those who helped with loans and provided information. But to Christian Bailly of the Musée de la Presse, Georges Cheyssial of the Musée National Jean-Jacques Henner, Christian de l'Epée at the Mairie de Gerardmer, Yvonne Brunhammer and François Mathey at the Musée des Arts Decoratifs, Pauline Reverchon at the Musée Municipal de Cognac, Phillipe Husson of the Musée de l'Ecole de Nancy, Philippe Thiébaut of the Musée d'Orsay, Michel Guillot of Musée Municipal René Sourdes in Suresnes—I owe special thanks. Elsewhere in Europe I owe particular gratitude to Phil Mertens of the Musée Royaux des Beaux-Arts de Belgique in Brussels, and to Jura Bruschweiler in Switzerland for his help with Hodler loans and insight into the artist's politics. For their information, assistance, and points of view I extend many thanks to Jean-Denis Bredin, Madeleine Rebérioux, Françoise Cachin, and Madeleine Malthête-Méliès.

The caveat about thanking every individual in Europe for their courtesy and assistance extends also to this country. Nevertheless, I owe special thanks to Roger Stoddard and Jenny Rathbun at the Houghton Library, to Sinclair Hitchings and Karen Shafts of the Boston Public Library, to Dennis Cate at the Jane Voorhees Zimmerli Art Museum, and to Menachem Schmelzer and Evelyn Cohen at the Library of the Jewish Theological Seminary of America. The people at these four institutions processed numerous loans for the exhibition and did much to accommodate the many requests for information and photographs. Other North American institutions, while lending fewer pieces, provided assistance and support. I am particularly grateful to Dean Walker at the Ackland Art Museum, Diantha Schull at the New York Public Library, Jay Fisher at the Baltimore Art Museum, and to Micheline Moisin at the Montreal Museum of Fine Arts, for their help and good will.

Many private lenders, both here and abroad, have been exceedingly supportive and generous. As previously mentioned, Herbert and Ruth Schimmel have been steady supporters of this project and made their superb and diverse collection accessible to me at all times. J. Robert Maguire, who has been collecting Dreyfusiana for over forty years, has also been enormously supportive and generous with both his time, knowledge, and materials. Of European private lenders, I owe particular thanks to Mr. and Mrs. Ronald Bouscher in Amsterdam and Henriette Guy-Loé in Sucy-en-Brie who have also contributed information and assistance as well as works from their collection. Thanks also go to Marc Knobel in Paris and Willa Silverman in New York for their help in directing me to particular lenders.

It has been very moving for me to have worked with the family of Alfred Dreyfus, who ironically noted a recent genealogical connection to my own family. These extremely sensitive individuals, whose lives no doubt bear the imprint of their relative's fate, have made great efforts to understand the Affair on both personal and historical levels. They have done all they can to assist and encourage me. I owe particular thanks to Dr. Jean-Louis Lévy and Simone Perl, two of Dreyfus's grandchildren, for the insight and information provided to my staff and myself for the exhibition and the numerous items they lent. Also to France Beck, his grandniece, I owe thanks for her help and knowledge.

The creation of a video introduction to the exhibition has demanded a great deal of time and thought. For having met the special challenges of both the subject and the medium through which it is conveyed, I owe special thanks to Peter Rosen, producer, Kit Fitzgerald, director, and Diane Dreher, scriptwriter.

For the advice and practical assistance of Marc Perrin de Brichambaut, Cultural Counsellor to the French Embassy in New York and Patrick Talbot, Deputy Cultural Counsellor, I add my deep appreciation. Their support was felt in many ways, not least in expediting important correspondence from France.

At the Jewish Museum, I am indebted to many individuals who have assisted with various aspects of the catalogue and installation. To Anne Driesse for her expert attention to the framing and preservation of the works, I am particularly thankful. Ginny Bowen and Belle Kayne also helped with this area. I thank also Caroline Goldberg who has provided a great deal of practical support over the last several months in the execution of numerous details attendant to this project, and Rachel Burton who assisted with organization during the past year. To Lynn Millinger who also pitched in to assist with a crucial deadline goes my special gratitude and to Gertrude Meyer who so willingly assisted with German translations. My thanks also to Elizabeth Ladenson for preparing translations of the copius body of French material, much of which is included here.

The members of the education department created meaningful public programs and special curricula for public schools; especially to Judith Siegel, Director of Education and Jean Bloch Rosensaft, Director of Public Programs, I owe very special thanks for their creativity, dedication, and friendship. I also remember with appreciation former Director of Education Andrew Ackerman. I am also grateful for the assistance of Fay Schreibman, Director of the National Jewish Archive of Broadcasting, who has given advice on audiovisual components of the exhibition. Also thanks to Ronnie Parker and Debra Case Tane on her staff, and to Lori Perlow formerly on her staff. The people who oversaw the shipping, handling, and installation of the exhibition deserve particular mention—special thanks to Rita Feigenbaum, Registrar, Susan Palamara, Assistant to the Regis-

trar, and to Al Lazarte, Director of Operations. To Ward Mintz, Assistant Director for Programs, and Diane Farynyk, Administrator of Exhibitions and Collections who saw to numerous details of coordination during the final phases of the exhibition (and curiously their first several months at the museum), I am most grateful. Anne Scher, Director of Public Relations, is to be complimented on her capability in disseminating information about the exhibition to the general public and to special interest groups. To my colleagues Vivian Mann and Susan Goodman go many thanks for their advice and support. I thank Ruth Dolkart, Carole Weisz, and Sybil Weingast for their expertise and assistance with this project as it related to contracts, finance, and membership respectively.

Several conservators and frame-makers have performed highly skilled tasks in order to prepare some of the objects for exhibition. I am most grateful for the attention to detail and the assistance of Konstanze Bachmann, Mariol Gallichio, Alan Farancz, Philip Feld, and Judith Eisenberg. John Parnell was unusually helpful and sensitive in his photography of the numerous objects as was Susan Jahoda during his absence from New York.

Many friends listened, advised, even assisted at different times and in various ways. They also offered useful suggestions and ideas. I am enormously grateful to Peter Prescott, who provided his own critical opinions at various stages of this project from grant proposals to catalogue contributions. Barbara Sloane has also been an interested and sensitive supporter throughout. Also to Alain Caillaud and Laurent Caillaud for their help in France; and to Janice Kuta, Richard Garretson, Lynn Gumpert, Bernard Friedman, and Virginia and Paul Strull go my heartfelt gratitude.

To the many others who have helped in various ways, I am most appreciative.

I close giving special acknowledgment and appreciation to the Director of The Jewish Museum, Joan Rosenbaum, who has given creative suggestions and analytic commentary on the many and complex facets of the exhibition catalogue. She was extremely supportive of me and devoted to the project, and provided the intellectual and practical expertise necessary to the realization of both catalogue and exhibition.

Norman L. Kleeblatt
Curator of Collections
The Jewish Museum

The Dreyfus Affair:
A Visual Record[1]

NORMAN L. KLEEBLATT

Captain Alfred Dreyfus, a Jewish officer in the French army, was accused of treason in late 1894. His court-martial, conviction, incarceration, re-trial, and ultimate rehabilitation in 1906 developed into a political event that divided France and had repercussions throughout England and Western Europe.

The ensuing political scandal known as the Dreyfus Affair resulted from problems rooted in the social and political contortions of nineteenth-century France. A complex and often contradictory cast of characters took part in the series of events that had transformed the first Dreyfus court-martial into "The Affair." These characters included both those who were actual participants in the mockery called a trial and the subsequent coverup[2] and others whose opinions and rhetoric created the public clamor which ultimately forced a retrial. The positions of the opinion makers vis-à-vis the military, the church, the fallen monarchy, capitalism, and the highly visible Jewish community were polarized into two perhaps too simplistic factions—the Dreyfusards and the anti-Dreyfus-ards. At both ends of the spectrum of opinion concerning Dreyfus's guilt or innocence, and the concomitant question of the importance of truth and justice over honor and national security, there were people who made rash and superficial judgments, out of the desire to reduce France's numerous social and political ailments to no more than a small surface blemish.

The Affair established for the first time in his-tory a new role of social and political activism for writers, artists, and academicians, setting the pace for the involvement of the same groups in the ever more pressing and harrowing dilemmas of the twentieth century.[3] In fact the term *intellectual* as it is understood today has its roots in the France of the Affair.[4] In 1898, at the height of the Affair, Henri-Gabriel Ibels, the artist who founded the illustrated journal *Le Sifflet* with the express pur-pose of aiding the cause for revision, recalled that "intellectual had become the synonym for anti-patriot, informer, spy, traitor, agent of the syndi-cates as if there had been a syndicate rich enough to buy all these consciences."[5]

Emile Zola, the distinguished and popular novelist, might be considered the personification of Ibels's definition. His article "J'Accuse," a ring-ing indictment of the military and the government published in Clemenceau's newspaper *L'Aurore* (13 January 1898), has become household knowl-edge even in America. Maurice Barrès, at the time a significant literary voice in France though less celebrated today, played an antagonistic role to Zola who made the search for truth surrounding the improper conviction of Alfred Dreyfus a per-sonal crusade. Barrès was an ardent nationalist and his many articles on the Affair included an inflam-matory description of Dreyfus during the Rennes trial.[6] Coming from this respected author, such words helped assuage any questions the public might have raised concerning the possibility that the Jewish officer was innocent. His articles smack of prejudice, racism, xenophobia, and blatant anti-Semitism. Zola and Barrès are paradigms of the polarization of the nation's literati, whose bitter arguments served to disseminate information and opinion to the French public.

The effect of the Dreyfus Affair on other French literary Olympians is discussed elsewhere in this volume (see the chapter by Susan Rubin Suleiman) but members of the intelligentsia from all over the globe offered their opinions. Literary luminaries from imperial Russia to the isolationist United States had their say, generally taking up the cause of the accused officer. Anton Chekhov and Mark Twain were two notable examples: they spoke out eloquently on behalf of the captain and denounced the injustice he suffered at the corrupt workings of the military and the legal system.[7]

Every professional discipline was split over the Affair. But none is more fascinating to examine in a museum context than the response of painters, sculptors, illustrators, and the pioneers of the newest visual media—photography and film. It is still unsettling to realize that it was the Dreyfus Affair that caused the break between the two important artists Degas and Pissarro, who had formerly been fast friends.[8] Once again we find two archetypical examples of a much broader phenomenon: Monet, Signac, Cassatt, and Vuillard sided with the Dreyfusards against the anti-Dreyfusards Renoir and Cézanne. And this is only the beginning of a lengthy list. Few artists lived through this era without taking sides. Some refused to take a political stance, as in the case of Rodin, who found that the vagaries of the polarized camps would eventually affect the fate of certain of his sculptures.

.   .   .

The concept for a museum exhibition on the Dreyfus Affair seemed natural, given the proliferation of visual material during the twelve years it took for the Affair—and the struggle for truth and justice it represented—to unfold. Besides the copious polemical material the Affair generated, there was an abundant body of art that was created, affected, or interpreted in connection with the infamous scandal. This examination of the painting, sculpture, drawing, film, and decorative art related to the Dreyfus Affair can be just a beginning in the documentation of what is surely a much larger body of work.

Comprising high art, polemical art, and a great quantity of commercial ephemera, the works included in the exhibition and this volume convey a vivid sense of the texture of fin-de-siècle France. This was an era that thrived on information (the more skewed and sensational, the better) and materialism (which grew ever more commercialized and accessible). And it frequently fused and confused these two.

As its title suggests, this essay which serves to introduce these various types of images, aims for a visual summary of the Affair. Although there have been more than eight hundred titles published on the subject, many of which presented illustrative material, there has been little systematic review of the imagery. Most of the books that reproduce visual material limit themselves to about a dozen images, that seem to have been tacked on as dutiful addenda. Two books chronicling the visual polemics that arose around the scandal did appear during the Affair. These were John Grand-Carteret's *L'Affair Dreyfus et l'Image* (published c. 1899) and the *Dreyfus-Bilderbuch* (published in Germany in 1899).[9] Both are compilations of some of the array of political cartoons about the case, which make some attempt to classify the satirical imagery. Little has been done since these publications first appeared. And certainly no examination of the impact of the Affair on painters and sculptors has been undertaken, save for the occasional mention in scholarly articles or specialized books of the effect of the case on a particular artist or work of art. In this volume, it would be impossible to include more than a sampling of the various types of images created in response to the Affair. A complete compendium of Dreyfus imagery would entail illustrations numbering in the tens of thousands.

.   .   .

Beginning around 1880, the phenomenon of artists serving politics through involvement in journalism coincided with the general increase in the permissiveness and power of the press.[10] The Fourth Estate was frequently irresponsible in its reportage, and this lack of professional accountability is evident in the illustrations as well as in the textual material. Yet journalism was becoming a respectable pursuit for the first time in French history. Figures from politics and letters—fields where there were individuals with opinions on both sides of the Dreyfus issue who had the influence to shape the course of the scandal—found a meeting ground in journalistic activities. And often there was no clear line of demarcation separating writers from politicians. Many figures wore both hats as they jockeyed positions and careers.[11] Almost every major character in the fight for revision was in some way involved with the press, whether as writer, owner, or backer of the numerous vehicles of opinion. The Dreyfusards Clemenceau, Zola, Scheurer-Kestner, Lazare, Waldeck-Rousseau, Séverine, Fénéon, and the anti-Dreyfusards Drumont, Rochefort, Méline, and Meyer were all engaged in some form or other with the business of journalism.[12] Journalistic activities also saw many artists and writers through difficult economic times, during the periodic lulls in the market for books and fine art.[13]

Besides creating much of the material that went into the journals, artists had a significant role in advertising the publications. The kiosks of Paris and, indeed, all France, were plastered with posters and broadsides promoting commercial or cultural products and political or social ideas. These placards clearly demonstrate the aesthetic and political aims of the publishers, according to the nature of the image or the choice of artist. *La Revue blanche* was a journal that promoted new artistic ideas, and it was one of the first to publish articles questioning the irregularities surrounding the original Dreyfus court-martial of 1894. The journal employed many leading artists among the Symbolists and Nabis, including Vuillard, Ranson, Denis, Toulouse-Lautrec, Sérusier, and Redon. Vallotton, about whom more shortly, was an artist-in-residence there. Toulouse-Lautrec was an artist who could bring his commercial work to levels of exceptional artistic achievement. His poster (see fig. 1) depicting the wife of the publisher Thadée Natanson in a sinuous art-nouveau style was anything but political. Instead, it served to draw attention to the lofty aestheticism that dominated the intellectual, artistic, and liberally oriented publication.

Clemenceau's *L'Aurore,* was also liberal, but more distinctly concerned with news and politics than with art and society, to which it also paid some attention. *Aurore* means "dawn" in French, and Eugène Carrière's poster of 1897 (see fig. 2) shows Dawn arising from the uninformed darkness of the night, an allegorical representation of

Figure 1, Cat. 10
Henri de Toulouse-Lautrec
La Revue Blanche, 1895
Color lithographic poster

4

Figure 2, Cat. 6
Eugène Carrière
L'Aurore, 1897
Poster

the dependability of the information the journal purveyed.[14] This work may indeed be the poster in support of Dreyfus referred to in the literature on Carrière,[15] who was passionately Dreyfusard from the moment he witnessed the degradation of the army captain at the Ecole Militaire on 5 January 1895. He was one of the few artists present, and certainly one of the few whose presence was recorded. That he fervently believed the maligned captain's protestations of his innocence during that harrowing ceremony is shown in the artist's correspondence.[16]

Drumont, who can hardly be called a major patron of the arts, nonetheless employed some very competent artists for the illustrated supplement of his scandal sheet, called *La Libre Parole.* Yet the promotional poster executed for his newspaper can only be characterized as artless (see Marrus, fig. 7). What it lacked in aesthetic sensibility, however, it more than compensated for in size and vividness. The monumental poster contains a cartouche with a photographic portrait depicting none other than the egocentric and anti-Semitic owner of the paper himself. Drumont, who often called himself "the chief rabbi of anti-Semitism," was quite content to use his own fiery likeness as the logo for his paper. Its slogan, "France for the French," summarizes its anti-Semitic and xenophobic program.

Steinlen's poster for his journal, *La Feuille,* (see fig. 3 and Cate in this volume) is more a demonstration of the artist's socialist tendencies than it is an expression of his ambiguous stance vis-à-vis the Dreyfus case. The downpour of paper that inundates the proletarian masses in the image serves as terse critique of this era of journalistic excess.

With Rochefort's 1899 placard for his own viciously anti-Dreyfusard *L'Intransigeant,* the newspaper poster became directly involved in the Affair and was actually banned by the police.[17] (see fig. 4). Reproduced on this public announcement is a representation by the caricaturist J. Belon of a hooked-nosed and thoroughly semiticized Dreyfus stealthily leaving his Rennes prison cell. Prominently affixed to his valise are travel stickers from both Devil's Island and Berlin, the latter obviously implying that Dreyfus had a furtive connection with the enemy government. The torn document of Dreyfus's arrest shown in the picture must be a reference to the pardon granted shortly after the

Figure 3, Cat. 9
Théophile-Alexandre Steinlen
La Feuille, 1897
Poster

Figure 4, Cat. 5
J. Belon
L'Intransigeant, 1899
Poster

Figure 5, Cat. 14
Artist unknown
Here is the enemy (Voilà l'ennemi!)
La Lanterne, ca. 1898
Poster

second judgment at Rennes. Here is a poster that blatantly caters to an anti-Dreyfusard, anti-Semitic market.

Ironically, Rochefort had been the first editor of the republican and anticlerical *La Lanterne,* a paper that would become an ardently Dreyfusard vehicle because of its anticlerical stance. Its 1898 poster possibly coincided with the publication of a petition in support of Colonel Picquart. The poster shows The Church personified as an evil sorcerer emanating from the Basilica Sacre Coeur, a building that had come to symbolize the political dominance of the Church in the Republic (see fig. 5).

On the same side of the media marketplace is a handbill that was central to the heart of the Dreyfusard camp. It announces the reprinting of Zo d'Axa's weekly journal *En Dehors,* which was no longer in operation. This left-wing publication had been closed down with the antianarchist laws of 1894, but around 1898 it seemed possible to contemplate a reprinting. Louis Anquetin portrays the symbolic elements of the scandal, including the framed army captain himself (see fig. 6). Dreyfus, depicted as a puppet on a child's hobby horse, sits immobile near the end of a procession. This group is led by a judge, whom Anquetin ironically equips with a set of tipped scales of justice. He is followed by a haughty military offi-

cer and a bovine-faced courtier. Dreyfus is trailed by an aloof painter, canvas in hand, who seems unaffected by these personifications of societal ills. It is an unmistakable call to arms for unengaged artists, implying that their individual political commitment is needed against the sinister anti-militaristic, antiroyalist, and antijudicial forces.[18]

Besides the skill of the graphic artists, the technological advances that allowed inexpensive reproductions were another key factor in the media's ability to capitalize on the power of the image. The processes attendant to this revolution of photomechanical reproduction had actually carved new niches for artistic endeavor and expanded existing ones.[19] Using the potential of these processes enlarged markets for both artist and artwork. As a result, political cartoons proliferated as never before. Photomechanical reproductions form, by far, the most extensive category of the Dreyfus-related images as they spread through newspapers and illustrated journals. It was truly a golden age of visual polemic.

None better illustrates the power of the press during this period in general, and its impact for the Dreyfus Affair in particular, than Félix Vallotton's arresting cover for the weekly journal *Le Cri de Paris.* Titled "L'Age du papier" (see Cate fig. 46 and cover of this catalogue) the print appeared ten days after Zola's inflammatory article "J'Accuse" was published in the 13 January 1898 issue of *L'Aurore*. It depicts, with the artist's usual graphic economy, the effect of the more than fifty daily papers on the information-hungry Parisian public.[20] A worm's-eye view of a cafe scene shows patrons reading the various journals, including *Le Temps* and *Le Journal,* while one conspicuously devours Zola's incendiary headline "J'Accuse." The faces of all the readers are buried in the all-too-prominent sheets of printed matter. Vallotton's anarchist tendencies load the image with further political implications involving the consumers and their objects of consumption. The publishers and journalists, whose lucrative enterprises are represented by the scads of paper they produce, cater to a top-hatted bourgeois clientele. The poor news vendors depicted hawking their wares at the upper left are certainly victims of the capitalist system. But we might also ask if the bourgeois consumers are not also at the mercy of that system, albeit different aspects of it? The way the print uses the abundance of paper to express the dominance of the press is analogous to the way Steinlen's poster for *La Feuille* handles the theme.

The image the two works convey is indeed close to reality. For the Dreyfus Affair was certainly one of the first political issues in history that was so intensely managed by the media. The press continuously manipulated the scandal, if only to augment its fortunes. *La Libre Parole,* Edouard Drumont's anti-Semitic scandal sheet, revitalized its lagging readership by leaking news of the arrest.[21] Similarly, the newspaper shown in Vallotton's print, Clemenceau's *L'Aurore,* founded only a year earlier, sold over 300,000 copies on the day Zola's famous indictment was printed.[22] A document that corroborates the avidity with which the journalistic output was consumed is the photograph of the Mme. Bizet Straus circle (see fig. 7), an ardently pro-Dreyfusard group, here shown absorbed in reading the sensational headlines of the various newspapers. Here, Madeleine Bizet, daughter-in-law of the composer, Paul Hervieu, playwright, and Mme. Straus, widow of Georges Bizet are shown reading both pro- and anti-Dreyfusard journals to ascertain every nuance of fact and factual distortion.

Vallotton's involvement did not stop at this prelude to the next two years of journalistic hype that reached its peak during Dreyfus's retrial in Rennes of September 1899. The artist created numerous works, including a contribution to the album of twelve prints honoring the officer who

Figure 6, Cat. 3
Louis Anquetin
Endehors, ca. 1898
Lithographic poster

Figure 7, Cat. 469
Madeleine Bizet, Paul Hervieu, and
Geneviève Straus
Photograph, 1898

risked his career in announcing that the real culprit was Colonel Walsin-Esterhazy. His lithograph for *Hommage des artistes à Picquart,* perhaps one of the strongest and most original of the suite, depicts the anti-Dreyfusard Prime Minister Méline waking from a dream with the startled realization that Dreyfus is innocent (pl. 124). This revelation was a fictive mockery of that official's stated misconception "There is no Dreyfus Affair," words he uttered just moments before the scandal escalated.

Among Vallotton's other illustrations for the Natanson-owned paper *Le Cri de Paris* is the moving cover of 1 October 1899 issue, published shortly after Alfred Dreyfus was pardoned. His graphic reinterpretation of a much-reproduced photograph of the returned prisoner reunited with his children is made even more poignant by the children's close interaction with their father. Its ironic title "Père, Une histoire" ("Papa, a story!") heightens the poignancy still further. Surely the public already understood the convoluted tale of Alfred Dreyfus to be an epic whose complexity Hannah Arendt would later compare with that of a Balzac novel.[23] The artist Henri-Gabriel Ibels also drew an image of the pardoned captive with his children, this one titled "To the Glory of Scheurer-Kestner" (see pl. 164). This sentimental image has none of the bite of Vallotton's. On the contrary, it evokes the sad irony of the untimely death of the vice-president of the Senate. Scheurer-Kestner, an Alsatian and one of the first of the revision bandwagon, died the morning Dreyfus's pardon was announced.[24]

Many other illustrators took part in the campaign to disseminate information and opinions from both sides of the Affair. Most noteworthy are the anti-Dreyfusards Forain and Caran d'Ache and their arch enemy Ibels. They established two opposed illustrated journals, *Psst . . . !* and *Le Sifflet,* against and for Dreyfus respectively. These two weeklies demonstrate the trend toward papers generated in rival pairs, which often benefited more from their mutual opposition than from their specific points of view.[25] Dennis Cate discusses these artists and their made-for-the-Affair journals, as well as the participation of the Montmartre school.[26] It is, nevertheless, important to remember that these were by no means the only artists whose works appeared in the pages of the copiously illustrated journals.

A host of illustrators, both pro- and con-Dreyfus, dispatched their drawings to the various papers. Some even jumped sides as their own or their employers' political convictions and views of the case changed. One example of such a change of heart is the illustrator known as Pépin, who worked for the right-wing (though also republican) newspaper *Le Grelot.* His reevaluation of his anti-Dreyfusard stance forced him to sever a twenty-year-long association with that paper. The prodigious illustrators Alfred Le Petit and Moloch actually met at the offices of their employer *L'Etrille* (see pl. 38).[27] Other new draftsmen soon appeared on the scene, adopting such *au courant* pseudonyms as Cyrano (for Edmond Rostand's recently published play). *Le Figaro,* a conservative journal which had originally taken a moderate position on the scandal and then turned revisionist, was one of the few dailies that published caricatures several times a week. It engaged the talents of Forain, Léandre, Caran d'Ache, and Henriot among others. Forain's career there would end around the time *Le Figaro* began printing drawings relating to the Dreyfus Affair. The artist refused to compromise his views in line with the paper's newly liberalized ones. Caran d'Ache stayed with *Le Figaro,* probably making some ideological concessions as he continued to illustrate *Psst . . . !* (pl. 49).[28] Drumont's *La Libre Parole illustré* included among its contributors Chanticlair, Gravelle, and Maillotin, and they created a barrage of scathing images (see pl. 6).

Hermann-Paul and Couturier contributed designs to *Le Sifflet,* as did its founder Ibels. Couturier also assiduously recorded the Rennes trial for many other journals and magazines. Numerous examples of the original drawings for these still exist. They appear, for the most part, accurate if dull visual reportage (see pls. 142–148). His art was given freer rein in more complex pro-Dreyfus imagery of his own imagination. *En voulez-vous des aveux* (see pl. 41) is one such example. In this print, he hangs the lot of corrupt army officials in effigy for their many and varied crimes. These victims of the hangings are depicted as puppets of the corrupt military system. His *Apothéose Orphéonique* is an image of great iconographical complexity. The anti-Dreyfusards, Déroulède, Coppée and d'Esparlies, dressed in antique robes, appear to present Esterhazy with a sword to fall upon after a battle which ends in a Pyrrhic victory (see fig. 8). Many of his designs were so enormously successful that they were made into a series of popular postcards and other ephemera.

One cannot discuss the courtroom imagery generated by the Dreyfus Affair without mentioning Paul Renouard. Renouard produced a large body of graphic work that depicted scenes of the Zola trial, the Court of Appeal, and Rennes. He has been described as "master of the 'snap-shot' sketch"[29] and, indeed, his several views of the gesticulations of the lawyer Labori at the Zola trial are a case in point (see pls. 30a, b). A fervent Dreyfusard, he executed numerous sketches of the various proceedings and the individuals involved, using both lithographic and wood-engraving techniques. The several extant sets of these graphics recall the immediacy of his deft hand and reveal his ability to capture the emotion of events and people. A noteworthy example is the depiction of Dreyfus's lawyer immediately after the second conviction at Rennes (see pl. 141). Demange holds his heavy head in his hands as he sits in despair after the long and emotional proceedings of the second court-martial (as if the first trial and conviction had not been enough!). The sardonic note struck by the emphasis on the crucifix, a device used to similar effect by Daumier earlier in the century, adds currency to the repeated injustice of the second conviction in a society that purported to be democratic and Christian. Another view of the Rennes court-martial in process indicates the artist's ability to politicize his observations (see pl. 132). Renouard captures the pale figure of the defendant, physically immobile and mentally dazed. Pushed to an insignificant corner of the background, Dreyfus is rendered as a transparent, ghostly presence. The defendant seems to present his testimony, not to the judges, whose faces are obscured, but to the arrogant, cross-legged, military elite whose complicity in the returned prisoner's frame-up seems quite evident. The artist's depiction of the traditional guard of dishonor—that is, the soldiers, their backs turned on the "degraded" captain—renders it as civilized barbarism (see pl. 135).

Although far less artistic and seemingly unopinionated, several drawings for reproductions by an illustrator who must be known simply by his monogram (O.I.) are enlightening. They show the members of the working press engaged in getting the Dreyfus story. They also show the curious

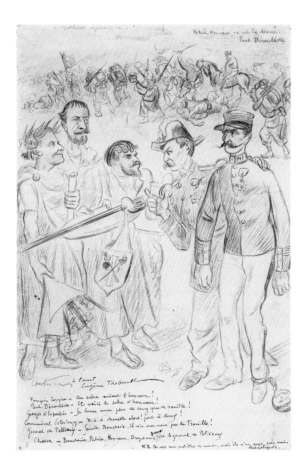

Figure 8, Cat. 127

Léon-Antoine-Lucien Couturier

Choral Apotheosis: Fatherland, Honor—It's the motto, Paul Déroulède (Apothéose orphéonique: Patrie, Honneur—c'est la devise, Paul Déroulède)

1898

Graphite on paper

means used to relay information from reporter to consumer. He depicted the many photographers awaiting their subjects during the retrial of 1899, and the use of homing pigeons to speed images to Paris in the rush to beat the competition. These offer privileged glimpses of journalistic life behind the scenes (see pls. 150 and 152).

The camera, one of the most revolutionary inventions for art in the nineteenth century, was bound to play a major role in the propagandistic flurry. The perfection of the halftone and the new technologies of improved photosensitive plates expanded the role for the political uses of photography. Photographic images could now be reproduced in magazines, newspapers, leaflets, and posters easily and cheaply.[30] Noteworthy among the photographers who provided illustrative material for newspapers is Gerschel. His two hundred photographs of the Rennes trial appeared in numerous publications, and the prints were compiled in albums and sold as souvenirs. Some examples of Gerschel's subjects include Madame Dreyfus arriving for her daily visit with Alfred, and candid shots of the military officers and attorneys who swarmed through Rennes during August and September of 1899 (see pls. 153–163).

The poster *Dreyfus est un traître* (see pl. 105) was one of the first to use the new halftone process to serve mass production. Employing photographic images of five former ministers of war, this visual and verbal diatribe might be categorized as an updated illustrated broadside. An anti-Dreyfus polemic appears beneath each image. The distribution of more than 136,000 copies of this mass-market propaganda compelled the Dreyfusards to retort. Using a nearly identical format and the very same commercial printer, their rejoinder showed a gallery of eleven Dreyfusard activists, including notable intellectuals and journalists (see pl. 106).[31] The history of these two posters supports the argument that the Dreyfusards attached less importance to the imagery contained in their publications than did the anti-Dreyfusards.[32] Accordingly, they were often content to play a defensive role, merely duplicating the latest efforts of the enemy camp.

The appearance of what was obviously a bogus photograph of Baron von Reinach in *L'Antijuif* caused quite a sensation. The baron, infamous for his connection with the Panama Scandal of 1892 and a relative of the esteemed Dreyfusard Joseph

Reinach, had died mysteriously at the height of that earlier scandal. The photograph's caption read "Von Reinach assassinated by Clemenceau." It was intended to discredit the two prominent Dreyfusards—Joseph Reinach and his uncle's purported assassin. Such apocryphal images were not new to the scene of political intrigue. The neo-Impressionist painter Signac had, ten years earlier, in 1889, created an illustrated pamphlet depicting the premature and fictitious death of General Boulanger, in order to mock the power-hungry general.[33]

Yves Guyot, director of the Dreyfusard daily *Le Siècle,* devised a clever method to show the public the virtually limitless possibilities for manipulating photographs. It also served to refute the veracity of the posthumous photo of von Reinach. His supplement *Les Mensonges de la photographie* (see pl. 107) showed several unlikely juxtapositions—mostly of anti-Dreyfusard figures—within the same photo. These images were created by the superimposition of several negatives into one print. The most ironic of them shows Colonel Henry awaiting a shave from his newfound barber, the former minister of war, Godefrey Cavaignac. This image sarcastically refers to the forger Henry's own suicide by razor (see fig. 9).[34]

Outside the realm of photographic images, but continuing the theme of propagandistic placards, is one of the most amazing efforts at large-scale visual character assassination: the series of more than fifty posters titled *Musée des horreurs* (see pls. 169–177). This suite of hand-colored lithographic posters, exceptional in their artistic quality, appeared around the time of the Rennes trial and continued for nearly a year thereafter. They appeared weekly and were also offered by subscription. These images were, no doubt intended to disgrace the victorious Dreyfusards who, following the compromise whereby the army captain was pardoned, had become more prominent in the leadership of the Third Republic. Signed with the pseudonym "V. Lenepveu," they portray the faces of various Dreyfusards and Jews (including Zola, Dreyfus, Clemenceau, Jaurès, Waldeck-Rousseau, Baron Rothschild, Joseph Reinach) with near-photographic accuracy. Their bodies, represented more fancifully in the form of mammals, serpents, and fish, serve the artist as metaphor for his own tawdry practice of social and political Darwinism.[35]

Given the rash of varied types of mass-produced images discussed thus far, it is not too difficult to conclude that the Dreyfus Affair had offered lucrative commercial, professional, and ideological rewards to those who manipulated it. Perhaps it is possible to believe that most of the aforementioned material was created out of genuine political conviction. Nevertheless, it is difficult to ascertain whether the ephemera that emanated from this media-hyped event served anything but material ends.

The market for materials created in this political cauldron seemed endless, and the range of manufactured paraphernalia showed that politics could propel cottage industries into big businesses (and not just in the area of journalism). Children were targeted as a market for materials that relayed the contorted tale of Captain Dreyfus. Comic strips appeared, both pro and con, naturally, to wit the sheets titled *Histoire d'un innocent* and *Histoire d'un traître* (see pls. 73–74). Colorful and charmingly illustrated, they were certainly one way to teach children recent history. Even Pierre Dreyfus, we are told, eventually learned his father's sad story through such a device.

Novelties relating to the scandal pose some mysteries: For what audience were they intended? Why do mostly anti-Dreyfusard images remain? For example, one could play with the elongated, phallic, and Semiticized nose of Dreyfus's brother in the toy called "Le Pif du Frère Mathieu"; or be assured that Zola's heart was in the right place as we lift the flap at the rear of the realist author's pants to discover the tattoo: "Mon coeur à Dreyfus" (My heart belongs to Dreyfus) (see pl. 66). Another card permits us to pull the figure of Truth from the bottom of her proverbial well through a tug-of-war of various Dreyfusard and anti-Dreyfusard figures (see pl. 67).

Yet another gimmick was the ten-part series of cigarette papers that offered the simplified tale of an honorable, but maligned captain (see pls. 68–70). It viewed the Affair from a Dreyfusard vantage point. Its trademark, "Le Papier du Bordereau," refers to the paper document whose misattributed authorship wrongly convicted Dreyfus. The series thereby equate, not at all subtly, the relative value of that piece of spurious evidence with the vaporous end-product of cigarettes—smoke! Adult board games, both pro and con, also appeared (see pl. 71). Dreyfusards could follow

ALLONS-Y!

Les malheurs d'un coiffeur.
Il vendait de l'eau pour faire pousser les cheveux, et la photographie prouve qu'il est atteint par la calvitie.
Il vient de dire :
— Le premier de ces messieurs, s'il vous plaît.
Et il se prépare à donner son premier coup de rasoir...

Figure 9, Cat. 346
"Allons-y"
Detail from *The Lies of photography (Les mensonges de la photographie)*
Le Siècle, 11 January 1899
Photomechanical print

the spiral trail titled "The Game of the Dreyfus Affair and the Truth" making visits to various pro- and anti-Dreyfusard characters in pursuit of the central and winning point of Truth. And the "Game of Thirty-Six Heads" published by *L'Antijuif* might be considered a panacea for anti-Dreyfusards seeking a break from Parisian nightlife (see pl. 72).

Political imagery was not new to the folding fan, that important accessory of the well-dressed woman. Examples from the period of the French Revolution were emblazoned with allegorical scenes commemorating the American Revolution of 1776, the treaty between America and France, and the French involvement in the wars of Spain. In an updating of the imagery on these coquettish yet practical appurtenances, visual references on fans of the late nineteenth century were made to the latest hot political topic. Several examples are preserved at the Musée Carnavalet in Paris. Their images, mostly culled from newspaper illustrations, relate both to Dreyfus and Zola (see figs. 10–11).

Another bountiful category of material was the recently invented postcard. The scandal created a flurry of examples of this popular new form of correspondence. The drawings of many illustrators mentioned previously were reproduced on these new vehicles for quickly jotted missives. Among the artists whose works found their way to the mailbox were Moloch, Couturier, and Orens. So desirable were Couturier's illustrated cards, that they were quickly out of print, soon to become cherished collectibles (see pls. 94–103).[36] Various photographs of the trials, especially at Rennes, and composite photographs of the important characters in both the Dreyfusard and anti-Dreyfusard camps were also widely used as illustrations for postcards (pls. 82–83).

. . .

The vast commercialization of the Affair, a phenomenon reflecting the late nineteenth-century's societal degeneration and seeming lack of propriety, appears amply evident from the preceding discussion. The bounty of images (and words) that were quickly, cheaply, and widely dispersed powerfully affected the transmission and formation of opinion. The commercial material, if only through its sheer quantity, gives a strong sense of popular preoccupation with the Dreyfus Affair. Needless

to say, many artists continued to work in the non-commercial realm and some of them produced art that was shaped by the hotly debated issues. To think that art of this kind was capable of exerting even a small fraction of the impact of the abundant commercial imagery is unrealistic. Some readers might even ask why the serious art that showed the impact of the Affair should be discussed at all: Its messages were often so personal, and its interpretation often so complex. Yet others might call into question the scrutiny already afforded the photomechanically reproduced images and the ephemera—both seemingly insignificant by-products of modern culture. Nevertheless, the fact that so-called high art and its makers on occasion fell prey, sometimes unwittingly, to political entanglement is in itself certainly worthy of examination in this context. Given the limitations of space and the scope of this book, the following must suffice as a cursory exploration for what may well be fertile territory for future investigation. Of particular note here is the different ratios of pro- and anti-Dreyfusard material that seems to obtain between the corpus of polemical images and ephemera and that of the fine art generated by the Affair. As previously mentioned, in the commercial category, the anti-Dreyfus output was seemingly greater than that of the Dreyfusards; whereas the work of the serious artists seems almost exclusively Dreyfusard. It would, nevertheless, be wrong to draw any conclusions from these empirical observations without a quantifiable study.

The intersection of politics and art was certainly not a new phenomenon sparked by the Dreyfus Affair. In fact, nineteenth-century France witnessed numerous examples of politics reflected in art, interacting with it, and sometimes even interrupting its production. Commissions for art by the various monarchies and republics resulted in the creation of works with specific programmatic goals; whether the portrayal of the power or heroism of the monarch (e.g., the portraits of Napoleon by Ingres and David) or as conciliatory offerings to the various factions of the French public (e.g., François Rude's *Marseilles* of 1836). Other artists commented either reportorially or allegorically on contemporary political issues and events (e.g., Delacroix's *Massacre at Chios,* or his *Liberty Leading the People*). Around mid-century and thereafter, many of the works of Courbet, Millet,

Daumier, and Manet took social and political issue with the dominant ideology of the day. No less politicized were the reactions of the Salon-going public to the various annual submissions, and in fact their response could often change the course of an artist's career.

Several examples here serve to show the artistic foreshadowing of the issues which were both inherent to the impending scandal and would remain central to it. These took the form of observations of powerful factions of government or society and depictions of the political arena itself. Pierre Bonnard's early picture *The Parade Ground* of 1890 is one such work. It shows the artist's indifference to the military and reveals a rather cynical view of it. The picture may reflect his own experience as a soldier nearly a decade earlier.[37] Its composition, content, and date relate quite closely to Vallotton's *At Twenty Years* (see Cate fig. 27). Jean-François Raffaëlli's *Portrait de M. Clemenceau en réunion électorale* (see pl. 184) depicts one of the major figures in the future Dreyfus campaign. It also already demonstrates his power to captivate the public. The artist wanted to show the politician in action and he actually followed his subject on various electoral campaigns to complete this work.[38] Demonstrated here is the intense degree of political activity in the Third Republic, made possible by the open nature of that government. One can but imagine many other such orations taking place throughout France under the freedom of speech it represents—the vocal equivalent of a free press.

In 1889, Alfred-Philippe Roll received a government commission to paint a monumental canvas commemorating the centennial celebrations of the French Revolution. Titled *La Fête du centenaire des Etats-Généraux celebrée à Versailles en 1889* (see pl. 185), it was not completed until 1893, when it was shown at the Salon. Its vision, depicting the unity of all factions of French political and social life under the leadership of President Sadi Carnot, is similar in its conciliatory purpose to that of Rude's *Marseilles*. Accommodating all the different classes and professions in one vast panorama, this grand-scale contemporary scene offers hommage to the success and harmony of the Republic.[39] One little suspects from this idealistic reportage that many of the participants, so charmingly brought together in this moment of national celebration, would become arch enemies in the wake of the Dreyfus Affair, or that Carnot, the master of cere-

Figure 12
Paul Cézanne
Portrait of Gustave Geffroy, 1895
Oil on canvas
Photo, Musée d'Orsay, Paris

Figure 10, Cat. 387
The Zola Case (L'Affaire Zola), 1898
Pleated paper fan; collage with news-
paper clippings; wooden blades

Figure 11, Cat. 389
*The Dreyfus Case at Rennes (L'Affaire
Rennes),* 1899
Pleated paper fan; collage with news-
paper clippings; wooden blades

monies at this event, would fall at the hand of an anarchist assassin the year after Roll completed his commission.

If the fate of the *Portrait of Gustave Geffroy* (see fig. 12) by Cézanne is not a direct result of the Dreyfus Affair, it is certainly a consequence of the prevailing political alignments that would be played out during the scandal. Geffroy was an art critic who championed the art of Cézanne. In 1895, he sat numerous times for this portrait, staged in his own study. Both artist and sitter were most enthusiastic about the joint venture. Then, with seemingly little provocation, Cézanne suddenly left for his native Aix in the south of France. Shortly after his abrupt departure—in April of 1896—he sent a messenger to fetch the materials he had left in Geffroy's home.[40] The por-trait was never completed and artist and sitter never saw each other again. An explanation given for Cézanne's behavior was the artist's apparent distaste for the writer's frequent mention of Georges Clemenceau.[41] While Clemenceau was not yet affected by the issues surrounding the Dreyfus case—the clues to the illegalities of the

first court-martial were not made public until later in 1896—he had always been connected with left-wing politics. Furthermore, the former anarchist and future Dreyfusard Geffroy was completing the biography of the French socialist and revo-lutionary Blanqui at the time of the sittings. It is not difficult to realize that Cézanne, who would later take a hard-line anti-Dreyfusard stance in accord with his own conservative politics, might have found himself at odds with Geffroy's radical views.[42]

Seen as a depiction of the activist engaged in the process of writing, Cézanne's portrait serves as an example of this then-popular image, a subject appropriate to an era that frequently invoked the maxim "the pen is mightier than the sword." In fact, these subjects might be called upon as proof of one positive aspect of the Dreyfus Affair. That is, the Affair, while provoking shrill and intense verbal responses, resulted in little physical vio-lence. The Dreyfus Affair was basically an ideo-logical battle fought with words, not weapons. Two nearly identical portraits of the critic and anarchist Félix Fénéon—one by Vuillard, the other

Figure 13, Cat. 464
Felix Vallotton
Fénéon à La Revue Blanche, 1896
Oil on cardboard mounted on canvas

Figure 14, Cat. 442
Henri Evenepoel
Portrait of Georges Clemenceau, 1899
Pencil on paper

by Vallotton (see fig. 13)—are excellent examples of this genre. In 1891, Vuillard also depicted the writer and future Dreyfusard Octave Mirbeau in a similar pose denoting his engagement in written communication. If not as aesthetically exciting, the 1899 *Portrait of Clemenceau* (see fig. 14), pen in hand, by the Belgian Evenepoel carries a similar message of activism through words, not deeds.

Among the paintings and drawings directly relating to the Affair, few refer so directly to current events or are as curious in their combination of news and fantasy as a pastel and two drawings by Henri–Gabriel Ibels. This is owing, in part, to the fact that Ibels, so actively involved in illustration, frequently dealt with reportorial images. The artist, previously discussed here as founder and contributor to the illustrated journal *Le Sifflet,* created a haunting pastel titled *La Dernière Dame voilée en place pour le quadrille* (see pl. 191). Taking historic license with the sequence of events and the cast of characters involved in the Dreyfus case, Ibels staged a scene in which poetic justice is accorded the antagonists. He has taken a triumvirate of military officials who helped frame Dreyfus and

has hung all three from gallows. At the right, du Paty de Clam, the officer who tried so ardently to get a confession from Dreyfus, twists in the wind. At the center hangs Mercier, the minister of war during the first court-martial and one of the conspirators involved in the cover-up. The figure at the left appears to be de Boisdeffre. The veiled female skeleton who plays for their execution, a reference to the fictitious veiled lady conjured up by Esterhazy as pretext, also serves as the dual personification of death and justice.[43] The scathing commentary, implying guilt of the military officials, is blatantly obvious.

Ibels adapts Christian imagery in two nearly identical drawings of Alfred Dreyfus crucified (see pl. 192). These drawings actually relate to a caricature for *Le Siècle* in 1900, but given the fact of their presentation to two friends, one of them the prominent Dreyfusard Joseph Reinach, permits us to put these in a more personal category. The imagery is a contemporary reworking of Matthew 27:48. Ibels has replaced the figure of Jesus with that of the artist's contemporary martyr Dreyfus. General Mercier, previously encountered in *La*

Dernière Dame, presents the captain, in an ignoble gesture, with the vinegar-soaked sponge.[44] The ironies attendant on this image are many. Dreyfus, the Jew, replaces the Christian savior. The general, as the personification of the military, replaces the taunting Jew. This curious inversion of the gospel text is for Ibels a means of equating biblical and contemporary tragedy and injustice.

In 1898, Edouard Debat-Ponson submitted to the Salon a monumental canvas titled *Nec Mergitur,* or *La Vérité sortant du puits* (see pl. 189). The picture's iconographical reference to the Affair, its association for a specific activist, and the reception it found at the Salon were to have far-reaching ramifications for the artist. The allegorical figure of Truth emerging from the well is one that had appeared frequently in late nineteenth-century art and it was utilized often in polemical works on both sides of the Affair.[45] Traditionally, the figure of Truth was hidden at the bottom of a well where she had to be sought. The aptness of this metaphor to the Dreyfus scandal is self-evident. Its offering by subscription to Emile Zola made the intent of this representation all the more cogent. Here is a work publicly exhibited at the height of the crisis, which pleaded for a revision of the original judgment. And it upheld the character of the recipient, who, risking his own career and well-being, had come to Dreyfus's defense. The adverse affects this painting was to have for the artist were manifold. Debat-Ponsan, the Languedoc-born student of the academician Alexandre Cabanel, suffered the rupture of family ties and lost many formerly devoted clients for his stock-in-trade portrait commissions.[46] A record of the work's impact on Emile Zola, who prominently displayed it in the entrance foyer to his home, is recorded by the dealer Ambrose Vollard. The noted author's great admiration for the canvas and the artist is aptly expressed in Zola's own words: "One seems to hear before this canvas the cry of the conscience of an honest man."[47]

Truth is also the title of an important painting by the Swiss artist Ferdinand Hodler, a work which was to occupy the painter for several years (see pl. 200). Two versions of this large composition exist; one of 1902, another of 1903. The work, in keeping with Hodler's explorations into basic questions of existence—life and death, faith and despair—shows the forceful female figure of Truth

unveiling the black-draped male figures who represent evil and deceit.[48] Numerous drawings for this work, which brought to a close Hodler's Symbolist period of the 1890s,[49] date from between 1898 and 1903. The picture's composition and conception came directly from the canvas titled *Day,* which preceded it. Its Symbolist allegory is certainly more imaginative, and also more allusive, than the hackneyed image of Truth emerging from the well. The Viennese art critic Franz Servaes recorded Hodler's connection of these works with the Dreyfus Affair at the time the two large murals were exhibited at the Vienna Secession in 1903.[50] Hodler's patron and friend Mathias Morhardt, a writer and one of the founders of the Dreyfusard organization, The League of the Rights of Man, is believed to have suggested this subject to the artist.[51] Given the basically apolitical nature of Hodler's oeuvre, the underlying theme of this work is even more unusual.[52] But the scandal's recurring ideological issues must have provided cogent analogues for Hodler's own philosophical inquiry.

The decorative artist Émile Gallé, whose works in glass and inlaid wood were objects of great aesthetic delectation, was a passionate Dreyfusard. His opinions and sentiments regarding the scandal and the personal affront he felt are well documented in his correspondence.[53] Gallé actually produced a corpus of works with both direct and implicit reference to the Affair. The inscriptions on his vases, their dedications to Dreyfusards, and the metaphoric meanings of the plants and animals depicted were combined to express his personal convictions. His vase *Hippocampes* (see pl. 196) dedicated to Joseph Reinach is a superb example of his craft as well as his devotion to the political cause. Its inscription, "Life depends on Truth," is a reference to Zola's famous statement "Truth is on the march" and a catchword frequently allegorized in Dreyfus imagery. It has been suggested that this work, in honor of the politician whose courage and zeal helped bring about the eventual realization of justice, may have been presented to Reinach after the appearance of the first volume of his seven-volume history of the Affair.[54] The Latin inscription on Gallé's 1898 table is apparently taken from Isaiah 61:11: "Just as the garden brings forth its seed, so God will bring forth Justice." Its meaning, once again, alludes to the scandal that so preoccupied the artist. The biblical passage deals with the salvation of Zion and justice for the oppressed; its clear reference to justice, one of the other issues central to the Dreyfus Affair, is evident (see fig. 15).

Several other Gallé vases have been associated with the Affair, again through their inscriptions and the metaphorical significance of both their representations and color. Among these is a vase of 1900 titled *Héracleum* (see fig. 16) and its pendant, which is inscribed "We like the idea with all its aspects, power, truth, liberty, peace, justice, innocence. Victor Hugo."[55] The funeral tone of another vase depicting elm trees in winter dormancy, symbolizing mourning and grief is another example (see pl. 197). This vase has been contrasted with a lamp inscribed more optimistically "Truth will glow like a lamp," which signifies hope for Dreyfus's rehabilitation.[56] Gallé made another table in 1899 for his wife; it has an inlaid inscription that refers to her dedication to the fight for humanistic principles, liberty, and justice. He signed this table as treasurer of the League of the Rights of Man. Not unlike the fate of Debat-Ponsan after his submission of *Nec Mergitur* to the Salon of 1898, Gallé's ardent political stance and his activity in this pro-Dreyfus group is thought to have lost for Gallé a number of his regular clients, who found themselves at odds with his political thinking.[57]

The monument to Auguste Scheurer-Kestner, commissioned from the eminent sculptor and ardent Dreyfusard Aimé-Jules Dalou, ranks as one of the most significant artistic testimonies to the scandal. As the Affair was the last major political involvement for the senator (who died the morning Dreyfus's pardon was announced), so this monument was Dalou's last major undertaking. Its iconographic program includes a portrait medallion of the senator on the base of the obelisk (see pl. 199). Invoked once again is the allegorical figure of Truth, standing to the right of the portrait, which is flanked on the left by the figure of Justice. Dalou seems to have been the perfect candidate for this commission. Through the classicism and austerity of his conception, he has evoked Scheurer-Kestner's nobility and unyielding high principles.[58]

Dalou had such a high profile as a Dreyfusard that some of his unrelated works became politicized. For example, when his *Triumph of the Republic* (see pl. 190) (which he worked on between 1879 and 1889) was finally unveiled in 1899, it was called by the anti-Dreyfusards "the Triumph

Figure 15, Cat. 447
Emile Gallé
Tea Table, 1898
Wood marquetry; bronze holders
Inscription:
Just as the garden brings forth its seed, so God will bring forth Justice, Is. ("Sicut hortus semen germinat, sic, Deus germinabit Justitiam, Is.").

18

Figure 16
Emile Gallé
Heracleum (Héracleum), 1900
Crystal in double layers; filigreed; engraved; inlaid; with applied elements
Inscription:
"Our arts will exhale the scents of the meadow / Altruism and beauty will perfume our lives. V. HUGO"
("Nos arts exhaleront des senteurs de prairie / altruisme et beauté parfumeront nos vies, V. HUGO")
Photo, Musée de l'Ecole de Nancy

of the Jews."[59] Dalou created numerous casts in plaster, bronze, and porcelain of his table sculpture of *Vérité méconnue* (see fig. 17), beginning in the 1890s. Through their iconographic relationship to the figure on the Scheurer-Kestner monument and the artist's own political convictions, these have sometimes been associated with the scandal. Claims also have been made that they were offered for sale to benefit the cause.[60]

The connection between figures of Truth in the art of the 1890s and the Dreyfus Affair was widespread, and it has given rise to a category of works that might be dubbed "le mensonge de la Vérité" (the error of Truth). What must be remembered in such interpretations is the fact that the Dreyfus Affair did not occupy the popular political consciousness until late 1896 at the very earliest, and consequently great caution must be exercised in the interpretation of such seemingly relevant allegories created prior to that date. It was really not until the appearance of Zola's "J'Accuse" that the issue moved to center ring. Therefore, it is also unlikely that Gérôme's figures of Truth emerging from the well, which have sometimes been connected with the Dreyfus Affair, should be so interpreted. These were begun in 1895 when the army captain was safely incarcerated on Devil's Island, and few felt that any injustice had occurred.[61]

The numerous works previously discussed are connected by the thread of allegorical or contemporary images relating to the issues, personalities, or events of the Dreyfus scandal. As already foreshadowed in the history of Cézanne's *Portrait of Geffroy,* the polarization of camps involved in the Affair could play havoc with art not related to the Affair. One of the most noted examples of political interference affected one of the key works of late nineteenth-century art: Auguste Rodin's brilliant Balzac monument (see pl. 194). The commission for this monument had been awarded to Rodin by the Société des Gens des Lettres in 1891 at the recommendation of Zola, its president.[62] Rodin, however, struggling for aesthetic originality and for conceptual and symbolic appropriateness to the memory of Balzac, did not finish his plaster model until 1898. During its exhibition at the Salon of that year, a controversy ensued. At the beginning, apparently, the issues of contention were aesthetic. The depiction of the celebrated author in his flowing robe and the unstable tilt of his figure must have contributed to the Société's rejection of the proposed monument. The furor over this piece escalated to such a degree that it now vied with the Dreyfus Affair for prominence in the press during May 1898.[63] Over a hundred articles about Rodin's sculpture appeared from May through July of that year.[64] Its political

Figure 17, Cat. 439
Aimé-Jules Dalou
Truth Denied (La Vérité méconnue),
ca. 1895
Bronze

entanglement with the Affair began when an alternative committee, seeing this work of art a new cause involving artistic freedom and freedom of expression in general, was formed. The purpose of the committee was to raise other funds for the casting of Rodin's *Balzac.* Many prominent liberals and radicals, mostly Dreyfusard in sentiment, contributed funds, and the goal was quickly realized. Many Dreyfusards—Clemenceau, Morhardt, France, to name a few—were among the supporters and the goal was quickly realized. Rodin, however, did not wish to become involved in politics, and indeed he had previously refused to sign a petition on Dreyfus's behalf for just this reason. Rodin, who might be likened to the unengaged artist depicted in Anquetin's poster for *En Dehors* (see fig. 6), art and politics did not mix. Seeing the substantial Dreyfusard contingent among his supporters, Rodin now refused to accept these funds and withdrew his sculpture from the Salon. Clemenceau in turn withdrew his support.

To many of the Dreyfusards who rallied to the support of this newest cause célèbre, Rodin's political indifference was a source of great disappointment.[65] The commission for a monument to Balzac was eventually turned over to the sculptor Falguière, who produced a dry, academic work. And, owing to all the controversy, Rodin's *Balzac*

was not cast until thirty years later.[66] It was only several years later that Rodin would see his first public sculpture, *The Thinker,* erected in Paris, under a much-changed political climate (see pl. 195). The intervening years between 1898 and 1904 had created a new era of political *rapprochement* in an effort to heal the wounds left in the wake of the Affair. With great sensitivity to bipartisan politics in general and Rodin's politics in particular, a new committee was formed, with great emphasis on the balance between Dreyfusard and anti-Dreyfusard constituencies. The sensitivity to the politics (or, perhaps, the lack thereof) was carefully choreographed. The radical, Dreyfusard Gustave Geffroy even asked the conservative, anti-Dreyfusard Paul Cézanne to contribute, in an effort to balance the list. The *Thinker* was installed in 1906, finally giving Rodin the prominence he deserved while creating a meeting point for many prominent Frenchmen who, at the height of the scandal, thought they might never again see eye to eye.

Aristide Maillol was another sculptor who seemed ambivalent to political issues. Nevertheless, the restructured complexion of more liberal politics in response to Dreyfus's pardon and its concomitant infusion of liberal ideas, brought him a commission that would have been unthinkable before or during the Dreyfus Affair. The revolutionary socialist Blanqui, whose biography Geffroy was completing when Cézanne dropped interest in the portrait of the writer, and for whom Dalou had created a funerary monument at Père Lachaise in 1883, was *persona non grata* with the prevailing regimes of the neo-conservative period of the 1890s. The ascendancy of a large proportion of Radical party members into the Chamber of Deputies around the middle of the first decade of this century is associated with the political victories of this group relating to Dreyfus's pardon and ultimate rehabilitation. It was only in such a reformed political atmosphere that a monument to Blanqui could have been contemplated. The sculptural monument to the revolutionary, commissioned from Maillol in 1904, was erected in Blanqui's home town Puget-Thèniers in 1907. Titled *L'Action enchainée* (see pl. 201), it was the only monument to a political figure during the Third Republic represented by a female nude.[67]

The themes of several works created at the height of the scandal, while not directly related to the Affair, conveyed strong sentiments about the problems that were at its core. Their messages were plainly evident to the public at the time and, because the rhetoric was for the most part pro-Dreyfus, the artists or their works frequently suffered critical opprobrium. The criticism generally concerned various much-debated issues—militarism, clericalism, patriotism, Zionism, and the division of the French nation over the Dreyfus Affair.

Jean-Jacques Henner, an Alsatian deeply affected by the separation of his native province from France in 1871, had sent a canvas to the Salon of 1898 (the one to which Debat-Ponsan submitted *Nec Mergitur*). Debat-Ponsan had used a popular allegory, the subject of Henner's entry was a representation of the biblical story of *The Levite of Ephraim and his Dead Wife* (see pl. 188). This complicated tale recounts the brutal and unnecessary slaying of Ephraim's wife by kinsmen of the tribe of Benjamin. The bloodshed that ensued in retaliation for this gross offense by the other Israelite tribes serves Henner as an allegory for the division of France during the Dreyfus Affair. The observation of Henner's pessimism at that time has been attributed, at least in part, to the Affair and the resulting factions that split the nation. One may also raise the possibility that the artist harbored feelings of kinship for his fellow Alsatian Dreyfus. We know with certainty that Henner was close friends with another fellow Alsatian, the vice president of the Senate, Auguste Scheurer-Kestner. Scheurer-Kestner was one of the earliest and most vocal Dreyfusards and he lost many friends when he spoke out for the revision of the first court-martial.[68] The artist's continued friendship with the senator, as well as his own basic ideology, firmly placed Henner in the Dreyfus camp. Scheurer-Kestner's letter to Henner of May 1898, in which the senator commends Henner on his *Levite* and remarks on the profound sadness of the Jew, could be a direct reference to the scandal.[69]

Paul Legrand's genre scene called *In Front of "The Dream" by Detaille* (see pl. 186) deals with the issue of patriotism in France while showing that ubiquitous late-nineteenth-century phenomenon, the newsstand. Exhibited in the Salon of 1897, the work shows several young boys in front of a newsstand in rapt admiration of a print of Detaille's monumental painting, *The Dream. The Dream,* first exhibited in 1888, shows soldiers in the field after battle, dreaming of the past military glories of Napoleon. The young men in Legrand's painting seem to admire this depiction of French militarism. To the right, a crippled soldier, a veteran of 1870, looks away with an indifference that borders on disapproval.[70] What is one to make of the contrasting attitudes of the different generations? Are these youths, certainly representative of unformed opinion, unaware of the dangers of war? And does the veteran not silently implore caution? While these interpretations may not be precise, Legrand certainly convinces the viewer of compromised feelings with reference to the military.

The Belgian, Evenepoel, who created numerous portraits of Clemenceau (including the one mentioned previously, see fig. 14) was strongly Dreyfusard. His letters are filled with references to the Affair. His painting *Fête aux Invalides* of 1898 (see pl. 187) is similar in intent to Bonnard's 1890 *The Parade Ground*. It recalls Bruegel's peasants frolicking, which heightens the sense of flippancy attending this event on the hallowed ground of the French army. And indeed it was seen immediately as such: A critic for the newspaper *Progrès Militaire* read the image as a derision of the French military.[71]

A Polish Jewish artist named Samuel Hirszenberg worked in Paris during part of the Affair. His artistic efforts had for quite some time been affected by social and political concerns. His *Wandering Jew* of 1899 is another link in the long chain of late nineteenth-century artistic preoccupation with the literary theme of a nation without a land.[72] The message of this vast and ominous canvas was no doubt meant to answer the prevalent anti-Semitism which aided the escalation of the Affair. His vision—of a sole, aged, and hunched Jew surrounded by a parabolic fence of crucifixes—can be read as nothing short of a diatribe against the power of the Church, with strong Zionist overtones (see fig. 18). Again, people's reaction to this work was influenced by its implied political message. Although it received a medal as a result of its inclusion in the Universal Exhibition of 1900, the dark, somber canvas was relegated to an obscure gallery.[73]

The year of Dreyfus's degradation—1895—witnessed the invention of the motion picture. The pioneers involved in the use of this new technological advance, the basis for the predominate media mode of today's video, soon employed their film to political advantage. As foreshadowed by *Le*

Siècle's "Mensonges de la Photographie" (see pl. 107 and fig. 9), the capabilities for deception inherent in film was even more limitless than that of still photography. And indeed, in 1898, one of Lumière's cameramen, seeing the potential market for film information on the Dreyfus Affair, fabricated a fake newsreel.[74] It was the excitement created around the Rennes trial in 1899 that really set filmmakers loose on the track of motion-picture reportage. But real footage of the prisoner and the proceedings was practically impossible to obtain given the security precautions taken by government and military. Some did attempt this, but their efforts were thwarted. A new manipulation of the motion picture medium was already in progress—the docudrama. And Georges Méliès used the Dreyfus Affair to such ends.[75] His 1899 film on the Dreyfus Affair was indeed the first docudrama in the history of film (see pl. 202). The pioneer filmmaker, who coincidentally began his career as caricaturist for such journals as *La Griffe* in 1889,[76] used newspaper photographs to restage the scenes for his then longest film to date—15 minutes![77] At the same time Méliès's piece was being produced, Pathé was busy reconstructing another interpretation (this film would be remade in 1907). The furor that ensued during the showing of these films was so great that Dreyfusards and anti-Dreyfusards actually became violent in the early movie theaters. So great was this hysteria that the government actually banned the films. This ban was the first instance of film censorship of any kind, and subsequently led to a prohibition on making or showing any films on the Affair in France. This restriction against the screening of such films remained in force until 1950, and it was not until 1974 that permission to produce a film on the scandal was granted.[78]

The debate which still continues about whether film is art or media expresses precisely the duality implied in the examination of the earlier polemical and photographic imagery.[79] Certainly twenty years ago, in the era immediately preceding the revisionism currently *de rigeur,* art historians would have even questioned the validity as art of some of the so-called academic works previously discussed. Lines of demarcation between the various categorizations of art—high art, folk art, popular art, commercial art—are certainly more blurred now than ever. And the development of a barometer to determine precisely the distinctions between

Figure 18, Cat. 450
Samuel Hirszenberg
The Wandering Jew (Le Juif Errant),
1899
Oil on canvas

all these levels (in addition to one capable of the quantification of quality of an artwork) would be as ludicrous a concept as the illustrator's image of the scale upon which Dreyfus weighs his level of culpability (see pls. 92–93).

Actually film is one of the few areas where the Dreyfus Affair has continued its visual life. One can hardly speak of the Affair without conjuring up the memory of having seen Paul Muni and Joseph Schildkraut in the Academy Award winning 1937 production "Life of Emile Zola" or the 1958 British film of "I Accuse" with Jose Ferrer and Viveca Lindfors. Currently, a new film on the subject is being planned by director Costa-Garvas.[80] Aside from the several watercolors and lithographs of the dramatis personae of the Affair by Ben Shahn in the early 1930s, an analogy for the artist to his then preoccupation with the injustices of the Sacco and Vanzetti case, it is hard to think of polemical or fine art created later in this century with reference to the Affair.

Recently, however, the French government's commission of a monument to Alfred Dreyfus showed that the scandal still had the capacity to provoke passions and to affect art. In 1982, as part of a program to create sculptural monuments to various figures of the late nineteenth and early twentieth century, the caricaturist for *L'Express,* sculptor Tim [Louis Mittelberg] was commissioned by the then minister of culture, Jack Lang, to create a monument to Dreyfus (see pl. 203). The completed sculpture was scheduled to be installed at the École Militaire, the precise and emotionally laden location of the captain's degradation. This plan was rejected by the minister of defense.[81] While the reasoning for its rejection there is complex, several other suggestions for the placement of this sculpture also have not panned out (although at the time of this writing, there is a proposal to place this work facing the Palais de Justice).[82] This piece, a veritable "wandering Jew" of late twentieth century sculptural monument, has still to find a home in Paris.

Notes

1. I wish to acknowledge with grateful appreciation the assistance of Anita Friedman and Irene Z. Schenck with regard to the research for this exhibition, the catalogue, and the present essay; they have labored closely with me on the project since its inception. I have benefited greatly from the thoroughness of their work, their dedication and enthusiasm for the subject, and not least, from the many topical discussions with them over the years. Although Stephen Brown entered the project at a late stage, his contribution to the research in this essay has been extremely valuable. The responsibility for the ideas expressed in this paper rests entirely, of course, with the author.

2. This point is discussed in some detail in this volume by Benjamin Martin.

3. This aspect of the Affair is elucidated, with particular reference to literary developments, by Susan Suleiman's contribution in the present catalogue.

4. See Jacques Barzun, *The House of Intellect* (Westport, Conn.: Greenwood, 1978), p. 1, and Suleiman's essay here.

5. Quoted from Judith Hansen O'Toole, "Henri-Gabriel Ibels: 'Nabi Journaliste,'" *Gazette des Beaux-Arts,* 36 (January 1982), 31–38.

6. Jean-Denis Bredin, *The Affair: The Case of Alfred Dreyfus* (New York: Braziller, 1986), trans. from the French by Jeffrey Mehlmann, 31 [First published as, *L'Affaire,* 1983].

7. See *Letters on Anton Chekhov,* selected and edited by Avrahm Yarmolinsky (New York: Viking, 1973), 302 and Justin Kaplan, *Mr. Clemens and Mark Twain: A Biography* (New York: Simon and Schuster, 1966), 353.

8. For further discussion of this point see the essay by Linda Nochlin in this volume.

9. John Grand-Carteret, *L'Affaire Dreyfus et l'Image* (Paris: Ernest Flammarion, n.d.). *Dreyfus-Bilderbuch; Karikaturen aller Völker uber die Dreyfus-Affäre* (Berlin: Eysler, 1899).

10. See Jacques Lethève, *La Caricature et la presse sous la IIIème république* (Paris: Armand Colin, 1961), 77–79.

11. For a discussion of the blurring of definitions between public and journalist see Walter Benjamin, "The Work of Art in the Age of Photo-Mechanical Reproduction," trans. by Harry Zohn, in *Illuminations* (Glasgow: Colin, 1973), 234.

12. See Theodore Zeldin, *France 1848–1945: Taste and Corruption* (Oxford: Oxford University Press, 1980), 153–155.

13. Robert F. Byrnes, "The French Publishing Industry and its Crisis of the 1890s," *The Journal of Modern History,* 23 (June 1951), 235.

14. The metaphor of light versus dark, truth versus falsehood, is the link that permits a comparison of the allegorically inclined works of Carrière and Hodler. Hodler's *Truth* is discussed below.

15. Martin Battersby, "Eugene Carrière, *Art and Artists*, 5, 2 (May 1970), 17.

16. Gabriel Séailles, *Eugene Carrière: Essai de biographie psychologique* (Paris: Armand Colin, 1922), 130.

17. Xavier Granoux and Charles Fontane, "L'Affaire Dreyfus": Catalogue descriptif des cartes postales illustrées, françaises et étrangères, parues depuis 1894 (Paris: Daragon, 1903), 48–49.

18. Ralph E. Shikes and Steven Heller, *The Art of Satire: Painters as Caricaturists from Delacroix to Picasso* (New York: Pratt Graphics Center and Horizon Press, 1984), 40–41.

19. Benjamin, *The Work of Art,* 221.

20. Zeldin, *France, 1848–1945,* ibid. "Newspapers and Corruption," 180.

21. *La Libre Parole* (November 1894). For further discussion of the status of this and other journals of the period, see Stephen Wilson, *Ideology and Experience: Antisemitism in France at the Time of the Dreyfus Affair* (London and Toronto: Associated University Presses, 1982), 9, 173 ff.

22. A figure cited in Jean Héritier, ed., *Histoire de la troisième république,* 2 vols. (Paris: Librairie de France, 1932–33), 1:202.

23. Hannah Arendt, *The Origins of Totalitarianism* (New York and London: Harcourt Brace Jovanovich, 1973), 91–92.

24. Bredin, *The Affair,* 181–186, 433 ff.

25. Zeldin, *France, 1848–1945,* 180.

26. See Cate in this volume.

27. Lethève, *La Caricature,* 83.

28. Ibid., 92.

29. Gabriel Weisberg, *The Realist Tradition: French Painting and Drawing, 1830–1900* (Cleveland: The Cleveland Museum of Art, 1980), 308.

30. An important contribution to our understanding of this aspect of the Affair is made by Donald English in his, *Political Uses of Photography in the Third French Republic, 1871–1914* (Ann Arbor: UMI Research Press, 1984). See esp. chap. 6, "The Dreyfus Affair and the beginnings of Modern Photographic Propaganda," 177–213.

31. Ibid., 180–182.

32. Ibid. and Lethève, *La Caricature,* 91.

33. John Rewald, *Post-Impressionism: From Van Gogh to Gauguin,* 2d ed. (New York and London: 1962), 154.

34. English, *Political Uses of Photography,* 200.

35. The series has been published by Ruth Malhotra, in her *Horror-Galerie; Ein Bestiarium der dritten französischen republik* (Dortmund: Harenberg, 1980).

36. Granoux and Fontane, *"L'Affaire Dreyfus,"* 5.

37. André Fermigier, *Pierre Bonnard* (New York: Harry N. Abrams, 1984), 48.

38. Musée des arts décoratifs, Paris, "Equivoques," exh. cat. 1973. See the entry for Jean-François Raffaëlli.

39. L. Roger-Miles, *Alfred Roll* (Paris: Lahure, 1904), 88.

40. John Rewald in William Rubin, ed. *Cézanne: The Late Work* (New York: Museum of Modern Art, 1977), 385–386.

41. Gerstl Mack, *Paul Cézanne* (New York, 1976), 343.

42. Rewald, *Cézanne: The Late Work,* 386.

43. Bernard de Montgolfier and Dominique Morel, "Pastels au Musée Carnavalet," *Bulletin du Musée Carnavalet,* 35 année, nos. 1–2 (1982):48–49.

44. Shepherd Galley: New York, "Christian Imagery in French Nineteenth Century Art, 1789–1906," exh. cat. 1980, no. 163, 402–404.

45. I am most grateful to Joan Diamond and Anita Friedman for sharing their thoughtful research and analysis of the allegorical figure of Truth. Their joint paper "Truth on the March: Art and Politics during the Dreyfus Affair," was delivered as the annual Phi Beta Kappa lecture, Hollins College, Roanoke, Virginia, April 1986.

46. Musée des Beaux-Arts, Tours, "Edouard Debat-Ponsan (1847–1913)," exh. cat., 7–11, 17.

47. Ambrose Vollard, *Paul Cézanne* (Paris, 1924), 162.

48. Sharon L. Hirsch, *Ferdinand Hodler* (New York, George Braziller, Inc., 1982), 22.

49. Ibid., 92.

50. Jura Bruschweiler, *Points de vue sur Ferdinand Hodler,* in "Ferdinand Hodler," Grand Palais: Paris, exh. cat. 1985, 275. It is interesting to note that Servaes wrote for the Viennese Journal *Die Neue Freie Presse,* the same paper for which the journalist Theodore Herzl was Paris correspondent. The formation of Herzl's Zionist ideology is generally considered to stem from his reaction firsthand to the anti-Semitism related to the Dreyfus Affair.

51. Ibid.

52. Conversation with Jura Bruschweiler, February 1, 1987.

53. See the letter by Gallé, included in the exhibition, now in the collection of Mr. and Mrs. Herbert D. Schimmel.

54. Françoise-Thérèse Charpentier and Philippe Thiébaut, eds. "Gallé," exh. cat. Musée du Luxembourg, Paris, 1985, 222.

55. Ibid., 213.

56. Ibid., 223.

57. Conversation with Phillipe Thiébault, April 1986.

58. Henriette Caillaux, *Aimé-Jules Dalou, l'homme, l'oeuvre* (Paris: Delgrave, 1935), 60 ff.

59. This point (and many others regarding Dalou scholarship) was kindly brought to my attention by Dr. John M. Hunisak in a letter dated October 17, 1986.

60. For the Dreyfusard connection, see H. W. Janson in Robert Rosenblum and H. W. Janson, *19th-Century Art* (New York: Abrams, 1984), 475. In the absence of conclusive evidence John Hunisak has, however, cautioned such interpretations. (Letter to author October 17, 1986.)

61. Gerald M. Ackerman, *The Life and Times of J. L. Gérôme,* (New York: Sotheby's Publications; Harper and Row, distributors, 1986), 142, 274, 276; and also Jacqueline Fontseré, "Moulins Musée departmental, Peintures et dessins du XIXe siècle"; *La Revue du Louvre:* vol. 30., nos. 5–6 (1980):344–348.

62. The commission had already gone to Henri Chapu who died before his maquette was fully realized. The choice of Rodin was controversial and was believed to have been rigged by Zola. John Tancock, *The Sculptures of Auguste Rodin* (Philadelphia and Boston: Godine, 1976), 444.

63. Albert Elsen, Stephen C. McGough, and Steven H. Wander, *Rodin and Balzac: Rodin's Sculptural Studies for the Monument to Balzac from the Cantor Fitzgerald Collection,* exh. cat. Stanford University, Spring 1973, 60–66.

64. Jacques de Caso and Patricia B. Sanders, *Rodin's Sculpture: A Critical Study of the Spreckels Collection, California Palace of the Legion of Honor, San Francisco* (Rutland, VT: Charles and Tuttle, 1977), 232.

65. John Tancock, *The Sculptures of Auguste Rodin,* 444.

66. The first bronze cast of *Balzac* was purchased in 1930 by the Koninklijk Museum voor Schone Kunsten in Antwerp.

67. Michele M. Facos, "Aristide's Maillol's *Blanqui Monument,*" *Arts* (January 1986), 42–48, 71.

68. Louise d'Argencourt and Douglas Druick, eds. *The Other Nineteenth Century: Paintings and Sculpture in the Collection of Mr. and Mrs. Joseph M. Tannenbaum* (Ottawa: The National Gallery of Canada, 1978), see Albert Boime, "Jean-Jacques Henner: The Levite of Ephraim and His Dead Wife," no. 40, 123–126.

69. Letter of Auguste Scheurer-Kestner to J. J. Henner, 29 May, 1898, Collection Musée Henner.

70. Royal Academy of Arts, London, *Post-Impressionism: Cross Currents in European Painting* exh. cat. 17 November 1979–16 March 1980, see no. 114, 88–89.

71. Ibid., no. 400, 265–266, and see also, Francis Edwin Hyslop, *Henri Evenepoel: Belgian Painter in Paris, 1892–1899* (University Park: Pennsylvania State University Press, 1975), 21, 90.

72. See, e.g., Galit Hasan-Roken and Alan Dundes, *The Wandering Jew: Essays in the Interpretation of a Christian Legend* (Bloomington: Indiana University Press, 1986).

73. Städtische Kunsthalle Düsseldorf, *Bilder sind nicht verboten,* exh. cat., 1982, 170.

74. Stephen Bottomore, "Dreyfus and Documentary," in *Sight and Sound* (Autumn 1984), 290.

75. Ibid., 292.

76. Paul Hammond, *Marvelous Méliès* (New York: St. Martin's Press, 1975), 26.

77. Bottomore, "Dreyfus and Documentary," 292.

78. Ibid., 293.

79. See Madeleine Malthête-Méliès and Anne-Marie Quevrain, "Georges Méliès et les arts: Etude sur l'iconographie de ses films et sur les rapports avec les courants artistiques," in *Artibus et historiae,* 1 (1980):133. The seminal speculative text, regarding the potential for change in cinema and "the media," vis-à-vis art and reproduction, is the work by Benjamin in n. 11 above.

80. Conversation with Jean-Denis Bredin, April 1987.

81. *The New York Times,* August 13, 1985 "Dreyfus, a Driver, and Disneyland."

82. *L'Express,* 17 April 1987, 47.

The French Jewish Community from Emancipation to the Dreyfus Affair

PAULA E. HYMAN

Five years before Captain Alfred Dreyfus was arrested for treason, the Jews of France joyously celebrated the centennial of the French Revolution and their own fortunate status as French citizens and French patriots. One rabbi gratefully proclaimed in a sermon on the occasion, "We have adopted the customs and traditions of a country which has so generously adopted us, and today, thanks to God, there are no longer any but Frenchmen in France."[1] In commemorating the Revolution with enthusiasm, French Jews gave public recognition to the fact that they were the first Jews in Europe to have been emancipated—that is, to have acquired, in 1791, the rights and obligations of citizenship.[2] A century later they were also arguably the most successfully assimilated Jewish community in Europe. They were at home in French culture, and some had managed to scale the heights of the prestigious *grandes écoles,* the civil service, and the army. Their early emancipation had shaped their social, cultural, and ideological development during the nineteenth century and constrained the ways in which French Jews responded to the surprising revival of French anti-Semitism that would find its sharpest expression in the Dreyfus Affair.

The Jews of France were not a large population, but they attracted attention not only because they constituted a social problem for the makers of the Revolution but also because they stemmed from diverse origins. Numbering some 40,000 in 1789, they lived in three distinct communities. The most highly acculturated were the several thousand Sephardic Jewish merchants of Bordeaux and Bayonne, the descendants of Marranos who had arrived in France in the sixteenth and seventeenth centuries. Gradually casting off their Catholic guise, by the beginning of the eighteenth century they had received rights of residence in France as Jews. Because of their relatively high degree of social integration, they were the first Jews in France to be emancipated, in January 1790. Another small Jewish community had long resided in Provence, in the areas under papal protection.

The vast majority of French Jews, however, were the Ashkenazic Jews of Alsace-Lorraine, numbering about 30,000. Dwelling in the villages and towns of France's two eastern provinces, the Jews of Alsace-Lorraine were traditional, Yiddish-speaking, and overwhelmingly poor. Banned from owning land and from guild membership, they eked out a living as peddlers, hawkers of old clothes, and commercial brokers. The wealthier among them were cattle and horse dealers and moneylenders. A classic example of an ethnic minority finding a modus vivendi as economic middlemen mediating between the countryside and the town, they earned the resentment of their peasant clientele, who were particularly resentful when they fell deeply into debt to Jewish moneylenders. It was concerning these Jews that the debates about the feasibility of emancipation raged during the 1780s. Could such Jews ever transform themselves into useful French citizens?[3]

If the ideal Jew in the enlightened opinion of eighteenth-century France was the Sephardic merchant or intellectual, the average Jew was the Ashkenazic peddler of Alsace-Lorraine. Such Jews

Figure 1, Cat. 20
Law Relative to the Jews (Loi Relative aux Juifs), 13 November 1791
Broadside
This law gave French citizenship to the Jews of Alsace and Paris.

were excoriated in the literature of the Enlightenment—even by those who supported Jewish emancipation—as superstitious, culturally backward, socially isolated, and economically exploitative of the naive French peasant. To become useful to the state and society, they would have to transform themselves culturally and economically and integrate themselves as individuals within the broader society—in other words, to assimilate, as the Sephardim had done. The supporters and opponents of emancipation differed not on the need for transformation, nor on its nature, but on its feasibility and its timing. Those who favored emancipation argued that the faults of the Jews were the result of their persecution, and that the Jews would change once their legal and political status were improved. Those who opposed emancipation contended that flaws in Judaism or in the very character of the Jews accounted for their behavior; the Jews could be emancipated only after correcting their social defects.

Because the logic of the Revolution tended to disband all corporate groups—and the autonomous Jewish community was such a corporation—and to extend liberties to the previously excluded, those favoring the emancipation of the Jews prevailed. The Jews were emancipated as individuals of the Jewish faith, who were not expected to maintain their ethnic identity. Indeed, in the most famous words of the debates on emancipation, as uttered by one proponent of the Jews, "To the Jews as individuals—everything; to the Jews as a group—nothing. They must constitute neither a body politic nor an order; they must be citizens individually."[4]

This was the official ideology of emancipation, accepted and promoted by Jewish leaders in France throughout the nineteenth century. Turning to their coreligionists, they called upon them to abandon their traditional commercial pursuits, to learn the French language and national customs, and to accommodate their religious practices to the needs of the state. However, the French government itself helped to perpetuate some measure of Jewish distinctiveness: During the reign of Napoleon I the "Jewish question" once more became an issue of public debate, as conservatives argued that emancipation had been a mistake that empowered Jews to take advantage of hapless peasants in Alsace. Sympathetic to this argument, Napoleon issued discriminatory decrees against Jews engaged in commerce. More important, he sought to organize the Jews as a religious community, much as he had arranged a concordat with the pope and had established an administrative system for French Protestants. Thus Napoleon instituted a hierarchical system of Jewish communal units, called consistories, all linked to a Central Consistory in Paris and under the jurisdiction of the government. Until 1831, when the state assumed responsibility for paying the salaries of French rabbis and cantors, as it already did for Catholic priests and Protestant pastors, all Jews had to belong to their local consistory and were assessed for the upkeep of the synagogue and its functionaries. The consistories remained the official link between the French government and individual Jews until the separation of Church and State (as a result of the Dreyfus Affair) in 1905. Finally, ever the showman, in 1807 Napoleon convened a Sanhedrin (the ancient Jewish political/legislative assembly) of Jewish delegates in Paris to address such questions as the loyalty of Jews to the state, the relationship of Jewish law to French civil law, and the role of the rabbi in an emancipated community. The delegates accepted the primacy of the state and denied the validity of the national or political elements in Judaism. In addition to teaching about Judaism, the rabbi was now to preach patriotism as well.[5]

The leaders of French Jewry learned well these lessons promoted by the Revolution and by Napoleon. Espousing what Michael Marrus has called the politics of assimilation, they defined Jewish interests as synonymous with French values and tried to facilitate the integration of Jews into all facets of French life.[6] Because French primary education was organized along confessional lines, the consistories established a network of state-recognized Jewish schools, which were more effective in teaching French than Hebrew. Their textbooks promoted patriotism and civic rectitude, pointed out that Jewish youth could dispense with those religious practices that conflicted with their military obligations, and defined contemporary Jews as a "religious society" in contrast to the civic and political society they had constituted prior to the destruction of the Second Temple. Since Jewish leaders internalized the new definition of Jews as followers of a faith rather than as members of a religio-ethnic minority, they refrained from any Jewish political activity except when the explicit interests of Judaism were at stake.[7]

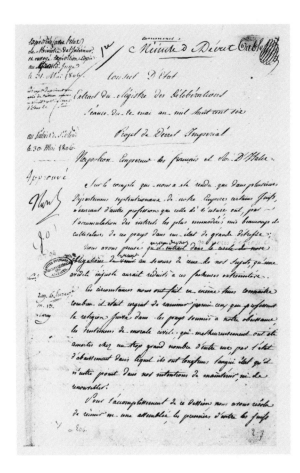

Figure 2, Cat. 15
Napoleon's Summons to the Jewish Community to Convene an Assembly of Jewish Notables
30 May 1806

Figure 3, Cat. 22
Artist unknown
Napoleon Presents the Law Re-establishing Judaism, 1806
Engraving, hand colored

The consistories modernized French Judaism as well as their definition of Jewish identity. Rabbis adopted clerical robes similar in style to those worn by Gentile clergymen and were now valued for their skills as preachers and pastors rather than as masters of Jewish law. The notables who dominated the consistories also introduced moderate reforms in synagogue practice and liturgy to enhance the aesthetic appeal of Jewish worship. However, the traditionalist sentiments of the Jews of Alsace—who even at mid-century constituted half of French Jewry—together with the fact that the consistorial system was monolithic prevented the adoption of more radical reforms of the sort that took root at that time in Germany.[8]

While French Jews took advantage of the opportunities provided by emancipation, they did not, as most proponents of emancipation had hoped, become indistinguishable from their Gentile compatriots. Ordinary Jews saw in emancipation a liberation from discriminatory taxation and from restrictions on their place of residence. In fact, the most dramatic response to emancipation on the part of Jews was to increase their geographic mobility and urbanization. In the course of the nineteenth century, thousands of Jews of Alsace-Lorraine, as well as a smaller contingent from Bordeaux and Bayonne, left their ancestral homes to establish new Jewish communities in places like Lyon, Lille, and Dijon, and especially Paris, which became the major center of Jewish life in France. Although Paris had harbored only about 500 Jews on the eve of the French Revolution, by 1831 it was by far the largest Jewish community in France, with a population of 8,000 Jews. The Paris Jewish community grew steadily throughout the century. After the loss of Alsace-Lorraine to Germany as a result of the 1870 Franco-Prussian War, about two-thirds of French Jews resided in Paris. At the time of the eruption of the Dreyfus Affair, France's Jewish population was no more than 75,000, but the concentration of 40,000 Jews in Paris, site of the national press, made France's Jewish population—though reduced in total numbers—all the more visible. Moreover, many of the Jews living in Paris were newcomers from the lost eastern provinces or from the Russian Empire. The former often spoke French with a strong Germanic accent; the latter, with a Yiddish accent or not at all. This situation confirmed hostile observers in their belief that all Jews in France were foreigners and hence not to be trusted.[9]

While the proponents of emancipation had anticipated a significant restructuring of the economic life of the Jews, most French Jews did not choose in the nineteenth century to abandon commerce for the supposed advantages of agricultural labor or artisanry. Even the Jewish notables who ran the consistories judged as impractical the establishment of Jewish agricultural colonies. Although they did establish a number of successful vocational schools that trained impoverished Jewish youth in a variety of artisan trades, these schools could accommodate only a small percentage of the population.

This failure to transform Jews into happy peasants and craftsmen is hardly surprising, given the limited opportunities available in those two sectors of the economy. Instead, the majority of Jews diversified their occupations within commerce and became settled shopkeepers rather than itinerant peddlers. In an era of capitalist expansion, they were able to draw upon their long experience with a market economy to achieve a visible degree of upward social mobility. Furthermore, a tiny fraction of French Jews made conspicuous fortunes in banking, through speculation on the bourse, and in industry. By the 1840s the Rothschilds, Pereires, and Foulds had taken their place among the preeminent banking families of France. The Rothschilds, who played a major role in the financing of the French railroad network, in particular became symbols of Jewish financial power and thus easy targets of anti-Semitic propaganda. Precisely because of their achievement of upward social mobility during the July Monarchy, the Second Empire, and the first decades of the Third Republic, the Jews of France were not fully assimilated with their Gentile neighbors. Their economic profile remained distinctively different.[10]

Yet their economic successes, along with their sense of political security, made it possible for young French Jewish intellectuals and professionals in 1860 to establish the Alliance Israélite Universelle, an organization for international Jewish defense. Grateful for their own enjoyment of equal rights and steeped in French culture, they sought to bring the benefits of emancipation as well as the glories of French civilization to their less fortunate coreligionists of eastern Europe and the Levant. Through the Alliance, and its educational institutions in particular, French Jews were to acquire influence and renown within the larger Jewish world.[11]

By the end of the century, when Jews were attacked it was no longer for being backward, poor, and self-segregated. Now they were por-

Figure 4
Artist unknown
The Grand Sanhedrin, 1807 Engraving
Photo, The Library of the Jewish
Theological Seminary, New York

trayed as successful manipulators of the capitalist system, who were in the vanguard of change, eroders of France's traditional institutions, and too strong a presence in French public life.[12] This new image of the Jew—popularized by such prolific anti-Semitic writers as Edouard Drumont, who presumed that the thoroughly acculturated Jew remained at heart a foreign element within French society—rested on the rise to prominence of a significant number of French Jews. From the days of Napoleon I, Jews had served with distinction in the army officer corps. A generation later a few entered politics; in the wake of the Revolution of 1848, two Jews, Adolphe Crémieux and Michel Goudchaux, became Minister of Justice and Minister of Finance respectively. By the middle of the century, to the chagrin of some observers, Jews excelled in the competitive examinations that were the hallmark of French education. Even in Alsace in the early 1860s Jewish lycée (high school) graduates were more than twice as likely as their non-Jewish classmates to enter the prestigious Ecole Normale Supérieur. By 1872 the French census indicated that nine percent of male Jewish household heads in Paris were liberal professionals, bankers, or industrialists. Among Jewish army recruits in 1885–1887, 15 percent earned their living in those fields.[13]

The French Jewish press exulted in the successes of French Jews and publicized them continually as proof of Jewish integration in French society. However, as one liberal French writer noted in his 1897 book on anti-Semitism: "Abandoning busi-

Figure 5, Cat. 19
Attributed to Georg Emanuel Opitz
Dedication of a Synagogue in Alsace,
Ca. 1828   Oil on canvas

ness and the Stock Exchange, leaving the trading occupations in which they had been forced to specialize for so long, many Jews rushed toward other careers. They turned to the liberal professions, to the Bar, to medicine, to teaching, to literature and to science. And what became of this effort to open up new outlets for themselves? Having been reproached for their long-standing preference for finance and business, they were now accused of invading the liberal professions."[14] Charles Maurras, the founder of the Action Française, interpreted this extraordinary social mobility of Jews from an anti-Semitic perspective. During the Dreyfus Affair, he noted, "Paris opened its eyes: Jewish salons had the upper hand. . . . People thought that the Jews were just financiers, in control of Money. But Money had delivered everything else into their hands: an important sector of the University, an equivalent sector of the judicial administration, a sector, less important but appreciable, of the army, at its highest levels."[15]

Besides the wide representation of Jews among the ranks of doctors, lawyers, and civil servants, some French Jews achieved renown in the world of the university and in the most glittering literary and cultural circles of Paris. Emile Durkheim was only the most prominent of a generation of Jewish academicians. Marcel Proust's society mixed the traditional French aristocracy of birth with a Jewish aristocracy of wealth. Before bursting upon the political scene, Léon Blum, while still in his twenties, was the literary critic of the *Revue blanche,* an avant-garde journal of arts and letters

of Symbolist and anarchist sympathies. The *Revue blanche* attracted a host of Jewish contributors, from Bernard Lazare, the anarchist critic and an important Dreyfusard, to Proust, and also including the poet Gustave Kahn and the writer Julien Benda. Its publishers, the financiers and art lovers Thadée and Alexandre Natanson, were also Jewish. Indeed, its historian has seen in the journal "extreme delicacy, an almost total absence of prejudices, a cosmopolitanism and eclecticism practically without limits, to which was added a troubling sensuality,"[16] which he attributed to the contingent of Jews on its staff. More important, contemporaries saw in the spirit of the *Revue blanche*—which welcomed new writing, promoted a social vision of art, published Blum's reflections on the Jewish mission in the modern world, and was militantly Dreyfusard—a profoundly Jewish element. Some found that element stimulating, but others rejected it as reflective of a purported Jewish domination of French culture.

Most prominent French Jews had little or no connection with the organized Jewish community. In their move to Paris and up the social scale, they abandoned the observance of Jewish ritual, except perhaps for rites of passage. Still, few converted to Christianity, in part because the universities, the army, and the civil service were relatively open, as they were not in Central Europe, to unconverted Jews. Perceived as Jews by the larger society, most also saw themselves as members of a group defined by an illustrious shared past, a religious heritage, and biological ties of common descent. Even half-Jewish individuals and converts from Judaism, as well as their descendants, like Ludovic Halévy, sometimes acknowledged a measure of Jewish identity, perhaps because they were still treated as Jews.

Because the prevailing ideological pronouncements surrounding their emancipation had presumed that within a generation or two Jews would differ from their compatriots in their religious practices alone, there was some confusion among nineteenth-century observers of French Jewry as to why nonobservant Jews did not completely abandon their Jewish identity, however attenuated. Like other modern European Jews, however, the Jews of France easily blended their Jewish identity, narrower in scope than that of premodern Jews, with a profound sense of their devotion to French culture and to French patriotism. In fact, the France that they cherished easily enough in the early years of the Third Republic was the France of the Revolution. As Zadoc Kahn, the Chief Rabbi of France, confidently declared in 1889, even after the emergence of the new anti-Semitism, "France will not repudiate her past, her traditions, her principles which constitute the best of her moral patrimony. . . . As for us . . . we will continue to love our country . . . and bear witness, in all circumstances to our gratitude and devotion."[17] The spokesmen of the French Jewish community thus saw no contradiction between their Jewish concerns and their French values, between their loyalties as Jews and their loyalties as citizens of France.[18]

That belief in France's continued commitment to her revolutionary ideals and of the harmony of French and Jewish interests was severely tested, though not destroyed, by the Dreyfus Affair. Whatever they believed concerning Dreyfus's innocence or guilt, French Jews maintained a discreet and quiet stance during the early years of the Affair. Disturbed by Dreyfus's arrest and conviction and by the shouts of "Death to the Jews" that accompanied his derogation, French Jews nonetheless assumed, along with most French citizens, that French institutions could be relied upon to dispense justice. Most Jews hoped that the storm of anti-Semitism would quickly blow over and experienced the Affair as a time of unease and anxiety that they expected would be short-lived. For some Jews, however, the anti-Semitism unleashed during the Affair produced more than mere discomfit. Social discrimination against Jews in schools, clubs, and business became rife. Moreover, after Emile Zola issued his famous indictment of French justice with his "J'Accuse" in mid-January 1898, anti-Semitic riots erupted in no fewer than sixty-nine places in metropolitan France during the following six weeks. In many cases Jews were targeted explicitly by the rioters, who shouted anti-Semitic slogans, threw stones, and attacked the property of Jews, and occasionally injured Jewish persons.[19]

As the Dreyfus case was transformed into the Dreyfus Affair, and the presumption of Dreyfus's guilt was challenged with convincing evidence, the response of Jews to the Affair became more complex and variegated. The official Jewish community never became formally involved in protest during the Affair. Reflecting in the 1930s, in the shadow of fascism, upon the community's lack of action, Léon Blum, socialist activist and Zionist

sympathizer, harshly attacked the Jewish bourgeoisie for its reluctance to become engaged in the fight against anti-Semitism (though he himself had, during the Affair, minimized the importance of anti-Semitism): "The rich Jews, the Jews of the middle bourgeoisie, Jewish civil servants feared the struggle undertaken on behalf of Dreyfus. . . . They thought only of lying low and hiding. They imagined that anti-Semitic passion would be deflected by their cowardly neutrality. . . . They did not understand . . . that no precaution . . . would delude the enemy and that they remained the victims offered to triumphant anti-Dreyfusism."[20] The Dreyfusard philosopher, Charles Péguy, remarked more sympathetically that "the great majority of Jews [were] . . . like the great majority of other voters. . . . They feared trouble."[21]

This official Jewish communal policy of neutrality, so surprising in retrospect, was the result of several factors. The consistories, the organs of the Jewish community, were not independent bodies but were linked to the governmental bureaucracy; French rabbis, as state functionaries, depended on the government for their salaries. This connection to the state tied the hands of the consistories and their leaders, both rabbinic and lay, for the Dreyfusards were impugning the trustworthiness of another branch of the state—the army. Moreover, the legacy of emancipation included an informal ban on the intrusion of Jews, as an organized group, into French politics. Having internalized that perspective on Jewish politics, Jewish communal leaders presumed that Jews would respond as individual citizens to the Affair and that the institutions of French democracy would not only protect all French citizens but would also ultimately yield a just solution. They saw anti-Semitism as an issue of French politics rather than as a Jewish problem. Thus, the Alliance Israélite Universelle regarded the Dreyfus Affair as outside its sphere of activity, in large part because it limited its task to defending unemancipated Jewries, which could not participate in the political process.

Still, despite the public adherence of the Jewish organizations to this ideology of political neutrality, in 1895 Chief Rabbi Zadoc Kahn privately convened a secret Committee of Defense against Anti-Semitism (le Comité de Défense contre l'Antisémitisme), composed of lay leaders active in the consistories or in the Alliance, to formulate

JACOB MEYER
Grand Rabbin et Président du Consistoire Israélite du dép. du Bas Rhin.

תמונת החכם הכולל כל בינה יודע הגאון הגדול כבוד שם מהורי
יעקב מאיר נר' אב״ד וראש הקהלות דהאנבסים נאריים דגליל התחתון רהין

ZADOC KAHN
GRAND RABBIN DE PARIS

an appropriate Jewish response to anti-Semitism. When the existence of the committee was discovered in 1902, anti-Semites attacked it as but another example of a "Jewish conspiracy."[22] This experience points to the quandary faced by the leaders of the organized Jewish community in attempting to find an effective response to anti-Semitism. Their silence was taken for shame, admission of guilt, or cowardice; their organized opposition as proof of a Jewish plot or of Jewish clannishness.

If the official Jewish community waited out the Affair, individual Jews, particularly intellectuals, were prominent in the Dreyfusard camp. The League for the Rights of Man (la Ligue des Droits de l'Homme), which was established during the Affair to fight for the republican vision of justice, included numerous Jews among its founders, members of its national board, and local activists.[23] This is not surprising, for Jews in the modern era have often chosen to combat manifestations of

anti-Semitism through nonsectarian institutions rather than through specifically Jewish organizations. Bernard Lazare, the anarchist writer who was later drawn to Zionism, was a central figure in the revisionist campaign, arguing for Dreyfus's innocence and for keeping the issue before the public eye.[24] Indeed, Léon Daudet described him in retrospect as "the Messianic Jew, who positively launched the Dreyfus Affair . . . like some wicked impresario"[25] while Charles Péguy saw in him the best examplar of "the prophetic race."[26] Lazare was not alone. Mathieu Dreyfus worked tirelessly on behalf of his brother; Joseph Reinach, who became the influential Dreyfusard chronicler of the Affair, labored for revision; Madame Emile Straus turned her salon into a Dreyfusard gathering place; and such political and cultural luminaries as Léon Blum, the Natansons, Emile Durkheim, Daniel Halévy, and the jurist Victor Basch—to name only the best known—used the resources at their disposal to support the Dreyfusard cause.

Figure 6
Artist unknown
Rabbi Jacob Meyer, 1830
Lithograph
Photo, The Library of the Jewish
Theological Seminary, New York

Figure 7
Gustave Levy
Rabbi Zadoc Kahn, 1889
Etching
Photo, The Library of the Jewish
Theological Seminary, New York

Figure 8, Cat. 17
Jean-Louis Forain
*The Jewish Peddler (Le Colporteur
Juif)*
Lithograph

For some Jewish intellectuals, among them the poet André Spire and the writer Edmond Fleg, the Dreyfus Affair stimulated a lifelong interest in probing the nature of Jewish identity and in exploring the Jewish cultural heritage they had previously abandoned.[27]

While the organized French Jewish community chose not to articulate a "Jewish position" on the Dreyfus Affair, the immigrant Jews from Russia who had settled in Paris in the 1880s and 1890s were less reluctant to take a public stand on this cause célèbre. Numbering some 20,000 at the turn of the century, they were primarily workers and impoverished artisans living in Montmartre and several immigrant neighborhoods, and especially in "the Pletzl," the immigrant quarter in the fourth arrondissement (a district in Paris). Their spokesmen, who had been influenced by the nascent Jewish workers' movement in Russia, were anarchists and socialists to whom ethnic politics came naturally because of their experience in the multiethnic Russian Empire. Calling themselves the Groupe des Ouvriers Juifs Socialistes de Paris (the Group of Jewish Socialist Workers of Paris), in 1898 they published a militant pamphlet addressed to the French Socialist party. The pamphlet decried the dangerous revival of anti-Semitism in France and called upon the party to follow its tradition of support for the oppressed and come to the aid of the victims of anti-Semitism. Dissatisfied with the lack of response to the pamphlet, the following year the group sponsored the only Jewish public protest meeting held during the Affair.[28]

While the immigrant Jewish socialists and anarchists analyzed the Affair primarily from a universalist perspective, which saw in the triumph of socialist principles a solution to the Jewish question, there were other Jews who learned from the Dreyfus Affair the lesson of Jewish nationalism. If the country which had been the first to emancipate its Jews now treated its assimilated Jewish citizens as an essentially foreign and potentially untrustworthy element, then the dream of the full acceptance of Jews into European societies had failed; further, such a dream could not be realized. Theodor Herzl, living in Paris as a correspondent for a major Viennese newspaper, did not become a Zionist because of the Dreyfus Affair. However, he witnessed several anti-Semitic incidents around the arrest and conviction of Dreyfus, which reinforced his conviction that only by reconstituting themselves as a nation would Jews be freed from the eternal problem of anti-Semitism. Similarly, the Dreyfus Affair had a profound impact upon Bernard Lazare, who was transformed from an assimilationist who denied the validity of Jewish identity into a Jewish nationalist who celebrated the value of Jewish distinctiveness.[29] Only a small group of French Jews rejected assimilation in favor of Zionism as a result of the Dreyfus Affair. However, the Affair did become for Zionist publicists a powerful symbol of the limits of emancipation.

Most French Jews welcomed with relief the conclusion of the Affair with Dreyfus's rehabili-tation in 1906. The ultimate vindication of the Dreyfusard cause, even after twelve years, persuaded Jewish communal leaders that the political system had functioned well and that their public stance of neutrality had been justified. When one member of the Central Consistory suggested that it send a letter of congratulations to Captain Dreyfus, the proposal was rejected as inappropriate.[30] And an article in one of the major French Jewish journals commented, with more optimism than insight, that "in giving birth to the Dreyfus Affair, anti-Semitism had died."[31]

The political legacy of the Dreyfus Affair for French Jewry was thus mixed. If some Jews had been sensitized to the potential power and fury of anti-Semitism in the modern era and to the consequent vulnerability of European Jews even in countries which had granted them full equality, most remained committed to the ideological stance and the political strategies of the hopeful era of emancipation.

Notes

1. Rabbi Felix Meyer in Benjamin Mossé, ed., *La Révolution française et le rabbinat français* (Avignon, 1890), 175.

2. For a general history of the process of emancipation in Europe, see Jacob Katz, *Out of the Ghetto* (Cambridge, Mass.: Harvard University Press, 1973), and Salo Baron, "Ghetto and Emancipation," *Menorah Journal* XIV (June 1928): 515–526 and "Newer Approaches to Jewish Emancipation," *Diogenes* XXIX (Spring 1960): 56–81. For the history of the terminology of emancipation, see Jacob Katz, *Emancipation and Assimilation* (Westmead, England: Farnborough, Gregg, 1972): 21–45.

3. For a survey of French Jewry in the eighteenth century, as well as the debate surrounding their emancipation, see Arthur Hertzberg, *The French Enlightenment and the Jews* (New York: Columbia University Press, 1968). On the role of the Sephardic Jews, see Frances Malino, *The Sephardic Jews of Bordeaux: Assimilation and Emancipation in Revolutionary and Napoleonic France* (University: University of Alabama Press, 1978).

4. National Assembly, 23 Dec. 1789 in *Réimpression de l'Ancien Moniteur* (*Gazette Nationale ou le Moniteur Universel*) (Paris, 1859), 2:456. Much of the debate is reproduced in Paul Mendes-Flohr and Jehudah Reinharz, eds., *The Jew in the Modern World* (New York and Oxford: Oxford University Press, 1980), 103–105.

5. Robert Anchel, *Napoléon et les juifs* (Paris: Presses Universitaires de France, 1928); Simon Schwarzfuchs, *Napoleon, the Jews and the Sanhedrin* (London and Boston: Routledge and Kegan Paul, 1979).

6. Michael Marrus, *The Politics of Assimilation: The French Jewish Community at the Time of the Dreyfus Affair* (Oxford: Oxford University Press, 1971).

7. Paula Hyman, *From Dreyfus to Vichy: The Remaking of French Jewry, 1906–1939* (New York: Columbia University Press, 1979), 8–11, 36–40.

8. On the limited nature of French reforms, see Phyllis Cohen Albert, *The Modernization of French Jewry: Consistory and Community in the Nineteenth Century* (Hanover, N.H.: Brandeis University Press, 1977), 50–55, 66–68, 197–198, 298–299; and Patrick Girard, *Les Juifs de France de 1789 à 1860* (Paris: Calmann-Lévy, 1976), 211–239.

9. For population developments until 1861, see Phyllis Cohen Albert, *The Modernization of French Jewry*, 3–25, 317–341; for the end of the century, see Marrus, *The Politics of Assimilation*, 29–34.

10. Albert, *The Modernization of French Jewry*, 26–34; Marrus, *The Politics of Assimilation*, 35–40; Patrick Girard, *Les Juifs de France de 1789 à 1860*, 119–130.

On the entrepreneurial role of nineteenth-century Jewish bankers in France, see Michael Graetz, *Haperiferya Hay'ta L'merkaz* (Jerusalem: Mossad Bialik, 1982), 138–153. For a survey of Jewish mobility during the Second Empire, see David Cohen, *La Promotion des juifs en France à l'époque du second empire*, 2 vols. (Aix-en-Provence: Université de Provence, 1980). On Jewish schools, see Zosa Szjakowski, *Jewish Education in France* (New York: distributed by Columbia University Press, 1980) and Paula Hyman, *Emancipation and Social Change*, forthcoming.

11. On the Alliance Israélite Universelle, see Andre Chouraqui, *Cent Ans d'histoire: l'Alliance israélite universelle et la renaissance juive contemporaine (1860–1960)* (Paris: Presses Universitaires de France, 1965), and Graetz, *Haperiferya*, 281–322.

12. For an elaboration of this argument, see Paula Hyman, "The Social Foundations of Jewish Modernity," *The Solomon Goldman Lectures* (Chicago, 1982), 3:71–82. For an exhaustive analysis of French anti-Semitic images of Jews, see Stephen Wilson, *Ideology and Experience: Antisemitism in France at the Time of the Dreyfus Affair* (Rutherford, Madison, & Teaneck, N.J.: Fairleigh Dickinson University Press, 1982).

13. The Alsatian figures are based upon my calculations from the 1864 governmental survey of French secondary school students found in the Archives Nationales, F^{17} 6849. The other statistics are from Doris Ben Simon-Donath, *Socio-démographie des juifs de France et d'Algérie* (Paris: Publications Orientalistes de France, 1976), 150, 166.

14. Anatole Leroy-Beaulieu, *L'Antisémitisme* (Paris: Ancienne Maison Michel Lévy Frères, 1897), 56, as cited in Wilson, *Ideology and Experience*, 401–402.

15. Charles Maurras, *Au Signe de flore: Souvenirs de vie politique, l'Affaire Dreyfus, la fondation de l'Action Française 1898–1900* (Paris: B. Grasset, 1933), 54, as cited in Wilson, *Ideology and Experience*, 394.

16. A. B. Jackson, *La Revue blanche (1889–1903): Origine, influence, bibliographie* (Paris: M. J. Minard, 1960), 115. On Proust's circle, see Seth Wolitz, *The Proustian Community* (New York: New York University Press, 1971).

17. Mossé, *La Révolution française*, 12.

18. Marrus, *The Politics of Assimilation*, passim; Hyman, *From Dreyfus to Vichy*, 6–8. With reference to the similar ideology of German Jewry, Uriel Tal pointed out that Jews saw no necessary conflict between Jewish identity and integration. See his *Christians and Jews in Germany*, trans. Noah Jonathan Jacobs (Ithaca and London: Cornell Univer-

sity Press, 1975). For a persuasive analysis of the possibility for Jews to assert a complex, multi-faceted identity, see Gary B. Cohen, "Jews in German Society: Prague, 1860–1914," in David Bronsen, ed., *Jews and Germans from 1860 to 1933: The Problematic Symbiosis* (Heidelberg: Winter, 1979), 306–337.

19. Wilson, *Ideology and Experience,* 106–124.
20. Léon Blum, *Souvenirs sur l'Affaire* (Paris: Gallimard, 1937), 97.
21. Charles Péguy, *Notre Jeunesse* (Paris, 1910), 101.
22. Marrus, *The Politics of Assimilation,* 240–242 and "Le Comité de Défense contre l'Antisémitisme," *Michael* IV (1976): 163–175.
23. Wilson, *Ideology and Experience,* 715–716.
24. On the career of Bernard Lazare, see Nelly Wilson, *Bernard Lazare: Antisemitism and the problem of Jewish identity in late nineteenth-century France* (Cambridge & New York: Cambridge University Press, 1978) and Marrus, *The Politics of Assimilation,* 164–195.
25. Léon Daudet, *Au Temps de Judas* (Paris: Nouvelle Librairie Nationale, 1933), 101, as cited in Wilson, *Ideology and Experience,* 714.
26. Péguy, *Notre Jeunesse,* 102.
27. For a list of prominent Jews involved in the Affair, see Wilson, *Ideology and Experience,* 714. On Spire and Fleg and new interest on the part of intellectuals in Judaism, see Hyman, *From Dreyfus to Vichy,* 43–45, 153, 156, 192–196.
28. Marrus, *The Politics of Assimilation,* 244–249. On eastern European immigrants in France in the Belle Epoque, see Nancy L. Green, *The Pletzl of Paris: Jewish immigrant workers in the "Belle Epoque"* (New York: Holmes and Meier, 1986) and David Weinberg, "'Heureux comme Dieu en France: East European Jewish Immigrants in Paris, 1881–1914," *Studies in Contemporary Jewry* 1 (1984): 26–54.
29. Marrus, *The Politics of Assimilation,* 164–195, 243–273. The best biography of Herzl remains, Alex Bein, *Theodore Herzl* (reprint New York: Atheneum, 1970). Also see David Vital, *The Origins of Zionism* (Oxford: Oxford University Press, 1975) and Henry J. Cohn, "Theodor Herzl's Conversion to Zionism" *Jewish Social Studies* XXXII (1970): 101–110.
30. Central Consistory, Minutes, July 20, 1906, HM 1070, Central Archive for the History of the Jewish People, Jerusalem.
31. "La Nouvelle revision," *Univers israélite* (22 June 1906): 360.

The Dreyfus Affair and the Corruption of the French Legal System

BENJAMIN F. MARTIN

From its inception, the Dreyfus "Affair" was at its core a legal case and had as its central issue "justice." On 22 December 1894, when the court-martial board unanimously declared Captain Alfred Dreyfus guilty of treason and sentenced him to confinement for life within the prison settlement on Devil's Island, Dreyfus's eminent Catholic attorney, Edgar Demange, exclaimed that the condemnation was the greatest crime of the century. Three years later, doubts had arisen about Dreyfus's guilt—and, even stronger ones about the fairness of his court-martial. Major A. Ravary, who was conducting an inquiry into the activities of the suspected traitor Major Ferdinand Walsin-Esterhazy, cautioned that military justice is not like other justice—to which Georges Clemenceau, one of the most prominent Dreyfusard politicians, riposted that there is only one sort of justice. And when France's highest court, the Cour de Cassation, on 3 June 1899, ordered a retrial for Dreyfus, Clemenceau bannered the single word JUSTICE across the front page of his newspaper, L'Aurore.[1]

But justice is not merely an ideal or even a goal. It is the entire process by which a crime is investigated and tried, and the expectation is that the truth will be discovered and that guilt and innocence will be duly apportioned. Despite her conventional image as a blindfolded goddess holding the scales, justice can never be perfectly impartial: It is the work of human beings, not gods; the result of decisions made by fallible minds, not divine balances. The Dreyfus Affair is cited as evidence that the system of justice failed in Third Republic France (because of the two convictions for a treason that Dreyfus certainly did not commit) or that it triumphed (because of Dreyfus's eventual exoneration and rehabilitation). Is this record comparable to that of other cases in France, particularly those outside the sphere of military justice? Even to attempt such an estimate implies that Dreyfus was hardly the only victim of a legal system whose practice departed excessively from the ideal.

Once a crime is discovered, the first step of criminal or military justice is to mount an investigation of the circumstances. Within the military, that responsibility usually belongs to the affected branch; and in cases of treason, to the unit concerned with counterespionage. During this period, for purposes of concealment, that unit was called the "Statistical Section," and it was under the overall supervision of the Deuxième Bureau, the intelligence division of the General Staff. Outside the military, such an investigation is the work of the judicial police, called the Sûreté. Any analysis of Sûreté methods during the last quarter of the nineteenth century reveals an appalling laxity in procedures. Lapses that received glaring publicity in the most famous criminal cases were matched in the less important ones. Depositions were carelessly drawn. Evidence was mishandled, lost, or sometimes fabricated. Too many police officials were venal or corrupt. Anatole France's character Crainquebille had, and was widely accepted as having, much basis in fact: a poor hawker arrested, tried, convicted, and imprisoned on charges trumped up by a policeman irritated that his path was briefly blocked by the sidewalk traffic in vegetables.[2]

By contrast, the Statistical Section's initial investigation of Dreyfus was almost professional. When the famous *bordereau,* the indication that a French officer had made treasonous contact with the German military attaché in Paris, came into the hands of the counterespionage unit on 27 September 1894, it was carefully photographed, and these photographs were circulated in an effort to identify the handwriting. Lieutenant-Colonel Albert d'Aboville's suggestion that the clues implied by the internal evidence of the bordereau should be followed was an entirely justified step, but one that would lead to the inclusion of Dreyfus among the suspects. Even then, there was no rush to judgment. It was only after a graphological examination by the appropriate military officials and by outside experts, including the Sûreté's famous criminologist Alphonse Bertillon, that a decision was made to consider Dreyfus the prime suspect. In fact, despite the anti-Semitic overtones that quickly emerged after Dreyfus's name was singled out, there is little to criticize in the military's initial investigation, which was completed on 13 October.[3]

At that point, if the case had been under civilian jurisdiction, it would have been turned over to a *juge d'instruction* (examining magistrate) for a formal judicial inquiry. Before the powers of his office were minimally circumscribed by the law of 8 December 1897, the juge d'instruction could order searches, seizures, and arrests on his own authority and without fear of being countermanded. He operated as a one-man grand jury, with the power to recommend indictment and trial or to dismiss the charges entirely. During the course of his inquiry into a case (the *instruction*), he could keep all of the details secret from the defense and hold the accused in custody, without access to an attorney, for as long as he chose. After 1897, the juge d'instruction had to bring charges within twenty-four hours against those he arrested (a French version of habeas corpus), advise those arrested of their right to legal counsel, and provide summaries of his investigations to the defense.

Further, he had the power to hold an accused incommunicado, except for visits by the accused's attorney, for only ten days (renewable once). The juge d'instruction was usually young and a junior member of the judicial bureaucracy, eager for promotion to a higher position, and often amenable when prosecutorial officials urged the ignoring (or overemphasizing) of ambiguities in the evidence, in order to set up the conditions for a conviction or an acquittal. In all the most notorious legal controversies of the Belle Epoque (the death of Emile Zola, the swindles by the Thérèse Humbert family, the suicide of Gabriel Syveton, the murders of the Marguerite Steinheil affair, and the assassination of *Le Figaro*'s editor by Henriette Caillaux), manipulations in varying degrees ethical, legal, and politically motivated were carried out by the juges d'instruction.[4]

The formal inquiry by the military judicial officer for the case, Major Armand Du Paty de Clam, did not depart from such practices. Du Paty arrested Dreyfus on 15 October (with Commissioner Armand Cochefert of the Paris Sûreté present), ordered a search of his apartment, and interrogated him in hopes of eliciting a confession. In an initial report to General Raoul de Boisdeffre, the chief of the General Staff, Du Paty concluded that apart from the bordereau (linked to Dreyfus by internal evidence and similar handwriting), there was no proof, no motive, and no admission of guilt. Certainly, if the charge had been anything other than treason, Dreyfus would have been released. But treason is a special kind of crime, one that by its very nature is difficult to prove unless the suspect is caught *en flagrant délit.* It is also a crime of honor—through the dishonor to the nation brought by traitorous acts, through the dishonor to the uniform brought when the traitor is a member of the officer corps. By arresting Dreyfus (and this news, like so much news, quickly leaked to the press), the army was committing its honor to the successful prosecution of the case. Much more important, the Statistical Section believed Dreyfus to be guilty, no matter how slight and circumstantial the evidence. Certain actions are taken for *raison d'état* (reasons of state); treason cannot be left unpunished. The Statistical Section compiled a secret dossier, taking from its archives any material that might seem to imply that Dreyfus was a traitor, and passed it to Boisdeffre. That secret dossier, the final report (on 31 October)

"The degraded officer had then to march round the entire square in front of the troops. He preserved his fortitude in an extraordinary degree, and never seemed to falter"

THE DEGRADATION OF CAPTAIN DREYFUS FOR SELLING STATE DOCUMENTS

THE LAST ACT OF THE CEREMONY IN THE SQUARE OF THE ÉCOLE MILITAIRE

Figure 1
*The Degradation of Captain Dreyfus for
Selling State Documents*, 1895
Photomechanical print
Bibliothèque Nationale

Figure 2, Cat. 106
Alfred Dreyfus Stripped of his Insignia
Police Photo, 1895

from Du Paty emphasizing suspicions despite the lack of proof, and the publicity about the arrest made inevitable the decision by the minister of war, General Auguste Mercier, on 3 November to take the case before a court-martial. Yet nothing thus far had gone irretrievably wrong for Dreyfus, because the charge of treason remained to be proved at the trial.[5]

A court-martial, such as Dreyfus would face, was not exactly a militarized version of France's civilian courts, where three-judge panels rendered the verdict in misdemeanor cases and twelve-member juries decided felony cases. French juries, an institution dating only from 1791, were capable of making determinations entirely at variance with the evidence, and often in favor of the defendant. Until 1945, the acquittal rate for jury trials was approximately thirty percent, three times higher than for trials before three-judge panels. The seven officers of the court-martial board were a panel of judges, but because they were not trained in law, they also resembled a jury. Courts-martial were otherwise similar to civilian courts. In both, the rules of evidence were remarkably lax by Anglo-Saxon standards, permitting the introduction of unauthenticated exhibits and hearsay. Witnesses and the defendant were allowed wide latitude in testimony to range beyond what was strictly applicable to the trial. Moreover, the defendant came before the court with considerable doubt as to his innocence. In criminal justice proceedings, the presumption of guilt stemmed from the preparation of the judicial inquiry by a supposedly impartial magistrate, the juge d'instruction. In military justice, it arose because the case had been sent to trial by superior officers, whose authority the court-martial board did not readily question.[6]

When the proceedings began on 19 December, Major Bexon d'Ormescheville presented the case for the prosecution. Because Mercier had not shown him the secret dossier, he had to rely on circumstantial evidence and on fervent testimony by Major Hubert Joseph Henry of the Statistical Section, who intimated that he knew more than he could reveal. Sensing that the judges appeared insufficiently convinced to convict, Mercier handed them the dossier on the last day of the trial (22 December). Neither the existence of this evidence nor the fact of its communication was revealed to Dreyfus or his attorney, Demange. The spurious proofs brought the board to their unanimous verdict.[7]

Dreyfus was convicted irregularly. The shame of the matter is not reduced by recalling that miscarriages of justice occurred in the criminal courts as well. For the military, reprimanding an act of treason justified extraordinary methods—but even so, there were apparently doubts. After the trial, Mercier ordered all of the officers in any way involved with the case to maintain strict silence about it and directed the Statistical Section to disperse the contents of the secret dossier among the archives. On 5 January 1895, Dreyfus suffered military degradation in public ceremony; by 21 February, he found himself aboard a prison ship bound for Devil's Island. The first phase of the Dreyfus case had come to an end.[8]

The central figure of the second phase would be Major Georges Picquart, an ambitious, and anti-Semitic, officer who in July 1895 became head of the Statistical Section. General Boisdeffre warned him that Dreyfus's family was agitating against the conviction, and Picquart appeared to take particular note of this problem and of the possibility that more traitors remained to be identified. He began a number of inquiries with no result, until in March 1896 an unmailed letter on blue paper, the *petit bleu,* apparently from the German military attaché and addressed to Major Esterhazy, was brought to the Statistical Section. The petit bleu was altogether a curious and suspect document, because spies are rarely so careless that they name their contacts openly. Nevertheless, Picquart launched an investigation of Esterhazy that included surveillance and the surreptitious opening of his mail—the latter an illegal act in the absence of higher authorization. Picquart undertook this risky endeavor without consulting his superiors, probably hoping that he would have a quick and dramatic success that would give impetus to his career. By August, he had nothing but rumors about Esterhazy's dissolute life and need for money, but while reviewing old files, Picquart came upon the bordereau and recognized in it a close resemblance to Esterhazy's handwriting. On 1 September, Picquart carried a report to Boisdeffre detailing his suspicion that the Dreyfus and Esterhazy cases were related. Boisdeffre replied that Picquart should look for more positive proof against Esterhazy and leave the Dreyfus case alone.

Accounts of the Dreyfus Affair usually emphasize that it was at this point, the autumn of 1896, that the military committed its fundamental blunders, and from them the most serious corruptions of the judicial process; that if excuses can be made for the treatment of Dreyfus before and during his trial, nothing can condone the decision to overlook the possibility that an innocent man was in chains on Devil's Island. A better assessment of what happened, however, would be more complicated and less moralistic.

Boisdeffre was displeased by Picquart's independent and illegal actions in the Esterhazy investigation, actions all the more blameworthy because no evidence against Esterhazy had turned up. In fact, Boisdeffre suspected that Picquart had fallen into a trap set by the Dreyfus family—against whom he had been warned—to shift the blame to another officer through some machination like the petit bleu. It is to play history in the subjunctive to ask how the military would have treated the results of a further investigation under Picquart if there had not been other, outside influences. On 18 September 1896, Lucie Dreyfus formally requested a new trial for her husband, because a report four days earlier in *L'Eclair* indicated that a secret dossier had been shown only to the court-martial board. On 7 and 8 November, Bernard Lazare distributed his famous pamphlet, *Une erreur judiciaire: La vérité sur l'affaire Dreyfus,* in which he indicated his knowledge of several documents from the secret dossier. On 10 November, *Le Matin* published a facsimile of the bordereau. Military officials were stunned because the revelations threatened to take the case before a public ill-prepared to understand the nature of counter-espionage and the difficulty of proving treason—and because the news appeared to indicate that classified information from the Statistical Section was being selectively disclosed to undermine confidence in Dreyfus's conviction. This assumption led the General Staff to suspect that Picquart, the man best situated to have betrayed the secrets, must have acted against Esterhazy not because of real evidence or because he fell into a trap (the petit bleu in either instance), but because he was in the hire of the Dreyfus family. Quite naturally, the military began to mistrust Picquart and to defend Esterhazy.

In November 1896, Picquart was sent on a series of missions that took him away from Paris and the Statistical Section for six months. By June 1897, he became aware that the General Staff regarded him as a primary contributor to the grow-

Figure 3, Cat. 193
Pépin
The Truth (La Vérité)
Le Grelot, 19 December 1897
Photomechanical print

ing agitation about the "affair," as it was coming to be perceived, and he decided to confide his belief that Dreyfus was innocent and Esterhazy guilty to his friend Louis Leblois, a member of the Paris bar. From this conversation on 21 June, Esterhazy's name and the resemblance of handwriting to that of the bordereau were made public.[9]

When Madame Dreyfus had first requested a new trial for her husband in September 1896, the Ministry of Justice refused the initiation of an appeal and stood on the letter of the applicable statute, Article 445 of the Code of Criminal Instruction. By its terms, which dated from 1808, a retrial could be granted only when there had been an error in the application of the law codes in three specific instances: When after a conviction for homicide there was clear evidence that the purported victim was alive; when after a conviction another defendant was judged guilty of the same act and the two verdicts could not be reconciled; and when a witness for the prosecution has been convicted of false testimony against the accused. Clearly, the petition could not satisfy any of these provisions, but a fourth instance had been added by legislation on 8 June 1895, stipulating that when, after a conviction, a new fact has been established or when documents unknown at the time have been discovered tending to prove the innocence of the person convicted, a retrial could be considered. The opinion rejecting Madame Dreyfus's petition declared that an illegal communication of evidence did not come under any of the specific provisions of Article 445 and questioned whether the amendment of June 1895 could be invoked retroactively, even if applicable.[10]

The situation was considerably altered by the autumn of 1897. Now, Esterhazy's name and possible role were known, and Picquart seems to have divulged even the existence of the petit bleu to Leblois. To trigger Article 445, Esterhazy could be brought to trial and convicted—from that, the retrial and exoneration of Dreyfus would follow automatically. But what the Dreyfusards knew (and the conclusions they drew from that) and what the military believed (based on their point of view) were dramatically different. The military insisted that Dreyfus was guilty and considered the attacks on Esterhazy a conspiracy. The Dreyfusards insisted that Dreyfus was innocent and considered the failure to prosecute Esterhazy a plot to protect the true culprit. Ironically, the Dreyfusards had begun their defense of Dreyfus by complaining that the evidence of the bordereau was flimsy, yet they were willing to condemn Esterhazy on the basis of the bordereau alone.

To defend the Dreyfus verdict and to determine whether Esterhazy was a traitor, the Ministry of War appointed General Georges-Gabriel de Pellieux to conduct a preliminary investigation into his conduct. Pellieux's report on 3 December was remarkably similar to the report about Dreyfus that Du Paty had submitted in October 1894: The bordereau might be in Esterhazy's handwriting, but there was no motive (apart from rumors), no proof (little credence was given to the petit bleu, and the earlier Statistical Section surveillance had produced nothing), and far from avowing his guilt, Esterhazy demanded a court-martial to clear his name. Dreyfus had protested his innocence just as resolutely, but the Statistical Section prepared a dossier to prove his guilt. Why not do the same to Esterhazy—in another act of *raison d'état* against possible treason? Dreyfus would then likely have to be retried, with all of the accompanying embarrassment, but there was more to it than that: The military had believed, and continued to believe, that Dreyfus was guilty; they did not believe that Esterhazy was guilty. Another factor was the military's suspicion of Picquart, the instigator of the Esterhazy case. Pellieux's investigation turned up evidence of Picquart's misconduct, in particular the opening of mail and then his divulging secrets to Leblois. It was too easy for a military mind to see in all of this an intrigue to free Dreyfus, the convicted traitor.

Because it appeared certain that Esterhazy would be acquitted by a court-martial, the General Staff readily took up his challenge for a trial. The judicial officer for the case, Major A. Ravary, went over the same ground that Pellieux had covered and for good measure brought in four new graphologists to examine the bordereau. Their opinion was that Esterhazy could not have written it. And with that conclusion, the case against him evaporated. The court-martial convened on 10 January 1898 and adjourned the following day after a unanimous verdict of not guilty.[11]

The military believed that the result of the Esterhazy court-martial would block the attack on the Dreyfus verdict. It was only a day before they were proved wrong: On 13 January, *L'Aurore* headlined Emile Zola's "J'Accuse," an open letter

charging that the military and the government had knowingly convicted an innocent man and acquitted a guilty one. Later the same day, Jean Jaurès, the tribune of the Socialist party, raised the issue of the Dreyfus Affair before the Chamber of Deputies and alleged that the military had plans to overthrow the Republic. Far from cutting short the public debate, the Esterhazy court-martial widened and politicized it. By 24 January, when Jules Méline, the conservative premier, warned the deputies not to arrogate to themselves the right to confirm or reject legal decisions, he was too late. A "case" might be decided by tribunals; an "affair" would be judged outside the legal process. The danger was assessed cogently by Albert de Mun, the famous Catholic social reformer, who in February wrote sadly, "If a verdict cannot be accepted by citizens except on condition that it may be revised in all of its elements by public opinion at the pleasure of whoever would put it in doubt, there would be an end to all justice, civil or military." Once this happened, just as de Mun predicted, the most blatant corruptions of justice were committed—and by both sides—by the military, believing that innocent or not, Dreyfus should remain on Devil's Island; by the Dreyfusards, believing that righting a wrong justified bending the rules.[12]

The new assaults on justice began with Zola's trial in February 1898 for libel in publishing "J'Accuse." The Dreyfusards wanted to use the judicial proceedings for propaganda purposes, to make public the irregularities in the Dreyfus and Esterhazy cases. To prevent this abuse, the Ministry of Justice committed one of its own—bringing the charges on an extremely narrow basis. The presiding justice, Jules Delegorgue, strictly controlled the introduction of any extraneous evidence. When the jury returned a guilty verdict (which was upheld after some complicated appeals), Zola completed the mockery by traveling to England to avoid serving the prison sentence he had courted.[13]

A second blow to the judicial process came after elections in May shifted the alignments in the Chamber of Deputies slightly and led to the replacement of Méline's cabinet with one slightly more moderate. The new minister of war, Godefroy Cavaignac, hoped to make his reputation by issuing a definitive *civilian* opinion on the Dreyfus Affair. His speech before the Chamber on 7 July

1898 justified the verdict of 1894, affirmed the proofs against Dreyfus, and had the effect of turning the Chamber into a court of appeal superior to that of the regular courts. The majority that day was overwhelmingly for Cavaignac and *against* Dreyfus, but the Dreyfusards grasped that if a legislative majority turned in Dreyfus's favor, the judicial process could be compelled to follow.[14] A third phase of the Dreyfus case was beginning.

During the next fourteen months, the principal events took place in the ministries and the courts, with results that began to turn the tide of opinion in the Chamber. Emboldened by Cavaignac's speech, the General Staff acted openly against Picquart. He was arrested on 13 July and charged with having communicated secret information to Leblois and having fabricated the petit bleu. At almost the same time, Cavaignac belatedly deputized his aide, Captain Louis Cuignet, to review thoroughly all of the files relating to Dreyfus. On 13 August, Cuignet discovered that one of the documents to which Cavaignac had specifically referred in his July speech was a forgery. It had been prepared, probably on 2 November 1896, by Lieutenant-Colonel (formerly Major) Henry to strengthen the circumstantial case against Dreyfus. Henry was arrested and committed suicide in prison on 31 August. Esterhazy immediately fled to Belgium. Humiliated by these developments, Boisdeffre resigned as chief of the General Staff. The revelations forced Cavaignac's own resignation, but they could not *directly* prove Dreyfus innocent, because the forgery had not been used to convict him initially.[15]

Nevertheless, Madame Dreyfus used the *faux Henry* (the false document prepared by Henry) as the basis for a new appeal on 3 September. Wary of direct involvement, Jean Sarrien, the minister of justice, formed a consultative committee (of three magistrates and three ministry representatives) to evaluate the request, but when the committee deadlocked, he assumed responsibility for rejecting the petition. The premier, Henri Brisson, objected. Thinking that there had been changes in general political opinion since July, he insisted that the entire cabinet decide the issue—a serious interference in the normal legal process. When the cabinet voted to overrule the minister of justice, the appeal came before the criminal chamber of the Cour de Cassation, France's highest court. Lacking complete power of judicial review, it could not (except in unusual instances) reverse the verdicts of lower tribunals. Instead, it was limited to "breaking" (*casser,* thus the name) a previous decision, and could then order retrial at the original jurisdiction.

The news that the Dreyfus case would be considered by the Cour de Cassation created a sensation. Already, both the supporters and the opponents of Dreyfus were well organized, with politicians, newspapers, and legions of dedicated believers. As the "case" became an "affair," the fate of Dreyfus the man became subsumed beneath the grander politico-philosophical question: Which is more important, raison d'état or absolute justice? The Dreyfusards, many of them enrolled in the League of the Rights of Man, claimed that justice for each individual was the paramount issue. Comprising, for the most part, liberals, freethinkers, and some socialists, the Dreyfusards deeply distrusted the military and what they perceived to be a clerical influence within the officer corps. Some of them, Jaurès, for one, feared a military coup d'état. The anti-Dreyfusards, who in late 1898 formed their own organization, the League of the Fatherland, vowed that a *hypothetical* injustice must not damage the reputation of the army, because if ever defeated, France could then defend justice for no one. Blind allegiance to the military, anti-Semitism, and a conservative disdain for "fainthearted idealists" characterized many anti-Dreyfusards, but their position on the case could claim an intellectual and juridical validity. The men like Méline and de Mun who opposed Dreyfus did so because a legal decision, however improper, should be overturned by another legal decision—not by legislation or public sentiment. Unfortunately, such reasoned opinion was overwhelmed by the violent wing of the anti-Dreyfusards, men who justified Jaurès's fears and who denounced every Dreyfusard as the henchman of anti-French Jews and traitors.

Léon Loew, the presiding justice of the Cour de Cassation's criminal chamber, found himself in the center of controversy, his honest effort to consider the petition objectively exposing him to vicious personal slander. Loew appointed Alphonse Bard, one of the fifteen associate justices, to prepare an evaluation of the appeal, and on 29 October, by a majority vote, the criminal chamber endorsed Bard's recommendation that it hear an inquiry into the Dreyfus case. Once this vote was taken, the anti-Dreyfusards sought to remove the appeal from the jurisdiction of justices whom they claimed were under Jewish control. Although the criminal chamber finished its inquiry on 9 February 1899 and would have voted to grant Dreyfus a new trial, the Chamber of Deputies and the Senate, with a majority still against Dreyfus, were debating a proposal to force the inquiry before all three chambers of the Cour de Cassation. The legislation, which became law on 1 March, nullified the work of the criminal chamber. The inquiry had to begin again, this time before forty-nine justices, and was completed on 29 May. On 3 June, a majority vote of the Cour de Cassation's entire bench reversed the verdict of 22 December 1894 and ordered a retrial. As its rationale, the court cited controversy over the authorship of the bordereau, and the secret communication of evidence.

The proceedings before the Cour de Cassation occurred under conditions that seriously compromised judicial impartiality. The justices deliberated under enormous public and private pressure, with more than a hint of violence, from both Dreyfusards and anti-Dreyfusards. The threat by the legislature—first implied and then carried out—to transfer jurisdiction of the case would imply that the legislature was the ultimate court of appeal. Throughout the second inquiry (the one before the three chambers), details from the proceedings of the first inquiry (before the criminal chamber alone) were illegally communicated by Dreyfusards to *Le Figaro,* which in publishing them contributed significantly to prejudicing a fair hearing of the evidence. Despite all interference, the Cour de Cassation ruled impeccably in requiring a new trial. It invoked retroactively the 1895 addition to Article 445 and cited the controversy over the bordereau as meeting the standard of "a new fact."[16]

It was in this super-heated and emotional climate that the new trial—a second court-martial—took place in Rennes, beginning on 7 August. The attitude of the military had not changed toward Dreyfus, and the intervention of civilian justice had, if anything, hardened the prejudices. The best efforts of the Dreyfusards were handicapped by the rules of trial procedure and by the defendant himself. Brought back from his hellish prison stay, Dreyfus appeared a broken man and inspired little confidence. In contrast, the military officers who

Figure 4, Cat. 221
The Esterhazy Case: Absolute Identity of the Handwritings, (Affaire Esterhazy—Identité absolue des Ecritures), 1898
Poster

testified against him, especially General Mercier, were much more impressive. Because of the lax rules of evidence, they were permitted to make impassioned denunciations and to repeat hearsay, much of it long since discredited. Trained magistrates might have sorted through the maze of testimony, but the seven officers on the court-martial board were hardly that. The prosecution argued that Dreyfus's guilt was proved not by a single document or act but by a cat's cradle of evidence that resolved into a pattern indicating that he was a traitor. Unable to discredit every accusation and every document, the defense could not prevail against this nebulous case. On 9 September, the board retired for deliberations that lasted less than an hour. By a vote of five to two, Dreyfus was again found guilty of treason, but with extenuating circumstances. The sentence of confinement for life was to be reduced to confinement for ten years, half of which had already been served.[17]

The verdict was ludicrous: Treason *has* no extenuating circumstances. The court-martial board was attempting a compromise, the closest that the military would come to admitting that perhaps a mistake had been made, but it was clearly unwilling to certify Dreyfus innocent—whatever else any other court might suggest. The military would not have another chance. A majority sympathetic to Dreyfus now existed in the legislature, finally turned his way by the ruling of the Cour de Cassation, and judicial decisions would be compelled to follow where politics led. René Waldeck-Rousseau, who had become premier in June with a mandate to resolve the affair, convinced the president of the Republic, Emile Loubet, to issue a pardon. Dreyfus had no alternative but to accept, because he could not have survived more time on Devil's Island. For many of his supporters, this conclusion was unsatisfactory. By accepting the pardon, they argued, Dreyfus acknowledged guilt and relinquished the chance for vindication; by offering it, the government endorsed the verdicts of the two courts-martial and the actions of the Statistical Section and General Staff. This righteous (and proper) indignation overlooked the point that, in issuing a pardon to reverse the process of justice because of disagreement with its outcome, the president of the Republic committed a further and grievous assault, the penultimate in the Affair, against the legal system.[18]

One final corruption of the system brought the Dreyfus Affair to a close. In April 1903, General Louis André, the minister of war in the cabinet of Emile Combes, undertook an exhaustive review of the evidence relating to Dreyfus and Esterhazy in the Statistical Section's files. He submitted a report to Combes on 19 October, demonstrating conclusively that most of the evidence alleged at the Rennes court-martial to form a pattern of guilt either did not relate to Dreyfus or had been altered to make it appear that it did. Dreyfus was alerted, and he formally requested Ernest Vallé, the minister of justice, to petition the Cour de Cassation for a revision of the Rennes verdict. The court's criminal chamber, with Jean-Antoine Chambareaud the presiding justice (he had succeeded Loew on his retirement), met on 3 March 1904 and voted to conduct yet another inquiry. It was completed on 19 November, following a tortuous nine months of testimony, which established as clearly as André's report had done the lack of solid evidence against Dreyfus. After so many efforts to discover the truth, the misconceptions and deceptions were finally revealed for what they were. In conformity with the legislative fiat of March 1899, the entire bench of the Cour de Cassation had to rule on the appeal, but that meeting did not take place for another nineteen months. The delay was primarily a result of the political reverses suffered by the Dreyfusard majority: André's disgrace for having used the Freemasons to report on the religious practice of Catholic officers; Combes's resignation soon after; the first Moroccan crisis with Germany; the violent demonstrations associated with enforcement of the law separating church and state; and the legislative elections of May 1906. With Dreyfus rescued from Devil's Island, his case seemed less pressing.

The Cour de Cassation finally assembled on 15 June 1906 to begin its deliberations on the petition and met until 12 July. From a review of the criminal court's inquiry, it was apparent that there were many instances of "new facts" to support "breaking" the Rennes decision. But that would lead to a third court-martial, granting the military an opportunity either to bring another verdict of guilty or to admit publicly and ultimately that an error had been made in 1894 and repeated in 1899. The justices were unwilling to gamble. By a majority vote, they annulled the conviction without refer-

Figure 5
Our Case: The Verdict (Notre procès—le verdict)
L'Aurore, 24 February 1898 Bibliothèque Nationale

ring the case back to any other court. A second vote, this one unanimous, pronounced Dreyfus innocent of all charges. Alexis Ballot-Beaupré, the chief justice of the court, explained the rulings by declaring that no credible evidence existed against the man twice convicted of treason.[19]

The decision of the Cour de Cassation was as surely an example of raison d'état as the first conviction of Dreyfus had been: A *final* exoneration was necessary in 1906; a conviction for treason had been necessary in 1894. The decision rendered "justice"—innocence was duly acknowledged—but it was not through sound jurisprudence. Article 445, on which the rulings were based, specified that the Cour de Cassation could decide the case itself under circumscribed conditions (as when the appellant was dead and a new trial thus impossible) or if no punishable crime would exist after the judgment. The court's action meant that no one had been a traitor in 1894—not Dreyfus, not Esterhazy, not anybody else. All evidence of treason, beginning with the bordereau, was ignored as inconvenient. The law was made to bend to political majorities and necessities.[20]

One of the most eloquent of the Dreyfusards, Charles Péguy, passed judgment on many of his allies by writing in 1910, "Tout commence en mystique et finit en politique."[21] He was referring to the way idealism is compromised in the struggle to maintain it: "Everything begins in faith and ends in politics." So many of the Dreyfusards acted out of a determination to right an injustice,

Figure 6, Cat. 331
Jean-Louis Forain
*Joseph to Dreyfus: Get Out of Here,
You'll Give Us Away (Joseph à Drey-
fus—Fous le camp, tu nous trahirais),*
1904 Black chalk on paper

only to commit injustice themselves in the process. Eventually, for both sides, the end justified the means. And few on either side appeared to understand what damage to principle was done when the legal system was politicized. Another version of Péguy's famous line appears in *Jean Barois,* Roger Martin du Gard's novel about these times, "We lanced the abscess, we counted on a cure—and now gangrene's set in."[22]

The injustice of the Dreyfus Affair should also be considered in relation to the injustice not uncommonly rendered by the French judicial system to others. Stripped of the accusation that Dreyfus was an *unusual* victim of political pressure, the fabrication of evidence, the flouting of trial procedures, and the pliability of magistrates, the case can be explained as a series of errors compounded by the fear of admitting mistakes at such a level and envenomed by the prejudice of anti-Semitism. Most miscarriages of French justice went unnoticed, their victims helpless and unrecognized. That enough citizens cared for a wrong to be righted and for justice to be done in at least this one instance saved Dreyfus and is to their eternal honor. We should not, however, forget the price.

Notes

1. The most recent and fullest account of the Dreyfus Affair is Jean-Denis Bredin, *L'Affaire* (Paris: Julliard, 1983), translated by Jeffrey Mehlman as *The Affair: The Case of Alfred Dreyfus* (New York: George Braziller, 1986). Two other excellent guides are Douglas W. Johnson, *France and the Dreyfus Affair* (London: Blandford Press, 1965), which includes an annotated bibliography, and Guy Chapman, *The Dreyfus Case: A Reassessment* (New York: Reynal and Company, 1955). For the reaction by Demange, Ravary, and Clemenceau, see Johnson, *France and the Dreyfus Affair*, 2, 224.

2. For the police in France during this period, see Marcel Le Clère, *Histoire de la police* (Paris: Presses Universitaires de France, 1964), 90–99; Henri Dupoy, *La Police des moeurs et la liberté individuelle* (Paris: Agenda-Annuaire, 1913), 25–80; Georges Aubert, *Organisation et méthodes de la police française* (Tours: Arrault, 1938), 116–123, among the many studies that might be cited.

3. Bredin, *The Affair*, 40–47, 54–78, analyzes the inquiry. For a discussion of the bordereau and the other documents in the case, see Marcel Thomas, *L'Affaire sans Dreyfus* (Paris: Fayard, 1961).

4. For the role of the juge d'instruction, see Benjamin F. Martin, *The Hypocrisy of Justice in the Belle Epoque* (Baton Rouge: Louisiana State University Press, 1984), passim, and "The Courts, the Magistrature, and Promotions in Third Republic France, 1871–1914," *American Historical Review* 87 (October 1982): 977–1009, particularly 979–980.

5. Johnson, *France and the Dreyfus Affair*, 43–53, provides a perceptive argument; see also Bredin, *The Affair*, 78–83.

6. Martin, "The Courts, the Magistrature, and Promotions," 977–982. Raoul de la Grasserie, *De la justice en France et à l'étranger au XXe siècle*, 3 vols. (Paris: Sirey, 1914); René David and Henry P. de Vries, *The French Legal System: An Introduction to Civil Law Systems* (New York: Oceana Publications, 1958); and R. C. K. Ensor, *Courts and Judges in France, Germany, and England* (Oxford: Oxford University Press, 1933), supply detailed background.

7. There is no transcript of the 1894 court-martial. Major Bexon d'Ormescheville's presentation is published in Yves Guyot, *La Révision du procès Dreyfus, faits et documents juridiques* (Paris: Stock, 1898). See also Bredin, *The Affair*, 83–97.

8. Johnson, *France and the Dreyfus Affair*, 30–31.

9. Ibid., 64–83; Bredin, *The Affair*, 140–152, 161–186.

10. *Code d'instruction criminelle*, Article 445. For a commentary, see Adhémar Esmein, *Histoire de la procédure criminelle en France, et spécialement de la procédure inquisitoire depuis le XIIIe siècle jusqu'à nos jours* (Paris: Larose et Forcel, 1882), translated by John Simpson, with a revision by the author, as *A History of Continental Criminal Procedure with Special Reference to France* (Boston: Little, Brown, and Company, 1913), 565–568.

11. Bredin, *The Affair*, 187–212, 217–242; Johnson, *France and the Dreyfus Affair*, 84–118. Guyot, *La Révision du procès Dreyfus*, publishes a partial transcript of the Esterhazy court-martial.

12. The general political context is described in Benjamin F. Martin, *Count Albert de Mun: Paladin of the Third Republic* (Chapel Hill: University of North Carolina Press, 1978), 109–128, with de Mun's words from 119. For Jaurès and Méline, see the *Journal Officiel*, Chambre des Députés, Débats, 13, 24 January 1898.

13. *Le Procès Zola devant la cour d'assises et la Cour de Cassation*, 2 vols. (Paris: Le Siècle et Stock, 1898). See also Bredin, *The Affair*, 245–275.

14. *Journal Officiel*, Chambre des Députés, Débats, 7 July 1898.

15. Bredin, *The Affair*, 313–332; Johnson, *France and the Dreyfus Affair*, 134–145.

16. Bredin, *The Affair*, 275–285, 332–384; Martin, *Count Albert de Mun*, 129–136. *La Révision du procès Dreyfus à la Cour de Cassation*, 3 vols. (Paris: Stock, 1899).

17. *Le Procès Dreyfus devant le Conseil de Guerre de Rennes*, 3 vols. (Paris: Stock, 1900). See also Bredin, *The Affair*, 397–429.

18. Bredin, *The Affair*, 429–451; Johnson, *France and the Dreyfus Affair*, 179; Chapman, *The Dreyfus Case*, 302–304.

19. Bredin, *The Affair*, 461–481. *La Révision du procès de Rennes. Enquête de la chambre criminelle de la Cour de Cassation*, 3 vols. (Paris: Ligue Français pour la Défense des Droits de l'Homme et du Citoyen, 1908).

20. For differing evaluations of the 12 July 1906 decision of the Cour de Cassation, see the *Recueil général des lois et des arrêts en matière civile, criminelle, administrative et de droit publique, 1907 (Recueil Sirey)* (Paris: Sirey, 1907), 1–49, criticizing it; and Albert Chenevier, "L'Article 445 et la Cour de Cassation," *Pages Libres* 411 (14 November 1908): 527–548; 412 (21 November 1908): 563–575, defending it.

21. Charles Péguy, *Notre Jeunesse* (1910), in *Oeuvres en prose, 1909–1914* (Paris: Librairie Gallimard, 1957), 516.

22. Roger Martin du Gard, *Jean Barois* (Paris: Librairie Gallimard, 1913), translated by Stuart Gilbert (Indianapolis: The Bobbs-Merrill Company, 1969), 269, spoken by the character François Cresteil d'Allize.

Popular Anti-Semitism

MICHAEL R. MARRUS

Popular anti-Semitism permeated the atmosphere of the Dreyfus Affair. It wormed its way into the culture of daily life, affecting events at every moment. But this anti-Semitism cannot be understood in isolation from other important historical developments. That anti-Jewish feeling in France had grown so strong and pervasive was part of the extraordinary politicization that occurred in the western world during the course of the nineteenth century. Politicization meant the commitment of ever greater numbers of people to particular causes of national or universal relevance, causes hitherto championed only by social or academic elites. Politicization also entailed an increasing tendency to couch such issues in a popular idiom and the ritualistic celebration of ideological positions before great masses of people. Finally, politicization involved new forms of political expression: mass-circulation newspapers, posters, popular parties and leagues, and political rallies.

It was not until the 1880s that hardened anti-Semites in France discovered that fear and hatred of Jews could have a broad popular appeal. Before that time, anti-Jewish writers had attracted relatively little attention, and they did not normally connect with serious political issues of the day. These writers came chiefly from the socialist Left, those who since the end of the Revolutionary and Napoleonic era had envisioned a new society free of the exploitation and social inequities associated with the liberal bourgeois order. Because Jews appeared to them to be the chief beneficiaries of the social arrangements they decried, such authors took to excoriating Jews as a group. As Jews were beginning to find their way in early nineteenth-century French society—and as some, such as the Rothschilds, achieved quite spectacular successes—people who looked back to a communalistic society or a preindustrial mode of production often considered Jews their enemies. Such were the views of some famous early socialists in France—men like Charles Fourier, Pierre-Joseph Proudhon, and Pierre Leroux. As regards anti-Semitism the most important was Alphonse Toussenel, a journalist and follower of Fourier whose first book had the inflammatory title *Les Juifs, rois de l'époque* (The Jews, Kings of the Era) (1845).

In retrospect, these left-wing thinkers appear to us as cranky individualists, fundamentally unlike the mass propagandists who emerged later, in the decade before Dreyfus. Toussenel, for example, while yielding to none in the intensity of his anti-Jewish views, nevertheless did not devote his career to disseminating the message. He retreated to the countryside in disillusionment after the failure of the Revolution of 1848, and lived his life as a country gentleman—hunting, and writing books on birds and animal life. To be sure, spokesmen such as Toussenel left behind them a legacy of ideas and images, replete with references to "high finance," the Rothschilds, and the Jewish propensity for capitalist exploitation. Like other elaborate

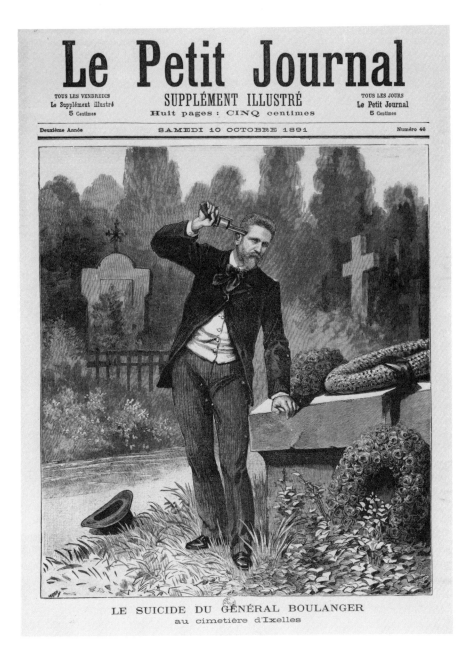

Figure 1
The Suicide of General Boulanger at the Ixelles Cemetery
Le Suicide du General Boulanger au cemetière d'Ixelles
Le Petit Journal, 10 October 1891
Photomechanical print
Bibliothèque Nationale

assaults upon capitalism, however, these notions failed to win adherents beyond a small coterie of intellectuals.

Popular anti-Semitism persisted in the eastern part of France, in the old Jewish population centers of Alsace and Lorraine, but such sentiment was guided more by traditional leaders of opinion, often local rural notables rather than by the modern urban rabble-rousers. In villages around Strasbourg, Metz, and Colmar, Jewish peddlers, wholesalers, and moneylenders continued to ply their trades until well into the nineteenth century. Hard times—or political upheaval, as in 1848—could bring to the surface a variety of ancient complaints rooted in custom and folklore. But this kind of disturbance occurred seldom after the middle of the century and was clearly on the decline as its social basis continued to erode. With the progressive integration of Jews into regional society, and with the gradual introduction of new institutions to perform traditionally "Jewish" functions, the old resentments against the Jews gradually subsided.

In 1882 the spectacular collapse of a Catholic banking house, the Union générale, sent anti-Jewish shock waves throughout France. While the old-style hostility was eroding, an event like the bank collapse catalyzed the development of a modern anti-Semitic ideology: an entire system of ideas that ascribed important disasters to Jews while proposing solutions to their supposed "domination" of French society.[1] The Union générale bank had been founded by Catholics specifically in order to break the hold of Jewish and Protestant families over the banking industry; it attracted deposits from Church institutions, distinguished Catholic families, and tens of thousands of small investors. When the crash occurred, owing in reality to severe mismanagement, press accounts sympathetic to the bank attributed the ruin to the evil machinations of Jews—particularly the Rothschilds—who were pictured as leading an assault on French national interests. "Killed by the Jews," was the brief epitaph on the Union générale written by the French ambassador to St. Petersburg, the Viscount de Voguë; a chorus of similar charges echoed across the country, led by Eugène Bontoux, a former Rothschild employee and director of the newly defunct Catholic bank. The result was scandal: a carefully orchestrated horror story played out in mass-circulation newspapers before a huge public hungry precisely for sensational melodrama of this kind. Across France, people were duly scandalized; for many decades, people remembered the Union générale crash and saw in it a prime demonstration that when the world was not right, a Jew was likely responsible.

Ten years later, in 1892, came another such scandal: the bankruptcy of the Panama Canal Company, which had been formed originally by the creator of the Suez Canal, Ferdinand de Lesseps. In the lurid light cast by the press upon the company's shady dealings, the most grotesque caricatures that emerged concerned two Jews, Baron Jacques de Reinach, who committed suicide in the course of the affair, and Cornelius Herz. Here was another opportunity to defame Jews before the entire nation.

"Every regime," writes Jeannine Verdès-Leroux, "has the scandals it deserves."[2] In the Third Republic, relatively weak and irresolute governments presided over a sharply divided populace, eager to believe the worst about those in financial or political power. To this was added the availability of anti-Semitic myths about Jewish financial manipulation, which could explain complex, extremely obscure financial intrigues.

No one took better advantage of these scandals than Edouard Drumont, a shy, brooding publicist of genius, who became the most outstanding purveyor of anti-Semitism in French history. Drumont was both Catholic and republican; by no means conservative politically, he was a man with a sharp eye for what would sell. In the wake of the Union générale crash he wrote a sensational two-volume work titled *La France juive* (Jewish France) (1886), reading into the long course of history a seemingly endless struggle between "Aryans" and "Semites." At the bottom of France's problems, which were accumulating perceptibly with the economic recession of the 1880s, was a scheming, predatory Jewish race. His work was a stunning success: It sold over a hundred thousand copies by the end of the first year and became the most widely read book in France. Thereafter Drumont's tract had continued to enjoy a long, vigorous life: In subsequent editions it was abridged, illustrated, reissued, expanded, and translated. Around Drumont emerged a whole cluster of anti-Semitic writers, who made the Jews the chief scapegoat for the ills of France. According to the historian of French

Figure 2, Cat. 400
Emile Courtet
Jewish Virtues According to Gall's Methods (Les qualités du Juif d'après la méthode de Gall)
La Libre Parole, 23 December 1893
Photomechanical print
The Jewish Museum

Figure 3, Cat. 47
Jean-Louis Forain
Artist and Jews (Artiste et Juifs)
Wash drawing on paper

anti-Semitism Robert Byrnes, "literature attacking the Jews rose from an annual average of less than one publication from 1879 through 1885, to fifteen in 1886, fourteen in 1887, nine in 1888, and twenty in 1889. Attacks upon the Masons, conversely, fell from an annual average of nine from 1879 through 1886 to six in 1887, five in 1888, and one in 1889."[3] Six years after releasing his bestseller and just in time to capitalize on the Panama scandal, Drumont launched *La Libre parole,* a daily newspaper devoted to anti-Semitism. Once again his journalistic instincts proved sound: The paper floated on a tide of anti-Jewish feeling and had reached the unusually high circulation of 200,000 by the time Alfred Dreyfus was arrested.

With Drumont and his paper, along with the other anti-Jewish pamphlets, books, and articles that had been appearing since the mid-1880s, we see the creation of a popular anti-Semitic genre. But why at this particular moment in French history? Economic difficulties beginning in the 1880s provide one plausible explanation. Another is undoubtedly the arrival on the scene of mass-circulation newspapers. Cheap popular dailies, read by hundreds of thousands and distributed throughout France on the newly built railway network added a new dimension to popular culture in the 1880s. Reveling in the sensational, stoking and feeding a popular hunger for novelty, these journals carried an anti-Semitic message to every corner of the land, awakening slumbering prejudices and inciting new fears of obscure forms of Jewish domination. Without press controversy and the wide circulation of stories related to his book, Drumont might never have achieved fame and notoriety with his *France juive*. And without the cynicism of journalists encouraged by the surprising popular response to such demagoguery, it seems unlikely that there would have been so many effective champions of modern anti-Semitic fantasies. By the last decade of the nineteenth century, according to Zeev Sternhell, the great majority of popular newspapers were anti-Semitic.[4] Journalists, not social theorists, spread the new anti-Jewish mythology.

To tap the current of anti-Semitic sentiment, activists attempted to build specifically anti-Jewish political movements. The first was the Ligue nationale antisémitique de France, organized in 1889 by a disparate group financed largely by a free-booting ex-officer and adventurer, the Marquis de Morès, a rancher in North Dakota and failed railway promoter in Indochina. De Morès and his followers were typical of anti-Semitic tendencies in the 1880s in being associated with Boulangism, a radical, plebiscitarian challenge to both organized socialism and the Republic. Its partisans rallied around the popular general and would-be dictator General Georges Boulanger.

Popular anti-Semitism could be allied with other causes besides Boulangism. In 1897 Jules Guérin, a disciple of both Morès and Drumont, began the Ligue antisémitique française, which eventually attracted thousands of members. While its heritage was Boulangist, its tendency was distinctly leftist and radical; its members proclaimed themselves "socialists," denouncing cosmopolitan speculators, department stores, and miscellaneous exploiters of the common person. The Ligue organized demonstrations, many of them violent, and achieved some success in the Paris municipal elections of 1900.

Throughout France in the 1890s, organizers like Morès and Guérin embarked on anti-Semitism as a political career. The movement provided politicians like these with money, popular standing, and a degree of authority. The French in Algeria proved particularly susceptible to energetic revolutionary demagogues. Among the settler population, Jews were often seen as the supporters of a liberal and more centralized rule from Paris. Within radical and strongly nationalist circles, which were often bitterly opposed to the central government, opposition to Jews was woven into the fabric of local politics by the end of the century. The great anti-Semitic tribune in North Africa during the Dreyfus years was a naturalized Italian named Max Régis, whose anti-Jewish effusions sometimes made those of Drumont and Guérin look mild by comparison. His followers would march through the streets of Algiers, sometimes singing an anthem, the *Marche antisémite*:

> A mort les juifs! A mort les juifs!
>   Il faut les pendre
>   Sans plus attendre.
> A mort les juifs! A mort les juifs!
>   Il faut les pendre
>   Par leur pif!

> Death to the Jews! Death to the Jews!
>   They must be hung
>   Without delay.
> Death to the Jews! Death to the Jews!
>   They must be hung
>   By their snouts!

In April 1898, at the height of the Dreyfus Affair, Drumont drew upon Régis's help and was elected to the Chamber of Deputies from Algiers. Later that year the French citizens of that city elected a new mayor: Max Régis.

Anti-Semitism clothed the ideals and aspirations of these agitators, lending form and apparent theoretical consistency to their diverse views. But the underlying reason for its success remains to be explained. Why did anti-Semitic mythology prove so popular? Behind it all, historians have suggested, lay a fundamental and widely felt enmity toward a world of change, a deep-seated anxiety and unhappiness in the face of a variety of forces

Figure 4, Cat. 43
Frédéric Régency
Today, thanks to the Jews, money has become Almighty (Aujourd'hui, grâce aux Juifs, l'argent est devenue taut-puissant)
La France Juive, 1886
Engraving

Figure 5, Cat. 242
A. Lemot
Each His Own Burden (Chacun Son Lot)
Le Pèlerin, 18 December 1898
Photomechanical print

that were transforming French society.[5] Anti-Semitism, in this view, had little to do with actual flesh-and-blood Jews; rather it was simply available as one of the most convenient and successful vehicles to oppose the dramatic new directions society was taking. The chorus of opposition sounded three broad predominant themes, each of which contributed its own mythical image of the Jew.

The first of these was the *cri de cœur* of the petit bourgeois—small shopkeepers, artisans, employees, and others for whom the growth in France of large-scale economic organization and the emergence of modern economic relationships seemed profoundly unjust. Many saw anti-Semitism as a way of protesting new inequities, which seemed such a shocking aspect of modern life. This anti-Semitism was populist, and its corresponding image of the Jew depicted a capitalist exploiter, linked to an international network of finance that was somehow seizing control of the fortunes of ordinary hard-working Frenchmen. In his *Testament d'un antisémite,* Drumont presented himself to the public as a defender of the poor and oppressed, a prophet of social justice. The anti-Semitic revolution for which he called would be an uprising of the downtrodden against the wealthy: "[T]he days of cosmopolitan high finance are numbered. Thanks to us, the names of the plutocrats who incarnate an avaricious and scheming Jewry are imprinted on the minds of the masses so that nothing can erase them."

These "masses" were the "people" of Michelet, rather than the proletariat of Karl Marx. They represented a vast brotherhood of Frenchmen united only by their misery and alienation—all of which could be blamed on the Jews. One day, Drumont wrote,

A man of the people will take up our campaign, a socialist leader who will refuse to be bought off by the Synagogue, as have been so many of his comrades; he will gather around him thousands of aroused persons, instructed by ourselves, those exploited people of all classes, small businessmen ruined by large department stores, those urban and rural workers crushed under the monopolies.

Here was a socialism for all classes, a political movement that did not require commitment to a class struggle in France. It was a socialism that dispensed with the elaborate theoretical baggage of the Left, seeing the enemy plain and undisguised. It was not a limited appeal to those who would identify with a workers' party, rather it was a call to the entire body of honest Frenchmen, who might feel themselves to be victimized by Jewish outsiders.

This "socialist" anti-Semitism had its origins in Boulangism, the enthusiastic popular mobilization of 1886–1889. But after the demise of that movement it persisted in a variety of political contexts, even within the established socialist parties. It is useful to realize how loose and adaptable were the terminology and ideology of popular politics a century ago. "Socialist," "nationalist," "anti-Semitic"—these denoted only broad affiliations, not carefully worked-out doctrines. Denunciations of "Jews" could be considered on the Left simply as a linguistic shorthand for populist leanings. Jean Jaurès, the revered Socialist party chief and eventual defender of the Dreyfusards, stooped himself to taking occasional swipes at Jews, while at the same time denouncing Drumont as a false socialist. For Jaurès, as for many others, "Jew" was a crude, shorthand way of saying "bourgeois"; until the height of the Dreyfus Affair in 1898, "anti-Semitism" was certainly not seen in such quarters as a serious menace to individuals or as a form of prejudice against a group.

A second anti-Semitic theme bore the stamp of popular Catholicism, itself a part of the late nineteenth-century politicization I have discussed in this essay. This form of anti-Semitism depicted Jews as the great challenge to the Church and the faithful; it rehearsed old charges against the Jews as a deicidal people, whose energies were now directed at the undermining of Christianity in France. The themes were old, and generations of Christian teachings regarding the Jews facilitated their acceptance. What was new was the extraordinarily wide distribution of such ideas at the end of the nineteenth century, and the widely respected authority the Church gave to the denunciation of Jews.

Often considered a period of secularization and dechristianization, the last decades of the nineteenth century nevertheless also witnessed a marked intensification of fervor in certain Catholic milieux, and even a popular religious revival associated with pilgrimages, the cult of the Sacré-Coeur, and ultramontanism, the movement with-

Figure 6, Cat. 72
Léon-Adolphe Willette
Anti-Semitic Candidate, 1889
Lithographic poster

Figure 7, Cat. 13
Artist unknown
La Libre Parole (poster), 1892
Photomechanical print

in the Church that was zealously supportive of papal authority. Modern means of transport and communication carried the new messages of commitment. Those who have studied this energizing of popular religion have detected a powerful current of anti-Semitism among the various new articles of belief. Verdès-Leroux, for example, examined diocesan bulletins, a form of Church communication becoming considerably more significant during the period than ever before. Of seventy-five of those issued during the year of the Panama scandal that were examined, only fifteen were *not* hostile to Jews. Nineteen went to extreme lengths—accusing Jews of ritual murders or describing the invasion of France by a predatory horde of Jews.[6]

One of the most modern newspapers in France from a technical standpoint, *La Croix,* the journal of the Assumptionist Order, reached a huge audience during the Dreyfus era, and mixed lurid anti-Semitism with other themes of interest to the Catholic laity and clergy. According to *La Croix* the Jews had virtually taken over the Republic, and they had invented socialism, anticlericalism, and materialism to further their godless aims. Both violent and racist, the paper left to the imagination no wrongdoing on the part of Jews. Every incident was linked to the purported conspiracy of Jews to subvert Christianity and French society.

This anti-Semitism provided a means for Catholics to legitimize their position in French society, which was severely challenged by anticlerical activists in the 1880s. Anti-Semitism was also a way of establishing the social relevance of Catholic teaching and belief. Some Catholic publicists found in its rhetoric a means to proclaim the socially progressive character of their religiosity, borrowing from the populist or "socialist" anti-Semitism. Catholics who would excoriate the Jews before a mass audience were often people who were nervously defensive—they felt their world engulfed by alien forces and saw themselves as the innocent victims of modernity. In the end, as Pierre Sorlin points out in his remarkable monograph on *La Croix,* Catholic anti-Semites created a diabolic image of Jews that took on a life of its own. The Jews of their own paranoid imagining really frightened these publicists; consumed with anxiety themselves, they encouraged the apprehensions of thousands of their fellow Catholics.[7]

Nationalist elements accounted for the third anti-Semitic theme sounded in the Dreyfus period. Anti-Semitic nationalists harped less on the external enemies of France than on the threat within—the danger that corrosive forces would eat away at the very foundations of French society, rendering the nation helpless and demoralized. The Jew, in this vision, was the rootless cosmopolitan, devoid of national loyalties and incapable of defending any interest but his own. For Maurice Barrès, one of the most celebrated nationalist writers at the turn of the century, Dreyfus's guilt was evident simply from the Jewishness of the convicted officer: "I need no one to tell me why Dreyfus committed treason. . . . That Dreyfus is capable of treason, I conclude from his race."[8]

Riding the coattails of nationalism, anti-Semitism was thus carried by the most powerful popular ideology in Europe in the decade before World War I. During this era people throughout Europe were deeply moved by the concept and symbols of the nation state; practically no sphere of life escaped this influence. Not every nationalist was anti-Semitic, of course; practically everyone became nationalists—liberals, conservatives, radicals, moderates, clericals, anticlericals, socialists, and antisocialists—and so did the Jews among them. But nationalists had a tendency to look about, questioning the national "belongingness" of others, and often when they did so they found Jews wanting. It is important to remember that until recent times nothing was easier than to single out the Jews as outsiders: There were no blacks or Orientals to speak of in Europe in the nineteenth century, no large Muslim minority such as today assumes the role of outcasts in French society; moreover, there was no tradition of religious pluralism. Historically, the Jews seemed uniquely "different." From this it was a short step to depict them as strangers, a different race of people—or indeed, the enemies of the nation: the unremissible sin, as the Catholic liberal Anatole Leroy-Beaulieu described it in his generally sympathetic book about Jews published in 1893.

How strong was popular anti-Semitism during the Dreyfus years? Robert Byrnes argued that the organized anti-Semitic movement was heading into decline in early 1893, on the eve of Dreyfus's arrest. Although it had real national strength, its organizations were weak and fractious, weakening

Figure 8, Cat. 397
Charles Huard
Dreyfus, Reinach and Company
Photomechanical print

the political cause. If Byrnes is correct, this would parallel a similar development in Germany, where the influence of anti-Jewish parties slipped significantly near the turn of the century. But while the political fortunes of anti-Semitism may have been waning in 1893–94, it seems also true that anti-Jewish ideas were deeply ingrained and widely disseminated. Once the press had thrust Jews prominently before the public with the Affair, groups and individuals had no trouble grasping the anti-Jewish message. According to Stephen Wilson, there were anti-Semitic demonstrations and riots in nearly seventy towns and cities in France in early 1898, with troops called in at least five times; that year twenty-two declared anti-Semitic deputies were elected to the Chamber of Deputies, together with forty more who would back anti-Semitic legislation.[9] The political strength of anti-Semitism certainly declined after the Dreyfus Affair, Wilson notes, but the reason does not seem to have been a lack of popular support.

Eventually other issues, other causes, and other myths largely displaced the image of the Jewish bogeyman in the popular consciousness. Anti-Semitism did not disappear, but it proved less compelling as a defensive, integrating ideology than it had earlier. Perhaps that is the shred of comfort one may draw from the sordid tale of popular anti-Jewish ideology. Anti-Semitism offered a temporary palliative for those who abhorred class division, secularization, social mobility, or economic modernization in French society. Anti-Semitism both explained these mysterious processes—*c'est la faute aux juifs* (it's the Jews' fault)—and created in the national community a fictional refuge for those who sought an escape from the disorienting challenges of modernity. But change triumphed in the end. Popular anti-Semitism, for a time at least, slipped into France's folkloric past.

Notes

1. Jeannine Verdès-Leroux, *Scandale financier et antisémitisme catholique: le krach de l'Union générale* (Paris: Editions du Centurion, 1969), 12.
2. Verdès-Leroux, 206.
3. Robert F. Byrnes, *Antisemitism in Modern France: The Prologue to the Dreyfus Affair* (New York: Howard Fertig, 1969), 155.
4. Zeev Sternhell, *La Droite révolutionnaire, 1885–1914: les origines françaises du fascisme* (Paris: Editions du Seuil, 1978), 217. On popular anti-Semitism in the countryside, and its limitations, see Michael Burns, *Rural Society and French Politics—Boulangism and the Dreyfus Affair 1886–1900* (Princeton: Princeton University Press, 1984).
5. Stephen Wilson, *Ideology and Experience: Anti-Semitism in France at the Time of the Dreyfus Affair* (Rutherford, N.J.: Fairleigh Dickinson, University Press, 1982), passim.
6. Verdès-Leroux, *Scandale financier,* 148.
7. Pierre Sorlin, *"La Croix" et les Juifs (1880–1899): contribution à l'histoire de l'antisémitisme contemporain* (Paris: Editions Bernard Grasset, 1967), 183.
8. *Scènes et doctrines du nationalisme* (Paris: Félix Juven, 1902), 152.
9. Wilson, *Ideology and Experience,* 734.

The Paris Cry: Graphic Artists and the Dreyfus Affair

PHILLIP DENNIS CATE

During the nineteenth century, artistic journal illustration was one of the most effective vehicles for social and political propaganda. The lithographic work of Daumier from the first half of the nineteenth century served as an influential precedent for the satirical journal illustrations of the eighties and nineties. By the 1880s, however, photomechanical printing processes had usurped the artistic role of lithography and the more documentary role of wood engraving in the illustration of journals. The new photoprinting processes allowed an artist's drawing to be reproduced and printed more quickly and economically than ever before.[1]

Along with this new technology, the 1881 Freedom of the Press law, which greatly reduced censorship, spurred the proliferation of illustrated journals that used the talents of a number of young avant-garde artists for often biting and witty designs. *Le Chat noir, Le Courrier français, Le Rire, Le Cri de Paris, Le Canard sauvage,* and *L'Assiette au beurre* were some of the most prominent satirical journals that employed the talents of such artists as Jean-Louis Forain, Théophile-Alexandre Steinlen, Henri de Toulouse-Lautrec, Félix Vallotton, Caran d'Ache, Adolphe Willette, Hermann-Paul, Henri-Gabriel Ibels, Charles Léandre, and others.

In 1898 the Dreyfus Affair generated a whole body of journalistic illustration and caricature, including in particular imagery both pro and con Dreyfus, as well as images of a more generally anti-Semitic cast. Prints and journal illustrations directly related to the Dreyfus Affair, however, only mark the climax of a decade-long period of anti-Semitic imagery, which had evolved with the popular response to Drumont's publication of *La France Juive* in 1886, and of images dealing with social and political issues, which developed in the late 1880s as artists and writers became socially and politically active.

In the early 1880s, with the establishment in Montmartre, the northernmost section of Paris, of the artistic and literary cabaret Chat Noir and its similarly titled illustrated journal, the neighborhood quickly became the center of avant-garde activity in the arts. This impoverished part of Paris was, as Jerrold Seigel has recently described it, the hub of Bohemian society in the 1880s and 1890s.[2] Artists, writers, and composers found that they could live and work there cheaply. They displayed their art and performed their poems, songs, and music at the Chat Noir and eventually at a number of other *cabarets artistiques* that flourished in Montmartre during the last decades of the century.

Throughout this period Montmartre was not only a sanctuary for nonestablished artists and writers but also a hotbed for literary and cultural activities with social and political themes.

Figure 1
Caran d'Ache
Study for a zinc cut-out for the
Epopée shadow theater performance,
1888 India ink

The Jane Voorhees Zimmerli Art
Museum
Gift of Carleton Holstrom

The community of artists and writers who associated together at the Chat Noir and, beginning
in 1885, at Aristide Bruant's cafe Le Mirliton, and
from 1893, at the Quat'z'Arts cabaret often collaborated on books, journals, song sheets, shadow-
theater productions, and programs for the performances at the Théâtre Libre and the Théâtre de
L'Oeuvre.[3]

By the end of the 1880s, among the artists Steinlen, Willette, Caran d'Ache, Forain, Louis Anquetin, Henry Somm, and Lautrec, there had been
many artistic collaborations and personal friendships; many relationships involved both. During
the next few years, Ibels, Vallotton, Hermann-
Paul, and Luce joined the diverse artists who were
connected by proximity, by respect for one another's art, and by commissions for their work,
but primarily by a mutual contempt for the bourgeois values of society exemplified and promoted
by the government of the Third Republic. These
artists, in general, had in common an empathy
with the disadvantaged and the downtrodden,
who were outcasts from society, estranged from
the status quo—like the artists themselves. However, the fact that artists tended to share a disdain for the principles of the Third Republic did
not necessarily align them politically and philosophically. The alternatives they posed to the status quo were extremely varied. Steinlen, Ibels,

Vallotton, and Luce were positioned to the left as
antimilitary, anarchist/socialists; Forain and Caran
d'Ache were promilitary, favoring a reactionary,
oligarchical form of government; Willette was a
promilitary, anarchist/socialist; while Toulouse-
Lautrec considered himself totally apolitical.

If by 1899 the position vis-à-vis Dreyfus of each
of the above artists was not clear, the album *Hommage des artists à Picquart* made it evident, either by
inclusion or in some obvious cases by exclusion.[4]
The album comprises twelve black-and-white lithographs honoring Picquart and sympathetic to his
case, along with 142 pages of signatures of artists,
writers, publishers, and other intellectuals appealing his imprisonment. Anquetin, Hermann-Paul,
Luce, and Vallotton (pl. 124) were among the
twelve artists who created the lithographs for the
album, while the names of Ibels and Steinlen are
listed within the petition. Willette, Caran d'Ache,
and Forain, all of whom had for some time displayed their deeply anti-Semitic bias in their illustrations, appear in neither section of the album,
nor does the noncommittal Toulouse-Lautrec.

The earlier graphic work by these artists would
place them, if not always among the most active,
certainly among the most prominent figures in the
social/political and anti-Semitic milieu in which
the Dreyfus Affair of 1898 unfolded. All but Lautrec eventually took sides in the Affair, and as is

suggested by Caran d'Ache's humorous cartoon (pl. 54), battle lines were drawn between one-time colleagues and friends of the Parisian artistic circles at the end of the century.

Willette and the writer Emile Goudeau were two of the first to become closely involved with the Chat Noir cabaret and its journal in the early 1880s. Goudeau, at the invitation of Rodolphe Salis, the owner and founder of the cabaret, was established at the end of 1881 as the official poet-in-residence of the Chat Noir. He brought with him the Hydropaths (a nonsense name which he had given to the group of poets and writers he had formed in 1878), which had met regularly until 1881 at a cafe on the rue Cujas in the Latin Quarter to perform their songs and poems. Willette, as a member of the Hydropaths, joined Goudeau at the Chat Noir and began creating illustrations for the journal in March 1882 a month after its inception.[5]

Salis commissioned Willette to create several works: a distinctive three-dimensional metal emblem showing a black cat jumping over a crescent moon for the cabaret's exterior, a large stained glass window called *La vierge*, and a painting called *Parce Domine*. In 1886, after the Chat Noir had moved to its new larger home at 12 rue Victor Massé, Willette's stained glass, *Le Veau d'Or* was on display in the cabaret's large "Salle des Gardes" (public hall).

In 1883 Willette introduced Steinlen to the Chat Noir group, and, he too became one of the early regular contributors of illustration to the cabaret's humorous journal. In addition, Caran d'Ache and other artists such as Henry Somm, Henri Rivière, George Auriol, and Eugène Grasset, defined with Willette and Steinlen the artistic atmosphere of the cabaret. In 1887 Salis published the *Chat Noir Guide*, which not only facetiously describes the interior of the cabaret and lists the artworks within but also names the early "members" of the Chat Noir.[6] These *membres fondateurs* (founding members) were the most prominent regular visitors to the cabaret from the artistic, literary, scientific, and political circles of Paris. For our purposes we can cite from this extraordinary list of over two hundred names representing *le tout Paris* such later participants in the Dreyfus Affair as Goudeau, Edgar Degas, Willette, Somm, Caran d'Ache, Steinlen, Emile Zola, Henri Rochefort, Arthur Meyer, Paul Renouard, and Anatole France.

Though not listed, Lautrec and his young artist friends also frequented the cabaret.[7]

In 1886 Rivière and Somm initiated the now famous Chat Noir shadow-theater performances, which for a period of ten years presented a total of forty-four different protocinema productions. Caran d'Ache's *L'Epopée* was first shown at the Chat Noir in 1888.[8] This elaborate two-act military history comprised fifty different scenes on Napoleonic themes (fig. 1), and reveals Caran d'Ache's respect for and fascination with the army, a predilection manifested earlier, in 1883–84, in his illustrations for the journal *La Vie militaire*.

The *Chat Noir* journal is essentially an apolitical chronicle of Montmartre that makes fun of all established things, including itself. This is also true of the *Courrier français*, which under the direction of Jules Roques began publication in November 1884, using a number of the *Chat Noir* artists as its illustrators. In 1885 Willette created the lithographic poster for the *Courrier français*. In it he subtly reveals his continued close relationship with Goudeau by depicting Goudeau's novel *La Vache Enragée* lying on a small table. The relationship between the poet and the artist continued throughout the period of the Dreyfus Affair. In addition to that of Willette, the work of Somm, Steinlen, and eventually Lautrec, Hermann-Paul, Anquetin and Vallotton appeared in the *Courrier français*. Beginning in 1887, Jean-Louis Forain became, along with Willette, one of the most dominant illustrators of the journal with works that lashed out satirically at bourgeois values and hypocrisies and recorded the Bohemian life of Montmartre.

The publication of Drumont's *La France Juive* in April 1886 did not unleash widespread anti-Semitic journal illustration. Indeed, throughout the 1880s such imagery was at a minimum. However, the artists who were the first to create images of this kind were Willette, Caran d'Ache, and Forain—these were three of the main figures involved in the anti-Semitic illustrated press during the next decade.

Exactly one year before the publication of *La France Juive*, Willette presented his fully developed anti-Semitic views in a double-page illustration for the 5 April 1885 issue of *Le Courrier français*. With *Les Juifs et la Semaine Sainté* (The Jews and Holy Week) (fig. 2) he not only expresses Drumont's basic arguments but also establishes essential iconographic elements for anti-Jewish—and

Figure 2, Cat. 69
Adolphe Willette
*The Jews and Holy Week (Les Juifs et
La Semaine Sainté)*
Le Courrier français, 5 April 1885
Photomechanical print
The Jane Voorhees Zimmerli Art
Museum

LE COURRIER FRANÇAIS

ÉDOUARD DRUMONT, l'auteur de la *France Juive*.

Figure 3, Cat. 70
Adolphe Willette
Edouard Drumont, author of La France
Juive
(Edouard Drumont l'auteur de la
France Juive*)*
Le Courrier français, 16 May 1886
Photomechanical print
The Jane Voorhees Zimmerli Art
Museum

eventually anti-Dreyfus—imagery of the following fifteen years. The text declares that Jews were the crucifiers of Christ and that Jews control the money of France but have no national allegiance. Willette seeks another "ninety-three" (meaning 1793) when, in the course of the struggle for civil liberty for France, the aristocracy was guillotined. Willette asks "quand le 93 de la race Juive?" and the prayer that appears at the lower left ends with a plea to find another means to destroy the Jews, since the pharaohs, the Philistines, and pestilence had failed in the past to do so. To use a pair of familiar twentieth-century terms, Willette was already seeking a "final solution" to the "Jewish question."

One vignette in F. Lunel's cartoon, *Une Poignée de predictions pour 1886,* which appeared in the 3 January 1886 issue of *Le Courrier français* has a caption that reads "Willette fera une Saint-Barthélemi de tous les Juifs de Montmartre." ("Willette will massacre all the Jews of Montmartre.") Willette's reputation as an avowed anti-Semite had such wide currency within the Montmartre artistic community that it warranted a satirical reference in the *Courrier français,* a reference that was expected to be understood by the journal's readers, who were by and large Willette's colleagues and neighbors on the butte. Willette's 1885 illustration and Lunel's cartoon reveal that the former's hatred for Jews was already full-blown well before the appearance of Drumont's book and more than three and a half years before his own vicious campaign as an anti-Semitic candidate in the 1889 legislative election.

On 16 May 1886, one month after the publication of *La France Juive* and three weeks after the duel between Arthur Meyer and Drumont, the *Courrier français* published a letter by Drumont to the journal's editor, Jules Roques, which served as a brief autobiography of its author. For this issue, Willette produced a full-page *Portrait of Drumont,* which pictures its subject as an embattled crusader defeating Moses, while defending himself against a flurry of sharp quill pens symbolizing press attacks against him (fig. 3). One pen, labeled *Le Gaulois,* wounds Drumont in the leg. It refers to the wound inflicted on him by Meyer, the Jewish editor of *Le Gaulois* in their duel. An ironic twist to the story was the fact that Meyer, though Jewish, was himself anti-Semitic. The vicious anti-Semitism of Willette and Drumont never became the mainstay of *Le Courrier français;* there was,

Figure 4, Cat. 71
Adolphe Willette
Winter will be hard for the goyim (the Christians) this year (Address of S. M. Rothschild, king of France.)
(L'hiver sera dur pours les goymes [les chrétiens] cette année) (Discours de S. M. Rothschild, roi de France)
Le Pierrot, 30 August 1889
Photomechanical print
Collection of Mr. and Mrs. Herbert D. Schimmel, New York

Figure 5
Jean-Louis Forain
Business (Les Affaires)
Monopoly—Misery! (Accaparement—Misère!)
Le Fifre, 30 March 1889
Photomechanical print
Collection of Mr. and Mrs. Herbert D. Schimmel, New York

however, no apparent effort made to condemn it.

The journal *Le Pierrot* was founded by Goudeau and Willette in July 1888. Its office was located in Willette's apartment at 79 rue Rochechouart, on the border of Montmartre within the cabaret district. Throughout its two-year existence, *Le Pierrot* was essentially a satirical journal without any particular political or anti-Semitic platform. Nevertheless, as the 1889 legislative election approached, Willette promoted his own candidacy and his anti-Jewish sentiments with his 30 August 1889 cover illustration (fig. 4), which depicts Baron Rothschild looking out over Paris, ready to set loose a horde of wolves and rats on the city. Its cap-

tion reads: "L'hiver sera dur pour les goymes (les chrétiens) cette année. (Discours de S. M. Rothschild, roi de France)." (The winter will be a hard one for the goyim [the Christians] this year. [Address by S. M. Rothschild, king of France].) Paranoid anti-Semitic sentiments of this kind were expressed four months earlier by Forain in his cover illustration for the March 30 issue of his short-lived satirical journal *Le Fifre* (fig. 5).[9] In it, he depicted a Jewish merchant hoarding food while the population of France starves.

In early September of that year Drumont founded the Ligue Nationale antisémitique de France, with headquarters at 48 rue Lepic in the

68

VISION ANTIQUE, par CARAN D'ACHE

Figure 6
Caran d'Ache
Ancient Vision (Vision Antique)
Figaro Illustré, 1886
Photomechanical print
Bibliothèque Nationale, Paris

heart of Montmartre; one of its first acts was to promote Willette as the anti-Semitic candidate for the ninth arrondissement (district). His lithographic poster announcing his candidacy makes its appeal by playing up the greatest fears of the workers: unemployment and poverty (See fig. 6 in Marrus's essay). The scapegoat it blames is the population of the "50,000 Jews" who, according to Willette, have enslaved thirty million Frenchmen: "It is not a question of religion, the Jew is a different race and enemy of ours." Willette's image patriotically appeals to the French to "close ranks and defeat their common enemy." In Willette's picture, the Talmud lies broken on the ground; in falling it has split open a bag of coins. Willette himself stands second from right, gun in hand, flanked by a general and a worker; to the left is a Gaul, symbol of native Frenchmen, holding the head of the slaughtered Golden Calf, the biblical false god of materialism, wearing the crown of a baron. The allegorical figure of France stands on the ramparts triumphantly blowing her trumpet. In the distance, Notre Dame Cathedral symbolizes Christian France; while off to the left the hated Jew is shown fleeing the country.

Willette's poster manages to combine the powerful themes of nationalism, Catholicism, purity of race, and the sanctity of the military, serving as a major pictorial summation at the end of the 1880s of French anti-Semitic propaganda. It was, however, a poster before its time, requiring something more tangible in the air—such as the Panama scandal or the Dreyfus Affair—to allow it to produce results. Willette lost the election in 1889; the anti-Semitic campaign, however, was merely postponed.

Indeed, while conceptually fully developed, anti-Semitic illustration during the 1880s is sporadic; it is basically confined to a few images by Willette and Forain and plays a relatively insignificant role in the dissemination of anti-Jewish propaganda. This is especially apparent with Willette's journal *Le Pierrot* and Forain's *Le Fifre,* in which anti-Semitic images are the exception to the otherwise standard satire on the bourgeois mores of contemporary French society.

The stereotypical notion that the control of wealth was in the hands of the Jewish bankers produced the dominant form of anti-Semitic iconography after the publication of *La France Juive*

Figure 7
Henri Rivière
The Stock Exchange (La Bourse)
from the album *The Temptation of
Saint Anthony (La Tentation de St.
Antoine)*, 1888
Stencil colored photo relief
The Jane Voorhees Zimmerli Art
Museum
Gift of Sara and Armond Fields

and at the time of the Panama scandal. Caran d'Ache's 1886 illustration, *Vision antique* for the *Figaro Illustré* (fig. 6) depicts within a humorously envisioned pastoral Greek landscape a Jewish family—designated as such by large noses—in which the corpulent father reads a paper titled *La Bourse.*

Since the Bank of France was directed by Baron Alphonse de Rothschild, it and the Bourse (stock exchange) became synonymous with Rothschild himself, and by association with avaricious businessmen, who were typically depicted as overfed, large-nosed, top-hatted Jews, often wearing fur-collared coats, portfolio in hand. Images of Rothschild wearing his baron's coronet and stereotypic images of the Jewish businessmen became symbols of the moneyed establishment and, by extension, all that was wrong with France.

In Henri Rivière's 1888 album *La Tentation de Saint-Antoine*—created in the style and as a permanent record of his popular Chat Noir cabaret shadow-theater production—avarice is symbolized by three scenes: "Le Jeu" (gambling), "Le Veau d'Or" (the Golden Calf), and finally by "La Bourse" (fig. 7).[10] In the last of these the devil, in the guise of a Jewish banker, tempts St. Anthony in front of the Paris stock exchange. Directly challenging the piety of the saint, a statue of the Golden Calf with a pink halo stands boldly in front of the Bourse, while an immense image of a thousand-franc note from the Banque de France serves as a backdrop to the entire scene.

Roedel's illustration for the 9 October 1892 issue of *Le Courrier français* (fig. 8) satirically depicts Christian reverence contrasted with supposed Jewish materialism. His montage of "Notre-Dame de Paris" and "Notre-Dame de la Galette" depicts a French artist—identified by his long hair, beard, large hat, and what appears to be sketch-box in hand, paying his respects to Notre Dame Cathedral; in contrast, a stereotyped Jewish banker pays his respects to the Bank of France. The caption, "Notre Dame de la Galette," makes a double pun: A *galette* is a small, flat, round cake, which for purposes of snide humor and double entendre refers here to a coin. The name also refers to the famous Montmartre dance hall, The Moulin de la Galette, popular with artists on the butte and for which Roedel later designed a poster.

The corpulent Jewish banker/businessman became a special genre of the "types Parisiens." The image was an integral part of the visual vocabulary used by the artists of the day and could be used to

LE COURRIER FRANÇAIS   11

Notre-Dame de Paris.   Notre-Dame de la Galette.

Figure 8
A. Roedel
Notre-Dame de Paris. Notre-Dame de la Galette
Le Courrier français, 9 October 1892
Photomechanical print
The Jane Voorhees Zimmerli Art Museum

make social or political references that artists could assume to be readily understandable to its viewers. This is apparent in work by both Toulouse-Lautrec and Steinlen, in particular.

Lautrec's 1892 poster for Victor Joze's novel *La Reine de Joie* (fig. 9) depicts such a figure in the arms of a demimondaine. The book—its full title was *La Ménagerie social Reine de Joie moeurs du demi-monde*—tells the story of a young woman named Alice Lavary, who becomes the mistress of a Baron de Rozenfeld. It is clear that the old baron comes from a long line of wealthy Jewish businessmen. He promises Alice riches and all the comforts of life; in return his only demand is that she not take other lovers from his social milieu, such as Rothschild or the King of Belgium. He has no objection to her having affairs with artists, writers, and the like. Her role is to create the kind of social life and environment that he has had no time to develop on his own—she is to arrange soirées at home, visits to the Opera, and the like. Indirectly—and this was fine as far as the baron was concerned—everyone would be aware that it was he who supported Alice.

The incipient anti-Semitism reflected in the novel can also be discerned in Lautrec's poster for it, in which the baron's negative—that is, Jewish—physical characteristics are sharply contrasted with those of the handsome non-Semitic-looking young man at the right. Another image by Lautrec, the lithograph *Pourquoi pas? . . . Une fois n'est pas coutume* (Why Not? . . . Once is not a Habit) (fig. 10) which was made to be reproduced in the 12 November 1893 issue of the journal *L'Escarmouche,* once again employs the formulaic attributes used to depict Jewish businessmen: here a man shown negotiating with prostitutes is given stereotyped features. Steinlen, too, used this formula in his depictions of wealthy but lonely men seeking a liaison with prostitutes.[11] The Baron de Rozenfeld type emerged in images of the 1890s as a generalized sinister character who found solace only in the relationship with prostitutes and, as we will see, in the exploitation of the French worker.

Joze's *Reine de Joie* was planned to be one of a series of novelettes dealing with contemporary social mores. A later novel, however, *La Tribu d'Isidore* (1897), was described by Joze as the "first volume in a series of novels which will form the history of a modern Israelite family in the process of conquering old Europe, thanks to these four qualities: intelligence, energy, guile and pa-

Figure 9
Henri de Toulouse-Lautrec
Queen of Pleasure (Reine de joie), 1892
Color lithographic poster
Collection of Mr. and Mrs. Herbert
D. Schimmel, New York

Figure 10, Cat. 62
Henri de Toulouse-Lautrec
*Why Not? . . . . Once is not a Habit
(Pourquoi pas? . . . Une fois n'est pas
coutume),* 1893
Lithograph

tience."[12] In the preface to the novel Joze denies
anti-Semitic intent: "One would be greatly wrong
to believe that my end is to make a series of pamphlets against the Jews. First, I am an enemy of
novels with a thesis, and then I am not an anti-
Semite in the precise sense of the word. I am not
of any Aryan league, of any anti-Jewish committee. I am only a spectator, a 'passant' who travels
the highway of life and interests himself in the
battles of the human insect.

"I observe the diverse manifestations of the social movement, I am philosophically incapable of
hating. I do not curse, I record."[13]

Figure 11 (right)
Théophile-Alexandre Steinlen
The Street (La Rue), 1896
Color lithograph
The Metropolitan Museum of Art
Harris Brisbane Dick Fund, 1936

Figure 12 (below)
Hermann-Paul
*The Beautiful Jewess Goes Shopping
(La Belle Juive va aux provisions)*
Le Rire, 23 May 1896 (checklist date
May 23)
Photomechanical color proof
The Jane Voorhees Zimmerli Art
Museum

Steinlen's 1896 life-sized color lithographic poster, *La Rue* (fig. 11) "records" an assembly of "types Parisiens," which was a system of categorizing people based upon their social rank and role in society. Among the stereotypical figures of nurses, laundresses, and laborers there is the "Jewish banker," dressed in black—to his right a lower-class rogue or pimp, and to his left, a beautiful member of the wealthy bourgeoisie. She is elegantly dressed with a hat in full plumage and is similar to Lautrec's portrait of Misia Natanson in the *Revue blanche* poster (see fig. 1 in Kleeblatt's essay) and to Hermann-Paul's illustration, "The Beautiful Jewess Goes Shopping," (fig. 12) in the 25 May 1896 issue of the journal *Le Rire*. Paul had previously created a series of illustrations in 1894 for *Le Courrier français* titled "Dames de France" in which a young Jewish "Virgin" is included (fig. 13). That same year Hermann-Paul illustrated Laurent Taihade's book *Pays du Mufle* (Country of Snouts) in which he uses the Jewish stereotype for his caricature called "En Israel."[14] Other works from the period show Paul's consistent use of this stereotype (fig. 14). "The Jew" and "The Jewess" were by the mid–1890s distinct, recognized figures in the "ménagerie Parisienne."

It is with a similar profession of objectivity in the analysis of a "race" as that described by Joze

Figure 13 (left)

Hermann-Paul

Young Virgin (Jeune vierge)

Ladies of France VII (Dames de France)

23 December 1894, *Le Courrier français*

Ink, pencil, crayon, and gouache

The Jane Voorhees Zimmerli Art Museum

Gift of Marion and Allan Maitlin

Figure 14 (above)

Hermann-Paul

The grotesques (Les Grotesques), ca. 1894–1896

Lithographic illustration for a song sheet

The Jane Voorhees Zimmerli Art Museum

Norma Bartman Purchase Fund

in *La Tribu d'Isidore* that almost a year later Clemenceau published his naive and condescending stories of Jews in Poland and France in a collection titled *Au Pied du Sinaï* (figs. 15, 16, 17). Both books were written just before Zola's "J'Accuse," that is, just before the Dreyfus case became the Dreyfus Affair. Lautrec's connection with the two publications must be more than coincidental; before Zola's accusations against the government in Clemenceau's *L'Aurore* Lautrec was, in fact, becoming the dominant illustrator of soft-core anti-Semitic literature—writing that, because of its moderation, would not appeal to staunchly committed anti-Semites such as those in league with Drumont.

Lautrec's cover for *La Tribu d'Isidore* (fig. 18) and his cover and ten lithographs for Clemenceau's *Au Pied du Sinaï* by no means place him in the category of Willette and Forain yet they do suggest that he, like Clemenceau, was sympathetic to the established view of the Jews—which, as Joze declared, was "not anti-Semitic in the precise sense of the word." Lautrec's first, but unpublished, cover design for *Au Pied du Sinaï* (fig. 19) depicts a kind of "wandering Jew" in the desert who is reaching out for what could be taken for a crowned German eagle in the distance.[15] The political implications of this lithograph may have been too strong for Clemenceau; the version he accepted instead depicts the Golden Calf dislodged from its altar, while Moses, Tablets of the Law in hand, looks on from the summit of Sinai.

Lautrec's position vis-à-vis the anti-Semitic currents of the 1890s is unique. He was closely involved personally and professionally with the Jewish Natansons, the directors of *La Revue blanche*. He not only produced lithographs for the journal but, as already mentioned also designed a poster for it, which portrays Misia Natanson, the wife of Thadée, chief editor of the journal. In February 1893 Thadée wrote a glowing review of Lautrec's exhibition at the Boussod and Valladon Gallery; he even went so far as to make approving mention of his poster for *Reine de Joie*.[16] Much has been written about the artists of the Nabi group who, along with Lautrec, worked for the journal—the record shows that they also socialized and vacationed with the Natanson family;[17] it is, therefore difficult to fully explain how it is that Lautrec could work on projects such as *La Tribu d'Isidore* that were indirectly critical of his friends the Na-

Figure 15, Cat. 61
Henri de Toulouse-Lautrec
At the foot of Sinai (Au pied du Sinaï),
cover, 1898 Lithograph

Figure 16
Henri de Toulouse-Lautrec
The Detention of Schlomé Fuss (L'Arrestation de Schlomé Fuss)
From *Au pied du Sinaï,* 1898 Lithograph
Georges Clemenceau, *Au pied du Sinaï*

Figure 17
Henri de Toulouse-Lautrec
Georges Clemenceau and the Oculist Mayer
From *Au pied du Sinaï*, 1898
Lithograph
Georges Clemenceau, *Au pied du Sinaï*

Figure 18
Henri de Toulouse-Lautrec
The Tribe of Isidore (La Tribu d'Isidore), cover, 1897
Lithograph
Collection of Mr. and Mrs. Herbert
D. Schimmel, New York

Figure 19, Cat. 60
Henri de Toulouse-Lautrec
At the foot of Sinai (Au pied du Sinaï),
unpublished cover, 1898
Lithograph
Collection of Mr. and Mrs. Herbert
D. Schimmel, New York

76

Figure 20
Henri de Toulouse-Lautrec
La Vache enragée, 1896
Color lithographic poster
Collection of Mr. and Mrs. Herbert
D. Schimmel, New York

tansons, nor how he could support the efforts of two avowed anti-Semites, Willette and Roedel, producing a poster in 1896 for their short-lived journal, *La Vache enragée* (fig. 20).[18] No other artists of the *Revue blanche* group divided their allegiance so radically. Indeed, the majority of the journal's artists signed the petition for Picquart and were strong Dreyfusards.

The Panama scandal, which erupted at the end of 1892, elicited a strong response from the socialist and anarchist segments of society and offered new ammunition for anti-Semitic propaganda. Drumont's *La Libre Parole* broke the news of the corruption in September 1892. *L'Echo de Paris,* which at this time included as its illustrators Forain, Toulouse-Lautrec, Caran d'Ache, Willette, Hermann-Paul, Renouard, and Ibels, made note of the revelations in *La Libre Parole* with an illustration by Ibels in the 20 November 1892 issue, which expresses the general public reaction. The caption reads:

What! all the same, Rothschild subscribed for twenty thousand francs!
—Twenty thousand francs! But, my good friend, what is that to them.[19]

The blame for the bribes to members of the Chamber of Deputies and to the French press was placed on the three Jews involved in the last stages of the canal's financing: Baron Jacques de Reinach, Cornelius Herz, and a man called Arton. Herz was French-born but both Reinach and Arton were German Jews who had become naturalized Frenchmen.[20] These facts played into the hands of those who subscribed to *La Libre Parole*'s slogan "La France aux Français!" and accepted the anti-Semitic premise that Jews had no allegiance to France.

A compilation of Forain's journal illustration related to the Panama scandal were published as an album in 1893 under the title *Les Temps difficiles (Panama).*[21] One of the first images depicts a German-Jewish husband speaking with an accent to his wife: "Since there is nothing more to gain here, let's return to Germany!" (fig. 21).[22] This image parallels in substance the more horrendous scene envisioned by Willette for the first issue of the illustrated *La Libre Parole,* which appeared on 17 July 1893 (fig. 22). Ironically it is Forain who uses the popular Dreyfusard metaphor of "Truth at the Well" (fig. 23) in reference to the Panama scandal.

— Buisqu'il n'y a blus rien à cagner ici, nous allons enfin poufoir retef'nir Allemands !

LA LIBRE PAROLE
ILLUSTRÉE

— Ohé ! la Vérité, ohé ! n'sors pas de c'froid-là..... tu t'enrhumerais !

Figure 21
Jean-Louis Forain
Since there is nothing more to gain here, let's return to Germany! (Buisquil n'y a blus rien à cagner ici, nous allons enfin poufoir retef'nir Allemands!)
From the album *Les Temps Difficiles (Panama),* 1893
Photomechanical print
The Jane Voorhees Zimmerli Art Museum

Figure 23
Jean-Louis Forain
Hey Truth, hey, don't come out—it's too chilly here. You'll catch a cold.
(Ohe! La Vérité, ohe! n'sors pas de c'froid-là . . . . tu t'enrhumerais!)
From the album *Les Temps Difficiles,* 1893
Photomechanical print
The Jane Voorhees Zimmerli Art Museum

Figure 22
Adolphe Willette
The Drought (La Sécheresse)
It's drying up, this old land of France. He [the Jew] thirsts again for blood and tears. It will be necessary to irrigate it incessantly.
(Elle devient sèche, cette vieille terre de France. Il encore a soif de sang et de larmes . . . . . il faudra l'arroser incessamment)
La Libre Parole, no. 1, 17 July 1893
Photomechanical print

Figure 24, Cat. 64
Félix Vallotton
The Anarchist (L'Anarchiste), 1892
Woodcut

Figure 25, Cat. 66
Félix Vallotton
The Demonstration (La Manifestation),
1893
Woodcut

Steinlen, Luce, Vallotton, and Ibels, as well as Willette and Forain, were artists who viewed the government of the Third Republic as corrupt and exploitative of the working class; these artists sought in their own way to either clean up corruption in order to save the Republic or to replace the system completely. Each artist had deep social concerns that surfaced en masse around 1892–93 at the time of the Panama scandal and the period of greatest anarchist agitation.

Vallotton's anarchist sympathies are specifically evident in three woodcuts of 1892 and 1893; *L'Anarchist* (fig. 24), *La Manifestation* (fig. 25), and *La Charge* (fig. 26) in all three of which street riots instigated by anarchists are the subject. An obvious antiestablishment position is evident in *L'Anarchist* and *La Charge;* in both, police brutality becomes the overwhelming theme. Vallotton's woodcuts *A Vingt Ans* (fig. 27) and *L'Execution* (fig. 28) both from 1894, take up the subject of the exploitation of the young soldier of lowest rank, the "petit piou-piou," by the powerful and corrupt bourgeois establishment. This subject of the young soldier drawn from the uneducated prole-

Figure 26, Cat. 65
Félix Vallotton
The Charge (La Charge), 1893
Woodcut

Figure 27, Cat. 68
Félix Vallotton
At Twenty Years (A Vingt Ans), 1894
Woodcut

Figure 28
Félix Vallotton
The Execution (L'Execution), 1894
Woodcut
Musée Cantonal, Lausanne

Figure 29
Théophile-Alexandre Steinlen
Civil rehabilitation and military execu-
tion (Réhabilitation Civile et Exécution
Militaire)
La Feuille, no. 4, 17 December 1897
The Jane Voorhees Zimmerli Art Museum
Gift of Norma Bartman Purchase Fund

Figure 30
Félix Vallotton
Edouard Drumont, 1894 Woodcut

tariat class for a mandatory three years of service in the army is also the theme of work by Ibels, Steinlen (fig. 29), and Luce.

In 1894–95 Vallotton created a series of eleven woodcut portraits of selected contemporary men and women that included the old communard, Louise Michel, as well as Alphonse de Rothschild, Georges Clemenceau, Henri Rochefort, and even Drumont (fig. 30). Drumont's strong support of the anarchist activities must have appealed to Vallotton directly. In 1891 André Ibels, brother of Henri, founded the journal *La Revue anarchiste;* that same year Henri Ibels and Willette contributed illustrations to the special issue on anarchism of the journal *La Plume.* Vallotton, Willette, Ibels, and Luce also contributed in the early nineties to the anarchist journal *Le Père peinard.* Luce's anarchist sympathies were so strong and well known that in April 1894 he was arrested and imprisoned

in Mazas until, along with Félix Fénéon, critic for *La Revue blanche,* he was acquitted.[23] His color lithograph for the literary supplement to *Les Temps nouveaux* (fig. 31) confirms his commitment to the leftist cause.

Steinlen's empathy for the impoverished and the exploited working class was heightened in 1878 when he read Zola's sensational novel of Montmartre poverty, *L'Assommoir.*[24] Beginning in 1885, he contributed illustrations to Aristide Bruant's journal *Le Mirliton* and illustrated his book *Dans la Rue* of 1888; these illustrations reveal the artist's deep and fully developed social concerns and his sympathy for the anarchist/socialist cause. On 15 December 1893, one week after the bombing of the Chamber of Deputies by the anarchist Auguste Vaillant, the Marxist periodical *Le Chambard socialiste* began publication, with Steinlen, using the pseudonym of Petit Pierre, as its chief

Figure 31
Maximilien Luce
*Our enemy is our master (Notre ennemi
c'est notre maître)*
Published by *Les Temps Nouveaux,*
1904 Color lithograph

The Jane Voorhees Zimmerli Art
Museum
Gift of Marion and Allan Maitlin

Figure 32, Cat. 57
Théophile Alexandre Steinlen
One Hundred Million! (Cent millions),
Reproduced in *La chambard socialiste,*
24 February 1894
Lithograph

illustrator for the first thirty-two of its seventy-eight issues. Gerault-Richard, the editor of the journal stated its purpose:[25] Indeed the enemies of the socialists and the anarchists included not only the ruling government and the Church but (especially) the wealthy capitalists, who were epitomized in a number of Steinlen's cover illustrations for *Le Chambard* by the stereotypical Jewish banker/businessman.

In *Cent Millions!* (fig. 32) the capitalist culprit depicted is probably Baron Jacques de Reinach, who, along with others, had robbed the public of millions of francs through the fraudulent Panama Canal investment scheme.[26] Although Reinach had two years earlier committed suicide rather than face the scandal, he is used by Steinlen to symbolize those who had become rich by the scheme but were acquitted later by the courts. It is compelling to compare Steinlen's satirical image of two

soldiers respectfully saluting the Jewish baron with images made of Dreyfus at his degradation (pl. 11) less than a year later and with photographs of the Rennes trial (pl. 162). in which Dreyfus walks between two lines of soldiers with their backs disrespectfully turned to him.

It was this kind of transformation of the Jew—from subjugator to subjugated—that is the topic of Steinlen's two covers for *Le Chambard* titled *Today* (fig. 33) and *Tomorrow* (fig. 34), and it was this transformation that became a momentary reality in Drumont's mind almost overnight (pl. 6).

Steinlen's socialist sympathies were expressed in his illustrations for *Le Chambard* as anticapitalist/anti-Semitic. By 1898 his overriding concern for human justice had converted him to a staunch Dreyfusard; similarly, Gerault-Richard, who in December, 1894 had commissioned a cover for his journal that depicted Dreyfus as a traitor, be-

Figure 33, Cat. 58
Théophile-Alexandre Steinlen
Today (Aujourd'hui)
Le chambard socialiste, March 1894
Stencil colored lithograph

Figure 34, Cat. 59
Théophile-Alexandre Steinlen
Tomorrow (Demain)
Le chambard socialiste, April 1894
Stencil colored lithograph

came the editor of *La Petite République,* a pro-Dreyfus socialist journal. In contrast, *La Libre Parole,* which intermittently used the talents of Willette for its hate-filled cover illustrations, throughout the decade kept up a relentless and virulent attack on Jews and on Dreyfus. Nevertheless, Willette shared to a considerable extent the socialist sympathies of Steinlen and in fact in 1894 participated in the May Day convocation organized by the socialist members of the Chamber of Deputies by illustrating the cover for the group's official organ *Les Trois-Huit* (fig. 35).[27]

During the first half of the 1890s Willette, Forain, Steinlen, Toulouse-Lautrec, Anquetin, Ibels, Vallotton, Hermann-Paul and Henry Somm were, to varying degrees, colleagues. They lived in close proximity to one another in and around Mont-martre and often worked together as illustrators of the same journals and of programs for the Théâtre Libre and Théâtre de L'Oeuvre, exhibited together at independent salons, and sold work through the same dealers. They were prolific printmakers who all, with the exception of Forain and Steinlen, contributed to the important print publication of the period called *L'Estampe origi-nale.*[28] There was inevitably a great deal of social and professional interaction among them, some-times limited to the *Revue blanche* group of artists, at other times broadened to include Steinlen, Willette, Forain, and eventually Caran d'Ache, as when all these artists were involved in the satirical journal *Le Rire,* which began publication in November 1894. This group of generally socially conscious Montmartre artists responded strongly

Figure 35
Fortune's Favor (L'Aumône à La Fortune)
Adolphe Willette
Study cover of *Les Trois Huits,* 1894
Crayon

The Jane Voorhees Zimmerli Art Museum
Gift of Carleton Holstrom

Figure 36
Heidbrinck
The Day of the Illustrators at Le Rire (Le Jour des dessinateurs au Rire)
Le Rire, 8 January 1898
Photomechanical print
The Jane Voorhees Zimmerli Art Museum

to the Dreyfus case as it dramatically came to a head with the publication of "J'Accuse." As we have seen it was also these artists who in large part established the iconography of pro- and anti-Dreyfus imagery.

The 8 January 1898 issue of *Le Rire* carries a full-page illustration titled *Le Jour de dessinateurs au Rire* (The Day of the Illustrators at *Le Rire*) (fig. 36), in which appear portraits of a majority of the artists for the journal, including Toulouse-Lautrec, Vallotton, Steinlen, Somm, and Couturier. The visages of the two prominent illustrators for *Le Figaro illustré,* Forain and Caran d'Ache, are paired in the foreground, as if to forecast their future partnership in the anti-Dreyfus journal *Psst. . .!*

Le Rire was a satirical weekly that took full advantage of the state of the art of the economical photorelief printing process. Vivid color illustrations by the foremost artists and illustrators of the day provided sharp, witty social and political commentary. Among these commentators, the comtesse de Martel de Janville and Charles Léandre were two of the most caustic. Madame Sibylle Gabrielle Aimée Marie-Antoinette de Riquetti de Mirabeau, comtesse de Martel de Janville used, fortunately, pen names: "Gyp" for her written satire and "Petit Bob" or "Bob" for the drawings she created to accompany much of her writing. Born in 1853, the countess began her literary career in the early 1880s, producing such humorous works as *Autour du Mariage ce que femme veut* (1883) and *Joies conjugales pour ne pas l'etre. . . ?* (1887).[29] Gyp collaborated with Drumont on *La*

84

Figure 37 (above left), Cat. 35
Gyp
*One thing's for sure, France isn't enjoy-
ing herself (—Sûr qu'elle n'est pas à la
noce, la France)*
Le Rire, no. 60, 28 December 1895
Photomechanical print

Figure 38 (left)
Gyp
On a Stroll (En Balade)
Illustration
Medium
The Jane Voorhees Zimmerli Art
Museum

Figure 39 (above right), Cat. 38
Gyp
*History of the Third Republic (Histoire
de la Troisième Republiqúe)*
Le Rire, no. 106, 14 November 1896
Photomechanical print

Libre Parole; her illustrations for *Le Rire* (fig. 37) are pointedly anti-Semitic and reflect the standard views of Drumont's journal as well as of her own satirical novels of the period such as *En Balade* (fig. 38) (1897) and *Israel* (1898).[30]

Although anti-Semitism was not the sole emphasis of *Le Rire,* in 1895 a short-lived series titled "Contes Juifs" (Jewish tales) that catered to the half-hearted anti-Jewish sentiments of the general public began to appear. Gyp's *Histoire de la Troisième République* (fig. 39), a special issue of *Le Rire* for 14 November 1896, and Léandre's "Gotha" series of satirical caricatures (fig. 40) of noted contemporary figures eventually tilted the journal to the side of the anti-Dreyfusards.

Nevertheless, *Le Rire*'s position regarding the Dreyfus Affair is moderate to the extent that Hermann-Paul, Vallotton, and Steinlen relied on other more partisan journals such as *Le Cri de Paris* and *La Feuille* to vent their views on the case, while Ibels, Forain, and Caran d'Ache went so far as to initiate their own publications *Le Sifflet* and *Psst. . . !,* focused specifically on the Affair—with diametrically opposed views of it. Hermann-Paul, Forain, and Caran d'Ache all created Dreyfus-related illustrations for *Le Figaro illustré* but, as with Caran d'Ache's cartoon, their work generally stayed above the real battle. In Forain's 1898 series "Doux Pays" for *Le Figaro illustré,* however, his anti-Semitic views were plainly expressed; yet his cover for the 24 December 1898 issue of *Le Rire* (pl. 57) reveals how he, too, could create generalized references to the case for more moderate journals.

On 6 October 1897 the long-time anarchist Zo d'Axa began publishing his journal *La Feuille* (see fig. 3 in Kleeblatt's essay) for which over a one-and-a-half-year period Steinlen illustrated seventeen out of the total of twenty-five issues. The talents of Willette, Léandre, Couturier, Anquetin, and Luce were used for one issue each and that of Hermann-Paul for three issues. Zo d'Axa (1864–1930) was born Alphonse Gallaud. After serving a short time in the army he deserted and left France. With the amnesty of 1889, he returned to Paris, where in 1891 he began publishing the journal *L'En Dehors,* for which during the anarchist activities of 1893–94 he was arrested, along with the editors of *La Révolte* and *Le Père peinard.*[31]

One month after the first issue of *La Feuille,* Emile Goudeau and François Trombert, owner of the Quat'z'Arts cabaret, began publishing the

Figure 40, Cat. 173
Charles Léandre
Mr. Arthur Meyer, Director of Gaulois
(M. Arthur Meyer, Directeur du Gaulois)
Le Rire, no. 240, 10 June 1899
Photomechanical print
Caption: Arthur, when he defends the throne. Meyer, when he defends the altar.
(Arthur, quand il défend le trône. Meyer, quand il défend l'autel)

journal *Les Quat'z'Arts,* which lasted for two years and included the illustrations of Charles Léandre and Abel Truchet. The office of *La Feuille* was located on the rue Navarin two blocks from the Quat'z'Arts cabaret at 62 boulevard de Clichy, where the office of its journal was also located. Following its establishment in 1893, the Quat'z 'Arts was among artists and writers the most popular of the "cabarets artistiques" in Montmartre and it soon usurped the role that had been played by the Chat Noir during the preceding decade.

In 1898 Grand-Carteret stated that "like all the journals of the butte and even the Montmartre hills, *Les Quat'z'Arts*, founded on the first [*sic*] of November, 1887, . . . declared itself right then and there against the 'Dreyfus Affair' and thus against all the people who, of whatever fashion, began to intervene for the revision of the trial."[32] Nine years later Jacques Ferny, a popular composer of cabaret songs, concurred in observing that the "Montmartre cabarets were anti-Dreyfus."[33] Aristide Bruant published an anti-Zola song in his *Lanterne de Bruant no. 35*. Yet the observations of Grand-Carteret and Ferny are not totally correct. First of all the statements were made by men who were, themselves, anti-Dreyfusards; secondly, broad generalizations about people's positions on the Dreyfus case are not reliable.

For instance, one may state that Gyp's anti-Semitic and anti-Dreyfusard leanings resulted from her aristocratic, conservative, Catholic background. Yet one could just as easily place in the same camp Senator René Bérenger a fervent Catholic and the self-appointed censor of pornography whose nickname was Père la Pudeur (Father Modesty).[34] It was Bérenger who brought to trial the artists who organized and the models who participated in the 1893 Quat'z'Arts ball, which took place at the Moulin Rouge. The Ecole des Beaux-Arts had instituted this annual costume ball just the year before. Bérenger's spies, which included La Goulue, the notorious dancer of the Moulin Rouge who was a favorite subject of Lautrec, informed him that some models at the ball had posed as subjects in particular paintings, carrying accuracy to the point of nudity when required. Although the ball was closed to the public, Bérenger won his case and those pronounced guilty were fined one hundred francs with a suspended sentence. On 3 June, the day after the verdict, art students of the Latin Quarter rioted against this act of censorship. During the melée a student was accidentally killed by the police; this led to three more days of rioting that was quelled only when 30,000 extra police officers were brought into Paris.[35] Bérenger's conservativism and the accidental death that had been the indirect result of his censorship action were never forgotten by the artistic community. The notoriety gained by the Quat'z'Arts ball inspired Trombert to name his new cabaret after it. Yet even though his background and his activities as a censor would seem to belong to a rightist perspective, Bérenger was

a man of moral conviction and as such was an active Dreyfusard in the Senate, unexpected as that stand may seem. In one of those ironies of history, many of those who protested Bérenger's small-mindedness in 1893 later opposed him in the conflict over the Dreyfus case, with Bérenger supporting revision and the anti-Dreyfusards opposing it.

Montmartre, like the rest of Parisian society, was split by the Dreyfus issue. While the sentiment of the majority of the clientele and performers of cabarets may have been against Dreyfus, a number of the artists and writers who were their patrons were Dreyfusards, as is demonstrated by the signatures on the Picquart petition. As with no other time, it was a period in which artists collaborated at one moment and opposed each other politically at another. The psychological shifts must have been, at the least, confusing if not schizophrenic.

As an anarchist Zo d'Axa used *La Feuille* to criticize what he considered to be the irrational, unjust, and hypocritical aspects of society, which were seen as the result of the actions of the establishment and the powerful. It was rational, therefore, as the weaknesses and falsehood of the military evidence against Dreyfus became obvious in the fall of 1897 for *La Feuille* to defend Dreyfus against the military establishment. Yet the Dreyfus case was seen by Zo d'Axa as only one example of social injustice among many. *La Feuille* endeavored to place the Dreyfus affair in context with the other ills of society. Therefore, as the journal lamented Dreyfus's situation, it also condemned the irrationality of Drumont, of anti-Semitic demonstrations, of blind allegiance to the military (fig. 41), of defenders of secrecy for purposes of national security, and of the rabble rousing press, *Le Petit Journal* (fig. 42) being one of the offenders. At the same time it condemned the "grands Juifs," who Zo d'Axa viewed as "more bourgeois than Jewish." These were the "high barons and the rich bankers" who were treated by the anti-Semites as the "rich pariahs" of society but, as Zo d'Axa complained, would not use their wealth or influence to aid the "poor pariahs" of society, the workers.[36] According to Zo d'Axa, the "grands Juifs" reserved their liberalism, sympathies, and support for members of their own class, such as the rich Captain Dreyfus, while normally siding with the military to control the impoverished workers.

Steinlen's images for *La Feuille* were pro-justice and pro-Dreyfus. Yet that did not necessarily

Figure 41 (above left), Cat. 213
Théophile-Alexandre Steinlen
Boisdeffre's Sheep (Les Moutons de Boisdeffre)
La Feuille, 28 February 1898
Photomechanical print

Figure 42 (above right)
Hermann–Paul
Mr. Judet's Daddy (Le papa de M. Judet)
La Feuille, 2 June 1898
Photomechanical print
The Jane Voorhees Zimmerli Art Museum

Figure 43 (left), Cat. 169
Charles Léandre
Scheurer-Kestner consults the clairvoyant (M. Scheurer-Kestner consulte la Voyante)
Les Quat'z'Arts, 28 November 1897
Photomechanical print

Figure 44, Cat. 107
Abel Truchet
I accuse! . . . (J'accuse!)
Les Quat'z'Arts, 23 January 1898
Photomechanical print

Figure 45, Cat. 215
Théophile-Alexandre Steinlen
Striking Arguments (Arguments Frappants)
La Feuille, 21 January 1898
Photomechanical print

mean Steinlen was totally unmoved by the aspect of Drumont's rhetoric that equated the Jews with the "rich pariahs" of France. It also was not inconsistent for *La Feuille* to include Willette among its illustrators, since he was foremost an anarchist. The journal never, however, employed the inflammatory stereotype of the Jewish banker or other anti-Semitic imagery within its pages.

La Feuille was committed to the basic principal of right against wrong and to defending the powerless against the powerful. The Dreyfus case afforded one very prominent platform from which to wage Zo d'Axa's campaign against social injustice. The case was not, however, the raison d'être for *La Feuille* as it was for *Psst. . . !* and *Le Sifflet.*

The Dreyfus case was also not the main focus

of Goudeau's journal *Les Quat'z'Arts.* Nevertheless, by the fourth issue, 28 November 1897, its anti-Dreyfusard tendencies were revealed with Léandre's farcical illustration (fig. 43) depicting Scheurer-Kestner consulting the seer, Mademoiselle Couesdon, who, it was said, received her revelations from the Archangel Gabriel. Couesdon's mystical powers had been discovered earlier in the decade by Gaston Méry, a writer for *La Libre Parole;* the preface of Méry's biography of Couesdon was in fact written by Drumont, whom Couesdon had predicted would eventually become president of the Republic.[37] The relationship of Couesdon with *La Libre Parole* makes Léandre's caricature of the Dreyfusard Scheurer-Kestner all the more ludicrous.

Figure 47, Cat. 153
Hermann-Paul
From the album, *Guignols,* 1899
Photomechanical print

Figure 46, Cat. 218
Félix Vallotton
The Age of Paper (L'Age du Papier)
Le Cri de Paris, 23 January 1898
Photomechanical print

But it is Abel Truchet's cover for the 23 January issue of *Les Quat'z'Arts* (fig. 44) and Goudeau's editorial in the 27 February issue that places this Montmartre journal squarely in the camp of the anti-Dreyfusards and anti-Semites.[38]

In contrast to Truchet's and Goudeau's specific anti-Zola and anti-Semitic reactions to "J'Accuse" in *Les Quat'z'Arts,* Steinlen's *Arguments Frappant* (fig. 45) for *La Feuille* reflects the general humanistic thesis of Zo d'Axa—the condemnation of the domination of passion over reason—and refers specifically to the attacks by mobs on Jews and on supporters of Zola after the 13 January publication of *L'Aurore.*

On 23 January Vallotton's *L'Age du papier* (fig. 46) brings *Le Cri de Paris* into the fray on the side of the Dreyfusards. Vallotton and Hermann-Paul are the principal illustrators of the journal supporting the Dreyfus cause. Later in 1899 *La Revue blanche* published the album *Guignols,* a compilation of Hermann-Paul's illustrations for several journals, including *Le Cri de Paris.*[39] Images related to the Dreyfus Affair comprise almost half the album and include Paul's eloquent response to "J'Accuse" in the 16 January edition of *Le Cri de Paris* (fig. 47).

In their Dreyfus-related imagery Steinlen and Paul imposed a temporary moratorium on the use of Jewish stereotypes previously found in their work. This freeze ends, however, with their work in *L'Assiette au beurre* and *Le Canard sauvage* (fig. 48) after the turn of the century.

Figure 48
Hermann-Paul
*Except pig, everything is permitted
(Exepté le cochon, tout nous est permis)*
Le Canard sauvage, no. 4, 11–17 April
1903
Photomechanical print
Jane Voorhees Zimmerli Art
Museum

Figure 49
*Principal Caricatures and Principal
Caricaturists of the 'Affair' (Principales
Caricatures et Principaux Caricaturistes
de L''Affaire')*
La Vie Illustrée, ca. 1899
Photomechanical print
Bibliothèque Nationale, Paris

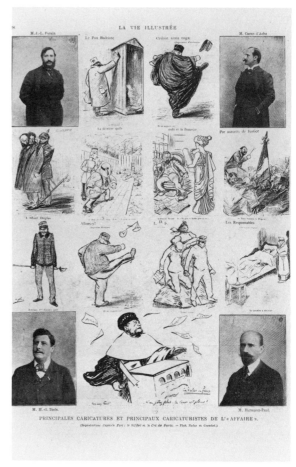

The implication of Vallotton's *L'Age du papier*
is, indeed, that the power of the press is more
powerful than the sword. During the next year
and a half, Zola's challenge to the French army
was replayed on the pages of the illustrated press.
The *Vie illustrée* (fig. 49) proclaimed Forain, Caran
d'Ache, Ibels, and Hermann-Paul as the principal
caricaturists for the two sides of the Dreyfus Affair. The battle between the Dreyfusards and anti-
Dreyfusards is no more energetically or artfully
fought by either side than on the illustrated pages
of *Le Sifflet* and of *Psst. . . !* These two journals
contain no text, only illustrations and captions;
each existed for very specific and limited purposes:
one to promote the revision of the Dreyfus case
and the other to reiterate Dreyfus's guilt and up-
hold the honor of the army. Surprisingly, both
publications were for a brief time successful in
their efforts.

Figure 50, Cat. 143
Jean-Louis Forain
The Good Patriot (Le Pon Badriote)
"I accuse" (—Ch'accuse . . . !)
Psst. . . !, no. 1, 5 February 1898
Photomechanical print

Figure 51
Henri-Gabriel Ibels
Is it a Cross or a Sabre (Est-ce une Croix ou un Sabre? . . .)
Reproduced in *Allons-y*, 1898
Photomechanical print
The Jane Voorhees Zimmerli Art Museum

Psst. . . ! began publication on 5 February 1898; this represented Forain and Caran d'Ache's immediate challenge to Zola. After eighty-five weekly issues, it terminated on 16 September 1899, one week after Dreyfus was found guilty again by the Rennes trial, at which time Forain felt that the goal of the journal had been achieved.

On 17 February 1898, in opposition to *Psst. . . !*, Archille Steens and Ibels began publishing *Le Sifflet*. It existed for seventy-two issues, folding on 16 June 1899, two weeks after the High Court of Appeals voted in favor of revision of the Dreyfus case and three days after the dismissal of all the charges against Colonel Picquart.

Forain's cover illustration (fig. 50) for the first issue of *Psst. . . !* clearly reveals the tenor of its anti-Dreyfus arguments. "Ch'accuse" exclaims the stereotypical Jewish banker, alias Zola, in a German accent, as he drops his letter to the president

Figure 52, Cat. 339

Théophile-Alexandre Steinlen

Small Penny (Le petit sou), 1899 or 1900?

Color lithographic poster

The Jane Voorhees Zimmerli Art Museum

David A. and Mildred H. Morse Art Acquisition Fund

of the Republic into the window of an outhouse. Maintaining the general anti-Semitic tone established during the previous decade, the primary thesis of the journal went further in holding that the Jews, Zola, and Germany were in collusion in support of revision; they are the dreaded "syndicate." Not only did Forain and Caran d'Ache create images that defended the army, but in response to the growing support of Dreyfus from anarchists, *Psst. . . !* attacked anarchists in general, despite the fact that Willette and Drumont were sympathetic to them.

While *Psst. . . !* ridiculed Zola, Joseph Reinach, Scheurer-Kestner, Brisson, Picquart, and other Dreyfusards, *Le Sifflet* in contrast challenged the evidence against Dreyfus and the credibility of Esterhazy, du Paty de Clam, Cavaignac, Rochefort, and Drumont, among many other anti-Dreyfusards. While *Psst. . . !* blames the Jewish "syndicate" for the weakness of the Third Republic, *Le Sifflet* credits that weakness to the alliance of the Church and the army (fig. 51).

Anticlericism had always been a solid part of the socialist platform; it was graphically expressed by Steinlen in *Le Chambard* (1893–94), and by the end of the century had become a major political issue for France. Steinlen's 1899 poster for the socialist journal *Le Petit Sou* (fig. 52) is a fitting contrast to Willette's anti-Semitic poster (see fig. 6 in Marrus's essay) ten years earlier and a striking example of the political metamorphosis undergone by similar iconography during the Dreyfus Affair. Steinlen's poster depicts the Church, the military, and the capitalists united, this time as the enemy of the people, and portrays the allegorical figure of the Republic as their savior. The Golden Calf no longer serves as a specifically anti-Semitic symbol but is a more general reference to the evils of capitalism.

In the fall of 1898, Ibels published his album *Allons-y!*[40] Dedicated to Zola, it comprises all of Ibels's illustrations for *Le Sifflet* up to that point. *Allons-y* ("Let's go") was the title of an illustration by Caran d'Ache for the 10 September 1898 issue of *Psst. . . !;* in it, Brisson is depicted igniting the bomb of revision. Ibels took the title "Allons-y" and its political implication and appropriated it for the revisionist purpose of his album. Forain's cover design (pl. 42) for the 19 February 1898 issue of *Psst. . . !* is the other source for the cover of Ibels's album.

La Vérité au Conseil de Guerre
N. de D!! Allez-vous habiller, c'est pas ici le conseil de Revision ???

Figure 53
Maximilien Luce
Truth at the Court-Martial (La Vérité au Conseil de Guerre)
"For God's sake get dressed! This isn't a draft board physical!"
(N. de D!! Allez-vous habiller, c'est pas ici le conseil de Revision???)
1899 Lithograph

Figure 54, Cat. 157 (above right)
Henri-Gabriel Ibels
Truth (La Vérité)
Drawing for *Le Sifflet,* 14 July 1898

To show the disrespect accorded the military by the courts, Forain had depicted a Dreyfusard lawyer kicking the *kepi* (hat) of a general and in the caption asks the reader, "Do you support that?" Ibels transformed the image to show a general kicking the scales of justice—using the same caption—in order to make the point that it is the unquestionable legal right of the defense to interrogate its accusers, generals or not, but not the right of the military to obstruct justice (pl. 43).

Within the rich visual iconography related to the Dreyfus Affair, the most poignant metaphorical image was one used often by both sides, "la verité,"—the truth, the naked truth, or one of numerous variants thereof. As we have seen, Forain's 1893 reference to the Panama scandal depicts Truth holding a mirror, contemplating her reflection as she attempts to climb from a well (fig. 23). Gyp created an unflattering image of a Jewish Truth for the 21 May 1898 issue of *Le Rire*; the Picquart album includes four images of Truth (pls. 114, 116, 118, 120) and Luce's lithograph (fig. 53) of 1899 shows the undressed female figure standing in front of a military tribunal as the embarrassed presiding officer yells "For God's sake get dressed! This isn't a draft board physical!"[41]

Inevitably it is the Dreyfusard's interpretation of Truth that is most eloquent and often universal (fig. 54), and it is the anti-Dreyfusards' depictions that are crass and demeaning (pl. 46). The visual counterattacks found in *Psst. . . !* and *Le Sifflet* serve as an encyclopedia of Dreyfus Affair iconography. Both journals vented their arguments and biases in the name of the French Republic; as history has proved, the position of Ibels and of the other Dreyfusard artists—Vallotton, Luce, and Couturier—is one of common sense, reason, and compassion whereas that of Forain and Caran d'Ache is blind commitment to the military, and bigotry. Most importantly *Psst. . . !* and *Le Sifflet* epitomize the embittered battle of an artistic community once tied by aesthetics, common interests, and ideals.

Notes

1. For photoprinting processes, see Phillip Dennis Cate, "Printing in France, 1850–1900: The Artist and New Technologies," *Gazette of the Grolier Club* June/December 1978:57–73.

2. Jerrold Seigel, *Bohemian Paris* (New York: Viking, 1986), 336–365.

3. For a detailed discussion of the artistic community in Montmartre, see Phillip Dennis Cate and Patricia Eckert Boyer, *The Circle of Toulouse-Lautrec,* exhibition catalogue (New Brunswick: The Jane Voorhess Zimmerli Art Museum, Rutgers, the State University of New Jersey, 1985).

4. *Hommage des artistes à Picquart,* preface by Octave Mirbeau (Paris: Société libre d'édition des gens de lettres, 1899).

5. For more on the Chat Noir, see Cate and Boyer, *The Circle of Toulouse-Lautrec,* 11–19; and Mariel Oberthur, *Cafés and Cabarets of Montmartre:* (Salt Lake City: Gibbs M. Smith, Inc., 1984), 58–65.

6. Rodolphe Salis, *Chat-Noir Guide* (Paris, 1887).

7. Lucien Goldschmidt and Herbert Schimmel, *Unpublished Correspondence of Henri de Toulouse-Lautrec,* (New York: Phaidon, 1969), 101.

8. Paul Jeanne, *Les Théâtres d'ombres à Montmartre de 1887–1923* (Paris: Les Presses modernes, 1937), 67–74.

9. *Le Fifre* existed for fifteen issues, from 23 February 1889 to 1 June 1889.

10. Henri Rivière, *La Tentation de Saint-Antoine,* (Paris: E. Plon, Nourrit et cie: n.d.), 18–23; the album is based on Rivières shadow-theater production first performed at the Chat Noir on 28 December 1887.

11. See especially Steinlen's illustrations in Aristide Bruant, *Dans la Rue,* (Paris, 1895).

12. "est le premier volume d'une série de romans dont l'ensemble formera l'histoire d'une famille d'Israélites modernes en train de conquérir la vieille Europe, grace de ces quatre qualites de leur race: l'intelligence, l'énergie, la ruse et la patience." Victor Joze, *Les Rozenfeld, histoire d'une famille Juive: La Tribu d'Isidore* (Paris: Antony, 1897), vii.

13. "On aurait le plus grand tort de croire que mon but est de faire une série de pamphlets contre les Juifs. D'abord, je suis un ennemi des romans à thèse, et puis je ne suis point un antisémite dans le sens précis du mot. Je ne suis d'aucune ligue aryenne, d'aucun comité anti-juif. Je ne suis qu'un spectateur, un passant qui se promène sur la grand'route de la vie et s'intéresse aux batailles des insectes humains.

    J'observe les manifestations diverses du mouvement social, en philosophe incapable de haïr. Je ne maudis pas, je constate." *Ibid.* p. x.

14. Laurant Taihade, *Pays de Mufle* (Paris: Bibliothèque artistique et littéraire, 1894).

15. Also see Riva Castleman's interpretation of this image in *Henri de Toulouse-Lautrec* (New York: The Museum of Modern Art, 1985), 15.

16. Thadée Natanson, "Oeuvres de M. de Toulouse-Lautrec," *La Revue blanche* no. 16, February 1893:146.

17. Bret Waller and Grace Seiberling, *Artists of la Revue Blanche,* exhibition catalogue (Rochester: Memorial Art Gallery of the University of Rochester, 1984).

18. For *La Vache enragée* see Cate and Boyer, *The Circle of Toulouse-Lautrec,* 16–17.

19. "Hein! Tout d'meme, Rothschild vient de souscrire pour vingt mille francs!
    —Vingt mille francs! Mais, mon bon ami, qu'est-ceque c'est pa pour eux."

20. D. W. Brogan, *France Under the Republic* (New York: Harper and Brothers, 1940), 79.

21. Jean Louis Forain, *Les Temps Difficiles* (Paris: G. Charpentier et E. Fasquelle, 1893).

22. "Buisqu'il n'y à blus rien a cagner ici, nous allons enfin poufour retef'nir Allemands!" (the spelling conveys a German accent).

23. Eugenia W. Herbert, *The Artist and Social Reform* (New Haven: Yale University Press, 1961), 188.

24. Phillip Dennis Cate and Susan Gill, *Théophile-Alexandre Steinlen* (Salt Lake City: Gibbs M. Smith, Inc., 1982), 23.

25. "Il s'attaquera directment aux hommes. Il combattra à outrance par le crayon et la plume, par la caricature et la satire, par la charge et la polemique violente, les ennemis des travailleurs sans distinction de poil ou de plumage.

Le Chambard dénoncera, sans peur ni merci, les inequités sociales et leurs auteurs, les exactions des exploitants, les canailleries et les corruptions gouvernementales. Il ne reculera devant aucune responsabilité, il ne menagera aucun pouvoir.

Les ennemis du Chambard? Tous les ennemis du Socialisme." Le Chambard no. 1, 15 December 1893:2.

26. Cate and Gill, Théophile Alexandre Steinlen, 93–95.

27. Les Trois-Huit (the Three-Eights) took their name from the socialist goal of an eight-hour work day.

28. Donna Stein and Donald Karshan, L'Estampe originale: a Catalogue Raisonné (New York: Museum of Graphic Art, 1970).

29. Jules Martin, Nos Auteurs et Compositeurs Dramatiques (Paris: Flammarion, 1897), 267.

30. Gyp, En Balade (Paris: Librairie illustrée, 1897); Gyp, Israel (Paris: Flammarion, 1898) (not illustrated).

31. Léo Campion, La Feuille par Zo d'Axa (Besanson: Le Vent du Ch'min, 1978).

32. "Comme tous les journaux de la butte et même des hauteurs Montmartroises, Les Quat'z'Arts, fondé le lre [sic] Novembre, 1897 par Mss. Emile Goudeau et Trombert, . . . s'est d'emblée déclaré contre 'l'affaire Dreyfus' et, par conséquent, contre tous les hommes qui, d'une façon quelconque, devaient intervenir en la circonstance, pour la révision du procès." ["Like all the newspapers from the Montmartrian mound and even from its heights, Les Quatr'z Arts, founded November 1, 1897 by Messieurs Emile Goudeau and Trombert, . . . immediately declared itself against "the Dreyfus Affair" and, consequently, against all men who, in whatever way, had to intervene in the matter, to bring about a retrial."] John Grand-Carteret, L'Affaire Dreyfus et L'Image (Paris: Flammarion, 1898), 143.

33. Jacques Ferny, "Le Cabaret des Quat'z'Arts," Les Chansonniers de Montmartre no. X, 25 October 1906:5.

34. Flax, "René Bérenger," Les Hommes du jour no. 20, n.d.

35. Charles Rearick, Pleasures of the Belle Epoque (New Haven: Yale University Press, 1985), 46.

36. Zo d'Axa, "En Grève," La Feuille no. 18, 20 October 1898.

37. Raphael Viau, Vingt Ans d'antisémitisme (Paris: Bibliothèque-Charpentier: 1910), 109–111.

38. In response to Zola's accusations in L'Aurore, Goudeau declares: "Et quand il °Zola§ a songé à détruire les grands chefs, que, dans son cauchemar, il accusait de tous les méfaits, il aboutit à ce cri désormais universel: Vive l'Armée!

Et si les intellectuals continuent à suivre cette piste, cela les ménera si loin, que, quand ils voudront retourner à leur bonne petite Tour d'Ivoire ou, jadis, ils éxecutaient des sonates et des vers libres, sous le regard alangui des riches juives, il n'y aura plus de Tour d'Ivoire.

Vive la Patrie et vive l'Armée."

[And when Zola dreamed of destroying the big leaders, that, in his nightmare, he accused of all the ill deeds, he ended up with the cry that has henceforth become universal: Long Live the Army!

And if the intellectuals continue to follow this path, it will lead them so far, that, when they want to return to their nice, little Ivory Tower where, formerly, they performed sonatas and free verse, under the languishing look of rich Jews, there will be no more Ivory Tower.

Long Live the Country and Long Live the Army.]

Emile Goudeau, Les Quat'z'Arts no. 17, 27 February 1898:2.

39. Hermann-Paul, Guignols, 60 dessins par Hermann-Paul (Paris: Editions de La Revue blanche, 1899).

40. H. G. Ibels, Allons-y! (Paris: P. V. Stock, 1898).

41. For a detailed analysis and history of "Truth" imagery as related to the Dreyfus Affair see Joan Diamond and Anita Friedman, "Truth on The March: Art and Politics During the Dreyfus Affair," Annual Phi Beta Kappa lecture. Hollins College, Roanoke, Virginia, April, 1986.

Degas and the Dreyfus Affair: A Portrait of the Artist as an Anti-Semite

LINDA NOCHLIN

Anti-Semitism, is a free and total choice of oneself, a comprehensive attitude that one adopts not only toward Jews but toward men in general, toward history and society; it is at one and the same time a passion and a conception of the world.

Jean-Paul Sartre, Anti-Semite and Jew

At the time of the Dreyfus Affair, many members of the artistic avant-garde took sides: Monet and Pissarro, with their old friend and supporter Zola, were pro-Dreyfusard, as were the younger radical artists Luce, Signac and Vallotton and the American Mary Cassatt; Cézanne, Rodin, Renoir, and Degas were anti-Dreyfus. Monet, who had been out of touch with Zola for several years, nevertheless wrote to his old friend two days after the appearance of "J'Accuse" to congratulate him for his valor and his courage; on 18 January, Monet signed the so-called Manifesto of the Intellectuals on Dreyfus's behalf.[1] Despite the fact that at the outset of the Affair many anarchists were unfavorably disposed toward Dreyfus—an army officer and wealthy to boot—Pissarro, who was an ardent anarchist, nevertheless quickly became convinced of his innocence. He too wrote to Zola after the appearance of "J'Accuse," to congratulate him for his "great courage" and "nobility of . . . character," signing the letter, "Your old comrade."[2] Renoir, who managed to keep up with some of his Jewish friends like the Natansons at the height of the Affair, nevertheless was both an anti-Dreyfusard and openly anti-Semitic, a position obviously linked to his deep political conservatism and fear of anarchism. Of the Jews, he maintained that there was a reason for their being kicked out of every country, and asserted that "they shouldn't be allowed to become so important in France." He spoke out against his old friend, Pissarro, saying

that his sons had failed to do their military service because they lacked ties to their country.[3] Earlier, in 1882, he had protested against showing his work with Pissarro, maintaining that "to exhibit with the Jew Pissarro means revolution."[4]

None of the former Impressionists, however, was as ardently anti-Dreyfusard and, it would seem, as anti-Semitic as Edgar Degas. When a model in Degas's studio expressed doubt that Dreyfus was guilty, Degas screamed at her "you are Jewish. . . you are Jewish. . ." and ordered her to put on her clothes and leave, even though he was told that the woman was actually Protestant. Pissarro, who continued to admire Degas's work, referred to him in a note to Lucien, as *"the ferocious anti-Semite."* He later told his friend Signac that since the anti-Semitic incidents of 1898, Degas, and Renoir as well, shunned him. Degas, at the height of the Affair, even went so far as to suggest that Pissarro's painting was ignoble; when reminded that he had once thought highly of his old friend's work he replied, "Yes, but that was before the Dreyfus affair."[5]

Such anecdotes provide us with a bare indication of the facts concerning vanguard artists and the Dreyfus Affair, and they tend to create an oversimplified impression of an extremely complex historical situation. Certainly, there seems to be little evidence in the *art* of any of these artists, of such essentially *political* attitudes as anti-Semitism or Dreyfusard sympathies.[6] Yet there are certain ways of reading the admittedly rather limited visual evidence that can lead to a more sophisticated analysis of the issues involved. Two concrete images reveal, better than any elaborate theoretical explanation, the complexity of the relation of vanguard artists to Jews and "Jewishness" and, at the same time, the equally complex relation which obtains between visual representation and meaning. The first, a work in pastel and tempera on paper of 1879 is by Edgar Degas, and it represents Ludovic Halévy,[7] the artist's boyhood friend and constant companion, writer, librettist, and man-about-town. Halévy is shown backstage at the opera with another close friend, Boulanger-Cavé (fig. 1). The image is a poignant one. The inwardness of mood and the isolation of the figure of Halévy, silhouetted against the vital brilliance of the yellowish blue-green backdrop, suggest an empathy between the middle-aged artist and his equally middle-aged subject, who leans, with a kind of resigned nonchalance, against his furled umbrella.[8] The gaiety and make-believe of the theater setting only serves as a foil to set off the essential solitude, the sense of worldly weariness, established by Halévy's figure. Halévy himself commented on this discrepancy between mood and setting in the pages of his journal: "Myself, serious in a frivolous place: that's what Degas wanted to represent."[9] The only touch of bright color on the figures is provided by the tiny dab of red at both men's lapels: the ribbon of the Legion of Honor, glowing like an ember in the dark, signifying with Degas's customary laconicism the distinction appropriate to members of his intimate circle—though Degas himself viewed such institutional accolades rather coolly.[10] Halévy, of course, was a Jew; a convert to Catholicism, to be sure, but a Jew, nevertheless, and when the time came, a staunch Dreyfusard. His son, Daniel, one of Degas's most fervent admirers, was to be, with his friend, Charles Péguy, one of the most fervent of Dreyfus's defenders.[11] No one looking at this sympathetic, indeed empathetic, portrait would surmise that Degas was (or would become) an anti-Semite or that he would become a virulent anti-Dreyfusard; indeed, that within ten years, he would pay his last visit to the Halévy's home, which had been like his own for many years, and never return again, except briefly, on Ludovic's death in 1908, to pay his final respects.[12]

The second image to consider is a pen-and-ink drawing, one of a series of twenty-eight by Ca-

Figure 1
Edgar Degas
Ludovic Halévy and Albert Boulanger-Cavé, ca. 1879
Pastel and tempera on paper
Musée d'Orsay, Paris

mille Pissarro, titled *Les Turpitudes Sociales*. Created in 1889,[13] the series, representing both the exploiters and the exploited of his time was intended for the political education of his nieces Esther and Alice Isaacson.[14] The drawing in question is titled *Capital* (fig. 2) and represents, in a highly caricatural style, reminiscent of Daumier or the English graphic artist, Charles Keene, the statue of a fat banker clutching a bag of gold to his heart. The features of the figure—the prominent hooked nose, protruding ears, thick lips, slack pot belly, soft hands, and knock-knees—could almost serve as an illustration for the description of the prototypical Jew concocted by the anti-Semitic agitator Drumont.[15] In a letter accompanying *Les Turpitudes Sociales*, Pissarro describes this drawing as follows: "The statue is the golden calf, the God Capital. In a word it represents the divinity of the day in a portrait of a Bischoffheim [*sic*], of an Oppenheim, of a Rothschild, of a Gould, whatever. It is without distinction, vulgar

and ugly."[16] Lest we think that this stereotypically Jewish caricature glossed by a list of specifically Jewish names is a mere coincidence, figures with the exaggeratedly hooked noses used to pillory Jews appear prominently in the foreground of another drawing from the series, *The Temple of the Golden Calf* (fig. 3), a representation of a crowd of speculators in front of the Bourse. A third drawing, originally intended for the *Turpitude Sociales* album but then omitted, is even more overtly anti-Semitic in its choice of figure type. The drawing represents the golden calf being borne in procession by four top-hatted capitalists, the first two of whom are shown with grotesquely exaggerated Jewish-looking features, while several long-nosed attendants follow behind in the cortege. The whole scene is observed by a group of working-class figures with awed expressions (fig. 4).

It is hard for the modern viewer to connect these anti-Semitic drawings with what we know about Pissarro: the fact that he was, after all, a Jew

Figure 2
Camille Pissarro
Capital
from *Les Turpitudes Sociales,* 1889–1890
Pen and ink
Private collection, Geneva

Figure 3
Camille Pissarro
The Temple of the Golden Calf
from *Les Turpitudes Sociales,* 1889–1890
Pen and ink
Private collection, Geneva

Figure 4, Cat. 53
Camille Pissarro
The New Idolators, 1889–1890
Pen and ink

himself; that he was an anarchist; that he was an extremely generous and unprejudiced person; and, above all, with the fact that when the time came he became a staunch supporter of Dreyfus and the Dreyfusard cause.

Yet lest we reach the paradoxical conclusion that the anti-Dreyfusard Degas was more sympathetic to his Jewish subjects than the Jewish Dreyfusard, Pissarro, one must examine further both the art and the attitudes of the two artists. What, for instance, are we to make of a Degas painting, almost contemporary with the Halévy portrait, titled *At the Bourse* (fig. 5)? It represents the Jewish banker, speculator, and patron of the arts, Ernest May, on the steps of the stock exchange in company with a certain M. Bolâtre.[17] At first glance, the painting seems quite similar to the *Friends on the Stage,* even to the way Degas has used some brilliantly streaked paint on the dado to the left to set off the black-clad figures, but if we look further, we see that this is not quite the

case. The gestures, the features, and the positioning of the figures suggest something quite different from the distinction and empathetic identification characteristic of the Halévy portrait: what they suggest is "Jewishness" in an unflattering, if relatively subtle way. If *At the Bourse* does not sink to the level of anti-Semitic caricature, like the drawings from *Les Turpitudes Sociales,* it nevertheless draws from the same polluted source of available visual stereotypes. Its subtlety owes something to the fact that it is conceived as "a work of art" rather than a "mere caricature." It is not so much May's Semitic features, but rather the gesture that I find disturbing—what might be called the "confidential touching"—that and the rather strange, close-up angle of vision from which the artist chose to record it, as though to suggest that the spectator is spying on rather than merely looking at the transaction taking place. At this point in Degas's career, gesture and the vantage point from which gesture was recorded were everything in

Figure 5
Edgar Degas
At the Bourse, ca. 1879
Oil on canvas
Musée d'Orsay, Paris

his creation of an accurate, seemingly unmediated, imagery of modern life. "A back should reveal temperament, age, and social position, a pair of hands should reveal the magistrate or the merchant, and a gesture should reveal an entire range of feelings," the critic Edmond Duranty declared in the discussion of Degas from his polemical account of the nascent Impressionist group, *The New Painting* (1876).[18] What is "revealed" here, perhaps unconsciously, through May's gesture, as well as the unseemly, inelegant closeness of the two central figures and the demeanor of the vaguely adumbrated supporting cast of characters, like the odd couple, one with a "Semitic nose," pressed as tightly as lovers into the narrow space at the left-hand margin of the picture—is a whole mythology of Jewish financial conspiracy. That gesture—the half-hidden head tilted to afford greater intimacy, the plump white hand on the slightly raised shoulder, the stiff turn of May's head, the somewhat emphasized ear picking up the tip—all this, in the context of the half-precise, half-merely adumbrated background, suggests "insider" information to which "they" are privy, from which "we," the spectators (understood to be gentile) are excluded. This is, in effect, the representation of a conspiracy. It is not too farfetched to think of the traditional gesture of Judas betraying Christ in this connection, except that here, both figures function to signify Judas; Christ, of course, is the French public, betrayed by Jewish financial machinations.

I am talking, of course, of significances inscribed, for the most part unconsciously or only half-consciously, in this vignette of modern commerce. If my reading seems a little paranoid, one might compare the gesture uniting the Jewish May and his friend with any of those in Degas's portraits of members of his own family who, after all, were also engaged in commerce—banking on the paternal side, the cotton market on his mother's—there is never the slightest overtone of what might be thought of as the "vulgar familiarity" characteristic of the gesture of May and Bolâtre in their images. Instead, Degas's family portraits, like *The Bellelli Family* or, in a very different vein, *The Cotton Market in New Orleans,* suggest either aristocratic distinction or down-to-earth openness of professional engagement.

Yet I am not suggesting that Degas was an anti-Semite simply through my reading of a single portrait any more than I would suggest that Pissarro was an anti-Semite because of the existence of a few drawings with nefarious capitalists cast in the imagery of Jewish stereotype. The real evidence for anti-Semitism, in Degas's case, or against it in Pissarro's is both more straightforward and, as far as Degas is concerned, more contradictory. Both artists reenact scenarios of their class and class-fraction positions; both of their practices in relation to what might be called the "signifying system" of the Dreyfus Affair are fraught with inconsistencies: they are not total, rational systems of behavior but rather fluctuating and fissured responses, changing over time, deeply rooted in class and family positions but never identical with them.[19]

Let us start to look at the evidence for Degas's attitudes toward Jews, Jewishness, and the Dreyfus Affair in greater detail, keeping in mind the fact that the Degas who sided with the anti-Dreyfusards in the late nineties was no longer the same Degas who sympathized with the fate of the vanquished Communards in 1871 or worked with the Jewish Pissarro in the eighties.[20] Attitudes change over time, vague propensities stiffen into positions; events may serve as potent catalysts for extremist stances.

First, then, evidence of what might be called "pro-Jewish" attitudes and behavior on Degas's part prior to the Dreyfus Affair—and there is a good deal of it. It is, to begin with, undeniable that Degas's circle of intimate friends, as well as that of his acquaintances, included many Jews, not merely Ludovic Halévy, and his son Daniel, who, as a young man, worshiped Degas,[21] but Halévy's cousin Geneviève, daughter of his uncle Fromenthal and widow of Georges Bizet, who, as Mme. Straus, wife of a lawyer for the Rothschild interests, ran one of the important Parisian *salons* of the later nineteenth century. The Halévy circle included such prominent Jewish figures as Ernest Reyer, the music critic for *Le Journal des Débats;* Charles Ephrussi, founder of the *Gazette des Beaux-Arts;* and Charles Haas, the elegant Jewish man-about-town who served as a model for Proust's Swann.[22] And of course, Degas was intimately associated with the Jewish artist Pissarro, both in connection with the organization of the Impressionist exhibitions, in which both played an important role and to which both exhibited untiring loyalty, but also in the practice of print-

Figure 6
Edgar Degas
Henri Michel-Lévy, ca. 1878
Oil on canvas
Foundation Calouste Gulbenkian,
Lisbon

making later.[23] Degas was one of the first to have bought Pissarro's paintings, and Pissarro admired Degas above all the other Impressionists, maintaining that he was "without doubt the greatest artist of the period."[24]

Indeed, it would have been difficult to participate in the vanguard art world of the later nineteenth century without coming into contact with Jews in one way or another;[25] even so, the number of Degas's Jewish friends and acquaintances was unusually large. It is equally undeniable that he portrayed a considerable number of Jewish sitters. In addition to the depictions of Halévy and May considered above, there are such portraits as those of a painter friend, Emile Lévy (1826–1890), a study for which dates from August 1865–1869; M. Brandon, father of the painter Edouard Brandon (1831–1897), who was also a friend of Degas's, of the mid-seventies; and the *Portrait of the Painter Henri Michel-Lévy* (1844–1914) (fig. 6), another friend of Degas's, with whom he exchanged portraits. The painter, a minor Impressionist, son of a wealthy publisher, is represented slouching rather morosely in the corner of his studio, with a large mannequin at his feet and his paintings on the walls behind.[26] Degas, in his letters, mentions sketches for a portrait of Charles Ephrussi, but the work itself has not been identified.[27] Perhaps most surprising of all, in view of Degas's later political stance, there is the double portrait of *Rabbi Elie-Aristide Astruc and General Emile Mellinet* of 1871 (fig. 7). Astruc, an authority on Judaic history, was chief rabbi of Belgium and assistant to the chief rabbi of Paris. Mellinet, a staunch republican, anticlerical, and Freemason, worked with Astruc in the ambulance service, during the siege of Paris, caring for the wounded. They asked Degas to paint them together to "recall their fraternal effort." The result is a striking little picture, loosely handled, casual and unpretentious, in which Degas, although emphasizing the comradely unity between the two men, nevertheless brings out contrasts of age, type, and character by means of subtle elements of composition and quite striking ones of color.[28]

Yet it is the Halévys who figure over and over again in Degas's work, both as subject and as site, as it were, of his practice as an artist. "We have made him," declared Daniel Halévy in his journal in 1890, "not just an intimate friend but a member of our family, his own being scattered all over the

Figure 7, Cat. 16
Edgar Degas
*Rabbi Elie-Aristide Astruc and General
Emile Mellinet,* ca. 1871
Oil on canvas

world."[29] It could, of course, be maintained, that as completely assimilated Jews, Halévy and his sons could hardly be considered "Jewish" at all. While it is true that Ludovic Halévy does not talk about his Jewishness in the pages of his *Carnets,*[30] and seems to have been without any particular religious beliefs or practices, there is at least one piece of evidence, long before the Dreyfus Affair brought him to greater self-consciousness and activism, that Ludovic Halévy in fact considered himself to be, irrevocably, a Jew. That evidence is in the form of a letter that appeared in the *Archives israélites,* a publication dedicated to Jewish political and religious affairs, in 1883, a time when Degas was having Thursday dinner and two or three lunches a week with Ludovic Halévy and his family at 22 rue de Douai. The occasion of the letter was an obituary for Ludovic's father, Léon Halévy. After thanking the editor for the articles, Halévy states: "You are perfectly right to think and say that the moral link between myself and the Jewish Community has not been broken. I feel myself to be and will always feel myself to be of the Jewish race. And it is certainly not the present circumstances, not these odious persecutions [the current pogroms in Russia and Hungary] that will weaken such a feeling in my soul. On the contrary, they only strengthen it."[31]

Although Halévy may have been guarded about expressing such sentiments to Degas, it is hardly likely that the artist could have been completely unaware of them—or of the fact that, from an anti-Semite's point of view, his close, indeed, one of his closest, friends was a Jew "by race," whether or not Halévy chose to be one. If Degas were in fact, an anti-Semite at this time, it would appear that the virus was in a state of extreme latency, visible only in the nuances of a few works of art and intermittently at that.[32] Or perhaps one might say that before the period of the Dreyfus Affair, Degas, like many other Frenchmen and women, and even like his erstwhile Impressionist comrade, Pissarro, was anti-Jewish only in terms of a certain *representation* of the Jew or of particular "Jewish traits," but his attitude did not yet manifest itself in overt hostility toward actual Jewish people, nor did it yet take the form of a coherent ideology of anti-Semitism.

In the case of the Halévys, Degas felt enough at home among them to work as well as to enjoy himself in their affectionate company. It was at their house on the rue de Douai that Degas made the drawings contained in the two large "Halévy Sketchbooks," in one of which Ludovic Halévy wrote: "All the sketches of this album were made at my house by Degas"[33] (fig. 8). The

Figure 8
Edgar Degas
Six Friends at Dieppe, 1885
Pastel and black chalk on paper
Museum of Art, Rhode Island
School of Design, Museum
appropriation

Halévys made frequent appearances in Degas's *oeuvre.* Besides the backstage portrait discussed above, both Ludovic and his son Daniel figure in one of Degas's most complicated group portraits, *Six Friends at Dieppe,* a pastel made in 1885, during a visit to the Halévys at this seaside resort. It is a strange picture. Most of the sitters are jammed against the right-hand margin, and Degas was not flattering to many of his subjects. The sitters include Halévy's son Daniel, peeking out at the spectator from under a straw boater; the English painter Walter Sickert; the French artists Henri Gervex and Jacques-Emile Blanche; and Cavé, "the man of taste," as Degas called him, whom the artist had portrayed before with Halévy behind the scenes at the Opéra. In this rather heterogeneous company, Ludovic Halévy stands out as a special case. As Jean Sutherland Boggs put it: "In the noble head of the bearded Halévy in the upper right of the pastel we can suspect a possible idealization which would reveal the easily satirical Degas' admiration and respect."[34]

At other times, however, Degas seems to have been less respectful of his old friend, most notably in the series of monotype illustrations he created for Halévy's light-hearted but pointed satire of backstage mothers and upwardly mobile young ballet dancers, *La Famille Cardinal,* in the late seventies. Taking Halévy's first-person narration quite literally, Degas has his friend appear in at least nine of the compositions,[35] most notably in the one entitled *Ludovic Halévy Meeting Mme. Cardinal Backstage* (fig. 9). Here, Degas's mischievous sense of caricature and his synoptic, suggestive drawing style are put to good use in the way he contrasts the stiff, reticent pose of the narrator with the more vulgar expansiveness of the mother of the two young dancers, whose careers, on stage and off, is the subject of the book. In another illustration, it is Degas himself, perhaps, who chats with the girls in the company of Halévy and another gentleman backstage; in still another, Halévy visits Madame Cardinal in the dressing room.[36] Halévy evidently failed to appreciate Degas's illustrations, and his refusal to accept them for publication evidently put some strain on their friendship.[37] Various reasons have been put forth for Halévy's displeasure: the author is said to have thought Degas's illustrations to have been "too idiosyncratic" or "more a recreation of the spirit and ambience of Halévy's book than authentic illustrations."[38] While both these reasons may be true, it seems to me that other considerations may also have figured in Halévy's rejection of his friend's pictures: that in some of them, he appears too *engaged,* too much a part rather than a mere spectator, of the rather *louche* business of selling young women's bodies behind the scenes at the Opéra. Did Halévy notice a disturbing resemblance between himself, as represented in the *Famille Cardinal* monotypes, and the single male visitor, leaning on a cane or umbrella, who is a constant, though often partial, presence in the famous *Brothel* monotypes of the same period, monotypes which the *Famille Cardinal* prints often resemble so closely?[39] Degas was perhaps not reticent enough in suggesting, through visual similarity, a more material connection between the life of the ballet dancer and that of the prostitute, plain and simple, than Halévy had been willing to make explicit in his light-hearted text about parental venality and female availability.[40] And as a final reason for the author's rejection of his friend's illustrations, is it too farfetched to suppose that Halévy saw a fleeting resemblance between himself as represented by Degas in the *Cardinal* monotypes and some of the coarse Semitic-featured "protectors" who appeared leering down the *décolletages* of ballet-girls in caricatures of the time? Obviously, a certain amount of tension existed between Halévy and Degas, as it so often does in extremely close male friendships, where a competitive relation with the world may conflict with intense intimacy.[41] Love and hate, support and antagonism are often not so far apart. Clearly, Degas's representation of Halévy in the *Cardinal* illustrations is a quite different, and more ambiguous, one than that embodied in the "noble head" from the Dieppe group portrait.[42]

The Halévys also played a significant role in Degas's intense if not always successful engagement with photography. Not only did Ludovic's wife, Louise, serve as the developer of his plates—he jokingly referred to her as "Louise la révéleuse" in one of his letters—[43] but members of the Halévy family posed for many of his prints and photographed *tableaux vivants,* among them the memorable parody of Ingres's *Apotheosis of Homer,* in which the two "choirboys," as Degas called them, worshiping in the foreground are Elie

Figure 9
Edgar Degas
Ludovic Halévy meeting Mme. Cardinal Backstage, ca. 1878
Illustration for Ludovic Halévy's *La Famille Cardinal*
Monotype
Private collection, Paris
Photo courtesy Harvard University Press

Figure 10
Edgar Degas
The Lemoisne sisters with Elie and Daniel Halévy, ca. 1885
Posed by Degas as a parody of Ingres' *Apotheosis of Homer*
Bibliothèque Nationale, Paris

seemed to have any political opinions."[47] Daniel Halévy describes the circumstances of the break in considerable detail: "Thursday, 25 November 1897. Last night, chatting among ourselves at the end of the evening—until then the subject [the and Daniel Halévy[44] (fig. 10). In addition, Degas photographed Daniel Halévy, in a thoughtful pose, seated in an armchair, his hand supporting his chin; Mme. Ludovic Halévy, pensive, in the same antimacassar-backed armchair; Elie in a leather chair with his mother reclining on a nearby sofa, several intriguing pictures of ballet dancers on the wall behind them (fig. 11). In another photograph, Ludovic is featured in a double exposure with other members of his family.[45]

All this came to an end, more or less abruptly, as the time of the Dreyfus Affair. As Daniel Halévy wrote: "An almost unbelievable thing happened in the autumn of 1897. Our long-standing friendship with Degas, which on our mother's side went back to their childhood,[46] was broken off. Nothing in our past relationship indicated that politics could cause such a break. Degas never

Dreyfus Trial] had been proscribed as Papa was on edge, Degas very anti-Semitic—we had a few moments of delightful gaiety and relaxation. . . . It was the last of our happy conversations," Daniel Halévy declares in his retrospective commentary on this journal entry. "Our friendship was to end suddenly and in silence. . . . One last time Degas dined with us . . . Degas remained silent. . . . His lips were closed; he looked upwards almost constantly as though cutting himself off from the company that surrounded him. Had he spoken it would no doubt have been in defense of the army, the army whose traditions and virtues he held so high, and which was now being insulted by our intellectual theorizing. Not a word came from those closed lips, and at the end of dinner Degas disappeared."[48]

The break with the Halévys was in many ways less sudden than it appeared; nor could it be attributed solely to the intensification of the Dreyfus Affair at the time it occurred, although without the Affair, it might not have taken place. One might almost liken the process of becoming an

Figure 11
Edgar Degas
Elie Halévy and his mother Louise, ca.
1896–1897
Photograph
Bibliothèque Nationale, Paris

anti-Semite to that of falling in love, a process, according to Stendahl, in his famous essay on the subject, culminating in "crystallization"; anti-Semitism may perhaps be thought of as "falling in hate," a process in which all the negative structures come together, and the subject assumes a new identity vis-à-vis the Other. This requires an often startling redefinition of former friends and associates: for example, in Degas's case, of Pissarro, with whom he had worked, whom he had admired and who admired him in return, or of Ludovic Halévy. The Dreyfus Affair was, of course, one of these crystallizing agencies, pushing equivocators over the brink, spurring to action people like Degas who before had perhaps merely grumbled and read Drumont with a certain degree of approval, but who didn't have a *cause* until the Affair served as a catalyst.

By 1895, Degas was already, in addition to being a violent nationalist and uncritical supporter of the army, an outspoken anti-Semite.[49] He had begun to have his maid Zoé read aloud at the breakfast table from Drumont's *La Libre Parole* and from Rochefort's scurrilous *L'Intransigeant,* which he thought was "full of a miraculous sort of good sense."[50] He became closer to people who shared his ideas: the painter Forain, who viciously caricatured the Dreyfusards in the weekly *Psst . . . ;*[51] his old friend Henri Rouart, and the four Rouart sons, the latter of whom were anti-Dreyfusard extremists.[52] With such companions, the aging Degas could, so to speak, let himself go: "In the town house in the Rue de Lisbonne [the Rouarts' home] Monsieur Degas was completely himself. . . . With people of whose friendship he was sure, he unbridled his frenzy as a dispenser of condemnations, as a fanatic, as a flag-waver from a past era. The others humored him in his manias and shared his prejudices."[53]

Degas, as a devoted follower of *La Libre Parole,* must have read the so-called *Monument Henry,* published in its pages in 1898–99. This was a subscription on behalf of the widow and child of Lieutenant-Colonel Henry, who had committed suicide when his fabrication of evidence incriminating Dreyfus was discovered, and who was made into a martyr of the anti-Dreyfusard cause; many subscribers sent overtly anti-Semitic messages along with their donations. One wonders what Degas made of them, how he managed to reconcile these obscenities with his actual experience of Jewish friends and supporters. Did Degas think of Ludovic Halévy when Zoé read to him at the breakfast table such sentiments as "for God, the Nation and the extermination of the Jews"[54] or "for the expulsion of the race of traitors"[55] or "French honor against Jewish gold"?[56] Did he think of the happy evenings spent at the rue de Douai when he read the comment from an inhabitant of Baccarat "who would like to see all the yids, yiddesses and their brats in the locality burned in the glass furnaces here"?[57] Did he think of Pissarro, once his companion in the Impressionist venture, his fellow experimenter in new printmaking techniques, and one of his most sincere admirers, when he read the numerous entries, such as the following, betraying what Stephen Wilson has termed "personal sadistic involvement in detailed tortures. . . ."? "A military doctor . . . who wishes that vivisection were practiced on Jews rather than on harmless rabbits"; or this: "a group of officers on active service. To buy nails to crucify the Jews." Or this: "to make a dog's meal by boiling up certain noses"?[58] Or, for that matter, what might Degas, an artist deeply concerned about his own rapidly failing vision, have thought about the anti-Dreyfusard donor from Le Mans who "would like all Jews to have their eyes put out"?[59] Or what might his reaction have been to the highly imaginative recommendation, again involving eyes and blinding, offered by Rochefort in the pages of *L'Intransigeant* in October of 1898 for the treatment of the magistrates who purportedly favored revision of the Dreyfus case: "A specially trained torturer should first of all cut off their eyelids with a pair of scissors. . . . When it is thus quite impossible for them to close their eyes, poisonous spiders will be put in the half-shells of walnuts, which will be placed on their eyes, and these will be securely fixed by strings tied round their heads. The hungry spiders, which are not too choosy about what they eat, will then gnaw slowly through the cornea and into the eye, until nothing is left in the blind sockets."[60] One would like to think that Degas was horrified or contemptuous of such grotesque lucubrations, which, for the modern reader, have clear sexual

connotations in their use of eye symbolism,[61] yet there is nothing to suggest that he was: on the contrary, Degas was a faithful reader of both journals, and evidently agreed with and took satisfaction in what they printed.

One must conclude that although Degas was indeed an extraordinary artist, a brilliant innovator, and one of the most important figures in the artistic vanguard of the nineteenth century, he was a perfectly ordinary anti-Semite. As such, he must have been capable of amazing feats of both irrationality and rationalization, able to keep different parts of his inner and outer life in separate compartments in order to construct for himself what Sartre has referred to as a personality with the "permanence of rock," a morality "of petrified values," and an identity of "pitiless stone"—choices, according to Sartre, constitutive of the anti-Semite.[62] To comprehend the mechanisms of Degas's anti-Semitism, one must conceive of the processes of displacement and condensation taking place on the level of the political unconscious functioning in a manner not dissimilar to those of the dreamwork on the level of the individual psyche, processes in which contradictory elements can be effortlessly amalgamated, painful conflicts torn asunder and safely kept apart. The sleep of reason produces monsters, and "The Jew" was produced in the sleep of Enlightenment ideals of reason and truth and justice, in the minds of nineteenth-century anti-Semites like Degas, secure in the knowledge that most of their more outrageous aggression-fantasies would be fulfilled on the level of text rather than in practice.[63] *Text* is the key word here. For it was editors, columnists, and pamphleteers who constructed the anti-Semitic identity of men like Degas. Without the discourse of the popular press—books, pamphlets, and journals, some of it to be sure, with high claims to "intellectual distinction" and "scientific objectivity"—which formulated and stimulated it, Degas's anti-Semitism would be unthinkable.[64] It was at the level of the printed word that anti-Semitism, flowing from, yet at the same time fueling the fantasies of the individual psyche, achieved a social existence and took a collective form.[65]

There was a specific aspect of Degas's situation in the world that might have made him particularly susceptible to the anti-Semitic ideology of his time: what might be called his "status anxiety."[66] According to Stephen Wilson: "The French anti-

Semites' attacks on social mobility, and their ideal of a fixed social hierarchy, suggest that such an interpretation applies to them, particularly when these ideological features are set beside the marginal situation of many of the movement's supporters."[67] Degas was precisely such a "marginal" figure in the social world of the late nineteenth century and had ample reason, by the decade of the nineties, to be worried about his status.

Although it is asserted in most of the literature that Degas came from an aristocratic family, recent research has revealed that the Degas family fortune in fact had originated in rather shady adventurism less than fifty years before the birth of the artist. Degas's grandfather, René-Hilaire Degas, made his money first as a professional speculator on the grain market during the Revolution, at a time when food shortages were provoking riots in Paris; then as a money changer, first in Paris, later in the Levant; and then as a banker and real estate operator in Naples.[68] In other words, the Degas family moved up in the world by precisely the same questionable means Jews were accused of employing: speculation and money changing. Neither did Degas possess the "pure" French blood or the age-old roots in the French soil valorized by Drumont, Barrès, and the ultranationalists. His paternal grandmother was an Italian, Aurora Freppa, and his mother, Célestine Musson, was a native of New Orleans, where her father was a wealthy and adventurous entrepreneur, whose main activity was cotton export, but who also speculated in Mexican silver mining.[69] Although members of the Degas family in both Naples and in Paris began to sign themselves "de Gas" in the 1840s, thereby implying that they were entitled to the *particule*, that is, the preposition indicating a name derived from land holdings, and although one Paris relative even hired a genealogist to create a family tree legitimizing such pretensions, in point of fact, these forebears were, to borrow the words of Roy McMullen, "indulging in the foolish little parvenu trickery that was laughed at . . . as 'spontaneous ennoblement.'" when Degas began signing himself "Degas" rather than "de Gas" after 1870, he was not rejecting an aristocratic background; he was simply signing his name as it really was. The parish register for the year 1770 that records the birth of Degas's grandfather lists his great-grandfather as "Pierre Degast, *boulanger*." Degas,

far from being a scion of the aristocracy, was the descendant of a provincial baker,[70] and the class into which he was born was in fact the *grande bourgeoisie,* a *grande bourgeoisie* of rather recent date and uncertain tenure haunted by memories of revolution and displacement. It was a family that moved a lot, even in Paris, during Degas's childhood, rather than being rooted in a permanent family *hôtel*. By the time of Auguste Degas's death in 1874, the Degas bank was near collapse;[71] by 1876, it had failed; and two years later, the artist's brother René, then living in New Orleans, reneged on his debt to the Paris bank, abandoned his blind wife and six children, and ran off with another woman. The family, in short, disintegrated, both morally and materially.[72] Degas's position at the time of the Dreyfus Affair offers a classic example of the "status anxiety" associated with anti-Semitism.[73] Not only had he chosen the marginal existence of an artist—and a nonconformist artist at that—but the family banking fortune had vanished; the family honor was besmirched, and the artist was obliged to sacrifice his comfortable private income to pay his brother's debts. Degas, then, had come from a background as *arriviste* as that of any of the nouveau riche Jews his fellow anti-Semites vilified, but by 1898, even this recently acquired upper-class position was an insecure one, despite his success as an artist.[74] Anti-Semitism served not only as a shield against threatening downward social mobility but as a mechanism of denial, firmly differentiating Degas's fragile *haut bourgeois* status from that of the newly wealthy, recently cultivated upper-class Jews whose position was, to his chagrin, almost indistinguishable from his own.

What effect did Degas's anti-Semitism have on his art? Little or none. With rare exceptions, one can no more read Degas's political position out of his art, in the sense of pointing to specific signifiers of anti-Jewish feeling within it, than one can read a consistent anti-Semitism out of Pissarro's use of stereotypically Jewish figures to personify capitalist greed and exploitation in the *Turpitudes Sociales* drawings. In Pissarro's case, it was simply that no other visual signs worked so effectively and with such immediacy to signify capitalism as the hook nose and pot belly of the stereotypical Jew.[75] There is, of course, always something repugnant about such representations, as there is always something suspect in representations in which women are used to signify vices like sin or lust, because in such representations there is inevitably a slippage between signifier and signified, and we tend to read the image as "all Jews are piggish capitalists" or "all women are seductive wantons" instead of reading it in a purely allegorical way.

The representation of anti-Semitism was a critical issue in the work of neither Pissarro nor Degas. In general, the subjects to which they devoted themselves did not involve the representation of Jews at all. By the time of the Dreyfus Affair, Degas had more or less completely abandoned the contemporary themes that had marked his production from the late 1860s through the early 1880s, a period when, of all the Impressionists, he had been "mostly deeply involved in the representation of modern urban life," to borrow the words of Theodore Reff.[76]

There was, however, one sustained work of art by a vanguard artist at the time of the Dreyfus Affair in which the question of anti-Semitism plays a central role, and that is the set of illustrations that Toulouse-Lautrec did for Clemenceau's *Au Pied du Sinaï* (1898), a series of vignettes of Jewish life. Although this is not the place for a detailed examination of Lautrec's ambiguous position vis-à-vis Jews, anti-Semitism, and the Dreyfus Affair—a subject well worth pursuing—certain aspects of his representation of Jews in these rather undistinguished lithographs are relevant to the present investigation. Once again, it is difficult to tell the artist's position from the images alone, without knowing something of their context: how they are to be read; who is doing the reading; and at what moment in history the reading is taking place.[77]

Clemenceau's collection of stories and anecdotes is mainly about Eastern European Jews, not about educated French ones; it is related to the popular *fin-de-siècle* genre of the travel book. It tends to puzzle the few modern readers who bother to look at it, because it's almost impossible to tell whether the book is meant as a sympathetic picture of specific Jewish types or a piece of anti-Semitic slander. Clemenceau, on some level, meant this as a plea for greater understanding of the Jews of Eastern Europe who were then being threatened with systematic persecution.[78] In contrast to the racists of his time, Clemenceau insists on the racial diversity of the Jewish types he met

in Carlsbad, where he went for the cure and with whose colony of Polish Orthodox Jews he is largely concerned. He insists nevertheless on one trait he deems common to all Jews—something he denominates "the subtile ray which seeks the weak point like the flash of a fine blade of steel."[79] Although he implies that the religious ceremonies of the Chassidim are bizarre, even grotesque, and consistently emphasizes the "sharp practices" of all Jews, rich and poor, his descriptions are in no way different from those of other travel writers of the time taking on the picturesque customs of exotic peoples. Readers familiar with the travel literature of the nineteenth and early twentieth century devoted to the Near East or North Africa would find nothing surprising in Clemenceau's descriptions of unwashed clothing or irrational behavior on the part of the "natives"; it is simply that this time the natives are Jewish. Modern Jews, not unreasonably, associate such discourses with those of anti-Semitism, rather than seeing them as one aspect of a wider phenomenon: the late nineteenth-century construction of the Other—Blacks, Indians, Arabs, the Irish—any relatively powerless group whose customs are different from those who control the discourse. Indeed, Clemenceau tries to redeem himself at the end of his section on the Chassidim with a plea for religious tolerance, asking whether it is "any more ridiculous to shake one's head like a duck, than to do any other movements in honor of God?" He answers his own question by saying: "I do not think so. Christians and Jews are of the same human stock."[80] Lautrec provided some rather amorphous vignettes of Polish Jews with the sidelocks, beards, and prayer shawls exhaustively detailed by Clemenceau, but there is one lithograph in the series that stands out: the one titled *A La Synagogue,* for Clemenceau's story, "Schlome the Fighter" (fig. 12).[81] This story tells of a poor Jewish tailor who is drafted into the Russian army owing to the cowardice of his richer and more powerful co-religionists. He endures his years of conscription, returns to make his enemies pay for their betrayal, and then assumes his former humble role. It is the sort of David-and-Goliath fable beloved of Yiddish humorists like Sholem Aleichem, stories where the wily little Jew triumphs over more powerful adversaries in the end, except "Schlome the Fighter" is a story with a piquant irony at its heart, because it is the detested Russian army that is instrumental in strengthening the Jew in question, and it is his co-religionists, not the Russian oppressors, who are assigned the role of villains in the piece. Schlome the Fighter can take charge of his life—can become a folk hero, in fact—only when he becomes "un-Jewish" at the dramatic climax of the story; when his manly deed is done, he reverts to his previous state of impotence and humility.

Lautrec has chosen to illustrate the scene when Schlome forces the wealthy Jews gathered in the synagogue for the Day of Atonement to pay him a large indemnity. He represents Schlome exactly as Clemenceau describes him; with his prayer shawl flung over the shoulder of his uniform, he stands on the top step of the temple, the point of his saber against the floor, addressing the terrified crowd.[82] It is a kind of witty, reversed *Ecce Homo*, where the persecuted figure actively confronts his tormentors, takes speech, and demands justice. Lautrec plays the forceful curve of his hero's left arm and saber against the curve of the plume on his cossack's helmet; with his muscular legs and strong back appealingly revealed by his tight-fitting uniform, Schlome is a virile, and eminently attractive figure. This is the only time that a Jew is represented as strong and sympathetic in the series—when the figure is totally unrecognizable *as* a Jew. We have to discover from the context, and the label, that this is a Jew not a cossack; or rather that this is an anomaly: a Jewish Cossack. This is a token not so much of Lautrec's personal anti-Semitism as it is of the fact that there was no visual language available with which he might have constructed an image at once identifiably Jewish and at the same time "positive" in terms that would be generally legible. The signifiers that indicated "Jewishness" in the late nineteenth century were too firmly locked into a system of negative connotations: picturesqueness is the closest he could get to a relatively benign representation of Jews who *look* Jewish.[83] As a result, the *Pied du Sinaï* illustrations make us uneasy. We don't know quite how to take them: as anti-Semitic caricatures or as misguided but basically well-intentioned vignettes of life in an exotic foreign culture.

Degas, in his last years, when the storm of the Dreyfus Affair had subsided, seems to have drawn back to some degree from overt anti-Semitism, although the evidence is equivocal. According to Thadée Natanson, publisher of *La Revue Blanche,* Degas's voice trembled with emotion whenever

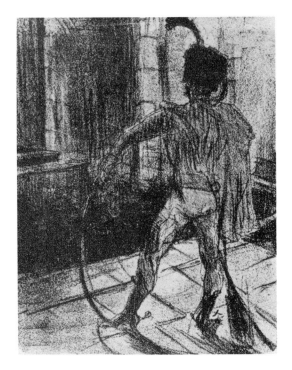

Figure 12, Cat. 61
Henri de Toulouse-Lautrec
A La Synagogue (LD 239)
Au Pied du Sinaï, 1898
Lithograph
Georges Clemenceau, *Au Pied du Sinaï*

he had to pronounce Pissarro's name.[84] Although he did not attend Pissarro's funeral in 1903, he sent Lucien Pissarro his regrets, saying that he had been too ill to be present: "I was in bed Sunday, dear sir, and I could not go to take the last trip with your poor father. For a long time we did not see each other, but what memories I have of our old comradeship."[85] Nevertheless, in another letter, probably referring to the recently deceased Pissarro, he talks about the embarrassment one felt, "in spite of oneself," in his company and refers to his "terrible race"—hardly phrases he would have used if Pissarro's Jewishness had ceased to be an issue.[86] And while it is true that Degas paid a final visit to the Halévys' house on the occasion of Ludovic's death[87] and continued to see the adoring Daniel for the rest of his life, he continued to cherish his anti-Dreyfusard opinions. "There are no signs," according to his most recent biographer, Roy McMullen, "that he ever thought he had taken the wrong side in the great clash of the two Frances."[88] When his old friend, Madame Ganderax, complimented him in front of one of his paintings, saying "Bravo Degas! This is the Degas we love, not the Degas of the Affair," Degas, without blinking an eyelash, replied "Madame, it is the whole Degas who wishes to be loved."[89] He was implying, with a touch of bitter humor, that one could not love the artist without loving the anti-Dreyfusard as well.

This is of course not the case. One can separate the biography from the work, and Degas has made it easy for us by keeping, with rare exceptions, his politics—and his anti-Semitism—out of his art. Unless, of course, one decides it is impossible to look at his images in the same way once one knows about his politics, feeling that his anti-Semitism somehow pollutes his pictures, seeping into them in some ineffable way and changing their meaning, their very existence as signifying systems. But this would be to make the same ludicrous error Degas himself did when he maintained that he had only thought Pissarro's *Peasants Planting Cabbage* an excellent painting *before* the Dreyfus Affair; Degas at least had the good grace to laugh at his own lack of logic in that instance.[90]

Notes

I would like to thank Irene Z. Schenck, research associate at the Jewish Museum, also Anita Friedman of that institution, and Thomas Wotjas, my research assistant at the City University Graduate Center, for their help in preparing this article. My thinking about Degas has always been stimulated by the work of and my conversations with Eunice Lipton of the State University of New York at Binghampton.

1. For the letter of 14 January 1898, see Daniel Wildenstein, *Claude Monet: Biographie et catalogue raisonné* (Lausanne: La Bibliothèque des Arts, 1979), vol. 3, no. 1399, 296. There are several other letters in which Monet expresses his admiration for Zola, in one of which he says, "C'est de l'héroisme absoluement" (to Geffroy, no. 1403, 296). He refused, however, to become a member of the Ligue des Droits de l'Homme. See Wildenstein, 3:82–83 for an analysis of Monet's position.

2. Cited in Ralph E. Shikes and Paula Harper, *Pissarro: His Life and Work* (New York: Horizon Press, 1980), 306. For a general account of Pissarro's course of action during the Affair, see ibid., 304–309.

3. Barbara Ehrlich White, *Renoir, His Life, Art, and Letters* (New York: Abrams, 1984), 210–211.

4. Ibid., 121.

5. Shikes and Harper, *Pissarro: His Life and Work*, 307–308. The underlining is Pissarro's.

6. I am excluding from this discussion artists of the second rank, like Forain, or draftsmen like Caran d'Ache, whose work was overtly anti-Semitic on a large scale; who functioned, in effect, as anti-Semitic caricaturists.

7. Halévy, besides being a popular and highly esteemed dramatic author and novelist, had also served as secretary-editor of the French Legislature, a post he abandoned in 1865 to devote himself exclusively to his literary career. His best known libretti were written in collaboration with Henri Meilhac and included *La Belle Hélène, La Grande-Duchesse de Gérolstein,* and *La Vie Parisienne,* all with music by Offenbach. He was awarded the Legion of Honor and was the first Jewish member of the Academie Française. For good accounts of Degas's relation with Halévy, see Roy McMullen, *Degas: His Life, Times, and Work* (Boston: Houghton Mifflin Company, 1984), 369–370, 383–386, 436, 440–441, 460; and Theodore Reff, *Degas: The Artist's Mind* (New York: Harper & Row, 1976), 182–188. For a good brief account of Halévy's career, see the *Universal Jewish Encyclopedia* (1941), 5:179–180 and *La Grande Encyclopédie,* 19:756–757. For a more extended account, see

Alain Silvera, *Daniel Halévy and his times: a Gentleman-Commoner in the Third Republic* (Ithaca: Cornell University Press, 1966), 1–41, passim.

8. Ludovic Halévy, like Degas, was born in 1834; both men were therefore forty-five years old at the time the picture was painted.

9. L. Halévy, "Les Carnets de Ludovic Halévy," *Revue des Deux Mondes* 42 (1937):823.

10. For the importance of the decorations and how they were obtained, see Ludovic Halévy, *Carnets,* intro. by D. Halévy (Paris: Calmann-Lévy, 1935), 2:9, August 15, 1869: "I can say that I did not steal it [The Legion of Honor ribbon], for I worked hard for ten years at the Ministry of Algiers and the Colonies and at the Chamber. These were not sinecures!"

11. For Daniel Halévy, see Silvera, *Daniel Halévy and his times.*

12. For a moving account of this last visit, see Daniel Halévy, *My Friend Degas,* trans. of *Degas Parle,* trans. M. Curtiss (Middletown, Conn.: Wesleyan University Press, 1964), 104–105.

13. This is the dating of Shikes and Harper, *Pissarro,* 232. Other authorities date the *Turpitudes Sociales* to 1890. See *Pissarro,* exh. cat. (Hayward Gallery London, Cat. no. 142), 1980–1981, and Richard Bretell and Christopher Lloyd, *A Catalogue of the Drawings of Camille Pissarro in the Ashmolean Museum, Oxford* (Oxford: Oxford University Press, 1980), no. 170, 210.

14. Shikes and Harper, *Pissarro,* 231.

15. Edouard Drumont, in *La France Juive,* published in 1886, identified the Jew by "the well-known hooked nose, the blinking eyes, clenched teeth, projecting ears, fingernails that are square instead of round and almond-shaped, an excessively long torso, flat feet, round knees, extraordinarily turned-out toes, and the soft, velvety hand of a hypocrite and a traitor." Cited in McMullen, *Degas,* 422.

16. Shikes and Harper, *Pissarro,* 232.

17. In a letter of 1879, Degas wrote to Bracquemond saying "M. Ernest May . . . Il se marie, va prendre un petit hôtel, je crois, et arrange en galerie sa petite collection. C'est un Juif, il a organisé une vente au profit de la femme de Monchot, devenu fou. Vous voyez, c'est un homme qui se lance dans les Arts." See Jean Sutherland Boggs, *Portraits by Degas* (Berkeley and Los Angeles: University of California Press, 1962), 123. Degas also did two drawings of Mme. Ernest May, in 1881. See Götz Adriani, *Degas: Pastels, Oil Sketches, Drawings* (New York: Abbeville Press, 1985), nos. 139 and 140. May was evidently to be one of the backers of the Impressionists' ill-starred print publication, *Jour et Nuit,* in which Degas was deeply involved. See McMullen, *Degas,* 355–356. There is some confusion about just which of these figures is actually M. May. Jean Sutherland Boggs in *Portraits by Degas* says left; McMullen says right. It would seem that it must be the latter: May is the one who is clearly identifiable and portrayed; the bending figure to the left seems an auxiliary.

18. Exh. cat., *The New Painting: Impressionism 1874–1886* (San Francisco: The Fine Arts Museums and Washington, D.C.: National Gallery of Art, 1986), 44.

19. Indeed, it is important to stipulate that anti-Semitism, far from being immediately identifiable with a class position actually functions ideologically, as Sartre has pointed out in *Anti-Semite and Jew,* trans. J. G. Becker (New York: Schocken Books, 1965), to smooth over and obliterate actual class distinctions and antipathies in a spurious national or racial unity or harmony: "I may be only a shop-keeper and he an aristocrat, but we are both Frenchmen and as such, we both hate Jews," 29–30.

20. For Degas's sympathy with the Communards, see McMullen, *Degas,* 199.

21. See Silvera, *Daniel Halévy and his Times,* 36: "Beyond doubt the single person who left the most permanent impression on the young Halévy was the painter Degas." Also see ibid., 39: "The importance of Degas in shaping Halévy's development can scarcely be exaggerated." Ibid., 36–39, stresses the importance of Degas's political, artistic, and social beliefs for shaping Daniel Halévy's development. Of course, Daniel Halévy's *My Friend Degas* is a testimonial to Degas's importance for Daniel Halévy.

22. McMullen, *Degas,* 386.

23. See Michel Melot, "La pratique d'un artiste: Pissarro graveur en 1880," *Histoire et Critique des Arts,* no. 2 (June 1977), 14–38. Also, Shikes and Harper, *Pissarro,* 161–175.

24. *Letters,* May 9, 1883. Cited in Shikes and Harper, *Pissarro,* 162.

25. See, for example, the important role played by the Jewish and pro-Dreyfusard Thadée Natanson, both as a publisher (of the *Revue Blanche*) and as a *salonnier.* For a good brief account of the Natanson brothers and their circle, see Gerstle Mack, *Toulouse-Lautrec* (New York: Alfred A. Knopf, 1938), 263 ff.

26. For the identification of the painting and a discussion of the sitter, see Reff, *Degas,* 125–130. There is some doubt about whether the painting was actually exhibited in the Fourth Impressionist Exhibition in 1879 or was merely listed in the catalogue. See the exh. cat., *The New Painting: Impressionism 1874–1866* (San Francisco: Fine Arts Museums and Washington, D.C.: National Gallery of Art, 1986), 258.

27. See Boggs, *Portraits by Degas,* 117. The letter was to Henri Rouart and is dated 1 May 1880.

28. See McMullen, *Degas,* 194, for information about the subjects. One can also consult the *Jewish Encyclopedia* for information about Elie-Aristide Astruc. Astruc wrote a study of anti-Semitism, *Origines et causes historiques de l'anti-Sémitisme* in 1884. Jean Sutherland Boggs, *Portraits by Degas,* 34–35, analyzes this painting in considerable detail, and compares the figure of Mellinet to an El Greco.

29. Daniel Halévy, 1965, entry of 30 Dec. 1890, 45.

30. See for example, Ludovic Halévy, *Carnets* and idem, "Les Carnets de Ludovic Halévy," *Revue des deux mondes* XLII (1937):811–843 and XLIII (1938):95–126, 375–403, 589–613.

31. *Archives Israélites: Recueil politique et religieux* XLIV (1883):310.

32. See Stephen Wilson, *Ideology and Experience: Antisemitism in France at the Time of the Dreyfus Affair* (Rutherford, N.J.: Fairleigh Dickinson University Presses, 1982), 5: "What the Affair reveals . . . is the wide extent and great importance of anti-Semitic prejudice in France, latent, but ready to manifest itself when circumstances allowed or encouraged it."

33. For information about the Halévy Sketchbooks, which were originally owned by Ludovic Halévy, and which contained sketches relating to the famous weekly dinners arranged by Henry Meillac and Albert Wolff at the Pavillon Henri IV, see Theodore Reff, *The Notebooks of Edgar Degas: A Catalogue Raisonné of the Thirty-Eight Notebooks in the Bibliothèque Nationale and Other Collections* (Oxford, 1976), I:1–3 and 128–133. Also *Edgar Degas, 1834–1917,* exh. cat. (D. Carritt, London), no. 21.

34. Boggs, *Portraits by Degas,* 70.

35. Eugenia Parry Janis, *Degas Monotypes: Essay, Catalogue & Checklist,* exh. cat. (Cambridge, Mass.: Fogg Art Museum, Harvard University, 1968), xxii.

36. Janis, in her catalogue of the Degas monotypes, lists 12 monotypes relating to the *Famille Cardinal* series that include Ludovic Halévy in the scene. See idem, *Degas Monotypes,* nos. 195–215. For a good account of the illustrations, see Reff, *Degas,* 184–186. Reff, 187–187, also refers to another collaboration between the two friends, the stage production of Halévy's and Meilhac's *The Grasshopper,* a satirical comedy about contemporary artistic life.

37. See, for instance, Pierre Cabanne, *Degas* (Paris: Pierre Tisné, 1957), cat. nos. 99–100, 118. But for a different opinion, see Ronald Pickvance, *Degas 1879: Paintings, Pastels, Drawings, Prints and Sculpture . . . ,* exh. cat. (Edinburgh: National Gallery of Scotland, 1979), 68, who states: "The project was dropped. Without acrimony, Degas quietly kept his designs in portfolios."

38. For the first of these explanations, see Pickvance, *Degas 1879,* 68; for the second, Reff, *Degas,* 186. Also see Janis, *Degas Monotypes,* xxii, for a similar explanation.

39. Halévy's reticence, his choice of other illustrators, Edmond Morin, Henri Maigrot, called Henriot, and later, E. Mas to do the pictures for his popular *Cardinal* stories, rather than Degas's more pointed and personal ones, may have something to do with the different degree of "actuality" occasioned by printed as opposed to visual discourse. While one can "be there" in the sense of being the narrator of the story without acute embarrassment, there is something different about being *depicted* in the sexually questionable situations related by the same text, something more concrete perhaps, and more implicative of the physical self: Halévy must have seen himself objectified, becoming, like a woman, the "Object of the Gaze" in Degas's monotype illustrations. It would be interesting to see if the other illustrators included Halévy in their pictures, and with such unflattering directness as Degas did.

40. For the relationship between ballet dancers and prostitutes in the context of Degas's work, see Eunice Lipton, *Looking into Degas: Uneasy Images of Women and Modern Life* (Berkeley, Los Angeles, London: University of California Press, 1986), 73–115.

41. For an important investigation of the representation of male homosociality and its tensions, specifically in literature of the eighteenth and nineteenth centuries, see Eve Kosofsky Sedgwick, *Between Men: English Literature and Male Homosocial Desire* (New York, 1985).

42. Degas could be rather cutting about his friend's literary ability. He evidently criticized Halévy's novel *The Abbé Constantin* (1882) for sentimentality, leading the latter to note in his *Carnets:* "My friend Degas is indignant about *L'Abbé Constantin,* nauseated would be more like it. He is disgusted with all that virtue, with all that elegance. He said insulting things to me this morning. I must always do things like *Madame Cardinal,* dry little things, satirical, skeptical, ironic, without heart, without emotion. He called me Father Halévy." Ludovic Halévy, "Les Carnets de Ludovic Halévy," 42:398.

43. Letter of 29 Sept. 1895 to Ludovic Halévy, *Lettres de Degas,* ed. M. Guérin (Paris: Bernard Grasset, 1945), 208.

44. Degas calls them "choirboys" in a letter of September 1885 (*Lettres* (1945):112). The photograph is by Barnes and was taken at Bas-Fort-Blanc near Dieppe in 1885.

45. McMullen, *Degas,* 431.

46. Ludovic Halévy's wife, Louise Bréguet, had been a childhood friend of Degas's sister, Marguérite (Fèvre).

47. Daniel Halévy, *My Friend Degas*, 97.

48. Ibid., 100–101. Degas sent a letter to Mme. Halévy the next morning, which she read without comment. Daniel's friendship with Degas nevertheless continued after this incident, although he had to visit Degas at the latter's home.

49. See the entry in Daniel Halévy's diary for November 5, 1895: "Degas is very sad. . . . He has become a passionate believer in anti-semitism." Cited in McMullen, *Degas,* 427.

50. See McMullen, *Degas,* 427.

51. Forain explained that in creating his anti-Semitic cartoons he was "acting . . . quite simply, as the echo of the public"; see Stephen Wilson, *Ideology and Experience,* 606.

52. Daniel Halévy (*My Friend Degas*) claims that Rouart himself was "extremely moderate about the affair." His sons, however, were fanatics. See Halévy's journal entry of 10 August 1899, 102.

53. Jacques-Emile Blanche, "Propos de peintre," cited in McMullen, *Degas,* 440.

54. Wilson, *Ideology and Experience,* 148.

55. Ibid., 155.

56. Ibid., 149.

57. Ibid., 156.

58. Ibid.

59. Ibid.

60. Cited in ibid., 589.

61. This is Wilson's suggestion, 589.

62. Sartre, *Anti-Semite and Jew,* 27, 54.

63. Wilson, *Ideology and Experience,* 589.

64. "The 'new' antisemitism found expression primarily in newspapers, journals, pamphlets and books, and its proponents were writers and journalists." "The main vehicle of antisemitism was the newspaper press, symbol, symptom and maker of a homogeneous national culture." Ibid., 606 and 639.

65. See ibid., *Ideology and Experience,* 589.

66. For a somewhat different interpretation of Degas's status anxiety, see Lipton, *Looking into Degas,* 190–195.

67. Wilson, *Ideology and Experience,* 637.

68. This information comes from the new and very full account of Degas's family history provided by McMullen, *Degas,* 2–3.

69. Ibid., 5–6.

70. Ibid., 8–9.

71. Ibid., 243.

72. Ibid., 260.

73. Says Wilson (p. 637) of the anti-Semites at the time of the Dreyfus Affair: "It seems that, losing status themselves, they were obsessed by the rising status of others, and symbolically of the Jews; here it should be recalled that the criteria of status were themselves in question, both objectively, causing authentic disorientation, and also, to some degree, because antisemites deliberately refused to accept criteria which gave them low status. As has been argued . . . antisemitism in France offered a compensation for this anxiety. Uncertain of their place in a real world that was changing, more or less unattached to it, antisemites 'belonged' to 'the nation,' and, if they were militants, they 'belonged to the movement.'"

74. In the terms of anti-Semitic paranoia even, a successful artist might consider himself insecure in relation to the Jews. Forain, Degas's close friend at the time of the Affair, complained to a friend: "We artists, like you writers, we live from hand to mouth; we only earn just enough to stay alive and keep on working, while the most insignificant little Jew who sets up in business is the possessor of a fortune at the end of a year or two." Cited in ibid., 608 and n. 61.

75. In the accompanying text, Pissarro had hastened to add: "The masses . . . dislike the Jewish bankers, and rightly, but they have a weakness for the Catholic bankers, which is idiotic." As Shikes and Harper have pointed out in their biographical study of Pissarro: "Pissarro hated all bankers, Jewish and Christian." *Pissarro,* 232, 234.

76. Reff, *Degas,* 164. One might of course link Degas's rejection of an explicit subject matter of modern life with his increasing conservatism and with a certain aspect of anti-Semitic ideology as well: its emphatic antimodernism. See Wilson, *Ideology and Experience,* 612 ff. for a discussion of the antimodernist stance of anti-Semitism and its espousal of the values and aesthetics of "Old France." But Degas never returned to a historicizing subject matter, and his rejection of the painting of modern life by the 1890s cannot necessarily be considered "conservative" in terms of the art practice of the period, in which Symbolism rather than Realism might be considered "advanced"; yet, during the same period, the politically radical Neo-Impressionists, like Seurat, Signac, Luce, and Pissarro, who became one of their members, certainly insisted on contemporary, often socially significant, subject matter.

77. Of course it must be kept in mind that these are not based on Lautrec's original ideas, but are *illustrations,* dependent on specific incidents in Clemenceau's narrative.

78. See Riva Castleman in *Henri de Toulouse-Lautrec: Images of the 1890s,* exh. cat. (New York: The Museum of Modern Art, 1985), 15 and n. 10.

79. Georges Clemenceau, "In Israel," in *At the Foot of Sinai,* trans. A. V. Ende (New York: Bernard G. Richards Company, 1922), 65. (Originally published in Paris by Henri Flouri, 1898, with 16 lithographs by Henri de Toulouse-Lautrec.)

80. Ibid., 62–79, and passim.

81. For the story, see ibid., 39–61.

82. Ibid., 54.

83. See for example his illustrations *Juifs polonais* (LD 240) and *La Prière* (LD 241).

84. Shikes and Harper, *Pissarro,* 308.

85. Cited in ibid., 308.

86. Shikes and Harper and McMullen disagree about whether the letter in question (*Lettres,* CXXXIII), actually refers to Pissarro or whether it refers to some other Jewish friend. Shikes and Harper believe that it refers to Pissarro, nn. 308, 347; McMullen, *Degas,* 444, believes that it does not.

87. According to Ludovic Halévy's son, Daniel, Degas demanded to see his old friend, asked for lots of light and peered intently into the dead man's face, saying "This is indeed the Halévy whom we have always known with the additional grandeur that death gives. This must be kept—recorded." Daniel Halévy, 1965, 105.

88. McMullen, *Degas,* 444.

89, Daniel Halévy, *My Friend Degas,* 111.

90. The incident was recounted by Vollard. See Shikes and Harper, *Pissarro,* 308.

The Literary Significance of the Dreyfus Affair

SUSAN RUBIN SULEIMAN

*May all my works perish, if Dreyfus is not inno-
cent. [. . .] I did not want my country to remain in
lies and injustice. One day, France will thank me for
having helped to save its honor.*
                                        Emile Zola[1]

*What is M. Emile Zola? I look at him in his roots:
this man is not a Frenchman.*
                                        Maurice Barrès[2]

Before it had a literary significance, the Dreyfus Affair had a personal and collective significance for those who lived through it. If writers can lay any claim to being different from other people, it is because they not only live their experiences but transform them, however indirectly, into words; these in turn resonate with the experiences of their contemporaries and of those, writers and readers alike, who come after them. It is surely one of the more notable features of the Dreyfus Affair that the words to which it gave rise—whether in the form of novels, plays, memoirs, historical treatises, polemical essays, or even newspaper articles—still have the power to arouse our passions. Accordingly, the Affair continues to produce yet more writing: Jean-Denis Bredin's recent book, a scrupulously researched history with all the suspense and high color of a thriller, is only one of the latest manifestations of the Affair's continuing resonance and it certainly won't be the last.[3]

In this essay I want to discuss two related but independent questions: What role did the Affair play in French intellectual life (which overlaps with but is not identical to the life of French intellectuals, a category of people whose very existence as such became recognized at the time of the Affair) in the closing years of the nineteenth century and the first half of the twentieth? What fictional representations of the Affair were produced in France during that same period? Both of these are big questions, which an essay such as this can only hope to outline: The first concerns the whole history of modern French political, philosophical, and social thought; the second, although more circumscribed, opens out onto the general question of the relations between history and fiction, between the real and its possible (or impossible) representations. I shall devote more space to the second, for literature is my special interest and field of competence; but an even better reason is that this question (unlike the first, which has received extensive attention) has never been treated in a systematic way, either by literary historians or by literary theorists.[4]

Critical Choices: The Affair and the Intellectuals

"I have often thought that this affair was a good fortune for the men of my generation. . . . One rarely has such an occasion to make a clearcut choice, at the threshold of life, between two fundamental ethics, and to know immediately who one is." So wrote Julien Benda, the famous author of *La Trahison des clercs* (*The Treason of the Intellectuals*, 1927), in the memoirs he undertook when he was close to seventy years old.[5] For him, looking back on it, the Dreyfus Affair marked not only his entry into writing (he published his first essay, which was about the Affair, at age thirty, in the Dreyfusard literary journal, *La Revue blanche*); it also marked, once and for all, the direction of his life and thought—as he puts it, it revealed to him *who he was*. In *La Trahison des clercs*, Benda had argued that the duty of the intellectual was to defend universal values, over and above the politics of the moment. Those who lost sight of this calling by engaging in ordinary political battles, defending merely local or national interests, betrayed their highest obligation and no longer deserved the name of intellectuals. This argument did not prevent Benda from supporting the antifascist cause during the 1930s, just as it had not prevented him from espousing the cause of the Dreyfusards thirty years earlier. But he saw no contradiction there, for according to him what was at stake in both cases was precisely the defense of universal values—truth, justice, intellectual and social freedom—against the particularist doctrines of racism, nationalism, and reasons of State.

As a personality, Benda is not very appealing. The portrait he paints of himself as a young man is that of a haughty, solitary, even priggish, individual with no intimate friends and no strong emotional attachments—passionless, unless one considers his attachment to the ideal of "pure intellect" a kind of passion. At a time when Proust fought duels in defense of Dreyfus, and Léon Blum stopped speaking to an old schoolmate who turned out to be anti-Dreyfusard; when Péguy and others marched and demonstrated; when Anatole France went around giving speeches and Zola willfully faced legal sanctions and public vilification; when friendships were made and unmade over the signing of a petition protesting Dreyfus's innocence, Benda took pride in the fact that "pity for the martyr of Devil's Island played a very small role in my action." Bernard Lazare, whom Péguy called the first and purest Dreyfusard among writers, could proudly proclaim that he had "defended Captain Dreyfus, but also defended justice and freedom."[6] From Benda's point of view, only the last half of that sentence mattered.

If he lacked the kind of personal involvement and passion one finds admirable, especially in a young man, Benda's evolution is nevertheless extremely instructive for anyone who wants to understand the far-reaching effects of the Dreyfus Affair in French intellectual and political life. It is not by chance, nor only because he was a Jew, that Benda was for Dreyfus in 1898 and against fascism in the 1920s and 1930s. Nor, to evoke a different camp, was it by chance that Charles Maurras, a virulent anti-Dreyfusard, became the founder of the ultranationalistic, anti-Semitic Action Française, which maintained its activities throughout the twenties and thirties. Unlike some of the younger men (Georges Brasillach, for example) who came to the Action Française after World War I and eventually ended up glorifying Hitler's Germany (Brasillach was executed in 1945 for his collaborationist writings and activities), Maurras never actively collaborated with the Nazis and was often at odds with the younger, more radical French fascist groups during the interwar years;[7] there is, however, no doubt that the Action Française, which venerated him as "Le Maître," was a first formative influence on many fascists like Brasillach. Maurras himself, already a very old man, became an active supporter of Pétain and the Vichy regime, and never abandoned his authoritarian, anti-Semitic views—views which he had first elaborated in the heat of the battle around Dreyfus. (As late as 1931, he still repeated all the anti-Dreyfusard legends that had been current in his youth: Esterhazy was a poor devil hired by the Jewish "Syndicate" to take the blame for Dreyfus; the Affair was a "Jewish conspiracy" to weaken France, and led directly to the massacres of World War I; Colonel Henry was a great patriot who committed a "heroic forgery," etc.)[8]

It is one indication of the power of the Affair that for all those who were old enough to take a "pro" or "anti" position in it and lived long enough to take a position on the great divisive issues of the interwar period (fascism, racism, colonialism, the Popular Front, the Spanish Civil War), their mature position could practically be deduced from what had been their stance on Dreyfus. Besides Benda and Maurras, these figures included Léon Blum, the Socialist leader and Prime Minister during the Popular Front who had been among the earliest Dreyfusards; and André Gide, who was pro-Dreyfus (although not very actively so) and became antifascist and anticolonialist in the 1930s, positions he did not abandon even after he gave up his "flirtation" with Communism. One possible exception is Paul Valéry, who in 1898 was one of the few writers and the only poet among the Symbolists (the poetic avant-garde of the 1890s) to contribute to the *monument Henry*, a fund established by Drumont's anti-Semitic newspaper, *La Libre Parole*, to help the Colonel's

Figure 1, Cat. 340
Théophile-Alexandre Steinlen
Paris par Emile Zola
Color lithographic poster

widow defray legal expenses for various lawsuits following his suicide. Contributing to the *monument Henry* was one sure indication of violent anti-Semitic as well as anti-Dreyfusard sentiments (true, Valéry did write "not without reflection" on his contribution). Valéry's political sympathies in the 1930s, however, don't seem to have been particularly pronounced one way or the other—although he did visit Mussolini on a trip to Rome in 1933.[9]

What about the others, those who did not live long enough to see the 1930s? These included Zola, Péguy, Proust, Jules Renard, Daniel Halévy, Jean Jaurès, and Clemenceau among the Dreyfusards; Barrès, Bourget, Drumont, Léon Daudet, the poets Coppée and Hérédia, and the critics Lemaître and Brunetière among the "antis." It may be significant that for today's non-French readers, the first list contains more familiar names than the second—and even French readers, who at least know their names, are less likely to have actually read Barrès and Bourget than to have read Zola,

Péguy, or Proust. At the time of the Affair itself, however, only Zola and France among the Dreyfusards were well-known writers; Bourget, Coppée and Hérédia, on the other hand, were members of the Académie Française, and Barrès was soon to be elected. Péguy had not yet published any literary work; Proust had published only a slender collection of stories, *Les Plaisirs et les jours* (which he arranged to have smuggled into Colonel Picquart's prison cell while the latter was detained at the Mont-Valérien in 1898). What conclusion can we draw from these facts? Certainly that the younger generation of writers, whose major work still lay before them, seem to have been more drawn to the Dreyfusard side than were the older, established members of the literary community. In a recent article, Christophe Charle, a literary sociologist in the Bourdieu school, has proposed a more sweeping argument. Noting that those who were "outsiders" to the Establishment (including Zola, who, despite his enormous popular success, was considered too "scandalous" for

Figure 2, Cat. 185
Alfred Le Petit
Counting the Votes (Le Depouillement)
Ink on paper

the Académie) tended to be for Dreyfus, whereas the *Académiciens* and those around them tended to be against him (Anatole France being the one notable exception), Charle concludes that partisanship in the Affair was primarily a struggle for power in the literary field, between the *dominants* who had it and the *dominés* who wanted it.[10] Although this type of argument has a certain appeal, in that if offers a systematic, sociologically determined explanation for political and ideological choices, I find it troubling for that very reason. Ideological choices—which, as Benda so clearly saw, are also existential choices—cannot be explained in purely, or even primarily, sociological terms. Charle understands and acknowledges the importance of the Affair in French public life, but his single explanatory grid produces an oddly skewed effect; for to suggest that people adopted the positions they did exclusively on the basis of self- (or even group) interest is to reduce not only the stature of the people involved, but also the importance of the ideas over which they fought, often with great personal courage and passion.

．　．　．

If one were to look in recent American history for an event even vaguely comparable to the Dreyfus Affair in its national significance, the Vietnam War might be singled out for its power to divide national opinion; the Rosenberg case, however, provides even more points of similarity: Here, as in the Dreyfus Affair, was an accusation of high treason; the protestation of innocence by the accused; a possible miscarriage or corruption of justice; an element of anti-Semitism; international attention and concern; and a strong division between those who were convinced of the accused's innocence (with intellectuals being especially likely to take this view) and those who were convinced of their guilt. One can even, as in the Dreyfus case, take the position espoused by a given individual as an indication of future political choices: Those who demonstrated for the Rosenbergs' release were likely, twenty years later, to demonstrate against the Vietnam War.

Despite these striking surface similarities, however, it is not really fruitful to pursue the parallel; for what makes the Dreyfus Affair so special is that it was the first case of its kind, evoking a national and international furor thanks to the rapid communication made possible by the daily press.

It has often been noted (most recently by Ory and Sirinelli) that without the press, there would not have been an "Affair" as we know it. One has but to think of the explosive effect of Zola's "J'Accuse," first published in *L'Aurore* (13 January 1898), or of the daily fires fueled by sheets like *La Libre Parole* or the Catholic *La Croix*, to recognize the influence of the press in keeping the case before the public.

The Dreyfus Affair, moreover, marked the first time that intellectuals acted as a self-conscious group in attempting to influence public events. Throughout the nineteenth century in France, writers and philosophers had intervened in public affairs: Chateaubriand, Benjamin Constant, and Lamartine all held political posts for a number of years; Vigny served as an officer in the Army; Victor Hugo, after a short time as a deputy, went into exile to protest the coup d'état of Louis-Napoléon and fired broadsides at the "little emperor" for almost twenty years; Jules Vallès was a member of the government of the Commune and had to flee the country in 1871 in order to escape execution. A century earlier, Voltaire had successfully intervened in the Calas Affair (a kind of proto-Dreyfus Affair, with a Protestant victim), and, on a quite different scale, Rousseau and the *encyclopédistes* had expounded ideas (about social organization, individual freedom, and equality before the law) that contributed to the French Revolution. But in all these cases individuals acted on their own, not as part of an organized (or even disorganized) intellectual group. The *encyclopédistes* may appear as an exception, since one can argue that they constituted a genuine intellectual movement; still, when they were active in public affairs (as distinguished from their intellectual activities) it was as individuals, not as members of a group. It was the Dreyfus Affair that inaugurated not only the current usage of the term "intellectual," but also the *collective intervention* of intellectuals, as a self-conscious group, in public affairs. The day after Zola detonated his literary bombshell in *L'Aurore,* there appeared (also in *L'Aurore*) the first of the "protestations" that were soon to be called "protestations des intellectuels," calling for a revision of Dreyfus's trial. These consisted chiefly of lists of names followed by identifying professional tags: professor, writer, architect, member of the Academy (Anatole France was only one), *agrégé*, *licencié* in law, science, liter-

ature, and so on. (*Agregés* and *licenciés* were holders of degrees obtained through advanced examinations.) A few weeks later, in February 1898, the Ligue des Droits de l'Homme was founded, with a steering committee in which university professors were a majority (the Ligue is still in existence). In December of the same year, to prove that not all "intellectuals" were Dreyfusards, two university professors and a number of well-known writers (including the poet François Coppée, the literary critic Jules Lemaître, and the novelist Maurice Barrés) founded the nationalist and anti-Semitic Ligue de la Patrie Française (which became defunct not long after).

In terms of modern history, then, the Dreyfus Affair occupies a privileged inaugural place that makes it incommensurable with later events, like the Rosenberg case, that bear some resemblance to it. This inaugural privilege is not, however, sufficient to account for the importance and the far-reaching effects of the Affair in French intellectual life—effects that the Rosenberg case, to evoke it one last time, did not have in the United States. These must be sought, ultimately, in the issues that the Affair crystallized for several generations of French men and women.

It has become something of a historian's commonplace to see the Dreyfus Affair as a dividing line, or a catalyst that helped draw the dividing line, between two political, ideological, and spiritual "families" in France. Bredin calls the Affair a sign of a permanent division between two temperaments, both of them characteristically French: the defense of order and the defense of individual ethical values. François Goguel, in his book on the political history of the Third Republic, wrote of the Affair as the fountainhead of two broad modern political currents: the "party of order" and "the party of movement" (roughly, conservative and progressive respectively). For my part, I have argued, here and elsewhere, that there was a significant continuity between positions adopted during the Affair and later ideological positions.[11] In fact, it is fascinating to see how certain themes, and even certain repertories of images, survived not only in the writings or discourse of a given individual (that is not, after all, very surprising), but continued in a virtually unbroken line between generations, from their first full elaboration during the Dreyfus Affair right down to the 1930s and beyond. Zola's statement to the jury that con-

122

demned him, that he was fighting for truth and justice, was repeated in virtually identical terms by the writers who signed antifascist declarations in the 1930s and by those who went off to fight for the Spanish Republic. Barrès's statement, in turn, that Zola was "not a Frenchman" (his father was Italian), springs out of a philosophy and an imagery (to be of the "French race," one has to be "implanted" in local French traditions and history; other "races," especially Jews, constitute a harmful "foreign body" in the French organism) that one finds practically unchanged, more than thirty-five years later, in the fascist writings and the major novel, *Gilles*, of Drieu La Rochelle. Indeed, the imagery as well as the xenophobia behind it are still alive in France today, as the demagogic success of Jean-Marie Le Pen and his racist Front National party (which captured ten percent of the seats in the National Assembly in the 1986 elections) demonstrates.

To say all this is to look at the Affair in the perspective afforded by history. What is quite striking is that, at the time of the Affair itself, many of the major participants also saw the issues clearly drawn—not only between "Good" and "Evil," for that was to be expected, each side seeing itself in one role and its opponent in the other, but also between two conflicting philosophies and temperaments, two conflicting visions of the role of intellectuals and of France itself. For Barrès, undoubtedly the most persuasive spokesman for the "patriotic" doctrine, the proper role of intellectuals (whom he saw chiefly as *educators*) was not to evoke abstract principles or Kantian categorical imperatives, but to keep in mind the specific French interests of the moment—and those interests required that the army not be weakened and that the French state be protected from the "enormous power of the Jewish nationality."[12] Intellectuals who relied on universal principles were therefore both wrongheaded and harmful: "The Dreyfus Affair," Barrès wrote at the time of the founding of the Ligue de la Patrie Française, "is an orgy of metaphysicians. They judge everything in the abstract. We judge each thing in relation to France" (p. 80).

This was precisely the kind of statement that prompted Lucien Herr, the Alsatian (Protestant) librarian of the Ecole Normale Supérieure, who enrolled Blum and others among the first group of Dreyfusards, to write his open letter, "A M.

Maurice Barrès." In this letter/essay, published in 1898 in *La Revue blanche*, Herr sets forth a very different conception of the responsibility of intellectuals and of the interests of France:

The French soul was truly great and strong only at those moments when it was both welcoming and giving. You want to bury it in the tetanic stiffness in which rancor and hatred have placed it. The young men whose "semi-culture" you mock know that indeed they don't possess, any more than you do, the whole truth: but they have in them something of the absolute, the faith in a human ideal, and that naive force of generous action which will sweep away absurd hatreds. . . . You have against you both the real people [of France] and the men of thoughtful will. . . , who are capable of allowing right and an ideal of justice to come before their own person, before their natural instincts and their collective egotism.[13]

Against Barrès's passionate defense of "French particularism," here then was an equally passionate defense of universal ideals. In a subsequent issue of *La Revue blanche*, Charles Péguy, who much later was to deplore the moment when the "mystique" of Dreyfusism degenerated into politics, attacked all those, including the Catholic Church (Péguy later became a fervent if unorthodox Catholic) and some members of his own Socialist Party, who did not adopt the cause of truth and innocence. An international conscience had been awakened, Péguy wrote optimistically, and "The Dreyfus Affair will not be the last in which it will pronounce a judgment. For a veritable catholicity of justice, an opinion of the whole inhabited earth is already taking shape."[14]

By 1910, when he wrote *Notre Jeunesse*, Péguy felt (and he was not alone in this) that the high ideals and high hopes for social justice of the first Dreyfusards had been betrayed by the politicians, who had exploited the Dreyfus Affair for specific political ends; Péguy was especially hard on the anticlerical policies of the Combes government, which culminated in the 1905 Law of Separation of Church and State. What even Péguy admitted, however, was that one major positive political result of the Dreyfus Affair had been the consolidation of the Republic.

The details of this political aspect of the Affair need not concern us here. What is worth emphasizing is that the ideological debates of the Af-

Figure 3, Cat. 471
Marcel Proust (seated on left) with
Mme. Geneviève Straus and her
circle, ca. 1898
Photograph

fair, conducted chiefly by writers and intellectuals, led to a complete reshuffling of the political parties and a remapping of the French political landscape. Léon Blum remarked, in his wonderfully readable *Souvenirs sur l'Affaire* (1935), that from the vantage point of the 1930s it seemed natural that the Left had been Dreyfusard and the Right anti-Dreyfusard. But such a view, Blum hastened to add, was an anachronism, an "erreur d'époques": It was not the division between Left and Right parties that had determined the pro- or anti-Dreyfus alignments in the Affair, but the other way around—the Affair had "decomposed the existing combinations and alliances" and thus created the major political division between Left and Right that characterized French parliamentary politics from then on.[15] If Blum's analysis is correct (and one finds a similar analysis in the recent work of some French sociologists), then it suggests one of the truly unique aspects of the Affair in modern history: a case where "it was the professional politicians who reclassified themselves in function of the cleavages created by writers."[16]

Who would have thought that ideas had such power?

Fictions of the Affair

That the Dreyfus Affair gave rise to a great deal of writing, including writing by some of the major literary figures of the late nineteenth and early twentieth century, is indisputable. It is all the more striking to note how few novels or plays come to mind in which the Affair plays a significant role. Proust's *A la recherche du temps perdu*, of course— and his early, unfinished novel, *Jean Santeuil*, as well; Roger Martin du Gard's *Jean Barois*; Anatole France's *Penguin Island* and *Monsieur Bergeret à Paris* (but not many people read these any more); Zola's last novel, *Vérité*, also largely unread today; Romain Rolland's play, *Les Loups*, never performed nowadays and read only by specialists (who are in any case the only ones who will recognize the once obvious references to the Affair). And that's basically it. We can add to this list a few works by less well-known or totally forgotten writers: André Beaunier's *Les Dupont-Leterrier*, subtitled "The Story of a Family during the Affair"; Gabriel Trarieux's *Elie Greuze*, a fictional biography of an intellectual at the time of the Affair; Jean-Richard Bloch's short story, "Lévy," and so on. But seen in the perspective of French literary history, the Affair shines more by its absence in works of fiction than by its presence. It may be true that a single great masterpiece like *A la recherche du temps perdu* (together with a minor masterpiece like *Jean Barois*) is enough to guarantee the Affair a prominent place in the French novel; still, the absence— or certainly the paucity—of fictional representations of the Affair is worth pondering.

The question appears all the more interesting, given that the *history* of the Affair in its day to day unfolding is itself so dramatic, so "novelistic," ranging from the burlesque to the sublime, with a happy ending to boot. As Proust wrote in a letter after Captain Dreyfus's rehabilitation, "It is curious to think that for once, contrary to habit, life is like a novel. . . . Blessed are those who are victims of an error, judicial or other! They are the only human beings to obtain revenge and reparation."[17] Paradoxically, however, the novelistic quality of the real story may also account, to some degree, for its relative lack of fictional representation: since the facts themselves are so gripping, what need is there to fictionalize them? Truth, in this case, is not only stranger but more dramatic than fiction.

Reinforcing this paradox is another one: the many historians who have written detailed accounts of the Affair (starting with Joseph Reinach, who began publishing his seven-volume *Histoire de l'Affaire Dreyfus* in 1901, before the Affair was completely over) have themselves indulged in a great deal of speculation, and what might be called fiction-making, regarding the principal actors, their motives, and the events in which they were involved.[18] All this apart from the fact that there exist, even to our own day, two fundamentally different versions of the facts in the Affair, depending on the allegiance of the historian. Although it may seem impossible that anyone today can still claim Dreyfus guilty, Bredin cites a book published in 1981 which maintains, and even simplifies, the official Army version of the "facts," circa 1898. After all, there are also historians who claim that no crematoria existed at Auschwitz.

It may be tempting to conclude from this, especially if one has a taste for the paradoxes dear to modern literary theorists, that the Affair has not lacked fictional representation; on the contrary, it exists *only* as fictional representation, especially in works that claim to be history! Spinning out the argument, we would end up with a provocative blurring between fiction and nonfiction, indeed between fiction and fact. I will not follow this line, despite my own penchant for modern theorizing, because I believe that certain distinctions are worth maintaining even at the risk of appearing stubbornly empirical and old-fashioned. For example, I want to be able to call fiction, indeed fabrication, not fact, the historian Robert Faurisson's claim that no Jews were incinerated at Auschwitz; at the same time, I would not want to call Faurisson's book a novel.[19]

Maintaining the distinction between novels and non-novels (which, as Faurisson's book shows, is not identical to the distinction between truth and lies), I offer the following hypotheses: For its immediate contemporaries, the Affair needed no *direct* representation in novels—they got plenty of direct representation simply by reading their newspapers; meanwhile, they could appreciate satire, allegory, transposition, and other allusive fictional modes that evoked the Affair rather than directly representing it. As we shall see, almost all of the works I first cited that were written during or just after the Affair rely on such indirect representation.

Another notable feature of those works is that not a single one is written from an anti-Dreyfusard perspective—indeed, all of them are clearly Dreyfusard in their sympathies. This raises an extremely interesting question, which suggests one more reason for the paucity of fictional representations of the Affair by and for its contemporaries: Why is it that a militant anti-Dreyfusard novelist like Barrès, who wrote numerous articles about the Affair (which he later published in a book) and who was also writing his major fictional trilogy, *Le Roman de l'énergie nationale*, during the very years of the Affair, refrained from representing it in a novel? Could it be that for an anti-Dreyfusard writer, the Dreyfus Affair was not *representable in fiction*? Barrès's trilogy is deeply concerned with the representation of contemporary history; the second and third volumes, published in 1900 and 1902, narrate at great length the stories of the Boulanger crisis and of the Panama Scandal, which span the years 1889 to 1893.[20] Although it has been argued that Barrès's way of telling these stories bears the clear stamp of his involvement in the Dreyfus Affair,[21] the significant fact is that the fictional time of the trilogy antedates the historical time of the Affair by several years. It may be no exaggeration to conclude that for an anti-Dreyfusard writer, the Dreyfus Affair simply did not constitute a fictionally narratable story.[22]

It was from a later generation of writers and readers, who no longer had direct involvement in the Affair but were still aware of its importance, that one might expect the kind of interest that produced (or was receptive to) works of fiction in which the Affair would be directly represented and its significance explored. *Jean Barois*, whose author was too young to have taken part in the Affair (Martin du Gard was born in 1881), is just such a work: It is the only important French novel which actually stages some of the major events of the Affair, in quasi-documentary fashion. *A la recherche du temps perdu*, although it treats the Affair very differently than *Jean Barois*, also views the Affair in historical perspective. Proust, ten years older than Martin du Gard, had been actively involved in the Affair; but as we shall see, his narrative stance is that of a distant and dispassionate observer rather than that of a participant.

These two novels, then, each in its own way, succeed in integrating the Dreyfus Affair as historical event into their fictional worlds. It is not an accident, however, that both novels are essentially pre–World War I works. *Jean Barois* was published in 1913. *A la recherche*, although published mostly after the war (only the first volume, which contains no mention of the Affair, appeared in 1913), was conceived well before the war and much of it was written before as well. Although the effects of the Affair on French intellectual and political life were enormous and far-reaching, its representation in French fiction after World War I is virtually nonexistent.

The reasons for this eclipse must be sought both in world history and in French literary history. One need hardly insist on the historical importance of World War I, which ushered in a period of political and economic upheavals that transformed the face of Europe (as well as the rest of the world). Many French writers, especially in the 1930s, responded to these events by getting involved in politics, just as their predecessors had done during the Dreyfus Affair; many wrote novels in the realist mode, in which history played a prominent role: Malraux, Nizan, Drieu La Rochelle, Jules Romains, Aragon, Céline, Brasillach, followed after World War II by Sartre, Camus, Beauvoir—the list is impressive. It is not surprising, however, that these novelists considered 1914, or even 1939, *not* 1898, as their chief historical horizon. During the interwar period, even Martin du Gard shifted his time-frame: The largest part of his multivolume novel, *Les Thibault*, for which he won the Nobel Prize in 1937, is titled *Summer 1914*.

In more strictly literary terms, there is another, not unrelated reason for the Affair's disappearance from fiction: To many of the writers who came of age after World War I, the realist novel, inherited from the bourgeois nineteenth century, appeared as bankrupt as the other values of the age that had produced it. The surrealists, although involved in radical politics during the 1920s and 1930s, were adamant in their refusal of realist fiction; other young writers—Cocteau, Bataille, Queneau, Blanchot, Leiris—whether they were involved in politics or not, devoted their creative energies to the exploration of private obsessions or to experimentation with language games rather than to realist, historically oriented fiction. Although, with the exception of Cocteau, these writers' work remained marginal during the 1930s, their work (again perhaps with the exception of

Cocteau) became the dominant influence on the French literary scene from the 1950s on, when the "nouveau roman" rendered all forms of realism suspect. Over the past few years, the winds have shifted again and a certain realism (telling a story set in a specific time and place) is once again considered respectable in Paris. It is, however, not likely that a belated historical novel about the Dreyfus Affair will soon make its appearance.

.   .   .

After these sketchy speculations about the literary absence of the Affair, I want to return to its presence. In what forms do we find it represented in the French novel, and what do these tell us about the general problem of the relation between history and fiction? Put another way: What are some of the correspondences that works of fiction establish between themselves and certain traumatic historical events? As these questions imply, my discussion here will be typological rather than chronological. I wish to explore certain types of representation and types of fictional discourse "about" history, using the Dreyfus Affair as an exemplary but not unique case.

Allegory. "In the simplest terms, allegory says one thing and means another," writes Angus Fletcher.[23] Like its sister tropes, irony and metaphor, allegory is a veiled, indirect way of saying. Its etymology (Greek *allos*, other; plus *agoreuen*, to speak openly, to speak in the *agora*, or assembly) suggests that allegory is the inversion of the language of the marketplace, where words say what they mean and mean what they say. In allegory, words do not say all that they mean and do not mean only what they say—they also mean something "other." Some modern literary theorists have suggested that *all* language has this double status—that in fact there is no such thing as a language of the marketplace, in which the meaning of words is unambiguous, and totally present to their speakers and listeners. In our post-Freudian age, it would be difficult to contest the validity of this view—if one admits the existence of the unconscious, the rest necessarily follows. Nevertheless, once again, certain distinctions should be made: If all language use is to some degree allegorical (since words never mean all and only what they say), there still exists a particular, self-consciously allegorical use of language that not

only means something "other" than what it says, but points to that something and invites its hearer or reader to look that way. When Orwell writes the story of a group of farm animals who seize power from their exploiters and set up an egalitarian community, which soon degenerates into the worst kind of tyranny, he obviously wants his readers to understand that he is writing something other than a nursery tale. And he can expect his contemporary readers to establish certain equivalences, to *translate* the events and characters of *Animal Farm* into a modern political and historical vocabulary.

Orwell, in other words, is writing a transparent kind of allegory, in which the "veil" over the unstated meaning is easy to penetrate, provided that one has a modicum of historical and human experience. Even to someone who has never heard of the Russian Revolution, or Stalin, or the purges of the 1930s, *Animal Farm* will probably function as an allegory—perhaps of the fate of all political revolutions, or more generally of the human tendency to be corrupted by power. But if one has never heard of revolution and has no conception of human government—if, let us say, one is a five-year-old child—then *Animal Farm* becomes simply a story about talking pigs and horses, and perhaps not a very interesting one at that.

The possible allegorical readings I have just evoked (and there are certainly other possibilities as well) move from a specific, singular set of historical equivalences (the animals' seizure of power equals the Russian Revolution; the pig equals Stalin, etc.) to a generalized statement about people and power. We might hazard the guess that the most successful historical allegories are those that allow for such a wide range of readings, or in any case allow for more than the specific, singular equivalence. The reason for this is obvious: With the passage of time, the specific historical references may fade from knowledge or memory; if new generations of readers are to find pleasure in the allegory, it must be able to accommodate a nonspecific but still meaningful translation. At the same time, one should not underestimate the pleasure to be derived from the highly specific translation that only a detailed knowledge of the historical events makes possible. To readers who possess such knowledge, either because they "were there" or because they have read a lot of history books, it is precisely the close fit between the historical events and their allegorized version (which is also often satirical, as in *Animal Farm*) that demonstrates the author's cleverness—and no doubt their own as well.

Did the Dreyfus Affair have its *Animal Farm*? Yes it did, in Anatole France's *Penguin Island* (1908). The novel as a whole covers wider ground, since it purports to tell the history of "la Pingouinie" (read France) from its earliest times when its inhabitants were waddling birds through their miraculous transformation into humans, right up to "les Temps Futurs," a bleak capitalist dystopia brought to an end by a huge manmade explosion (Anatole France's prophetic soul!) which bombs the country back into the stone age. Thus the novel can be read as a bitter allegorical satire (or satiric allegory) of modern times: One effect of Anatole France's involvement in the Dreyfus Affair was to turn him toward socialist politics and a socialist critique of capitalism.

On its way to the future, *Penguin Island* lingers over some of the better-known episodes of French history. Of these, the longest section is devoted to the Dreyfus Affair. France recounts it, in terms at once precise and burlesque, as "The Affair of the 80,000 Bales of Hay." A Jewish army officer named Pyrot is accused of having stolen the bales of hay in order to sell them to the Marsouins, Penguinia's hereditary enemies. No sooner is Pyrot packed off, protesting his innocence, to a cage on a desert island, than there arises back home a growing group of devoted defenders, the Pyrots or pyrotins. In the army, the Generals Greatuk and Panther (Mercier and Boisdeffre, to those in the know) make sure that plenty of evidence is manufactured against him ("six months later, the evidence against Pyrot filled up two stories of the Ministry of War. The floors caved in under the weight of the dossiers and the landslide of evidence crushed beneath it two department heads, fourteen bureau chiefs and sixty copying clerks").[24] Before too long, however, the brave colonel Hastaing (read Picquart) discovers the real hay-thief, Maubec (read Esterhazy). The famous writer, Colomban ("author of 160 volumes of Penguinian sociology"—Zola, of course), publishes a pamphlet showing that Pyrot is innocent, whereupon mobs roam the streets screaming "Death to Colomban." And so it goes. A certain famous astronomer with his head in the clouds, Bidault-Coquille, also enters the fray—and the reader has the pleasure of identifying, beneath the exaggerated features of this dreamer, Anatole France himself.

One of the chief delights of this whole episode consists in recognizing the equivalences between France's cast of burlesque characters and their no less burlesque adventures, and the heroic or unheroic people and events of the real Affair. It is astonishing how complete a rendering of the Affair France manages to produce in the space of seventy pages, including not only details like the *bordereau* (the document on whose basis Pyrot/Dreyfus is condemned), but also broad social and political phenomena: the prevalence of anti-Semitism, in high places and low; various antirepublican movements which tried to exploit the Affair to their own ends; the ongoing debate within the Socialist party as to whether, and to what extent, the case merited their involvement; the cowardice, and then the opportunism, of the republican politicians who waited to see which way the tide was turning before declaring themselves Dreyfusard, and then used their newly consolidated political power to press their campaign against the Church. Finally, France's account even includes the disillusionment of the early Dreyfusards who discovered that the Affair had produced no profound social changes but rather a return to business and politics as usual—all this without leaving the allegorical/ satiric mode of the narrative or ever mentioning the word "Dreyfus." In short, France succeeds in giving us both a hilarious narrative account (hilarious because so obviously exaggerated, so "unrealistic," yet so closely modeled on the real thing) *and* a serious political interpretation of the Affair, complete with the disenchantment that had set in among the most idealistic of the surviving Dreyfusards—including France himself—by 1908. In terms of cost accounting—the economy of writerly means against the quantity of readerly pleasure—a good allegory ranks high indeed.

Penguin Island and *Animal Farm* are not only allegories but also satires, making sharp criticisms of the way things are (or were) by humorous means. The best political and historical allegories are probably those that have this satiric element, but it is not absolutely necessary. Camus's novel, *The Plague,* for example, is often called an allegory of the resistance to Nazism, or of Europe under Nazi rule. Yet its tone is anything but satiric. It would be interesting to speculate on whether certain historical events lend themselves more or less easily to satiric allegorical treatment—it may be the case, for example, that a phenomenon like Nazism, or the extermination of European Jews, while it *can* accommodate allegory, is too horrendous to accommodate satire. It may produce a kind of desperate absurdist humor, but that is not quite the same thing.

Transposition. What I am calling transposition, or "calque" (from the French *calquer*, to trace; copy; make an impression of) is closely related to allegory in that it is an indirect mode of representation requiring a double reading: The story that is told clearly refers to another, untold story, which it is up to the reader to uncover. In allegory proper, however, the manifest story tends to be fantastical and nonrealist: talking animals, penguins transformed into humans, much ado about bales of hay, or the bubonic plague in Oran in 1940. Such nonrealist elements (which one also finds in classic examples of the genre like *Pilgrim's Progress* or *The Faerie Queene*) function as so many signals pointing to the necessity of an "other" reading. In transposition, by contrast, the manifest story is in the realist mode, but it is presented in such a way that to anyone familiar with the "other" story, its tracing of that story will appear evident—indeed, the manifest story will appear only as a pretext, or an alibi (Latin: "elsewhere") for the other one.

Admittedly, this distinction between allegory and transposition may be tenuous, and in some works may be altogether blurred. We might want, simply, to see both these genres as instances of a symbolic mode. Yet, I can offer at least one "pure" example of a transposition relating to the Dreyfus Affair, which will justify the distinction I am making. Romain Rolland's play, *Les Loups* (*The Wolves*), dedicated to Charles Péguy, was first staged in Paris in May 1898, at the height of the battle for revision of Dreyfus's trial. Zola had already been tried and condemned in civil court for libel (a trial he had explicitly sought in publishing "J'Accuse"), and was awaiting a second trial after the first had been declared illegal on a technicality. Colonel Picquart had been imprisoned for two months and then stripped of his functions at the Ministry of War; anti-Semitic demonstrations were taking place all over France, and in the up-

coming parliamentary elections Jaurès and other Dreyfusards were about to lose their seats while Drumont and several other virulently anti-Semitic candidates were elected. In short, things did not look good for the pro-Dreyfus camp. (It was the discovery of Colonel Henry's forgery, followed by his suicide later that summer, that would turn things around—but that happened several months after the production of *Les Loups*.)

The action of *Les Loups* takes place in Mayence in 1793, at the headquarters of the French Revolutionary Army. No member of the 1898 audience could fail to notice, however, the transposition of recent events in Rolland's historical drama, which recounts the frame-up, on charges of treason, of d'Oyron, one of the officers among the Revolutionaries. The frame-up is manipulated by a demagogic fellow officer, Verrat, a pig butcher in private life, who hates the aristocrat d'Oyron for being "of another race." A third officer, Teulier, who in private life is a distinguished member of the Academy of Sciences (shades of the "intellectual"), discovers the frame-up and the identity of the real traitor, and tries to prevent d'Oyron's execution by the firing squad—this despite the fact that Teulier himself had earlier expressed his antipathy for and distrust of the aristocrat. What motivates Teulier is a desire for truth, independent of his personal feelings. As he states in one of the many speeches of the play that function as transpositions: "I have the principle, at once scientific and republican, of admitting nothing without close examination and believing nothing except what my reason shows me to be evident."[25] Teulier fails, unable to sway his fellow officers, who either adamantly maintain d'Oyron's guilt ("Why does one need proof, when one has one's convictions?" Verrat asks), or else fall back on reasons of state (the verdict of a court-martial in the middle of a war cannot be reversed). The play ends with d'Oyron's off-stage execution, as Verrat and his cohorts shout "Vive la nation" and Teulier sits awaiting his own punishment: He is to be sent before the Committee of Public Safety, on charges of demoralizing the army. But he remains undaunted and proudly proclaims that he would not want to change places with his accusers.

There is no need to insist on the tracing of the Affair's broad outline and major characters by those of *Les Loups*: d'Oyron as Dreyfus, Teulier as Picquart (with a touch of Zola and other intellectuals in his faith in reason and science), Verrat as the anti-Semitic "patriots" of the General Staff, and so on. In the guise of a historical drama situated in a time and place "elsewhere" (but *not* in some fantastic farmyard or Penguinia), Rolland created an accurate, if somewhat pessimistic, version of events he and his contemporaries were witnessing. The sympathies of the play are obviously on Teulier's side, and indeed the Dreyfusards took it up immediately as a statement for their cause. The irony is that by the time *Les Loups* was produced, Rolland himself had resolutely turned his back on the Affair, refusing to sign any pro-Dreyfus declarations and deploring the politicization of French life created by the Affair. What Rolland meant by "politicization," however, was not what Péguy meant by it ten years later, when he decried the degeneration of the Dreyfusard mystique into politics. Rather, Rolland had in mind the "fanaticism" of the early Dreyfusards and the threat that it posed to national unity! Rolland was an unabashed anti-Semite, despite his having a Jewish wife.[26] We recall that his hero, Teulier, had a profound antipathy for d'Oyron and others of his "race." All this notwithstanding, *Les Loups* functioned, in 1898, as a highly effective plea for the Dreyfusard cause.

To today's reader (to this one, at least), *Les Loups* appears more as a curiosity than as a work of intrinsic literary interest. This may be because it functions too exclusively as a transposition and not sufficiently as a genuine historical drama. Whereas a drama like Büchner's *Danton's Death* is of continuing interest because it tries to render, in all its "thickness" and complexity, a historic conflict of tragic proportions, *Les Loups* reduces and thins out the historical past in order to make it illustrate a specific conflict in the author's own time. The historical action is only an alibi, serving an immediate illustrative function; once that function is no longer relevant, the event to which it refers no longer current, the work loses its interest.

Could we say the same thing about the episode of the 80,000 bales of hay in *Penguin Island*? I think not. Even if we overlook the fact that this episode is part of a much longer work with broad symbolic implications, France's burlesque inventions and comic exaggerations do more than merely transpose the Affair for illustrative purposes; they positively transform it, calling attention to the verbal and artistic work (and "play")

of transformation that the text has accomplished. This would suggest that if one wants to represent a historical event in the indirect mode, telling one story by means of another, a frankly nonrealist rendering like that of allegory or myth is a better choice, aesthetically at least, than a "pure" but narrow realist transposition.

Zola's last novel, *Vérité* (1902), offers an interesting confirmation of this hypothesis. The third volume of a planned tetralogy titled "The Four Gospels" (Zola died before completing the project), *Vérité* is not read much today; it and its companion volumes (*Fécondité* and *Travail*) are generally faulted by critics for their overblown style, their lack of verisimilitude, their obvious allegorism. I would argue, however, that it is precisely its nonrealist elements that make *Vérité* interesting—and quite successful—as an indirect representation of the Dreyfus Affair. This is a transposition that increasingly veers off toward allegory, blurring the distinction between the two.

The action begins in a small French town, whose physical and social configurations correspond to Zola's time, circa 1901. A Jewish public school teacher, Simon, is unjustly condemned for the brutal rape and murder of his ten-year-old nephew, who is Catholic and attends a Catholic school run by monks. The real murderer is a teacher in the school, Brother Gorgias, but he is protected by his superiors who use the case as a means of attacking the public schools of the Republic and reinforcing the hold of the Church over the town. The novel's hero, Marc Froment, is a public-school teacher who believes in Simon's innocence and in all the values he sees as being threatened by the Church: faith in reason and science, the search for truth independent of any dogma, the equality of men and women and a healthy attitude toward sexuality, religious tolerance. Besides devoting his life to fighting the Church in the name of these values, Marc leads a crusade (together with Simon's brother and a dedicated lawyer, who call to mind Alfred Dreyfus's brother, Mathieu, and the lawyers Demange and Labori) to establish Simon's innocence. This endeavor lasts Marc's whole life, for it is only many years later, when he is already a great-grandfather, that Simon, now a very old man also, returns in triumph, exonerated, to his home town. Zola uses this mythic (and totally "unrealistic") stretching of time in order to show the complete transformation

Figure 4, Cat. 478
Ludovic, Elie and Daniel Halévy at
the funeral of Emile Zola, 4 October
1902
Photograph

of the town, and of French society, in the interim: By the end of "l'Affaire Simon," Church and State have been separated and all Church property put to public uses; Marc's and Simon's children have intermarried, thus transcending an anti-Semitism of which not even Marc had been completely free; the people of the town have become enlightened, reasonable citizens who would never repeat the obscurantist mistakes and prejudices of the past. In short, a new age has dawned: The time is utopian and the mode allegorical.

Meanwhile, Zola has given us (in more than seven hundred pages!) a detailed transposition of the major events and actors of the Dreyfus Affair as he knew it: The debates over handwriting and the testimony of "experts"; the various forgeries and the *dossier secret* used by the army at both of Dreyfus's trials; the trials themselves, especially the public one at Rennes (here called Rozan); and so on. One thing Zola leaves out, interestingly, is his own "J'Accuse" and its consequences: his hero's biggest exploits are in the classroom, educating generations of schoolchildren. Although there is an episode which can be considered a transposition of "J'Accuse" because of the public outcry against Marc it brings, it has nothing directly to do with the criminal case and therefore doesn't play the same structural role in the story. In addi-

tion, Zola completely rewrites at least one major event in the Affair: Whereas Dreyfus, after his second condemnation, accepted a presidential pardon rather than continuing the fight (which would have meant returning to prison), in Zola's version Simon refuses a pardon and it takes three generations before his innocence is established. (Zola did not live to see the exoneration of Dreyfus in 1906.)

Besides the mythic stretching of time and the larger-than-life heroism attributed to Simon and the other positive characters (the villain Gorgias is presented in similarly exaggerated terms), the novel exceeds the realist frame even in its use of language. Naturalistic descriptions and narration gradually merge with veritable paeans to Reason, Progress, and Truth, as in the following passage near the end:

Glory to the innocent who almost perished by the people's fault, and to whom the people will never give enough joy! Glory to the martyr who suffered so much for the unrecognized, stifled truth, and whose victory is at last that of the human spirit freeing itself from error and falsehood! Glory to the schoolteacher struck down at his work, victim of his effort to attain more light, who is all the more exalted today because he paid with such pain for each parcel of truth taught by him to the ignorant and the humble.[27]

As I suggested earlier, the distinction between (nonrealist) allegory and (realist) transposition is tenuous, and *Vérité* certainly bears that out. However, it also bears out a contention I would argue more strongly; namely, that allegory is a more successful mode for the indirect representation of historical events than is realist transposition. Had Zola simply transposed the Dreyfus Affair into a criminal case, with no allegorical overtones of the kind I have mentioned, *Vérité* might have been shorter and more "realistic," but it would have retained little *raison d'être* after the passions of the moment had died down.

Mimetic Representation. In both allegory and realist transposition, the historical event is never mentioned explicitly. No matter how obvious the equivalences between the manifest story and the untold story, it is still left up to the reader to make the necessary translation. In both cases, therefore, we are dealing with a symbolic, not mimetic, representation of the historical event: The reader is called upon to "see double"; to read the historical event back into its displaced, symbolic representation. As I suggested earlier, this kind of double reading is especially easy, and pleasurable, for an audience that is close enough to the historical event to recognize it even though it is never named.

In mimetic representation, by contrast, no such double reading is required: The fictional text (whether novel or play) functions not as a funhouse mirror offering a grossly distorted and/or displaced version of the "real." Rather, it functions (or purports to function) more like a trustworthy camera lens, providing an accurate picture of the historical event and its spatiotemporal context. As we might expect, there is a great variety of possible angles and perspectives even for such an apparently objective mode of representation, giving rise to quite different fictional "takes" on history and on public events in general. Pursuing the photography metaphor, we might use as distinguishing criteria what the camera focuses on and the camera's angle and distance in relation to its object. As concerns the Dreyfus Affair, there exists an interestingly wide range of mimetic representations. I shall discuss two broad types: the documentary and the depiction of effects.

In documentary representation, the focus is chiefly on the historical event (in this case, the Dreyfus Affair) as a significant action in its own right. Like novelized biographies of famous historical figures, the documentary novel or play claims to give a faithful account of the historical event: Its aim is to inform accurately, even while taking certain fictional liberties—representing the private thoughts of historical characters, for example, or recreating events for which there exist no detailed historical accounts, or, going one step further, introducing fictional characters who are shown participating in the historical event and interacting with historical figures.[28] This kind of representation is rarely found contemporaneously with the event, for two reasons: First, a "complete picture" is not possible without a certain temporal distance; second, contemporaneous readers do not need this kind of informative representation, since they are living in the midst of the event and can get their information from their daily newspapers (or, today, from their television sets).

Obviously, later readers can get their information from historical accounts as well, rather than relying on plays and novels—and indeed, as I mentioned earlier, the Dreyfus Affair has received more than its share of attention from historians, whose works often have the shape (as well as, occasionally, the inventiveness) of fiction. Nevertheless, there remains a public for the hybrid genre of the documentary novel or play, which is neither altogether fact nor altogether fiction and which provides information about past history in a fairly painless way. In its simplest form, such a work is intended for children or adolescents: Thus a recent novel by Bertrand Solet, *Il était un capitaine* (1972), tells the "complete" story of the Dreyfus Affair in less than two hundred pages, covering all of its major incidents from Dreyfus's arrest in 1894 to his rehabilitation in 1906, and managing to tell at the same time the love story of a fictional Parisian journalist who covers the Affair and eventually takes a small part in it as an ardent Dreyfusard. In its paperback version, the novel is explicitly designated as written for adolescents (age thirteen and up), and comes complete with illustrations. It is simply told and simply conceived; ambiguity and complications, whether of plot or of sentence structure, are kept to a minimum. At the same time, the history is generally accurate and the work claims such accuracy for itself by means of occasional footnotes (identifying certain historical figures or giving the source of a quotation) and a list of "works consulted" at the end.[29]

Admittedly, this kind of novelized history for young people or lazy readers (the hardback version of Solet's novel appeared in a historical series with a nonspecified audience) represents one extreme of the documentary genre. But I think that it illustrates, perhaps because of its very simplicity, the continuing appeal of the genre. The novelization of history makes it conform to familiar patterns of storytelling and characterization—hero, villain, betrayal, courageous action—which provide pleasure because they are familiar. The result may be banalization and trivialization, such as we have seen recently in telefilm versions of the Holocaust, for example. But as the popular success of those films demonstrates, the appeal of the genre is immense, even when it deals with historical events that are extremely painful to contemplate. Despite the trivialization that seems endemic to the enterprise, one could argue that it is better to have large numbers of people think about such events in fictionalized documentary terms than not at all.

Both the effectiveness and the appeal of this kind of representation were demonstrated, in the case of the Dreyfus Affair, by a play produced in Paris in 1931, which eventually had to be closed down because of violent protests outside the theater by members of the Action Française. The play, titled *L'Affaire Dreyfus*, was a French translation, by Jacques Richepin, of a work by two German authors, Hans J. Rehfisch and William Herzog.[30] It focused not on the Affair in its entirety but on its most dramatic few months, from the acquittal of Esterhazy in January 1898 (which provoked Zola's "J'Accuse") to Colonel Henry's suicide in August of that year. The major historical figures of the Affair, including army officers like Henry, Esterhazy, Boisdeffre, and Picquart, writers and journalists like Zola and Clemenceau, and political figures like Jaurès, are directly represented on stage, as are well-known events like the Zola trial of February 1898 or the discovery of Henry's forgery by an officer in the war ministry in August. A preface by Richepin claims absolute historical accuracy for the events represented; in the scenes of the Zola trial, the actual published transcripts were used as part of the dialogue. In other scenes, the authors took liberties—as when they show a love scene in prison between Picquart and his beloved cousin, for example, or present a private conversation between Esterhazy and his mistress. The chief focus of the play, however, is not

on private but on public events; the general effect is to leave no doubt about the innocence of Dreyfus; the heroism of Zola, Picquart, and other Dreyfusards; the villainy of Esterhazy, and the misguided patriotism of Henry.[31] Small wonder that the radical Right found the play objectionable, and feared it sufficiently to prevent it from being seen.

The best-known work of documentary-style fiction about the Dreyfus Affair is Roger Martin du Gard's *Jean Barois* (1913). Unlike the Richepin play, whose sole subject is the Affair, and unlike the children's novel, which arbitrarily yokes together the "human interest" story of the fictional journalist and a flat narrative account of the Affair, *Jean Barois* integrates the historical event into its fictional world by making it a turning point in the hero's life. Presented as a series of dramatic scenes consisting chiefly of dialogue, the novel recounts the life of a French intellectual confronted with the major challenge of his generation: the crisis of faith. Jean Barois, born in 1866, is the son of a doctor who believes only in scientific progress; by contrast, Barois's grandmother, who brought him up, is a devout Catholic. Barois himself, after years of soul searching, spends his active adult life fighting against the obscurantism of revealed religion and proclaiming the religion of progress. Although in his old age, sick and fearing death, he returns to the Church, the novel presents this as a capitulation. Barois' heroic years are those he spends writing books, giving speeches, and editing a journal he had founded with a group of like-minded friends in 1896. It is significant that the first major battle he and his friends engage in is precisely the Dreyfus Affair: In their journal, *Le Semeur* (*The Sower*), they are the first to publish an "open letter to the French people" by Luce, a well-known older intellectual, calling for a reopening of the case in 1897. This brings them immediate notoriety, and from then on *Le Semeur* becomes a major voice among the Dreyfusards and in French intellectual life in general.

Now obviously, the journal *Le Semeur* never existed. Martin du Gard accomplishes a daring, if quite problematic, blending of fiction with documentation here, as elsewhere in the novel. Luce's open letter titled "Conscience," for example, is a kind of fictional double of Zola's "J'Accuse"; at the same time, Martin du Gard inserts the real "J'Accuse" into the fiction by having Barois and his friends comment on it a few days after its publication, and then actually quoting part of it in the narrative, complete with a footnote.[32] In the same way, he sends the *Semeur* group to attend the Zola trial of February 1898; a footnote informs the reader that the trial scene "reproduces scrupulously the stenographic transcript of the tenth hearing" and even gives page references to the published transcript (p. 262). Two pages later, however, still in the midst of this same scene, we find Barois and another fictional character exchanging remarks and gesticulating next to Zola's lawyer, Labori. The novel thus literally inserts the invented characters and their words into the otherwise factual transcript. In later scenes, Barois and his friends discuss Colonel Henry's suicide (August 1898) and report in detail on Dreyfus's trial in Rennes (August 1899); later still, some members of the group comment with disenchantment on the transformation of the original "dreyfus*istes*" into what they see as the merely political "dreyfus*ards*." They thus echo, without actually quoting them, the ideas developed around 1910 by Péguy and other writers associated with the *Cahiers de la quinzaine*—a journal founded in 1901, which incidentally has several points in common with the fictional *Le Semeur*.

Martin du Gard's blending of fiction and fact is extremely interesting and deserves further study. What seems particularly significant in the present context is that for several generations of readers, this novel has functioned as their first reliable source of information about the Dreyfus Affair. It presents the highlights of the Affair in a vivid way for which it claims both fictional affect and documentary accuracy. As Emmanuel Berl, a well-known intellectual of the 1930s, once remarked, reading *Jean Barois* had transformed him and others like him (too young to have experienced the Affair directly) into "Dreyfusards by delayed action," *dreyfusards à retardement.*[33]

Returning once again to the photography metaphor, we can say that in documentary fiction the camera is trained at least part of the time on the Affair itself as object. Even *Jean Barois*, which is quite selective in what it shows and tells and which filters events through the eyes of Barois and his friends, nevertheless *represents* certain major events like the Zola trial or Dreyfus's trial at Rennes. In what I call "depiction by effects," in contrast, the camera is trained not on the Affair but only on

the reactions and results it produces. The Affair is thus not an object of representation *by* the fiction, but an object of representation *in* the fiction: People discuss it, fight over it, are transformed by it, and these discussions and transformations, like so many shadows cast by the Affair, are what we are given to see.

If allegory and transposition are particularly suitable for readers who are close to the historical event, and documentary fiction suitable for readers who are far from it, fiction that represents effects seems equally appropriate for both. Indeed, two of the best-known novels in which the Affair figures prominently belong in this category, and are situated at opposite ends of the temporal spectrum: Anatole France's *Monsieur Bergeret à Paris* was published in 1902, but most of it had already appeared in weekly installments in *Le Figaro* starting in July 1899; Marcel Proust's *A la recherche du temps perdu* was published (save for the first volume, which appeared in 1913) between 1918 and 1925. Despite the enormous difference in scope and style (to say nothing of quality) between these two novels, they share a common approach to the historical event; for what interests both France and Proust as novelists is not the event as such, but its repercussions on individuals and on French society as a whole.

Monsieur Bergeret à Paris is the last volume of a tetralogy France began in the early 1890s, under the general title of *Histoire contemporaine*. As the title implies, France was here attempting the rare and interesting feat of writing a "history of his times" contemporaneously with its unfolding. The first two volumes, (*L'Orme du Mail* and *Le Mannequin d'osier*), published in 1896 and 1897, contain no mention of the Affair. Instead, we have a rather weak plot line turning around the question: "Who will be named Bishop of Tourcoing?" In a manner reminiscent of Balzac's *Le Curé de Tours*, which also turns around the question of a clerical appointment, France uses this plot to explore the ins and outs of provincial politics (the two rival candidates both live in the same provincial capital and have different factions on their side), as well as the broader problem of relations between Church and State, which were becoming increasingly strained in France during the 1890s.

At the outset of the third volume (*L'Anneau d'Améthyste*, published in 1901 but serialized starting in 1897), the Bishop's appointment has still not been made; however, France has enlarged his political field to include Paris, and has also developed a subplot concerning the domestic life and the daily work life of the classics professor, Bergeret, whose appointment to a teaching position at the Sorbonne became the starting point of *Monsieur Bergeret à Paris*. Most important for our purposes by this third volume we find frequent mentions of the Affair: It is discussed in the provincial salons, which are unanimously in favor of the army, as well as by Bergeret and another professor, the only two people in town who think that Dreyfus is innocent. In the meantime, the "ordinary citizens" of the town take up the habit of "going to break some windows at Meyer's shoe-store, out of respect for the Army," and shouting "Death to Zola"[34]—we are in January 1898.

By the time France reaches the last volume, *Monsieur Bergeret à Paris*, the Affair occupies almost the entire fictional terrain—which is all the more extraordinary, given that not a single event of the Affair is directly represented in the novel. Instead, France multiplies the occasions for discussion of the Affair within the fiction by moving Bergeret to Paris: Here we see a provincial aristocrat come to consult Bergeret about his son's education and giving him his views about "the traitor" into the bargain (chap. 5); a class-conscious carpenter who praises Bergeret for his Dreyfusard views while constructing the bookshelves for his new apartment (chap. 7); an old schoolmate who gloatingly informs Bergeret that the anti-Dreyfusard press is printing defamatory articles about him (chap. 14), and so on. France indulges in a private wink to the reader by having Bergeret read one of his [that is, France's] own *Figaro* articles as he sits in the Luxembourg Gardens; the article is reprinted verbatim, but without mention of its author's name (chap. 13).[35]

In addition, France devotes considerable space to a new subplot involving the political conspiracy of a small royalist group, who attempt (without success) to exploit the Affair in order to overthrow the Republic: Here France is relying on his readers' knowledge of an actual failed coup, led by the rabble-rousing poet, Paul Déroulède—the "coup de la caserne de Reuilly," which occurred in February 1899. In my terms, this new subplot is an example of realist transposition rather than of mimetic representation. France also introduces a kind of satirical allegory that foreshadows *Penguin*

Island, by having Bergeret "discover" a sixteenth-century volume that recounts, in an archaic French modeled on Rabelais, the doings of a group of "Trublions" (*troublion*: troublemaker) who ally themselves with the Army and the Church to sow discord in the kingdom. Aside from the opportunity for playfulness and linguistic virtuosity that this pastiche allows him, France is once again counting on his readers' everyday knowledge to translate the allegory into contemporary terms. *Monsieur Bergeret à Paris* thus offers a multilayered representation of the Affair, consisting not only of mimetic depiction by effects, but also of transposition and allegory.

It would be interesting to study in detail the changes France made between the serialized version of the novel printed in *Le Figaro* at what was still the height of the Affair (1899–1900), and the final version published in 1902. My own impression, based on the comparison of a few key chapters, is that besides reordering and cutting (the order of the chapters printed in *Le Figaro* was changed in the novel and some chapters were omitted altogether), France toned down the explicitly polemical aspects of his *Figaro* pieces in favor of a more distant, ironic (albeit still pro-Dreyfusard) perspective in the final version. It is as though, by the time France published the novel, he was aiming for a more detached, less immediately engaged vision of "contemporary history"—which, one could well argue, novelists with an eye toward posterity have always tried to do.

That remark brings me, finally, to *A la recherche du temps perdu*. Proust's great novel is not only the most enduring work of French (or any other) literature in which the Affair figures prominently; it is also the only such work which views the Affair in a post–World War I perspective. Proust's narrator is able to see the Affair both as part of *his* "contemporary history" (the bulk of the novel's action takes place between 1895 and 1905, during the narrator's young manhood) and as part of a past forever gone—swept away by the cataclysm of the war and, even more importantly in Proustian terms, by the merciless advance of Time. The narrator who speaks to us from the very beginning of the novel is already an old man on the verge of death; he has seen all, experienced all; his view of the passions of his youth, whether amorous or political, is like that of someone looking through a telescope: sharp, clear, and infinitely distant.

In *Jean Santeuil,* the unfinished novel he was working on during the years of the Affair (and which remained unpublished until 1952, thirty years after his death), Proust devoted a number of documentary fragments to the Affair, especially to the Zola trial which he himself assiduously attended: The hero of *Jean Santeuil* is an ardent Dreyfusard who spends his days in court and his nights in the cafés discussing each day's testimony. By the time he wrote *A la recherche du temps perdu,* Proust attributed this passionate involvement not to his protagonist but to the latter's friend, the slightly buffoonish Jewish intellectual, Bloch:

He would arrive there in the morning and stay until the court rose, with a supply of sandwiches and a flask of coffee, as though for the final examination for a degree, and this change of routine stimulating a nervous excitement which the coffee and the emotional interest of the trial worked up to a climax, he would come away so enamoured of everything that had happened in court that when he returned home in the evening he longed to immerse himself again in the thrilling drama and would hurry out to a restaurant frequented by both parties in search of friends with whom he would go over the day's proceedings interminably and make up, by a supper ordered in an imperious tone which gave him the illusion of power, for the hunger and exhaustion of a day begun so early and unbroken by any interval for lunch. The human mind, hovering perpetually between the two planes of experience and imagination, seeks to fathom the ideal life of the people it knows and to know the people whose life it has had to imagine.[36]

This passage, which I have chosen practically at random from among the dozens and dozens devoted to discussions or evocations of the Affair in the novel, is a good indication of Proust's telescope vision. We have a beautifully sharp and detailed account of Bloch's activity and passion, but it is presented by a narrator who is seeing it from a great emotional distance. The overall effect is comical—not because Bloch's motives are impugned in any way (his passion is sincere, that is clear), but because the narrator's attitude is so detached, I am tempted to say so Olympian (note grand generalization with which the passage concludes) that we cannot help seeing Bloch as somewhat ridiculous. From the perspective of the gods, all human passions unfold as comedy.

Indeed, it is chiefly as human comedy, but of the highest and most serious kind (Proust was not an admirer of Balzac's *La comédie humaine* for nothing), that the Affair's effects and significance are studied and brilliantly analyzed in Proust's novel. Perhaps the most original, and unique, aspect of Proust's approach is that he uses the Affair as a peg on which to hang broad (and deep) generalizations about human nature, society, and finally about time and history. He shows not only the enmities and alliances, the psychological quirks and rationalizations, the social ups and downs, and the comedies of manners produced by the Affair; he also presents these phenomena as manifestations of general "truths" whose application extends far beyond this single historical event.

Take the psychology of partisanship, for instance. The duc de Guermantes, a not very intelligent but extremely arrogant aristocrat, is a self-righteous anti-Dreyfusard . . . until the day he goes to take the waters at a health resort and meets "three charming ladies" who impress him as being more intelligent than he, and who convince him with miraculous speed that "they can't keep a man in prison who has done nothing." The duke returns to Paris a "fanatical Dreyfusard," to the reader's comic delight. But the Proustian narrator is not content to leave it at that. "And of course," he remarks, "we do not suggest that the three charming ladies were not, in this instance, messengers of truth. But it is to be observed that, every ten years or so, when we have left a man imbued with a genuine conviction, it so happens that an intelligent couple, or simply a charming lady, comes into his life and after a few months he is won over to the opposite camp." Then the narrator generalizes even further, moving from individual to national psychology: "And in this respect there are many countries that behave like the sincere man, many countries which we have left full of hatred for another race and which, six months later, have changed their minds and reversed their alliances" (II, 767).

Another example: The narrator remarks about his old friend Swann—who, unlike the duc de Guermantes, is supremely intelligent—that "Swann's Dreyfusism had brought out in him an extraordinary naïvety," since "he subjected all his admirations and all his contempts to the test of a new criterion, Dreyfusism" (II, 604, 605). This specific observation is developed and substantiated by Swann's words and actions on several occasions, which the narrator recounts in some detail; but it is also generalized, in two different ways: First, Swann is typical of all other partisans of the case, Dreyfusards and anti-Dreyfusards alike, who judge everything by the criterion of "Dreyfusism." Second, his new way of choosing his friends and enemies is typical of a general tendency in human nature: "In reality we always discover afterwards that our adversaries had a reason for being on the side they espoused, which has nothing to do with any element of right that there may be on that side, and that those who think as we do do so because their intelligence, . . . or their uprightness, . . . has compelled them" (II, 738).

What Proust does for individuals, he also does for social groups. Thus, he shows in great (and often comic) detail how the affair helps Odette and other anti-Dreyfusard hostesses who would normally never be received by the high aristrocracy, to penetrate the Faubourg St. Germain. Madame Verdurin, on the other hand, suffers a temporary setback in her social climbing during the Affair, for her salon is Dreyfusard. Along with these details concerning individuals, Proust's narrator also gives us, from his Olympian perspective, some coruscating social generalizations. Thus: "Social people who refuse to allow politics into their world are as far-sighted as soldiers who refuse to allow politics to permeate the army. . . . The reason that they were Nationalists gave the Faubourg Saint-Germain the habit of entertaining ladies from another class of society; the reason vanished with Nationalism, but the habit remained" (III, 236–237). Or, even more far-reachingly, these remarks concerning Madame Verdurin:

Mme. Verdurin, thanks to Dreyfusism, had attracted to her house certain writers of distinction who for the moment were of no use to her socially, because they were Dreyfusards. But political passions are like all the rest, they do not last. New generations arise which no longer understand them; even the generation that experienced them changes, experiences new political passions which, not being modelled exactly upon their predecessors, rehabilitate some of the excluded, the reason for exclusion having altered. . . . It was thus that, from each political crisis, from each artistic revival, Mme. Verdurin had picked up one by one, like a bird building its nest, the several scraps,

temporarily unusable, of what would one day be her Salon. The Dreyfus case had passed, Anatole France remained. (III, 237)

Generalizations of this scope are only possible for one who is viewing things from very far indeed. And the further we advance in the novel, the more daring and sweeping they become. By the last volume, when the fictional time has almost caught up with the time of narration and World War I has become part of the novel's action, we find analyses and generalizations that bear not only on the vagaries of individual psychology or social change, but on the meaning of historical memory itself:

So the Dreyfusism of M. Bontemps, invisible and constitutional like that of every other politician, was no more apparent than the bones beneath the skin. No one troubled to remember that he had been a Dreyfusard, for people in society are scatter-brained and forgetful and, besides, all *that* had been a very long time ago, a "time" which these people affected to think longer than it was, for one of the ideas most in vogue was that the pre-war days were separated from the war by something as profound, something of apparently as long a duration, as a geological period, and Brichot himself, that great nationalist, when he alluded to the Dreyfus case now talked of "those prehistoric days." . . . The words Dreyfusard and anti-Dreyfusard no longer had any meaning then. But the very people who said this would have been dumbfounded and horrified if one had told them that probably in a few centuries, or perhaps even sooner, the word Boche would have only the curiosity value of such words as *sans-culotte, chouan* and *bleu*. (III, 748–749)

Here Proust gives us not only the long historical perspective that was impossible for a France or a Martin du Gard, writing before the war; he also furnishes, indirectly, an explanation for why no other novel, after his own, devoted sustained attention to the Dreyfus Affair: "Prehistoric" times, as Brichot put it, lack novelistic interest.

Perhaps the most radical, and paradoxical, observations about the Affair and about history come even later, close to the very end of the novel, when the narrator-hero sits meditating in the Guermantes' library about the novel he will finally write (and which is possibly the novel we have been reading). As often happens in *A la re-*

cherche, the narrator's own conclusions are first announced, in a disguised form, by or about another character with whom he has a curious affinity—the baron de Charlus. Earlier, while walking down the Champs-Elysées with the baron one night during the war, the narrator remarked:

M. de Charlus still retained all his respect and all his affection for certain ladies who were accused of defeatism, just as he had in the past for others who had been accused of Dreyfusism. He regretted only that by stooping to meddle in politics they had given a handle to the 'polemics of the journalists'. . . . So systematic was his frivolity that for him birth, combined with beauty and with other sources of prestige, was the durable thing and the war, like the Dreyfus case, merely a vulgar and fugitive fashion (III, 812).

For Charlus, public events like the war and the Dreyfus Affair (that is, history) were less important than his own respect for beauty and high birth. Translated into aesthetic terms, this is precisely the theory that we find the narrator developing in his meditation in the library. The only kind of book that is worth writing, he maintains, is the "inner book of unknown signs" that is within each human being and that only an act of artistic creation can "decode." But the task is difficult, and the temptation to avoid it great: "Every public event, be it the Dreyfus case, be it the war, furnishes the writer with a fresh excuse for not attempting to decipher this book" (III, 913).

History, in other words, is not what really matters and is not the true subject of art: Had not Swann, that other alter ego of the narrator, stated at the very beginning of the novel that newspapers should be switched with great books, the latter to be read every day and the former only every few years?

One might see in this final relegating of history to second place, far behind the sanctuary of Art, a sign of Proust's aestheticism, an elevated form of snobbery. Proust has never appealed much to those hardheaded realists, Marxist or other, for whom History (written with a capital H) is the touchstone of value; and indeed, his "religion of Art," if taken as itself an absolute value, cannot but be problematic, especially in the perspective of the late twentieth century. But *A la recherche du temps perdu* is far too complex and self-contradic-

tory a work to be pinned down to any simple conclusion. If it contests the value of history, and the value of fiction that sets as its chief task the representation of social reality, it does so in a profoundly paradoxical way. For as its treatment of the Dreyfus Affair indicates, Proust's novel can be read *both* as a subversion of history *and* as a superb historical analysis of the interrelations among public events, individual psychology, and social change. Apart from its other qualities, its value for us today may reside in that salutary self-contradiction.[37]

Notes

1. Emile Zola, "Déclaration au Jury," in *L'Affaire Dreyfus: La Vérité en marche* (Paris: Garnier-Flammarion, 1969), 134. Originally published in *L'Aurore*, 22 February 1898. Unless otherwise indicated, all translations from the French are my own.
2. Maurice Barrès, "Les Intellectuels ou logiciens de l'absolu," in *Scènes et doctrines du nationalisme* (Paris: Félix Juven, 1902), 40.
3. Jean-Denis Bredin, *The Affair: The Case of Alfred Dreyfus*, trans. Jeffrey Mehlman (New York: Braziller, 1986). Bredin's book appeared in France in 1983, and was a bestseller. Among the many responses it elicited, see Maurice Blanchot, "Les intellectuels en question," *Le Débat* no. 29 (March 1984), 3–28.
4. There exist very few books on literature and the Dreyfus Affair, and none at all on the more specific question I will be treating here. For an informative but outdated study, see Cécile Delhorbe, *L'Affaire Dreyfus et les écrivains français* (Paris: Victor Attinger, 1932); more recently, see the collective volume, *Les Ecrivains et l'Affaire Dreyfus*, ed. Géraldi Leroy (Presses Universitaires de France, 1983). Victor Brombert's *The Intellectual Hero: Studies in the French Novel, 1880–1955* (Chicago: University of Chicago Press, 1960) remains of interest and contains an excellent discussion of the Dreyfus Affair's influence on French fiction in its opening chapters. For more general recent discussions of the role of intellectuals (including university professors) in the Dreyfus Affair, see Antoine Compagnon, *La Troisième République des lettres, de Flaubert à Proust* (Paris: Editions du Seuil, 1983),

and Pascal Ory and Jean-François Sirinelli, *Les Intellectuels en France, de l'Affaire Dreyfus à nos jours* (Paris: Armand Colin, 1986).

5. Julien Benda, *La Jeunesse d'un clerc* (Paris: Gallimard, 1936), 204. Further page references to this edition will be given in parentheses in the text.

6. See Bernard Lazare, *Une Erreur judiciaire: L'Affaire Dreyfus* (Paris: Stock, 1897), 64.

7. For a detailed discussion, see Zeev Sternhell, *Ni droite ni gauche: L'idéologie fasciste en France* (Paris: Editions du Seuil, 1983), especially chap. 3.

8. See Charles Maurras, *Au signe de Flore: Souvenirs de vie politique* (Paris: Les Oeuvres Représentatives, 1931), 51–120.

9. On the *monument Henry*, see Bredin, *The Affair*, 350–353; also Stephen Wilson, "Le Monument Henry: La structure de l'anti-sémitisme en France, 1898–1899," *Annales ESC* March-April 1977:265–291. Valéry's visit to Mussolini is mentioned very briefly in Agathe Rouart-Valéry's biographical introduction to his complete works—see Valéry, *Oeuvres*, vol. I (Paris: Bibliothèque de la Pléiade, 1957), 59.

10. Christophe Charle, "Champ littéraire et champ du pouvoir: Les écrivains et l'Affaire Dreyfus," *Annales ESC* March-April 1977:240–264.

11. See Bredin, *The Affair*, 543–544; François Goguel, *La Politique des partis sous la Troisième République* (Paris: Editions du Seuil, 1946); Susan Rubin Suleiman, *Authoritarian Fictions: The Ideological Novel as a Literary Genre* (New York: Columbia University Press, 1983), 68–69.

12. Barrès, "Position de la question Dreyfus," in *Scènes et doctrines du nationalisme*, 34. Subsequent references to this collection of essays will be given in parentheses in the text.

13. Lucien Herr, "A M. Maurice Barrès," *La Revue blanche* Tome XV, January-April 1898:244.

14. Charles Péguy, "L'Affaire Dreyfus et la crise du parti socialiste," *La Revue blanche* Tome XX, September-December 1899:130.

15. See Léon Blum, *Souvenirs sur l'Affaire* (Paris: Gallimard, 1935), 101–109.

16. Christophe Charle, "Champ littéraire et champ du pouvoir," 242.

17. Marcel Proust, letter of 21 July 1906, to Madame Straus; in *Correspondance de Marcel Proust,* vol. VI, ed. Philip Kolb (Paris: Plon, 1980), 159.

18. For a good overview of the historiography of the Affair, see Bredin, *The Affair*, 506–515.

19. Robert Faurisson, *Mémoire en Défense: contre ceux qui m'accusent de falsifier l'Histoire* (Paris: La Vieille Taupe, 1980). Nancy Huston has trenchantly observed to me that some novels "tell the truth" even though they are not factual, whereas Faurisson's book, even while not being a novel, tells lies. I wish to thank her for this observation.

20. The Boulangist movement (1889-1891), united around the enormously popular General Boulanger, came close to overthrowing the Republican regime—Barrès himself was elected as a Boulangist deputy in 1889. The Panama Scandal (1892–1893) implicated a number of republican deputies and again came near to toppling the regime. Barrès was vitriolic (and virulently anti-Semitic) in his account of the scandal, which occupies all of *Leurs Figures* (1902), the last volume of his trilogy. The second volume, devoted to Boulanger, is entitled *L'Appel au soldat* (1900). For a detailed discussion of the trilogy and its relation to contemporary history, see my *Authoritarian Fictions*, 118–132.

21. See in particular Zeev Sternhell, *Maurice Barrès et le nationalisme français* (Paris: Armand Colin, 1972), 110 and passim.

22. Another important right-wing novelist one can cite in this regard is Paul Bourget, whose novel, *L'Etape* (1902), recounts the "conversion" of a young anticlerical Dreyfusard intellectual to Catholicism and right-wing politics. Curiously, Bourget never actually *names* the Affair but refers to it (only once) as "a highly publicized judicial affair" which "served as a pretext for an ill-fated civil war" (Paris: Plon, 1902, vol. I, 13–14). Although the action takes place in 1900 and 1901, Bourget never makes any further mention of the Affair—this despite the fact that his novel's thesis is barely comprehensible without it. (I discuss *L'Etape* at length in *Authoritarian Fictions*, chap. 2.)

23. Angus Fletcher, *Allegory: The Theory of a Symbolic Mode* (Ithaca and London: Cornell University Press, 1964), 2.

24. Anatole France, *L'Ile des Pingouins* (Paris: Calmann-Levy, 1908), 302.

25. Romain Rolland, *Les Loups* (Paris: Albin Michel, 1925), 81.

26. For a discussion of Rolland's complex attitudes toward the Dreyfus Affair and of his anti-Semitism, see Antoinette Blum, "Romain Rolland: face à l'affaire Dreyfus," *Relations Internationales*, 14 (1978):127–141.

27. Emile Zola, *Vérité* (Paris: Fasquelle, 1957), 705.

28. I am using the term "documentary" here in a quite specific sense, to designate a novel or play that focuses—if not exclusively, at least to a significant degree—on a historical event, and which claims factual accuracy for its representation of the event. A somewhat broader use of the term is made by Barbara Foley in her long and interesting recent study, *Telling the Truth: The Theory and Practice of Documentary Fiction* (Ithaca and London: Cornell University Press, 1986).

29. Bertrand Solet, *Il était un capitaine* (Paris: Laffont, 1972). The children's version is in the *Livre de poche* "Jeunesse" series (Hachette, 1979).

30. Hans J. Rehfisch and Wilhelm Herzog, *L'Affaire Dreyfus*, version française en 3 actes et 10 tableaux de Jacques Richepin. (Paris: Albin Michel, 1931). The closing of the play because of the Action Française demonstrations is recounted in Richepin's preface; it is also told in Eugen Weber, *L'Action Française* (Stanford, CA: Stanford University Press, 1962), 298.

31. Another, more recent play by a French author (Emmanuel Eydoux, *Capitaine Alfred Dreyfus*, Marseille: Roger Eisinger, 1967) presents a much more negative view of Colonel Henry, showing that he was out to get Dreyfus from the very beginning, for dishonorable personal reasons rather than out of a misguided patriotism. This play, also claiming a strict documentary status, deals with events from Dreyfus's arrest (23 September 1894) to the last day of his trial (22 December 1894), after a prologue which focuses on the ceremony that deprived him of his rank (5 January 1895).

32. Roger Martin du Gard, *Jean Barois* (Paris: Gallimard, 1921), 256. Subsequent page references will be given in parentheses in the text.

33. Quoted in David Schalk, *Roger Martin du Gard: The Novelist and History* (Ithaca: Cornell University Press, 1967), 27.

34. Anatole France, *Histoire contemporaine: L'Anneau d'améthyste/Monsieur Bergeret à Paris* (Paris: Calmann-Lévy, 1966), 107.

35. France's article, entitled "Le Bureau," appeared in *Le Figaro* of 16 August 1899, just after the opening of Dreyfus's trial at Rennes. It was not presented as part of *Monsieur Bergeret à Paris*, but as an independent piece castigating the "Deuxième Bureau" of the war ministry and painting a glowing portrait of Colonel Picquart. The polemical force of the article is somewhat attenuated in the novel because of the way it is framed: Bergeret reading it aloud to two friends on a bench in the Luxembourg Gardens, next to a statue of Marguerite d'Angoulême.

36. Marcel Proust, *Remembrance of Things Past*, trans. C. K. Scott Moncrieff and Terence Kilmartin (New York: Random House, 1981), vol. II, 240–241. Subsequent references to this edition will be given in parentheses in the text, indicating volume and page number.

37. I wish to thank Carrie Noland for helping me with the research on this essay, and Louise Wills for tracking down many a stubborn footnote or hard-to-find text. My student Robert Dujarric, who wrote a paper on the Dreyfus Affair in *A la recherche* a few years ago, turned my attention to that aspect of Proust's novel at a time when my own interests lay in a quite different direction.

The Dreyfus Family

MICHAEL BURNS

In the final days of December 1894, Alfred Dreyfus awaited his public "degradation" and prepared for exile. Letters from his Cherche-Midi prison cell record the anguished appeals of an innocent officer condemned by the army of the Fatherland to which he had devoted his life ("Oh, dear France, whom I love with all my soul, all my heart . . . how can you accuse me of such an appalling crime?"). But the passion that ran through every letter gave way, in postscripts, to the equanimity more natural to the methodical Dreyfus, the practical soldier of scrupulous discipline. Listing provisions needed for the journey out, he asked his wife, Lucie, to purchase a sturdy portable inkwell and an English grammar book with exercises suited for a classroom of one ("since I will be my own professor").[1] For over four years on Devil's Island, when not striken by fever or depression, Dreyfus studied English. And he used Shakespeare—his closest companion, with Montaigne—to articulate the measure of his despair: "I never understood the great writer better than during this tragic epoch," he later confided to Joseph Reinach; nor did he ever repeat any passage more often than Iago's speech from the third act of *Othello,* which he copied in his prison notebooks:[2]

> Who steals my purse steals trash; 'tis something, nothing;
> "Twas mine, 'tis his, and has been slave to thousands;
> But he that filches from me my good name
> Robs me of that which not enriches him
> And makes me poor indeed.

"The shapes of life" that Shakespeare created, writes critic George Steiner, "give voice to our inward needs"; he is the "common house of our feelings." So it was for the prisoner who read the playwright with an eye to discovering language that captured the primacy of honor and the dignity of one's good name. "Infamy covers my name," Dreyfus wrote Lucie, and he told his brother Mathieu that it was "unbearable" to see their name "debased and dragged through the mud." He would rather his children not live, he said in his most desperate moment, than "live with their name dishonored."[3]

The army committed its honor to the case, Benjamin Martin tells us, while the army's principal victim, on an island far from the drama of his own "affair," committed the honor of his family name.

It was an ancient patronym dating from the first century Roman town of Treveris (now Trier) on the banks of the Mosel river north of Strasbourg and west of the Rhine. Jews had migrated to the settlement with Roman colonizers, and many had adopted the place name as their family name. Following the German invasions of the fifth century, some families took the language of the new colonizers—the words *Drei* ("three") and *Füss* ("feet")—to approximate the sound of the original settlement, and across time and space Treveris evolved in a variety of forms: Trifus, Tréfousse, Dreyfous, and, in the eighteenth century, Dreÿfuss, the name used by Alfred's great-grandfather.[4]

The earliest reliable documents record the birth of Abraham Israel Dreÿfuss in 1749 in the village of Rixheim on the southern plain of French Alsace.

Abraham worked as a kosher butcher through the 1770s and married Brändel Meyer in 1780, a union undoubtedly arranged by a Jewish marriage broker (a *Shadkhan*) who had known the Meyer family in the German village of Müllheim, a short distance across the Rhine. The couple had two children, but only the first, born in 1781, survived. They named him Jacob.[5]

On the eve of the French Revolution over 20,000 Jews, more than half the French Jewish population, lived in scores of villages and small towns along the Rhine valley and the foothills of the Vosges and Jura mountains. It was a "veritable human and spiritual reservoir" of Judaism.[6] Unlike the shtetls of Eastern Europe, however, the Dreÿfuss quarter within Rixheim was not a clearly marked or strictly controlled area of quarantine; Christian and Jewish rituals followed their own rhythms in distinct locales, but the commercial networks of Alsace prevented rigid barriers of separation. While Brändel sewed the quilts or crafted the hairnets that were part of Rixheim's local industry, Abraham worked in a room that opened on the dirt road facing his family home. On occasion he would sell the excess parts of butchered animals to gentiles, and, like other merchants, he would lend money at interest rates determined, in part, by seasonal fluctuations of the village economy. A service necessary in a world where peasants searched for credit and where banking institutions were unknown, moneylending was also the principal cause of anti-Jewish feelings among the gentile populace. No matter that the majority of lenders in Alsace, as elsewhere in Europe, were Christian, or that Jews had been forced into the "commerce of money" over centuries by popes, princes, feudal lords, and kings; legend had it that usury was the "habitual practice" of the Jews, and in times of trouble local custom had it that Rixheim and other communities became the targets of peasant discontent.[7]

In 1789, agricultural crisis, a fever epidemic, and the outbreak of national revolution combined to shatter the relative calm that had marked Abraham and Brändel's first decade together. In response to rebellions that broke out at the time of the Great Fear and, later, during the Terror and revolutionary wars, Rixheim's Jews fled to the nearby city of Mülhausen or across the border to Switzerland in search of temporary refuge. When the various crises abated they returned to their

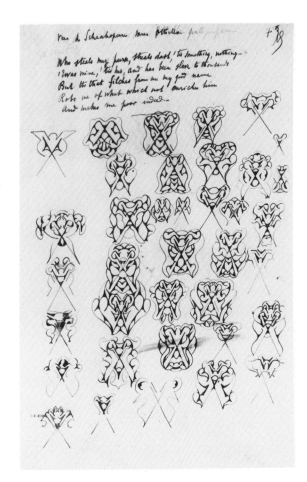

Figure 1, Cat. 80
Alfred Dreyfus
Notebook page, Devil's Island, August 1898
Pen and ink

homes to find doors, shutters, and floorboards torn away, ovens and stoves destroyed. In ransacked houses open to the cold wind that blew from the Jura mountains, they would, noted one observer, "thank God for a mild winter."[8]

For the Dreÿfuss family, as for the vast majority of French Jews, the age of emancipation was an age of paradox; an enlightened state promised equality and tolerance, while local country folk, acting on old memories and new fears, delivered violence. But if the 1791 edict of emancipation increased resentments and sparked conflict, it also struck down ancient barriers to Jewish migration. Descendants of families excluded from cities since the fourteenth century—Jewish peddlers and others who were allowed to visit town markets only if they paid the same tax as that levied on cattle, and left when church bells tolled at sundown—now had the choice of rural exodus and the option of city life. It was, however, an option postponed. Migration took resources, and resources took time. And through the early years of the new century most Jews remained in their native communities to work, and to wait.

Jacob Dreÿfuss was no exception. He became a *revendeur,* an all-purpose peddler hawking old clothes, farm tools, trinkets, religious engravings, and assorted other goods. Like his father, with whom he continued to live after Brändel's death in 1805, Jacob added moneylending to his services, and with the income from interest on loans and second-hand trade he soon purchased small parcels of land for rental to Rixheim villagers (another opportunity that had been made possible by emancipation). At the age of thirty-two, having saved enough to start a family, he married twenty-eight-year-old Rachel Katz. Five years later, in 1818, their first and only child, Raphael, was born.[9] The following year, young Raphael's grandfather died at the formidable age of seventy. The first member of the family to appear in written accounts, the first with a history in Rixheim, Abraham Dreÿfuss was the last to remain within its boundaries.

With the other Jews of Rixheim, the family had been largely untouched by Napoleon's attempts to suppress usury and hasten the assimilation of the "vile and debased" Ashkenazim into the French Fatherland.[10] Jewish rituals and Judeo-Alsatian dialect continued to thrive in their community, as did the practice of moneylending for Jews and gentiles throughout the region. The Emperor's legendary powers did not extend to the control of weather or harvests, and the need for rural credit became even more acute in the wake of the Napoleonic wars. Loans in the region nearly doubled in the decade after 1818, and records of Jacob's transactions suggest the steady, though modest, growth of his income.[11] He taught Raphael the lessons of second-hand trade and moneylending, and by the mid-1830s the family had the means to leave their ancestral village.

They also had the motivation. Pulled by urban opportunities for Jews with a knowledge of retail trade, they were pushed from the countryside by the threat of persecution. A number of communities in southern Alsace had experienced conflict in the preceding years, from Ribeauvillé to Zillisheim, and especially in Durmenach, near Rixheim, where drunken peasants beat down the doors of Jewish moneylenders and threatened to "exterminate them all." With varying degrees of effectiveness, authorities called in troops to protect local "Israelites," and the state's response was duly noted and appreciated by Jewish families. But troubles continued for more than a decade, reaching a climax during the revolution of 1848, when Jews who remained in the countryside suffered the most violent attacks since the summer of the Great Fear.[12]

By then, however, Jacob, Rachel, and Raphael had taken the western road out of Rixheim to settle in Mülhausen, a city long known to hinterland Jews as a center of sanctuary in a hostile world. It was also "la ville la plus française de l'Alsace," but, like Breton peasants moving to Paris, the Dreÿfuss family was not immediately "crushed into the mold" of French culture.[13] They settled in neighborhoods populated by other migrants, and by Jewish merchants whom Jacob and Raphael met on previous visits, and maintained, for a time, the customs and language of the countryside—*rus in urbe.* And they followed the familiar rhythms of worship in the new Mülhausen synagogue. In 1800 the city's Jewish population had numbered less than one hundred, but by the mid-1830s it approached 1200 and was growing rapidly.[14]

During these early years, city records listed Jacob and Raphael as merchants (*marchands*). The products they sold[15] were not specified, but the experience of others suggests that, like rural scrap-iron dealers who became hardware salesmen or tanners who took up the shoe trade, Jacob and Raphael would adapt the lessons of Rixheim to an urban *affaire commerciale* (business). The moment for such an enterprise was ideal. Mülhausen entered a period of brilliant economic growth and the opportunities available in textile and related businesses multiplied with the expanding economy. Though still part of a community of "demi-proletarians" struggling for a place in the urban world, Jacob and Raphael were determined to apply their background as country peddlers and intermediaries to a new city trade.[16]

Jacob, who shaped the dream, did not live to see it realized. He died in 1838, at the age of fifty-seven, only three years after the move to the city. The cause of his death was not recorded.[17] A few years earlier, Mülhausen officials had struck down ancient prohibitions and allowed Jews to be buried within city limits; and it was in that new section of the cemetery that Rachel and Raphael buried Jacob. Throughout his life he had used the Hebrew name and had never adopted the Gallicized "Jacques." But it appears on his tombstone, and the complete inscription is a striking document of both change and continuity: The name Jacques suggests the mingling of French and Ashkenazic cultures, while the year of death given as 5598, following the traditional Jewish system of reckoning, confirms the enduring faith that had traveled with the Dreÿfuss family from country to town.

Jacob's widow and son were not alone for long. In the spring of 1841, twenty-four-year-old Jeannette Libmann, daughter of a kosher butcher in the town of Ribeauvillé, came south to the city to work as a seamstress and to marry Raphael Dreÿfuss, one year her junior. The union was apparently arranged through a relative of Jeannette's and a merchant friend of Raphael's.[18]

Jeannette found a job in Mülhausen, and worked as a seamstress, while Raphael applied the lessons he had learned from his father as a trader along the backroads of Alsace and became a commission agent, an intermediary between textile manufacturers and buyers. He was responsible for finding clients who would pay the highest price for commissioned goods and he kept industrialists informed of what products were in demand. With other agents, he would extend loans to manufacturers in need of ready capital.[19] As important to the workings of urban commerce as Jacob's moneylending had been essential to the Rixheim mar-

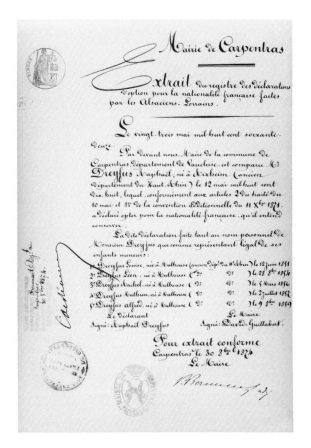

Figure 2, Cat. 26
Document certifying the choice of French nationality by the Dreyfus family after they left Alsace-Lorraine. Carpentras, 30 October 1874.

Ink on paper

CONSISTOIRE ISRAÉLITE DE PARIS

Temple de la rue _de la Victoire_

כתובה

[Hebrew ketubbah text]

KETOUBA OU ACTE DU MARIAGE RELIGIEUX

Aujourd'hui _Premier_ jour du mois de _Syar_ de l'année 56_50_ de la création du monde (21 _Avril_ 1890), les époux _Dreyfus Alfred_ _Hadamard (Lucie Eugénie)_ se sont présentés devant nous, à l'effet d'obtenir pour leur union l'n consécration religieuse et la bénédiction de Dieu.

En présence de Dieu, et dans le Temple consacré à son culte, après la récitation des prières d'usage, après avoir indiqué aux deux époux les devoirs qu'ils auront à remplir dans leur nouvelle carrière, après les avoir bénis au nom de la Religion et appelé sur eux les faveurs du Ciel, nous les déclarons unis par les liens du mariage, CONFORMÉMENT A LA LOI DE MOÏSE ET D'ISRAEL כדת משה וישראל

Le Grand-Rabbin de Paris,

Zadoc Kahn

Figure 3, Cat. 28
Jewish marriage contract (Ketubbah) of Alfred Dreyfus and Lucie Eugénie Hadamard, Paris. 21 April 1890.
Ink on printed form

ketplace, Raphael's brokerage business was also no less unpredictable. He dealt in fabrics and in fortune, in a trade of chance that was highly sensitive to market fluctuations and to the ability of clients to pay fees or repay loans. Contrary to the stereotype of Jews luxuriating in that middle ground of commerce and capitalism—a stereotype that, Michael Marrus reminds us, fed the resentments of mid-century anti-Semites—Raphael had another aim: security for his family, which meant the security of fixed capital. Through the 1850s, while he dealt with manufacturers, Raphael planned and saved in the hope of someday entering their ranks.

This was never an easy task, but the history of Mülhausen made it at least possible. The city that Raphael's father had chosen was known to Jews not only for its economic opportunities but for its unique tradition of accommodation: A center of French culture, Mülhausen was also an enclave of Protestantism in overwhelmingly Catholic Alsace. In cotton mills and chemical factories the majority of workers were Catholic, their dialects and customs Germanic, whereas the notables who owned the industries, controlled the politics, and fashioned the city's high and official culture were uniformly Calvinist and French. Descendants of Huguenots chased from France in the seventeenth century and forced into the textile trades of Switzerland and Mülhausen or into the commerce of money, these city entrepreneurs understood the history of their Jewish neighbors because, in some ways, their families had lived it.[20] People of two diasporas, both oppressed by the Old Regime and liberated by the new, French Protestants and Jews remained separate in private life and religious habits, while working together to make Mülhausen an international textile center and a powerful force of French culture on the German frontier. Not one major enterprise owned by a Catholic would be established in the city during the nineteenth century.[21]

For the manufacturing elite and, eventually, for the Dreÿfuss family, the French language provided a linguistic mark of social distinction, a sign of acculturation and, eventually, national allegiance. On the fiftieth anniversary of the former republic's _réunion_ with France, in 1848, the Germanic name Mülhausen gave way to the Gallicized Mulhouse. A decade earlier, the family had made a similar statement on Jacob's cemetery marker, and in

Figure 4, Cat. 29
*Alfred Dreyfus (on the first step at the
extreme right) with his class at the Ecole
de Guerre.* August 1891.
Photograph

1844, Raphael and Jeannette again blended French
and Jewish customs when they named their first
son after his deceased grandfather and called him
Jacques. Finally, a few years later, Raphael took
yet another step away from the countryside of his
ancestors and from the Germanic idioms of the
city's working class. On the birth certificate of
his daughter, Rachel, named after his mother who
had recently died, Raphael dropped the double
letters and distinctive marks that spoke of his
past and jeopardized his future: Dreÿfuss became
Dreyfus.[22]

The decade of the 1850s, the most prosperous
for city industries, was also the most advantageous
for Raphael's commission agency. By 1862 he

could abandon the lucrative but limited profession
of intermediary and build his own small cotton
mill on the rue Lavoisier in the city's western
industrial sector. Almost immediately plans were
underway to expand the factory and add more
powerful machinery, and by the end of the decade
"Raphael Dreyfus et Compagnie" was becoming
one of the major textile establishments in southern
Alsace.[23]

Like his Protestant counterparts, the Koechlins,
Miegs, Schlumbergers, and Dollfuses, Raphael
made his mill a family enterprise and had no
trouble recruiting partners. Between 1844 and
1859 Jeannette had nine children, of whom four
boys and three girls survived. With her income no

longer needed, Jeannette had left her seamstress job to care for the children in the family's small apartment on the bustling rue de Sauvage close by the Protestant church of Saint Etienne. Later the family moved to a spacious and stately home surrounded by a garden of trees on the quiet rue de la Sinne.

The youngest child, Alfred, was ten years old when the family moved in 1869. In a fashionable neighborhood some distance from the factory on the rue Lavoisier, Alfred lived in the secure and comfortable Dreyfus family circle, the setting of his earliest and fondest memories: "My childhood passed gently," he later wrote, "amid the kind influences of mother and sisters, a father deeply devoted to his children, and the affectionate protection of older brothers."[24]

His closest brother, Mathieu, born in 1857, shared with Alfred, Jeannette, and the three sisters—Henriette, Louise, and Rachel—the benefits provided by their father and two older brothers. While Jacques and Léon worked with Raphael among laborers who spoke Alsatian dialect and learned the industrial arts of carding machines and steam power, Mathieu and Alfred studied the lessons of French, German, history, literature, and science that were required of the children of a respectable bourgeois family. That division of private and public spheres—of generations within a family pursuing different tasks in separate spheres for a common goal—was typical of the age, especially among newly rich families eager to use their resources to smoothe the "coarse" edges of their Judeo-Alsatian culture and embrace the customs of the city's *grand patronat*.[25] If many habits were too hard for Raphael and Jeannette to break—if, for example, they never lost their Germanic accents—their children would compensate by announcing their preference for French over German and by working to refine their pronunciation, perfecting the subtle sounds of belonging.

For Mathieu and Alfred, the time spent together during these early years shaped the common interests and similar sensibilities that would unite them over the decades to come. Though never as timid as his younger brother, never as intensely interior, Mathieu understood Alfred's complex personality—as did the oldest sister, Henriette, who was like a mother to the boy. They knew that his "rigid manner" was reserved for strangers, while family and friends appreciated his lively curiosity. "He is a stoic," Mathieu later said of Alfred, "with a cold appearance but a warm heart." Shy in public, an "incorrigible dreamer" in private, there was good reason to call young Alfred, as his sisters did, "Don Quixote."[26]

The history of the family in Mulhouse in the 1860s—their prosperity, acculturation, and freedom to worship in an atmosphere of tolerance—confirms the view that the Second Empire was, for many French Jews, a "golden age," when economic opportunities and a climate of accommodation led to the realization of promises delivered decades earlier at the moment of citizenship.[27] But if the family's experience testifies to the accuracy of that picture, it also reveals the fragility of the Jews' position at that time. The privileges of comfort and stability had been hard won by parents who clung to memories of scarcity and persecution in Rixheim and Ribeauvillé. Their children knew only the security of the city, never the contrasts of the countryside, but they would hear the stories and the entire family would acquire a sense of the most important legacy of emancipation: the protection that the state had promised, and, in the end, provided. In the 1820s and 1830s, young Raphael and Jeannette had watched French troops attempt to suppress anti-Jewish rebellions in their native communities,[28] and they later learned with their children that Mulhouse, "the most French city of Alsace," was an enclave both of prosperity and, for the Dreyfus family at least, of social calm; an urban refuge from the upheavals of the countryside. Though brief, this period of equipoise in Mulhouse was long enough and its impact strong enough to shape the family's faith in France and sustain their belief that the state was a powerful and benevolent ally.

In the early fall of 1870, taking shelter in their home, the family watched Prussian troops invade and occupy Mulhouse. Later, Alfred pointed to that scene, his "first sorrow," as the moment of his commitment to the French Fatherland.[29] But his precocious patriotism was not an abstract allegiance or the chauvinism of a "civilized" Frenchman repulsed by "barbaric" Germans; all that, and more, would take time to learn. It was the despair of an eleven-year-old boy whose home the land of his father, was threatened. A tree-lined garden on the rue de la Sinne, and France, had been invaded.

The impact of the Franco-Prussian war and the

family's official "option" for France in 1872 provides the point of departure for those histories of the Dreyfus Affair that do not begin, as the vast majority do, with the Captain's arrest on a cold October morning in 1894. Invariably, brief allusions are made to the family's fortune, assimilation, and intense patriotism; to Alfred's time with his sister Henriette in the southern town of Carpentras before he entered the Ecole Polytechnique; and to the life he later enjoyed with Lucie Hadamard, daughter of a diamond merchant, and their children, Pierre, born in 1891, and Jeanne, born two years later. But, understandably, the high drama of the scandal unfolds not in family parlors, nor even in the prisoner's cell, but in the backrooms of the army General Staff, in the cloakrooms of anxious politicians, and among popular journalists and distinguished literati who made the Affair a Manichean struggle between Church and State, radicals and reactionaries, the intelligentsia and the mob, anti-Semites and the forces for tolerance.

But without "le dreyfusisme familial," as historian Madeleine Rebérioux has called it,[30] there would not have been an Affair. Without the plots uncovered by Mathieu or the official appeals submitted by Lucie, no stage would have been constructed for the Affair's more celebrated actors, virtually all of whom, Jews and gentiles, were at first indisposed to fight for a man whose guilt they assumed and whose manner attracted no sympathy and much contempt. While Dreyfus on Devil's Island could not influence the machinations of his own Affair, Mathieu, Lucie, and other family members congregating in Paris could work to determine its outcome.

They kept the case open and the prisoner alive. As much as Emile Zola, Mathieu was Voltaire to Alfred's Calas, a Calas tortured but not yet dead, and it is instructive that the mantlepiece of Mathieu's apartment later held two artifacts of the Affair that, for him, captured its essence: a photograph of Zola and a bust of Voltaire. In the Cherche-Midi and Santé prisons, on Devil's Island and awaiting his retrial at Rennes, Dreyfus recalled his childhood with Mathieu and the years with Lucie, and never doubted that his brother and wife would act to preserve the family's honor and the integrity of France ("above all, and no matter what the cost," he wrote Mathieu in 1897, "the interests of the country must be respected").[31] Essential and

inextricable, that communion of interests, the two faiths of family and Fatherland, sustained him. From the night of his arrest, when he hurled himself against the stone wall of his prison cell, through the hardest times on Devil's Island, when disease and depression brought dreams of release through suicide, Dreyfus was rescued and his spirits revived by letters from Lucie and Pierre, Mathieu and the other brothers and sisters. The stories these letters told of young Jeanne's humor or of Pierre's favorite books, and the tangible tokens of their presence, including the picture of Lucie and the children on the prisoner's spare table ("my talisman, my strength"), created a world of hope by conjuring the beloved family and keeping the prisoner's memory of them fresh and vivid. Souvenirs of "happiness and joy," they were, Dreyfus admitted, at once agonizing and inspirational; remembrances of things past that might never be recaptured and reminders that death on Devil's Island meant dishonor for the family in France.[32] "Je te dois tous," ("to you I owe everything") said Dreyfus in 1920 as he stood by Mathieu's coffin, and two decades earlier at Rennes he had said the same of Lucie: "If I am here, it is to her that I owe it."[33]

He owed his survival to his wife and brother, and at the end of five years in prison he owed his recuperation to the sister who had raised him. Emaciated, fever-ridden, and with hair turned white, he left Rennes in September, 1899, and went home to Henriette. At Carpentras he was alone with Lucie for the first time since October 1894, and in a garden that recalled Mulhouse and the rue de la Sinne, he met Jeanne and Pierre. "I feared the surprise they may have at the sight of a father unknown to them," he wrote, "but the moment they rushed into my arms . . . so much sadness, so much grief, was forgotten." It was a scene of "family intimacy" like the one that Emile Zola had foreseen in a letter to Lucie: The children will sit on their father's knee and hear him tell the "tragic story . . . and they will be proud of him and of the name they carry." "The abominations of the street," said Zola, who had witnessed the riots surrounding the Affair, "all die on the doorstep of the home."[34]

Exile had sheltered Alfred Dreyfus from those "abominations," but his family had lived through them. Whereas most historians writing after the fact never moved beyond the involvement of

Figure 5, Cat. 24
Miniature folding screen with photographs of Pierre and Jeanne Dreyfus, 1894–1899
Painted wood, photographs

Mathieu ("le frère admirable"), at the time of the case, commentators were obsessed with the family's role. Army agents and, later, Parisian police mobilized to follow family members in the hope of exposing a network of espionage. Journalists crafted scenarios, wildly fabricated but widely believed, of a secret Jewish syndicate led by Mathieu or by Lucie's father, and financed by the ill-gotten gains of Jewish industrialists and diamond peddlers. The family's background in Alsace loomed large for anti-Semites as a staging area for Jewish-German intrigues; willing to commend Alsatian Christians for their patriotic stand on the eastern frontier, anti-Semites were just as quick to condemn Alsatian Jews for their supposed treason.[35] And attacks went beyond mere words: One of Alfred's nephews was summarily expelled from his school in Belfort where Jacques lived, another was prevented from entering the Ecole Polytechnique. During the most critical years of the Affair, 1898–99, nearly every family member faced anti-Dreyfusard gangs. In Paris, Belfort, and Carpentras, hooligans shattered windows, trapped family members in apartment lobbies or along city streets, and forced them to take refuge in rented houses under assumed names. Gangs covered

Henriette's home with posters reading "Down with the Jews! Down with Dreyfus! Down with the Syndicate of Treason!," and other signs appeared in Carpentras, calling for a rally of "all patriots against the Jewish vermin." Pierre and Jeanne, who spent much of this time in Carpentras, had been told that their father was on a "long voyage" for the army and they never fully understood the events that surrounded them; but they never forgot the stones hurled at them from a bridge above Henriette's garden.[36]

The actions of police agents and angry crowds, if unforgiveable, were at least comprehensible in the climate of fear that had developed during the most dramatic months of the Affair. Less understandable are histories of the case that, with few exceptions, criticize the "bizarre tactics," as Hannah Arendt called them, of a family out to "rescue their kinsman." "In trying to save an innocent man," says Arendt, the family "employed the very methods usually adopted in the case of a guilty one. They stood in mortal terror of publicity and relied exclusively on back-door maneuvers."[37] Arendt accepted rumors fashioned by Dreyfus's enemies as objective evidence, and relied on an error-ridden article published four decades after

Figure 6, Cat. 105
Dreyfus's Prison Hut, Devil's Island.
Photograph

the Affair; her conclusions were the product of poor research and a rich imagination. But they were not unique. The basic view of a hesitant family cowed by authority and conservative in tactics is echoed in other, more responsible, accounts. Léon Blum, who fought for Dreyfus, questioned Mathieu's methods and his unrelenting respect for the government in power. For Blum, who spoke for others, the family's strategy was "political," not "revolutionary" like that of Jaurès or Clemenceau, and it was a "fatal error" that could only be explained as the noble attempt of one brother, who should have known better, to respect the wishes of another, who never could: Mathieu complied, goes this interpretation, with a prisoner whose faith in the state remained as unshakeable on Devil's Island as it had been three decades earlier when the family opted for France.[38] On this point, Blum was correct. More recently, Stephen Wilson has also noted that while the family was less cautious than some suggest, they were still "conditioned by defensive and deferential patterns of behavior." Wilson cites an 1899 police report describing the family's plans for the retrial at Rennes: They would not send paid demonstrators to protest on Dreyfus's behalf, goes the account, "on the contrary, they will remain in the strict privacy of the family," strangers to all confrontation and upheaval.[39]

The family's fear of publicity was real and their tactics were often defensive. But they resulted in the prisoner's release and exoneration and not in a "fatal error." The quiet pressure and personal influence employed by Mathieu was not simply the "classical recourse of the bourgeois in trouble";[40] it was a compelling habit formed across generations by a Jewish family of Alsatian origin whose security, from the time of their emancipation to the Affair, had depended on the state. Faith in France, in the "Justice" that Alfred Dreyfus always spelled with a capital "J" and never doubted, may have blinded the family to abuses of political power and isolated them from those who defined their deference as pusillanimity; but, as Mathieu noted, they had been isolated from the moment of his brother's conviction when "not one hand was extended," when "every door was closed," and when "those who knew us avoided us . . . We were the plague-striken."[41]

Abandoned by friends, they were surrounded by the crowd. And, consciously or not, they knew, as descendants of Abraham and Jacob, that

Figure 7, Cat. 32
The Family Reunited in Carpentras.
Autumn, 1899.
Photograph

the stones hurled at them in Paris or Carpentras were no different from the stones of Rixheim. Their generation, Alfred's generation, had flourished in the peaceful and prosperous intervening years in Mulhouse, but the older memories remained to confirm the contrast and strengthen the family's allegiance to France and to the promises France made to its citizens. In an age when honor mattered, they were honor-bound to respect *la Patrie,* and, as Alfred Dreyfus noted, they expected that *Patrie* to remember that "she, too, has a sacred duty to fulfill."[42]

Notes

Research for this essay was supported by the Rockefeller Foundation, the American Philosophical Society, and Mount Holyoke College. Above all, I thank those members of the Dreyfus family who generously shared their private papers and their memories.

1. For Dreyfus's prison letters, see Bibliothèque Nationale (hereafter BN), N.A.F. 16609; see also, N.A.F. 24895.
2. BN, N.A.F., 24909, Dreyfus notebook, August, 1898, 7; and N.A.F. 24895.
3. George Steiner, *Language and Silence: Essays on Language, Literature and the Inhuman* (New York: Atheneum, 1967), 198; BN, N.A.F. 17387 and 16609.
4. Paul Lévy, *Les Noms des Israélites en France* (Paris: Presses Universitaires de France, 1960), 124–125. Some historians point to other locales for the origin of the name (e.g., Troyes), but the majority, it seems, trace it to Treveris.
5. Archives départementales du Haut-Rhin (hereafter ADHR), C 1284, Dénombrement des Juifs en France, 1784; ADHR, 4 E, notary, February 4, 1780.
6. Robert Anchel, *Les Juifs de France* (Paris: J. B. Janin, 1946), 235; Michael Marrus, *The Politics of Assimilation: The French Jewish Community at the Time of the Dreyfus Affair* (Oxford: Oxford Univ. Press, 1971), 235; and Patrick Girard, *Les Juifs de France de 1789 à 1860: de l'émancipation à l'égalite* (Paris: Calmann-Lévy, 1976), 110.
7. On village customs in Alsace, see Freddy Raphael and Robert Weyl, *Juifs en Alsace: Culture, société, histoire* (Toulouse: Privat, 1977); on moneylending in Rixheim and Alsace, see ADHR, V 612–613; Raphael and Weyl, *Juifs en Alsace,* 370–371 and passim; and Léon Poliakov, *Histoire de l'antisemitisme,* vol. 2 (Paris: Pluriel, 1981), 106 and passim.
8. *Mulhouse et le Sundgau, 1648–1798–1848* (Mulhouse, 1948), 128; François-Georges Dreyfus, *Histoire de l'Alsace* (Paris: Hachette, 1979), 186–189; Béatrice Philippe, *Etre Juif dans la société française du moyen-âge à nos jours* (Paris: Editions Montalba, 1979), 107–108.
9. ADHR, 5 E 416, and 3 P 1434, cadastres.
10. Girard, *Les Juifs,* 75; and Paul Mendes-Flohr and Jehuda Reinharz, eds., *The Jew in the Modern World: A Documentary History* (New York: Oxford Univ. Press, 1980), 112–113.
11. ADHR, V 612–613; Paul Leuilliot, *L'Alsace au début du XIXeme siècle: essais d'histoire politique, éconmique et religieuse,* vol. 2 (Paris: S.E.V.P.E.N., 1959), 19.
12. ADHR, V 611 and 4 M 44; Leuilliot, *L'Alsace au début,* vol. 2, 184, and vol. 3, 245; Rina Neher-Bernheim, *Documents inédits sur l'entrée des Juifs dans la société française (1750–1850),* vol. 2 (Tel Aviv, 1977), 339; Moses Ginsburger, "Juifs et Chrétiens à Ribeauvillé en 1819," *7eme Bulletin de la société historique et archéologique de Ribeauvillé,* Colmar, 1937, 65–65, and the same author's "Les Troubles contre les Juifs de l'Alsace en 1848," *Revue des Etudes Juives* 64, 1912, 109–117.
13. Frédéric Hoffet, *Psychanalyse de l'Alsace* (Paris: Flammarion, 1951), 73–74; and Girard, *Les Juifs,* 251.
14. Ernest Meininger. *Histoire de Mulhouse* (Mulhouse, 1923), 100; ADHR 6 M 9.
15. ADHR 5 E 337.
16. Henry Laufenburger, *Cours d'économie alsacienne,* vol. 2 (Paris: Librárie du Recueil Sirey, 1932), 10; Georges Weill, *L'Alsace française* (Paris: F. Alcan, 1916), 109; Raphael and Weyl, *Juifs en Alsace,* 369.
17. ADHR 5 E 337.
18. ADHR 5 E 405, Ribeauvillé, 5 E 337, Mulhouse.
19. *Histoire documentaire de l'industrie de Mulhouse* (Mulhouse, 1902), 951ff.
20. Henri Sée, "Dans quelle mesure Puritains et Juifs ont-ils contribué aux progrès du capitalisme moderne?" *Revue historique,* 1927, vol. 155, 61–65; Laufenburger, *Cours d'économie,* vol. 1, 2 and vol. 2, 162, 226.
21. Dreyfus, *Histoire de l'Alsace,* 227.
22. ADHR 5 E 337; Meininger, *Histoire de Mulhouse,* 106.
23. *Histoire documentaire,* 498; ADHR 5 M 78.
24. Capitaine Alfred Dreyfus, *Souvenirs et Correspondance* (Paris: Bernard Grasset, 1936), 40–41; Alfred Dreyfus, *Cinq années de ma vie* (Paris: François Maspero, 1982), 57.
25. Jean Schlumberger, et al., *La Bourgeoisie alsacienne: Etudes d'histoire sociale* (Strasbourg: F. X. LeRoux, 1954), 12, 491; Raphael and Weyl, *Juifs en Alsace,* 406.
26. H. Villemar, *Dreyfus Intime* (Paris: P.-V. Stock, 1898), 7–8; BN, N.A.F. 14382, Mathieu Dreyfus, September 24, 1902.
27. For these years, the most thorough survey is David Cohen, *La Promotion des Juifs en France à l'époque du Second Empire,* 2 vols. (Aix en Provence: Université de Provence, 1980).

28. See, for example, ADHR V611, and note 12 above.
29. Dreyfus, *Cinq années,* 57.
30. Madeleine Rebérioux, *La République radicale?: 1898–1914* (Paris: Seuil, 1975), 6.
31. Archives Nationales (hereafter AN), BB^{19} 110, July 8, 1897.
32. BN, N.A.F. 14307, Dreyfus notebook, and N.A.F. 17387.
33. Josephine Lazarus, *Madame Dreyfus: An Appreciation* (New York: Brentano's, 1899), 8; and author's interview with Mathieu Dreyfus's granddaughter, Madame France Reinach Beck, Paris, June 20, 1983.
34. BN, N.A.F. 14308, Dreyfus notebook; Zola's letter is discussed in Alfred Bruneau, *A l'Ombre d'un grand coeur* (Paris, 1980), 163–164.
35. AN F^7 12473, police reports; AN BB^{19} 108, army reports.
36. Stephen Wilson, *Ideology and Experience: Antisemitism in France at the Time of the Dreyfus Affair* (Rutherford: Fairleigh Dickinson Univ. Press, 1982), 699; AN F^7 12467, perfect of the Vaucluse, January 21, 1898; AN BB^{19} 73, police, October 10, 1898; Archives départementales de Vaucluse, 1 M 809, Carpentras; and author's interview with France Reinach Beck.
37. Hannah Arendt, *The Origins of Totalitarianism* (New York: Harcourt Brace Jovanovich, 1973), 105–109.
38. Léon Blum, *Souvenirs sur l'affaire* (Paris: Gallimard, 1981), 57–60.
39. Wilson, *Ideology and Experience,* 712.
40. On the recourse of the bourgeois, see Eric J. Hobsbawn, *The Age of Capital* (New York: Scribner, 1975), 244.
41. BN, N.A.F. 14382, Mathieu Dreyfus, July 21, 1906; on the prisoner and "Justice," see N.A.F. 16609, June 1, 1899.
42. BN, N.A.F. 23819: ". . . comme le spectre de Banquo je sortirais de la tombe pour . . . rappeler à la Patrie [qu'elle] aussi a un devoir sacré à remplir" (". . . like the specter of Banquo, I shall come out of the tomb in order . . . to remind the Fatherland that it also has a sacred obligation to fulfill.") (October 2, 1897).

Plates

Plate 1

Henri de Toulouse-Lautrec

Ribot's Testimony (Déposition Ribot)
The Arton Trial (Procès Arton), 1896

Lithograph

Collection of Mr. and Mrs. Herbert
D. Schimmel, New York

Léopold-Emile Aron (known as
Arton) was accused of participating
in a scheme to bribe government
officials during the French attempts
to build the Panama Canal. The failure of the Panama Company—whose
financing had been undertaken by
two Jewish businessmen—fed an out-
burst of anti-Semitism.

Lautrec's interest in the courtroom
was short-lived and lay in depicting
its theater, rather than in politics or
social justice.

Plate 2

Jean-Louis Forain

In the Wings (Dans les coulisses), 1899

Oil on canvas

The Art Institute of Chicago, Mr.
and Mrs. Martin A. Ryerson Collection

Forain dedicated a series of paintings,
executed over a twenty-year period,
to backstage scenes involving dancers
and their admirers. In his depiction
of these men he hinted at anti-Semitic attitudes and stereotypes that
he openly declared in his anti-Dreyfusard journal, *Psst . . . !* . The figure in the foreground of this work
is said to be Joseph Reinach, one of
the major Dreyfus supporters.

Plate 3

Bob (Comtesse Sibylle Martel de
Janville, also called Gyp)

Algerian Jews

Le Rire, 14 November, 1896

Photomechanical print

Collection of Willa Silverman, New
York

The countess who wrote novels
under the pen name Gyp published
her drawings under another pseudonym: Bob. In her vitriolic *History
of the Third Republic,* Algerian Jews
who received French citizenship are
depicted as locusts.

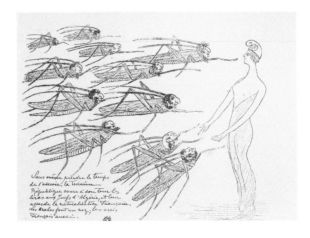

Plate 4

Bob (Comtesse Sibylle Martel de Janville, also called Gyp)

Kike-Rats

Le Rire, 14 November 1896

Photomechanical print

Collection of Willa Silverman, New York

In the same issue of *Le Rire,* she portrayed Drumont as a catcher of Jewish rats.

Plate 5

Louis Anquetin

Drumont and Vacher (Drumont et Vacher)

La Feuille, 3 November 1898

Photomechanical print

Collection of Mr. and Mrs. Herbert D. Schimmel, New York

The Dreyfusard artist Louis Anquetin viewed the anti-Semitic Drumont as an evildoer consumed by hatred, and paired him with a fanatic murderer named Vacher.

A propos de Judas Dreyfus

— Français, voilà huit années que je vous le répète chaque jour!!!

Savonnage infructueux

— Juifs, chez nous, en France, le sang, seul, lave une tache comme celle-là!!!

Plate 6

J. Chanteclair

On the subject of Judas Dreyfus (A propos de Judas Dreyfus)

La Libre Parole illustrée, No. 70, 10 November 1894

Photomechanical print

The Jewish Museum

The caption reads:

"—Frenchmen, I've been telling you this every day for eight years!!!"

(—Français, voilà huit années que je vous le répète chaque jour!!!)

Edouard Drumont, self-proclaimed champion of France and her army, praises himself for having alerted the public to the treachery of Jews as early as 1886, in his anti-Semitic diatribe *La France Juive.*

This cartoon appeared nine days after *La Libre Parole* proclaimed Dreyfus as the traitor.

Plate 7

J. Chanteclair

Fruitless Soaping (Savonnage infructueux)

La Libre Parole illustrée, No. 71, 17 November 1894

Photomechanical print

The Jewish Museum

The caption reads:

"Jews, for us in France, blood alone can get out a stain like that!!!" (Juifs, chez nous, en France, le sang, seul, lave une tache comme celle-la!!!)

Sixteen days after naming Dreyfus as the traitor, *La Libre Parole* warns the treasonous Jews, who wash themselves in money, that only a bloodbath will expiate their sins.

Plate 8

Frederic de Haenen

The Degradation of Captain Dreyfus,
1895

Ink wash, crayon, and white gouache
on cardboard

Collection of *L'Illustration,* courtesy
of Eric Baschet, Paris

This drawing was published as a
double-page spread in *L'Illustration,*
12 January 1895

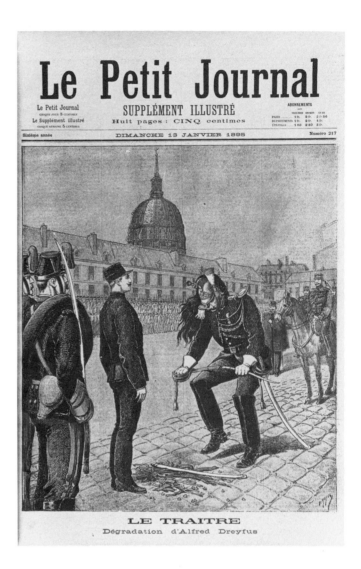

Plate 9

H. Meyer

The Traitor: The Degradation of Alfred Dreyfus (Le Traître. Dégradation d'Alfred Dreyfus)

Le Petit Journal, Supplément Illustré, 13 January 1895

Photomechanical print

Musée de la Presse, Paris

Courtesy of Christian Bailly

This neutral image of the ceremony does not reflect the violent anti-Semitism of the paper's editorial content.

The Degradation

On 5 January 1895 Alfred Dreyfus was ceremonially stripped of his badges of rank and his saber broken. He was marched around the courtyard of the École Militaire, where troops of the Paris garrison had assembled for the "execution parade." As he made his circuit of the courtyard, the crowd out on the street shouted, "Death to the traitor! Kill him! Dirty Jew! Judas!" He was then taken in a police van to prison to await deportation.

The event provided the press with the opportunity for graphic commentaries.

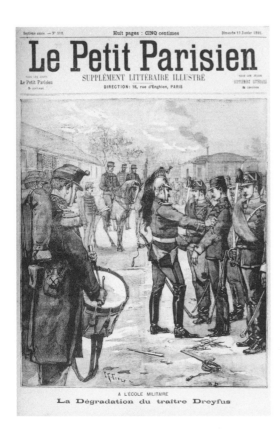

Plate 10

Artist unknown

*The Degradation of the Traitor Dreyfus
(La Dégradation du traître Dreyfus)*

*Le Petit Parisien, Supplément Litéraire
Illustré,* 13 January 1895

Photomechanical print

Musée de la Presse, Paris

Courtesy of Christian Bailly

Le Petit Parisien, another widely circulated newspaper, was initially anti-
Dreyfusard, but later it took his side.

Plate 11

Artist unknown

*Police Wagon, Drums, and Bugles (Voi-
ture Cellulaire, Tambours et Clairons),*
1899

Photograph

Collection of J. Robert Maguire,
Shoreham, VT

This photograph was probably taken
from the rooftop of a building over-
looking the courtyard.

Plate 12
Charles Paul Renouard
The 5th of January, 1895 at the Ecole Militaire (Le 5 janvier 1895 à l'école militaire)
L'Affaire Dreyfus, 1899
Lithograph, artist's proof
The Library of the Jewish Theological Seminary of America, New York

Renouard would publish this image in his 1899 album of lithographs, a sympathetic summary of the Affair.

Plate 13
A. Vignola
Execution Parade (Parade d'execution)
Le Pilori, 6 January 1895
Photomechanical print
Musée de Bretagne, Rennes

In this illustration from an anti-Republican, anti-Semitic journal, the outsiders witnessing the degradation include soldiers from Italy, Germany, and England.

Plate 14
Lionel Royer
The Degradation (La Dégradation)
Le Journal Illustré, 6 January 1895
Photomechanical print
Musée de Bretagne, Rennes

The characterization of Dreyfus as Judas was common in the anti- Semitic press.

Plate 15
Oswald Heidbrinck
The Traitor (Le traître)
Le Rire, 5 January 1895
Photomechanical print
The Jewish Museum

The caption reads:
"—What's Dreyfus?

—The *man* who for thirty *deniers* wanted to make all the women of France widows, make the small children weep tears of blood and give over his fellow soldiers to enemy bullets!"

(—Qu'est-ce que Dreyfus?

—C'est l'*homme* qui pour trente deniers a voulu rendre veuves toutes les femmes de France, faire pleurer des larmes se sang aux petits enfants et livrer ses compagnons d'armes aux balles de l'ennemi!)

Plate 16
Donville
At home (En famille)
La Libre Parole illustrée, No. 174, 7 November 1895
Photomechanical print
The Jewish Museum

The caption reads:

"I spent money for you to go to Polythechnic: but don't be as dumb as that poor Treyfus, don't get caught!"

(Ch'ai débensé de l'archent pour que tu endres à Bolytechnique: mais ne sois pas aussi pète que ce baufre Treyfous, ne te fais pas bincer!)

From 1892, the anti-Semitic *La Libre Parole* crusaded against the number of Jews in the Ecole Polytechnique (the military engineering school) and Jewish officers in the army, claiming that their loyalty to France was questionable.

Here, a rich father, speaking with a German-Jewish accent, warns his son, an army officer, to be more careful than Dreyfus in his treasonable activities.

Plate 17
Charles Paul Renouard
La Fronde
L'Affaire Dreyfus, 1899
Lithograph
The Library of the Jewish Theological Seminary of America, New York

This feminist Dreyfusard newspaper was founded in December 1897 by Marguerite Durand, center, and Caroline Rémy Guebhard, known as Séverine, right. An early contributor to *La Libre Parole* and close friend of Drumont's, Séverine broke with that circle and became a Dreyfusard.

The Case Against Esterhazy

Plate 18
Monogrammist LG
Petit Bleu Verdict
ca. 1898
Photomechanical print
Bibliothèque Nationale, Paris

The power of the press is demonstrated as the public scrambles for news concerning the authorship of the "*petit bleu*," the letter linking the spy Esterhazy to the German military attaché, Maximilien von Schwarzkoppen.

Plate 19
Charles Paul Renouard
Don't Ever Confess! (N'avouez jamais!), ca. 1898
Pen and ink on paper
Musée Carnavalet, Paris

In a meeting imagined by this Dreyfusard artist, Secretary of War Mercier orders the traitor Esterhazy to remain silent. A confession from Esterhazy could have exposed Mercier's involvement in the illegal proceedings during Dreyfus's court-martial.

Plate 20
Charles Paul Renouard
40 Upper Gloucester Road
L'Affaire Dreyfus, 1899
Lithograph, artist's proof
The Library of the Jewish Theological Seminary, New York

In his album on the Affair, Renouard depicts the traitor Esterhazy as an archvillain in his English hideout.

Plate 21
Léon-Antoine-Lucien Couturier
The Temple of Professional Secrecy—Psst! This way, Colonel!
(Le Temple du Secret Professionnel—Psst! Par ici! Colonel!), 1898
Watercolor
Musée de Bretagne, Rennes

Spoofing the inviolability of military secrets and the game of espionage, Couturier depicts the spy, Esterhazy, lying in wait for du Paty de Clam behind a public urinal.

This is the original drawing for the illustration in *Le Sifflet* of 18 August 1898.

Plate 22
Emile Zola
I Accuse (J'Accuse).
L'Aurore, 13 January 1898
Newspaper
Photo, courtesy of the Beinecke Rare
Book and Manuscript Library, Yale
University

Zola's famous, inflammatory letter
to the President of the Republic published in *L'Aurore* on 13 January 1898
accused the General Staff of crimes
and complicity in a plot against
Dreyfus.

Plate 23
I Prove (Je Prouve)
La Patrie, 16 January 1898
Newspaper
Musée Carnavalet, Paris

Rebuttals to Zola's *J'Accuse* surface
in the anti-Dreyfusard press which
includes the paper *La Patrie.*

Plate 24
I Accuse (J'Accuse)
La Libre Parole, 14 January 1898
Newspaper
Musée de la Presse, Paris
Courtesy of Christian Bailly

In response to the indictments printed in *L'Aurore,* Edouard Drumont, in his anti-Semitic newspaper *La Libre Parole,* counters Zola's *J'Accuse* with charges against the Dreyfusards.

Plate 25
B. Moloch
Zola the reckless (Zola le téméraire)
L'Image pour Rire No. 9, January-February 1898
Photomechanical print
Bibliothèque Nationale, Paris

The caption reads:

"I have all the evidence of Dreyfus's innocence, I'm making it my affair and it's going to get me in there." (J'ai là toutes les preuves de l'innocence de Dreyfus, j'en fais mon affaire et ça me fera entrer là.)

In Moloch's cartoon, Zola, the clairvoyant, erroneously predicts that his new novel *The Dreyfus Affair* will enable him to fulfill his long-cherished ambition to gain membership in the French Academy.

The Zola Trial

In his open letter to the president of France, Zola invited a charge of libel by accusing the General Staff of conspiring to find Dreyfus guilty, even though they knew he was innocent. His strategy of using his own trial to reopen the Dreyfus case was only partially successful, and Zola was found guilty.

Plate 26
Charles Paul Renouard
Lawyers for Both Sides (Avocats des 2 partis)
L'Affaire Dreyfus, 1899 Lithograph
The Library of the Jewish Theological Seminary of America, New York

At the start of the trial, Fernand Labori, Zola's lawyer, greets Edmond van Cassell, the advocate-general.

Plate 27
Charles Paul Renouard
Edgar Demange as a Witness
L'Affaire Dreyfus, 1899 Lithograph
The Library of the Jewish Theological Seminary of America, New York

The caption reads:
"M. Demange says: This proves that two men of good faith can have different opinions on the same subject."
(Mr. Demange dit: cela preuve que deux hommes de bonne foi peuvent avoir une opinion différente sur le même sujet.)

Dreyfus's lawyer testified that he believed that the judgment against Dreyfus was illegal because of the secret documents shown to the judges without the knowledge of the defense.

Plate 28
Charles Paul Renouard
Clemenceau
L'Affaire Dreyfus, 1899 Lithograph
The Library of the Jewish Theological Seminary of America, New York

Although he was not a lawyer, Georges Clemenceau was allowed to represent *L'Aurore* at Zola's trial. Clemenceau, the political editor of that paper, coined the title *J'Accuse* for Zola's article.

Plate 29a–d
Charles Paul Renouard
Four Heads of Esterhazy
L'Affaire Dreyfus, 1899
Lithographs
The Library of the Jewish Theological Seminary of America, New York

Esterhazy, accused and acquitted of having written the document that convicted Dreyfus, refused to answer any of the questions put to him by the defense counsel.

Plate 30a, b
Charles Paul Renouard
Labori's Closing Arguments for the Defense
L'Affaire Dreyfus, 1899
Wood engravings
The Library of the Jewish Theological Seminary of America, New York

Theatrical and passionate, Labori took three days to summarize his case.

Plate 31

The Zola Trial (Le Procès Zola)
The Verdict (Le Verdict), 1898
Poster
Bibliothèque Nationale, Paris

Poster announcing the session of the
Court of Assize on 23 February
1898, during which the verdict on
Zola's trial was delivered. He was
sentenced to one year in prison and
a fine.

Plate 32

Théophile-Alexandre Steinlen
Rochefort is Dying! Rochefort is Dead!
(Rochefort se meurte! Rochefort est mort)
La Feuille, 16 June 1898
Photomechanical print

Collection of Mr. and Mrs. Herbert
D. Schimmel, New York

In a mock funeral, the nationalist
leader—temporarily destroyed by the
reversal of Zola's first conviction—is
mourned by the General Staff.

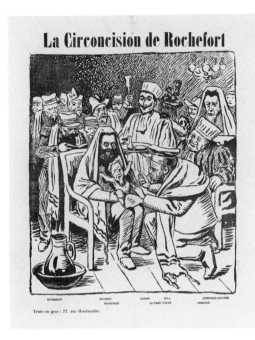

Plate 33

The Circumcision of Rochefort (La Circoncision de Rochefort) ca. 1898

Poster, woodblock print

The Jewish Museum; Gift of Mr. and Mrs. Herbert D. Schimmel

Dreyfusards and anti-Dreyfusards are pilloried through their joint participation in this travesty on the Jewish ceremony.

Zola, assisted by the lawyers, Labori and Demange, initiates the anti-Semitic publisher of *L'Intransigeant,* Henri Rochefort, who is seated on the lap of the virulent anti-Semite, Edouard Drumont.

Plate 34

L. Calot

Long Live the Army! (Vive l'Armée!) 1898

Photomechanical print

Bibliothèque Nationale, Paris

Dreyfus, Zola, and two Jews are swept away amid assorted garbage, including the Dreyfusard newspapers, *L'Aurore, Le Siècle,* and *La Fronde,* by a towering army officer.

172

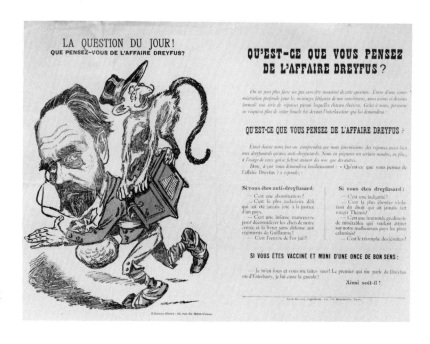

Plate 35

Artist unknown

The Question of the Day! What do you think about the Dreyfus Affair? (La Question du Jour! Qu'est-ce que vous pensez de L'Affaire Dreyfus?) ca. 1898

Poster

Boston Public Library

Zola as an organ-grinder carries the monkey Dreyfus on his back. This poster offers perplexed, besieged Dreyfusards and anti-Dreyfusards prepared answers to the controversial question, "What do you think about the Dreyfus Affair?"

Plate 36

Artist unknown

Zola and his "Intellectuals" (Zola et ses "Intellectuels") ca. 1898

Photomechanical print

Bibliothèque Nationale, Paris

Zola, as swineherd, leads his "flock" in a cartoon ridiculing and discrediting the intellectuals' support of Dreyfus. This newspaper clipping was preserved by the photographer Eugene Atget in his scrapbook.

The Debacle

After Zola's conviction, two anti-Dreyfusard journals both published covers alluding to his novel, *La Débâcle,* which was critical of the General Staff during the Franco-Prussian War.

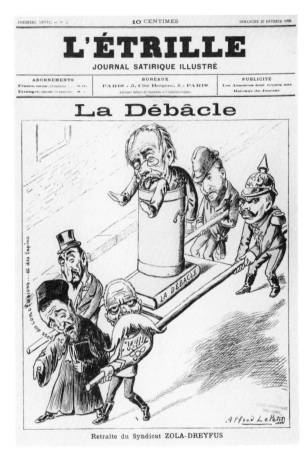

Plate 37
Fertom
The Debacle (La Débâcle)
Le Pilori, 27 February 1898
Photomechanical print
Musée de Bretagne, Rennes

The caption reads:
"Ah! Pity his poor plight (familiar tune)."
(Ah! plaignez son pauvre sort [air connu].)
Scheurer-Kestner is characterized as a blind man asking for pity, while Labori and foreign militia follow Zola's coffin to the garbage dump.

Plate 38
Alfred LePetit
The Debacle (La Débâcle)
L'Etrille, 27 February 1898
Photomechanical print
Musée Carnavalet, Paris

The caption reads:
"Retreat of the Zola-Dreyfus Syndicate"
(Retraite du Syndicat Zola-Dreyfus)

The Syndicate, a mythical Jewish conspiracy created by the anti-Semitic press, was seen as the guiding force of the revision movement. It was said to have German ties and to have hired the French intellectuals who supported Dreyfus.

174

Plate 39

E. Grenieux

Emile Zola and the Dreyfusards, or The Traitors' Debacle (Emile Zola et les Dreyfus ou La Débâcle des Traîtres)
1898

Photomechanical print

Musée Carnavalet, Paris

Zola, the perennial candidate to the French Academy, is stopped at its gates and vilified as a pornographer and offender of the French Army in league with the Jewish Syndicate. This brochure was published around the time of his trial before the Court of Assize.

Plate 40

de Haenen

Crisis in Algeria (Affaire d'Algérie)
1898

Photomechanical print

Bibliothèque Nationale, Paris

Jewish shops in French Algeria were plundered in January and February 1898, during anti-Semitic rioting following the publication of Zola's "J'Accuse."

Plate 41

Léon-Antoine-Lucien Couturier

You want confessions? Here are some!!!
(En voulez vous des aveux? En voilà!!!)
ca. 1898

Poster

Bibliothèque Nationale, Paris

In this Dreyfusard cartoon, the protagonists of the Dreyfus conspiracy confess their various crimes. Lt. Col. Henry admits his forgery; Esterhazy, his writing the bordereau and being the real traitor; and the General Staff, to lying and condemning an innocent man.

Plate 42

Jean-Louis Forain

Let arms yield to the toga (Latin: *Ce-dant arma togae*) (Impression d'audi-ence)

Psst. . . ! No. 3, 19 February 1898

Photomechanical print

The Jewish Museum; Gift of Charles and Beth Gordon

The caption reads:

"And we put up with it!" (Et on supporte ça!)

On this cover, a magistrate kicks an army officer's hat. Forain was concerned that the military was giving way to civil power.

Plate 43

Henri-Gabriel Ibels

Let's Go! (Allons-y!) (Impression d'audience)

Le Sifflet, No. 2, 24 February 1898

Photomechanical print

Collection of Mr. and Mrs. Herbert D. Schimmel, New York

The caption reads:

"And we put up with it!" (Et on supporte ça!)

In his rejoinder, Ibels draws an army officer kicking at the scales of justice.

Psst. . . ! and *Le Sifflet*

Two opposing journals established at the time of Zola's intervention on behalf of Dreyfus epitomize the polarization of the press. *Psst. . . !* was anti-Dreyfusard and *Le Sifflet* was Drey-fusard. These publications frequently used similar images or captions with contrary intent. Both papers were created by artists for the sole purpose of expressing their opinions on the Affair.

Plate 44

Jean-Louis Forain

Neighborhood Drudgery (La corvée de quartier)

Psst. . . !, No. 4, 26 February 1898

Photomechanical print

The Jewish Museum; Gift of Charles and Beth Gordon

The caption reads:

"What a trash-heap! . . . This could get 100,000 men killed" (Quel fumier! . . . Ça pouvait faire tuer 100,000 hommes!)

Forain's soldier sweeps up the refuse of the Zola trial: a judge's hat and a copy of "J'Accuse." The suggestion is made that Zola's efforts might end with a decimated French army.

Plate 45

Léon-Antoine-Lucien Couturier

For the King! (Pour le Roy!)

Le Sifflet, No. 5, Year 2, 3 March 1899

Photomechanical print

Collection of Mr. and Mrs. Herbert D. Schimmel, New York

The caption reads:

"To think this could get 100,000 men killed" (—Dire que ce fumier-là pouvait tuer plus de cent mille hommes!)

A year later *Le Sifflet* responded with a soldier cleaning up after an unsuccessful Royalist coup.

178

Coucou, le voilà!

La Vérité sort de son puits.

LA VÉRITÉ QUAND MÊME!

MÉLINE — Malgré tout, j'ai bien peur qu'elle ne sorte, la rosse!...

Plate 46
Caran d'Ache
There he is! (Coucou, le voilà!)
Psst. . . ! 10 June 1899
Photomechanical print
The Jewish Museum; Gift of Charles and Beth Gordon

The caption reads:

"Truth comes out of its well." (La Vérité sort de son puits.)

Zola, holding a Dreyfus doll, emerges from a toilet, in this scurrilous variation on truth rising from her well.

Plate 47
Raoul Barré
The Truth Even So! (La Vérité Quand Même!)
Le Sifflet, No. 5, 17 March 1898
Photomechanical print
Collection of Mr. and Mrs. Herbert D. Schimmel, New York

The caption reads:

"Méline—In spite of everything I'm afraid she'll come out, the beast! . . ." (Méline—Malgré tout, j'ai bien peur qu'elle ne sorte, la rosse! . . .)

Truth, traditionally represented as a nude woman rising from a well, strains against the force of the army for her freedom, as the anti-Revisionist Premier Méline and the spy, Esterhazy, watch with alarm.

L'ESPRIT DU SABRE

— Hon! hon!! *Intellectuels*... Hon! hon!! hon !!! *Tas de rossards!*... Hon! hon!!
moi Gouvernement... Hon! *Serrer la vis!* Hon! hon!!...

Salons intellectuels

CHŒUR DES DAMES : — « Un royaume pour un lieutenant de dragons! »

Plate 48

Henri-Gabriel Ibels

Rapier Wit (L'Esprit du Sabre)

Le Sifflet, 3 March 1898

Photomechanical print

Collection of Mr. and Mrs.
Herbert D. Schimmel, New York

The caption reads:

"Heh, heh!! *Intellectuals* . . . Heh,
heh, heh!! *Bunch of scoundrels!* . . .
Heh! heh!! *me Government* . . . Heh!
Tighten the vise! Heh! Heh!! . . . "
(Hon! hon!! *Intellectuels*. . . Hon!
hon!! hon!!! *Tas de rossards!* . . .
Hon! hon!! *moi Gouvernement* . . .
Hon! *Serrer la vis!* Hon! hon!! . . .)

In Ibels's cartoon envisioning an anti-
Dreyfusard salon, where loyalty to
the army reigns, two gentlemen
demonstrate their "rapier wit" by
scoffing at intellectuals.

Plate 49

Caran d'Ache

Intellectual Salons (Salons intellectuels)

Psst. . . !, 10 December 1898

Photomechanical print

The Jewish Museum; Gift of Charles
and Beth Gordon

The caption reads:

"Ladies' chorus: 'A Kingdom for a
Cavalry Lieutenant!' (Choeur des
Dames: 'Un royaume pour un
lieutenant de dragons!')

The term *intellectual* was used as a
derogatory epithet for Dreyfusards.
Here, the women's dissatisfaction
with their escorts, who are apparently engaged in political conversation, echoes the anti-Dreyfusard sentiments of the artist.

Plate 50

Jean-Louis Forain

Joseph's Epaulettes (Les Epaulettes de Joseph)

Psst. . . ! No. 21, 25 June 1898

Photomechanical print

The Jewish Museum; Gift of Charles and Beth Gordon

The caption reads:

"Here's something for my collection! . . . I already have Dreyfus's!" (Voilà pour ma collection! . . . J'ai déjà celles de Dreyfus!)

A ragpicker assembles a collection of military insignia, which apparently already includes the epaulettes torn from Dreyfus's uniform. He now hopes to add those of Joseph Reinach, who was one of the most hated and vilified of Dreyfus's supporters.

Plate 51

Jean-Louis Forain

For Dreyfus (Pour Dreyfus)

Psst. . . !, No. 75, 8 July 1899

Photomechanical print

The Jewish Museum; Gift of Charles and Beth Gordon

The caption reads:

"Package from His Serene Imperial Highness the Prince of MONACO" (Envoi de Son Altesse Sérénissime Monseigneur le Prince de MONACO!)

The theme of Dreyfus's lost epaulettes is reprised in this reference to the assistance given him by the Prince of Monaco.

Plate 52

Maximilien Luce

Soldiers' Girls (Filles à Soldats)

Le Père Peinard No. 102, 2 October 1898

Photomechanical print

The University of Michigan Library, Labadie Collection

The caption reads:

"To Forain, ex-Communard, and to Corporal Poiré, known as Caran d'Ache." (A Forain, ex-communard et au caporal Poiré, dit Caran d'Ache).

The caricaturists for the anti-Dreyfusard newspaper *Psst. . . !,* Forain and Caran D'Ache, are portrayed as prostitutes of the church and army.

Social Tensions

The movement for the revision of the Dreyfus verdict polarized the country, particularly after Esterhazy was acquitted of the charge of treason and Zola found guilty of libel. Cartoonists satirized the effects on daily life.

Plate 53

Pépin

A Portrait of Conjugal Love (Tableau de l'amour conjugal)

Le Grelot, 30 January 1898

Photomechanical print

Bibliothèque Nationale, Paris

The caption reads:

"The Dreyfus-Esterhazy Affair in the Bedroom" (L'affaire Dreyfus-Esterhazy à la Chambre . . . à coucher)

Households were divided when family members had different opinions.

L'affaire Dreyfus-Esterhazy à la Chambre... à coucher.

Plate 54
Caran d'Ache
A Family Dinner (Un dîner en famille)
Pen and ink on paper
Bibliothèque Nationale, Paris

This drawing was published in *Le Figaro,* 14 February 1898, during Zola's trial. The captions read: "Absolutely, no talk of the Affair." "They talked about it."

Plate 55
Félix Vallotton
At Home (En Famille)
Le Cri de Paris, 13 February 1898
Photomechanical print
Bibliothèque Nationale, Paris

Another family quietly demonstrates divergent points of view as husband and wife read the news of Zola's trial in the nationalist *L'Intransigeant* and the opposing *L'Aurore.* A third member of the family peruses the anarchist *Le Libertaire* which became a supporter of revision.

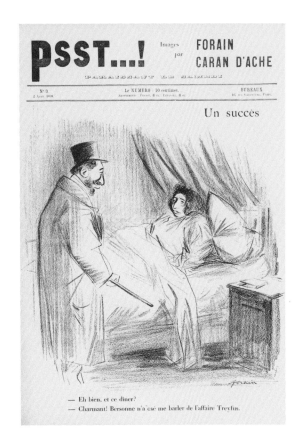

Plate 56
Jean-Louis Forain
A Success (Un succès)
Psst. . . ! No. 9, 2 April 1898
Photomechanical print
The Jewish Museum, Gift of Charles
and Beth Gordon, Connecticut

The caption reads:
"'Well, how was the dinner-party?'
'Luffly! No one dared zpeak to me
of the Treyfus Affair.'"
(Eh bien, et ce dîner? Charmant!
Bersonne n'a osé me barler de l'af-
faire Treyfus.)

Anti-Semitic writers often wrote
captions giving their characters a
stereotyped Yiddish accent.

Plate 57
Jean-Louis Forain
The Affair (L'Affaire)
Le Rire, 24 December 1898
Photomechancial print
The Jewish Museum

The caption reads:
"Another house we won't be dining
in again." (Encore une maison où
nous dinerons plus.)

Hostesses complained that the Affair
was spoiling social life.

Alfred Le Petit

One of the most prolific cartoonists to address the Affair, Alfred Le Petit published in *La France, Mon Droit,* and *L'Etrille,* the latter established as a propaganda vehicle during this period. His anti-Dreyfusard caricatures express his pungent comments on the personalities involved, although many of the specific allusions are now obscure.

Plate 58
Alfred Le Petit
The Affair (L'Affaire)
Pen and ink on paper
Collection of Artine Artinian, Palm Beach

Le Petit represented the Affair as a reptile with stereotyped Semitic features feeding on the body of France.

Plate 59
Alfred Le Petit
They Had to Use Forceps to Deliver It (Il a fallu les forceps pour accoucher le ça), 1899
Pen and ink on paper
Collection of Artine Artinian, Palm Beach

The revocation of the first judgment against Dreyfus was seen as a monstrous infant whose birth had been difficult.

Plate 60
Alfred Le Petit
Le Figaro: The Secret File (Le Figaro: le dossier secret), 1899
Pen and ink
Musée de Bretagne, Rennes

The inscription reads:

"This is very witty." (H. de Villenhart) (Elle est très bonne.)

When the judges of the Appeals Court requested the secret Dreyfus file, anti-Dreyfusards referred to them as "hirelings of Germany." Le Petit depicts them with the characteristic spike of Prussian helmets on their traditional judicial caps.

* Plate 61
Alfred Le Petit
He Repeats the Offense (Il Récidive),
1899
Photomechanical print
Bibliothèque Nationale, Paris

Zola's influence was felt during the
appeal process, although he was still
in England.

Plate 62
Alfred Le Petit
Zola Rabid (Zola hydrophobe), 1899
Pen and ink on paper
Collection of Artine Artinian, Palm
Beach

The caption reads:
"Rennes Court-Martial" ("Conseil
de guerre, Rennes")
"The Law" ("La loi")
"Another Attack" ("nouvel accès")

In another rebuke of Zola, the author
is portrayed as a mad dog confront-
ing the law during the Rennes court-
martial.

LOGIQUE

Traître dehors patriote dedans

APPRÉHENSION

— Ne tirez pas trop, vous allez nous faire tomber.

* Plate 63
Alfred Le Petit
Logic (Logique), 1899
Photomechanical print
Bibliothèque Nationale, Paris

The caption reads:
"Traitor outside, patriot inside"
(Traître dehors, patriote dedans)

Le Petit's title is ironic, while his caption expresses his true feeling. After Dreyfus's pardon, the nationalist leader Déroulède remained in prison for conspiracy against the state. Déroulède would be found guilty and exiled for ten years.

* Plate 64
Alfred Le Petit
Apprehension (Appréhension), 1899
Photomechanical print
Bibliothèque Nationale, Paris

The caption reads:
"Don't pull too hard, you'll make us fall." (Ne tirez pas trop, vous allez nous faire tomber.)

The weak Cabinet is threatened by the Senate in the aftermath of Dreyfus's pardon.

Songs and games

The proliferation of games, comic strips, toys, and songs is another example of the appeal to popular opinion during the struggle for revision.

Plate 65

Bob (Comtesse Sibylle Martel de Janville, also called Gyp)

Truth in Action (La Vérité en marche)

Le Rire, 21 May 1898

Photomechanical print

The New York Public Library

The caption reads:

Mr. Jaurès—We will not be put off our work, because we have the right to carry it out in broad daylight . . . (Speech on 24 Jan. 1898)

Truth in Action/Spectacular Drama

Down with the army/Long live Dreyfus/Long Live Zola

Song: Let's dance the carmagnole, long live the sound, long live the sound! Let's dance the carmagnole, long live the sound of the cannon!

The artist, a fervent anti-Semite and anti-Dreyfusard, employs the image of a bitter Truth in her reference to Zola's statement that truth had been set in motion and nothing could stop it. The socialist leader Jaurès sings a song of the French Revolution and dances to Zola's drumbeat.

ZOLA-MOUQUETTE
Le fondement de l'affaire Dreyfus

MON CŒUR À DREYFUS

Plate 66

Artist unknown

Zola-Mouquette. The foundation of the Dreyfus Affair (Zola-Mouquette. Le fondement de l'affaire Dreyfus) ca. 1898

Paper novelty

Musée Carnavalet, Paris

As his pants drop in this acerbic pull-toy, Zola's buttocks reveal the inscription "My Heart belongs to Dreyfus" ("Mon Coeur à Dreyfus").

Plate 67

Artist unknown

The Secret of the Veiled Lady (Le Secret de la Dame Voilée) ca. 1898

Paper novelty. Photomechanical reproduction

Boston Public Library

This paper novelty showing Dreyfus resting on bags of money on Devil's Island contains two windows for viewing an illustrated rotating wheel. Figures associated with the Affair, such as Esterhazy's "Veiled Lady," are visible in the opening over the well.

Dreyfus's story was told on the covers of books of cigarette papers humorously labeled "The *bordereau* paper," named after the infamous document that convicted him.

The ephemeral nature of this product is a comment on the value of this piece of evidence.

Plate 68

Artist unknown

At the Cherche-Midi. The foot exam and the dim lantern. (Au Cherche-Midi. L'épreuve du pied et de la lanterne sourde).

The bordereau paper (Le papier du bordereau) 1899

Book of cigarette papers

Musée Carnavalet, Paris

To catch him off guard, du Paty de Clam interrogated Dreyfus late at night during his imprisonment at Cherche-Midi in October, 1894.

This cigarette paper mockingly reveals du Paty examining Dreyfus's foot.

Plate 69

Artist unknown

At the Court of Appeal. The revision decided unanimously. (A la Cour de Cassation. La révision décidée à l'unanimité).

The bordereau paper (Le papier du bordereau) 1899

Book of cigarette papers

Musée Carnavalet, Paris

Plate 70

Artist unknown

Devil's Island. The hut and the palisade. (A l'ile du Diable. La case et la palissade).

The bordereau paper. (Le papier du bordereau) 1899

Book of cigarette papers

Musée Carnavalet, Paris

Plate 71

Artist unknown

The Game of the Dreyfus Affair and Truth (Le Jeu de l'Affaire Dreyfus et de la Vérité), ca. 1898

Photomechanical print, colored

Collection of Ronald Bouscher, Amsterdam

The goal of this popular Dreyfusard board game was to reach Truth. The image derives from the French saying "Truth lies at the bottom of the well."

Plate 72

A. Lambot

The Game of 36 Heads (Le Jeu des 36 Têtes)

L'Antijuif, 12 February 1899

Photomechanical print

Houghton Library, Harvard University, Cambridge

The newspaper *L'antijuif,* the official organ of the *Ligue Antisémitique Française,* also published its own game. Like the Dreyfusard game, the set of rules and description of characters contain elaborate puns on the names of enemies.

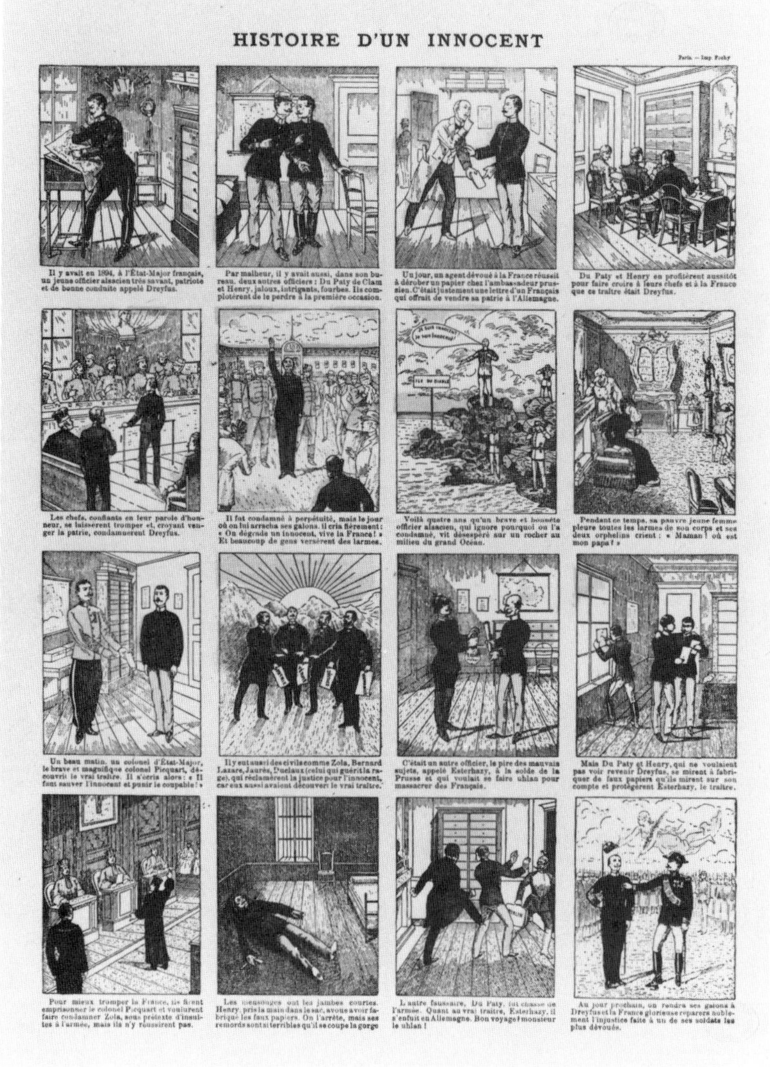

Plate 73

Artist unknown

History of an Innocent (Histoire d'un innocent), 1898

Stencil colored lithograph

The Boston Public Library

In his memoir of his father, Pierre Dreyfus writes of having had the Affair explained to him by means of such a colored print. He was eight years old when his father was pardoned.

Plate 74

Artist unknown

*History of a Traitor (Histoire d'un
Traître)*, ca. 1899

Stencil colored lithograph

Rodeph Shalom, Philadelphia
Museum of Judaica of Congregation

Anti-Dreyfusards also produced their
own version of the history of the Affair. It employs most of the standard
anti-Semitic imagery of the time.

Plate 75

Artist unknown

The Kitchen of the General Staff (La Cuisine de l'Etat-Major)

Le Père Peinard, no. 101, 25 September 1898

Photomechanical print

The University of Michigan Library, Labadie Collection

The caption reads:

"A thousand bolsters! The more I scrub the dirtier it gets!" (Mille polochons! Plus je frotte, plus c'est sale! . . .)

An officer curses the futility of the Dreyfus cover-up.

Plate 76

F. G. Keronan

The New Siamese Twins (Les Nouveaux Fréres Siamois)

Le Père Peinard No. 106, 30 October 1898

Photomechanical print

The University of Michigan Library, Labadie Collection

Fervent anti-Dreyfusard allies, the clergy and military, are here united both in body and spirit.

The anarchist paper *Le Père Peinard* delighted in lampooning both factions.

Plate 77

Georges Manzana-Pissarro

Miss Liberty Being Tortured on the Rack

Le Père Peinard, 8 January 1899 and 15 January 1899

Photomechanical print

The University of Michigan Library, Labadie Collection

The caption reads:

Part one: "'How will this end?' . . . 'We will tell you in the next issue, the good guys.'" (Comment ça finir-t-il? . . . On vous le dira au prochain numéro, les bons bougres.)

Part two: Liberty has a tough life . . . Watch out for squalls! When will this scene take place? (Elle a la vie dure la Liberté! . . . Gare la casse! A quand ce tableau?)

In a two-part cartoon in *Le Père Peinard,* an anarchist journal, Manzana ponders the fate of Liberty and includes a "Rothschild" among her anti-Dreyfusard torturers.

Postcards

The postcard, then a recent invention, became a propaganda tool as each faction expressed itself in this medium. Many cards were issued in limited editions and quickly became collectors' items. Publishers in many countries created cards referring to the Affair.

Plate 78
Seljenka & Szél, publishers
Budapest, Hungary
Dreyfus on Devil's Island, 1899
Photomechanical print
Musée de Bretagne, Rennes

Dreyfus hears the news of his retrial.

Plate 79
Origin unknown
The Ship Truth, 1899
Photomechanical print
Musée de Bretagne, Rennes

Picquart and Zola serve as dock-workers when Dreyfus returns from Devil's Island on the ship of Truth.

Plate 80

Monogrammist EE

Max Marcus, publisher

Berlin, Germany

The State in the State—Here's the Sad Result (L'Etat dans l'Etat—Voilà le triste resultat!), 1899

Photomechanical print

Musée de Bretagne, Rennes

The text reads:

"In the opinion of the civilized world Dreyfus is judged—France is found guilty."

A play on words in the heading is employed to express a common reaction to Dreyfus's second conviction—that it was a political act.

Plate 81

Four-Step (Pas-à-Quatre)

Photomechanical print

Musée de Bretagne, Rennes

Three anti-Dreyfusards and the traitor are humorously depicted as a music-hall chorus line.

Plate 82
A. M. Amiot, publisher
The Hague, Holland
Picquart, Dreyfus, and Zola, 1899
Photomechanical print
Musée de Bretagne, Rennes

Photographs of the protagonists were popular.

Plate 83
Max Marcus, publisher
Berlin, Germany
The Dreyfus Affair: Drumont, Rochefort, and Déroulède, 1898
Photomechanical print
Musée de Bretagne, Rennes

The caption translates:

The three great Frenchmen or the Triple Alliance. The modern three-leaf clover.

A German postcard with a sardonic caption depicts three enemies of Dreyfus.

Plate 84
G. Sternfeld, publisher
Venice, Italy
Affair Dreyfus—Spit on Zola (Affaire Dreyfus—Conspuez-Zola), 1899
Photomechanical print
Musée de Bretagne, Rennes

Henri Rochefort, publisher of the Nationalist newspaper *L'Intransigeant* is shown in a medallion on one of a series of twelve cards illustrating different aspects of the Affair. A soldier, a priest, and two peasants express their negative opinion of Zola.

Plate 86
Artist illegible
Drumont-Dreyfus
Photomechanical print
Musée de Bretagne, Rennes

There were two series of postcards designed to resemble playing cards with personalities of the Affair.

Plate 85
Difficult Cleaning (Nettoyage difficile), 1899
Photomechanical print
Musée de Bretagne, Rennes

The symbol of France attempts to clean up Dreyfus using mother's milk. This anti-Dreyfusard allegory suggests that it would be difficult to prove his innocence.

Plate 87
Gaston Noury
King of Hearts—Man of War, 1901
Photomechanical print
Musée de Bretagne, Rennes

This king of hearts is General Zurlinden, an anti-Dreyfusard minister of war who served briefly in 1895 and again in 1898.

202

Plate 88

Julio (?)

Noble Mission!

La Réforme, 6 August 1899

Brussels, Belgium

Photomechanical print

Musée de Bretagne, Rennes

The caption reads:

"And they're looking for the pearl of truth in all that sh . . . !" (Et c'est dans toute cette m. . . . qu'ils cherchent la perle de la vérité!)

The day before the second court-martial began, Rochefort and Drumont were depicted with another anti-Dreyfusard, Jules Quesnay de Beaurepaire, a justice on the Court of Appeal.

Orens

During the Affair, Orens created several groups of satirical postcards referring to the events.

Plate 89

Orens

Go in Peace (Allez en Paix), 1899(?)

Photomechanical print

Musée de Bretagne, Rennes

Orens takes a harsh view of Dreyfus's pardon.

Plate 90

The Jaurès-Dreyfus Cakewalk (Le Cake-Walk Jaurès-Dreyfus), 1903

Photomechanical print

Musée de Bretagne, Rennes

The artist is sarcastic about Jaurès's activities in the Chamber of Deputies on behalf of Dreyfus.

Plate 91

Orens

I Accuse (J'Accuse), 1904

Photomechanical print

Musée de Bretagne, Rennes

The caption reads:

"1898, E. Zola accuses the court of having acquitted Esterhazy by command." (1898 E. Zola accuse le Conseil d'avoir acquitté par ordre Esterhazy.)

Orens raises the question of who is to be crucified, Zola or Esterhazy. At this point the artist seems to be sympathetic to Zola, depicted carrying the torch of Liberty and the mirror of Truth.

Plate 92

Orens

The Thermometer of Truth,

Le Burin Satirique No. 12, second year, 250 examples, 1904

Photomechanical print

Musée de Bretagne, Rennes

The caption reads:

The Court of Appeal orders a new inquiry on the forgeries discovered in the Dreyfus Affair dossier, and announces a demand for revision, formulated by Dreyfus, and acceptable in form.

There are three possibilities on this thermometer: "Innocent," "Pardon," or "Guilty."

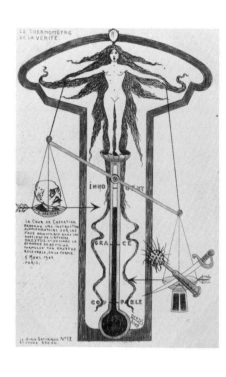

Plate 93a, b

Orens

The Dreyfus Weighing (Le Pesage Dreyfus), 1906

Photomechanical print

Musée de Bretagne, Rennes

The choices on the scale of appeal are "Innocence," "Charenton" (an insane asylum), "Guilty," and "Liar." Dreyfus is weighed and found innocent; Esterhazy is found guilty. The artist depicts both men with the same degree of acid humor.

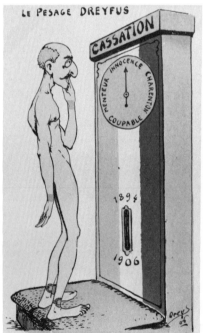

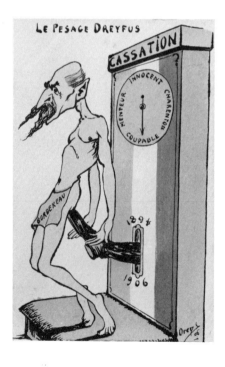

Couturier: History of a crime

The vigor of the drawings and the acerbic text contributed to the great success of this group of eighteen postcards, according to a contemporary critic. The events are described from the Dreyfusard point of view, and several of the cards are inscribed with the sender's comments.

There were two editions, tinted and black and white. Both sold out immediately.

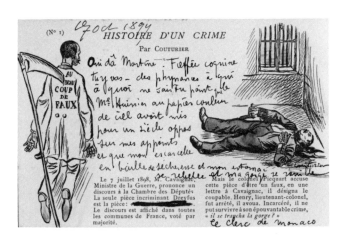

Plate 94

Léon-Antoine-Lucien Couturier

From the Good Thrust of the Scythe (Au beau coup de faux)

History of a Crime (Histoire d'un crime) no. 1, 1899

Photomechanical print

Musée de Bretagne, Rennes

The drawing of Minister of War Cavaignac on the left contains a typical visual and verbal pun. The word *faux* can be translated as either "scythe" or "forgery." A document that Cavaignac had declared was the most important evidence against Dreyfus turned out to be a forgery. The drawing on the right depicts the forger Henry, who committed suicide in his prison cell.

Plate 95

Léon-Antoine-Lucien Couturier

Esterhazy

History of a Crime (Histoire d'un crime) no. 4, 1899

Photomechanical print

Musée de Bretagne, Rennes

The portrayal of Esterhazy in a Prussian uniform derives from a letter he once wrote in which he said he could have happily been a Uhlan (a Prussian trooper) killing a hundred thousand Frenchmen. Esterhazy's handwriting in this letter established that he had also written the bordereau.

Plate 96

Léon-Antoine-Lucien Couturier

Public Building

History of a Crime (Histoire d'un crime)
no. 5, 1899

Photomechanical print

Musée de Bretagne, Rennes

Esterhazy and Commandant du Paty
de Clam often met secretly to discuss
the cover-up. The Dreyfusard artist
Couturier sets their meeting in a
public urinal. He published a variant
of this drawing in *Le Sifflet,* 18 August 1898.

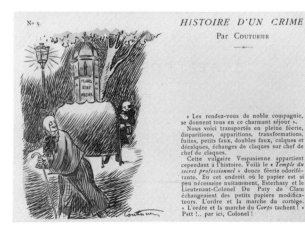

Plate 97

Léon-Antoine-Lucien Couturier

General Mercier

History of a Crime (Histoire d'un crime)
no. 7, 1899

Photomechanical print

Musée de Bretagne, Rennes

General Mercier, Minister of War in
1894, depicted with members of the
General Staff, du Paty de Clam,
Gonse, and de Boisdeffre, was responsible for Dreyfus's premature arrest on insufficient evidence. He is
described as having become an accomplice of the Army to avoid being
regarded as a "Milquetoast."

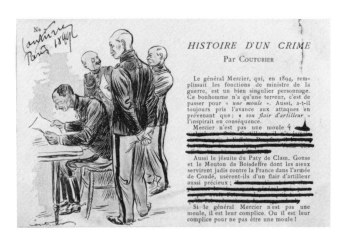

Plate 98

Léon-Antoine-Lucien Couturier

Drumont and du Paty de Clam

History of a Crime (Histoire d'un crime)
no. 8, 1899

Photomechanical print

Musée de Bretagne, Rennes

On the right, du Paty and Colonel
Henry prepare documents for General Mercier's use. Drumont, tipped
off about Dreyfus's arrest, published
the news in *La Libre Parole.* The
General Staff, afraid to back down,
continued to insist that Dreyfus was
guilty.

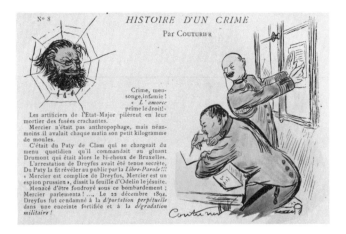

Plate 99
Léon-Antoine-Lucien Couturier
The Confessions
History of a Crime (Histoire d'un crime)
no. 9, 1899
Photomechanical print
Musée de Bretagne, Rennes

After the degradation of Dreyfus,
one of the officers guarding him
claimed that he had confessed. Actually, Dreyfus had reaffirmed his
innocence.

Plate 100
Léon-Antoine-Lucien Couturier
On Devil's Island
History of a Crime (Histoire d'un crime)
no. 10, 1899
Photomechanical print
Musée de Bretagne, Rennes

The text speaks of Dreyfus, the innocent martyr, an exile on Devil's
Island, victim of the high treason of
the General Staff.

208

Plate 101
Léon-Antoine-Lucien Couturier
Father du Lac and du Paty de Clam
History of a Crime (Histoire d'un crime)
no. 11, 1899
Photomechanical print
Musée de Bretagne, Rennes

Father du Lac played a minor role in
the conspiracy against Dreyfus, but
was seen by the latter's partisans as
a symbol of the role of the Church.
On the right Esterhazy, a notorious
gambler, bets with money he received as a spy.

Plate 102
Léon-Antoine-Lucien Couturier
General Gonse and General Picquart
History of a Crime (Histoire d'un crime)
no. 13, 1899
Photomechanical print
Musée de Bretagne, Rennes

When Picquart reported to his superior officer that Esterhazy, not
Dreyfus, was actually the traitor, he
was told to keep it quiet.

Plate 103

Leon-Antoine-Lucien Couturier

The Accuser at the Revision

History of a Crime (Histoire d'un crime)
no. 18, 1899

Photomechanical print

Musée de Bretagne, Rennes

Livid that the Court of Appeal had
overturned Dreyfus's 1894 conviction, the architect of the case, Mercier, leaves with two policemen.

Plate 104

Artist unknown

Rennes—La Salle des Pas-Perdus, 1899

Photomechanical print

Musée de Bretagne, Rennes

Couturier never realized his plan to
complete the *History of a Crime* series
with the story of the Rennes trial.
However, while in Rennes for the
trial, he embellished a number of
conventional picture postcards of the
town and sent them to friends in
Paris.

In September, 1898, the Cabinet sent Lucie Dreyfus's request for an appeal to the criminal chamber of the Court of Appeal.

Photographic Posters

Plate 105

E. Charaire, printer

Dreyfus Is A Traitor (Dreyfus est un traître), 1898

Poster

Archives Nationales, Paris

In November 1898, Déroulède's Ligue des Patriotes published this propaganda poster, which features photographs of five ministers of war with accompanying quotations, attesting to Dreyfus's treason.

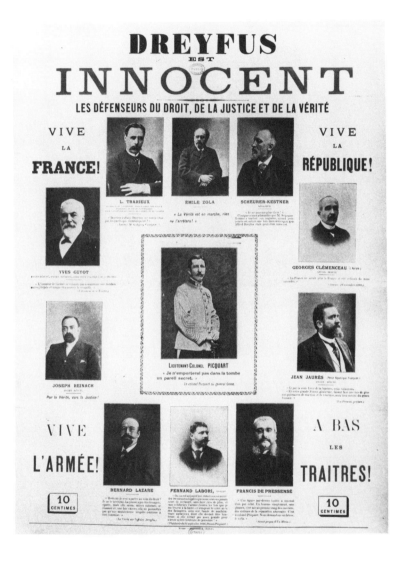

Plate 106

E. Charaire, printer

Dreyfus Is Innocent (Dreyfus est innocent), 1898

Poster

Boston Public Library

Employing a similar photograph-and-text format, the Dreyfusards responded with their own poster in December 1898, which displays eleven prominent men affirming Dreyfus's innocence.

The High Court of Appeal

After Dreyfus's appeal had been heard by the Criminal Chamber of the Appeal Court (Cour de Cassation), the government moved to transfer it to the united Court of Appeal, which consisted of three chambers: Civil, Criminal, and Petitions. The full court also found that there were grounds for a new trial.

Plate 107

The Lies of Photography (Les mensonges de la photographie)

Le Siècle, 11 January 1899

Photomechanical print

Collection of J. Robert Maguire, Shoreham, VT

To demonstrate to a gullible public the ability to easily falsify photographs, the Dreyfusards published this series of eighteen fictive, composite images, in which archenemies like Joseph Reinach and Edouard Drumont, and other implausible pairs, were juxtaposed.

Plate 108

Charles Paul Renouard

The Entrance of the Magistrates (Entrée des Magistrats)

L'Affaire Dreyfus, 1899

Lithograph

The Library of the Jewish Theological Seminary of America, New York

Plate 109

Charles Paul Renouard

The Combined Chambers of the High Court of Appeal (Toutes Chambres réunies)

L'Affaire Dreyfus, 1899

Lithograph

The Library of the Jewish Theological Seminary of America, New York

Forty-nine judges, dressed in scarlet and ermine, heard the appeal.

Plate 110
Charles Paul Renouard
*Judge Bard Reading his Report
(M. Bard lisant son rapport)*
L'Affaire Dreyfus, 1899
Lithograph
The Library of the Jewish Theological Seminary of America, New York

Alphonse Bard was the judge in the Criminal Chamber who undertook the investigation of the case.

Plate 111
Théophile-Alexandre Steinlen
Let's Salute Them! (Saluons-les!)
La Feuille, 18 January 1899
Photomechanical print
Collection of Mr. and Mrs. Herbert D. Schimmel, New York

For anarchist publisher Zo d'Axa and his contributors, the Dreyfus Affair became another opportunity to criticize the inequities in French society. In this illustration with its ironic caption, Steinlen attacks the judiciary and the army during Dreyfus's appeal.

Homage to Picquart

As head of Army intelligence, Lieutenant-Colonel Georges Picquart discovered evidence vindicating Dreyfus. In retaliation for trying to force a revision of the case, he was ordered before a court-martial. News of the charges against Picquart touched off massive public demonstrations on his behalf. Twelve artists paid their tribute in an album of lithographs.

Plate 112
Charles Paul Renouard
Portrait of Octave Mirbeau
L'Affaire Dreyfus, 1899 Lithograph
The Library of the Jewish Theological Seminary of America, New York

The playwright-critic Octave Mirbeau, who wrote the preface for the *Artists' Homage to Picquart,* was a member of the anarchist movement, along with several of the artists whose works appear in the following album.

Plate 113
Louis Anquetin
*To Colonel Picquart, 1 January 1899
(Au Colonel Picquart, Ier Janvier 1899)*
The Artists' Homage to Picquart (Hommage des artistes à Picquart), 1899
Lithograph
Collection of Mr. and Mrs. Herbert
D. Schimmel, New York

A bound hero confronts a dragon, symbol of destruction and evil. In the context of the Affair, it could also be a visual play on *dragoon,* a soldier, hence a reference to the Army.

Plate 114
Pierre-Emile Cornillier
Homage to Colonel Picquart (Hommage au Colonel Picquart)
The Artists' Homage to Picquart (Hommage des artistes à Picquart), 1899
Lithograph
Collection of Mr. and Mrs. Herbert
D. Schimmel, New York

In his cell, Picquart is comforted by Truth and Justice, allegorical figures which are recurring images in the art of the Dreyfus Affair.

Plate 115

Adolphe Ernest Gumery

To Picquart, Awakener of Souls (A Picquart, éveilleur d'Ames)

The Artists' Homage to Picquart (Hommage des artistes à Picquart), 1899

Lithograph

Collection of Mr. and Mrs. Herbert D. Schimmel, New York

A figure bearing Victory's laurel wreath and Liberty's torch of enlightenment comes to Hell with Picquart to free the damned. Picquart, Dreyfus's rescuer, is himself bound.

Plate 116

Hermann-Paul

Untitled

The Artists' Homage to Picquart (Hommage des artistes à Picquart), 1899

Lithograph

Collection of Mr. and Mrs. Herbert D. Schimmel, New York

Anti-Dreyfusard President Félix Faure prevents the military from seeing Truth. Her image derives from the traditional French saying "Truth lies at the bottom of a well."

Plate 117

Maximilien Luce

Don't Think about Your Sword; Take this Pickaxe. (Ne regrettes pas ton épée; prends cette pioche.)

The Artists' Homage to Picquart (Hommage des artistes à Picquart), 1899

Lithograph

Collection of Mr. and Mrs. Herbert D. Schimmel, New York

Labor is often symbolically portrayed as a stonebreaker. The artist suggests that only the efforts of the common man can demolish the wall between Picquart and truth.

Plate 118

Georges Manzana-Pissarro

Untitled, 1898

The Artists' Homage to Picquart (Hommage des artistes à Picquart), 1899

Lithograph

Collection of Mr. and Mrs. Herbert D. Schimmel, New York

Manzana, a son of Camille Pissarro, shared his father's radical politics; his cartoon employs a popular representation of Truth.

Plate 119
Lucien Perroudon
Untitled
The Artists' Homage to Picquart (Hommage des artistes à Picquart), 1899
Lithograph
Collection of Mr. and Mrs. Herbert D. Schimmel, New York

Perroudon's portrait was based on a photograph of Picquart taken while he was still in uniform.

Plate 120
Hippolyte Petitjean
Untitled
The Artists' Homage to Picquart (Hommage des artistes à Picquart), 1899
Lithograph
Collection of Mr. and Mrs. Herbert D. Schimmel, New York

Truth observes as the names of Dreyfus's supporters, Picquart foremost, are carved in stone.

Plate 122
Théo Van Rysselberghe
Untitled
The Artists' Homage to Picquart (Hommage des artistes à Picquart), 1899
Lithograph
Collection of Mr. and Mrs. Herbert D. Schimmel, New York

A massive hand stifles Truth.

Plate 121
Louis Armand Rault
Untitled
The Artists' Homage to Picquart (Hommage des artistes à Picquart), 1899
Lithograph
Collection of Mr. and Mrs. Herbert D. Schimmel, New York

A symbolic demonstration—the crowd includes Emile Zola, who had escaped to England after his conviction for libel.

Plate 123
Joaquín Sunyer
Untitled
The Artists' Homage to Picquart (Hommage des artistes à Picquart), 1899
Lithograph
Collection of Mr. and Mrs. Herbert D. Schimmel, New York

In Sunyer's impressionist style, the traditionally defined figure of personified Truth dissolves into pure light, which rises above the crowd.

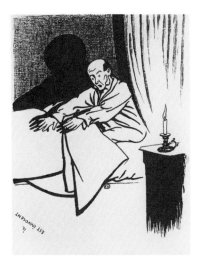

Plate 124
Félix Vallotton
He is Innocent (Il est innocent)
The Artists' Homage to Picquart (Hommage des artistes à Picquart), 1899
Lithograph
Collection of Mr. and Mrs. Herbert D. Schimmel, New York

Former premier Jules Méline, an anti-Dreyfusard, is now disturbed by Picquart's cry at the Zola trial: "He [Dreyfus] is innocent."

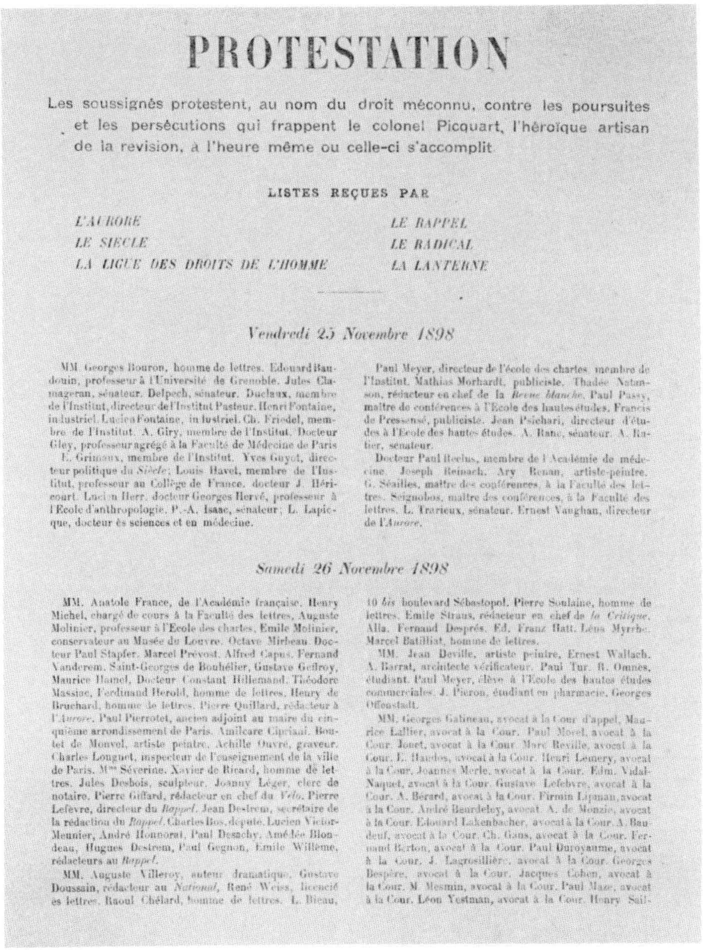

PROTESTATION

Les soussignés protestent, au nom du droit méconnu, contre les poursuites et les persécutions qui frappent le colonel Picquart, l'héroïque artisan de la revision, à l'heure même ou celle-ci s'accomplit

LISTES REÇUES PAR

L'AURORE — *LE RAPPEL*
LE SIÈCLE — *LE RADICAL*
LA LIGUE DES DROITS DE L'HOMME — *LA LANTERNE*

Vendredi 25 Novembre 1898

MM. Georges Bouron, homme de lettres. Edouard Baudouin, professeur à l'Université de Grenoble. Jules Clamageran, sénateur. Delpech, sénateur. Duclaux, membre de l'Institut, directeur de l'Institut Pasteur. Henri Fontaine, industriel. Lucien Fontaine, industriel. Ch. Friedel, membre de l'Institut. A. Giry, membre de l'Institut. Docteur Gley, professeur agrégé à la Faculté de Médecine de Paris

E. Grimaux, membre de l'Institut. Yves Guyot, directeur politique du *Siècle*; Louis Havet, membre de l'Institut, professeur au Collège de France. docteur J. Héricourt. Lucien Herr. docteur Georges Hervé, professeur à l'Ecole d'anthropologie. P.-A. Isaac, sénateur; L. Lapicque, docteur ès sciences et en médecine.

Paul Meyer, directeur de l'école des chartes, membre de l'Institut. Mathias Morhardt, publiciste. Thadée Natanson, rédacteur en chef de la *Revue blanche*. Paul Passy, maître de conférences à l'Ecole des hautes études. Francis de Pressensé, publiciste. Jean Psichari, directeur d'études à l'Ecole des hautes études. A. Ranc, sénateur. A. Ratier, sénateur.

Docteur Paul Reclus, membre de l'Académie de médecine. Joseph Reinach. Ary Renan, artiste-peintre. G. Séailles, maître des conférences, à la Faculté des lettres. Seignobos, maître des conférences, à la Faculté des lettres. L. Trarieux, sénateur. Ernest Vaughan, directeur de l'*Aurore*.

Samedi 26 Novembre 1898

MM. Anatole France, de l'Académie française. Henry Michel, chargé de cours à la Faculté des lettres, Auguste Molinier, professeur à l'Ecole des chartes, Emile Molinier, conservateur au Musée du Louvre. Octave Mirbeau. Docteur Paul Stapfer. Marcel Prévost. Alfred Capus. Fernand Vanderem. Saint-Georges de Bouhélier, Gustave Geffroy, Maurice Hamel, Docteur Constant Hillemand. Théodore Massiac, Ferdinand Herold, homme de lettres. Henry de Bruchard, homme de lettres. Pierre Quillard, rédacteur à l'*Aurore*. Paul Pierrotet, ancien adjoint au maire du cinquième arrondissement de Paris. Amilcare Cipriani. Boutet de Monvel, artiste peintre. Achille Ouvré, graveur. Charles Longuet, inspecteur de l'enseignement de la ville de Paris. Mme Séverine. Xavier de Ricard, homme de lettres. Jules Desbois, sculpteur. Joanny Léger, clerc de notaire. Pierre Giffard, rédacteur en chef du *Vélo*. Pierre Lefèvre, directeur du *Rappel*. Jean Destrem, secrétaire de la rédaction du *Rappel*. Charles Bos, député. Lucien Victor-Meunier, André Honnorat, Paul Desachy, Amédée Blondeau, Hugues Destrem, Paul Gegnon, Emile Willème, rédacteurs au *Rappel*.

MM. Auguste Villeroy, auteur dramatique, Gustave Doussain, rédacteur au *National*, René Weiss, licencié ès lettres. Raoul Chélard, homme de lettres. L. Bieau, 10 *bis* boulevard Sébastopol. Pierre Soulaine, homme de lettres. Emile Straus, rédacteur en chef de *la Critique*. Alla. Fernand Després. Ed. Franz Hatt. Léna Myrrhe. Marcel Batilliat, homme de lettres.

MM. Jean Deville, artiste peintre, Ernest Wallach. A. Barrat, architecte vérificateur. Paul Tur. R. Omnes, étudiant. Paul Meyer, élève à l'Ecole des hautes études commerciales. J. Pieron, étudiant en pharmacie. Georges Offenstadt.

MM. Georges Gatineau, avocat à la Cour d'appel, Maurice Lallier, avocat à la Cour. Paul Morel, avocat à la Cour. Jouet, avocat à la Cour. Marc Reville, avocat à la Cour. E. Hardes, avocat à la Cour. Henri Lemery, avocat à la Cour. Joannes Merle, avocat à la Cour. Edm. Vidal-Naquet, avocat à la Cour. Gustave Lefebvre, avocat à la Cour. A. Bérard, avocat à la Cour. Firmin Lipman, avocat à la Cour. André Beurdeley, avocat. A. de Monzie, avocat à la Cour. Edouard Lakenbacher, avocat à la Cour. A. Baudeuf, avocat à la Cour. Ch. Gans, avocat à la Cour. Fernand Berton, avocat à la Cour. Paul Duroyaume, avocat à la Cour. J. Lagrosillière, avocat à la Cour. Georges Bespère, avocat à la Cour. Jacques Cohen, avocat à la Cour. M. Mesmin, avocat à la Cour. Paul Maze, avocat à la Cour. Léon Yestman, avocat à la Cour. Henry Sail-

Plate 125
Petition: Title Page
The Artists' Homage to Picquart (Hommage des artistes à Picquart), 1899
Collection of Mr. and Mrs. Herbert D. Schimmel, New York

The album also included a listing from six newspapers of the names and occupations of over 30,000 people who declared their belief in Picquart's innocence. In the protestation, they note that Picquart was being persecuted at the same time that Dreyfus's case was being reviewed. Claude Monet and Edouard Vuillard were among the signatories.

Sampling of the thousands of cards and letters
of support sent to Captain and Madame Dreyfus.

Plate 126
Samuel W. Pascheles, publisher
Prague, Czechoslovakia
Capitaine Dreyfus, 1898
Photomechanical print
Musée de Bretagne, Rennes

Jewish New Year's card sent to
Dreyfus on Devil's Island in 1898.

Plate 127
L. Blümlein & Co., printer
Frankfurt, Germany
*Gruss aus Coblenz (Greetings from
Coblenz),* 1898
Photomechanical print
Musée de Bretagne, Rennes

Greeting card postmarked Coblenz
sent to Dreyfus on Devil's Island.

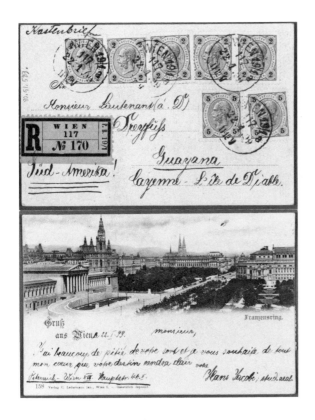

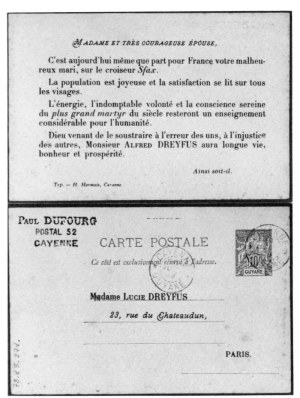

Plate 128
C. Ledermann, jun., printer
Vienna, Austria
Gruss aus Wien (Greetings from Vienna), 1899
Photomechanical print

Greeting card from Vienna sent to Dreyfus on Devil's Island.

Plate 129
H. Harmois, printer
Cayenne, French Guiana
1899
Photomechanical print
Musée de Bretagne, Rennes

Printed card sent to Lucie Dreyfus from Cayenne, French Guiana expressing joy and good wishes on the occasion of her husband's return to France aboard the "Sfax," on 9 June 1899.

Plate 130
Rumania
1899
Photomechanical print
Musée de Bretagne, Rennes

Jewish New Year's card sent to
Dreyfus during his retrial in Rennes
in August 1899, from Rumania.

Plate 131
Thank-you Card
Paris, 1899
Engraved paper
Musée de Bretagne, Rennes

Thank-you card sent to well-wishers
by the Hadamard family and Alfred
and Lucie (born Hadamard) Dreyfus
after the Rennes trial.

Plate 132
Charles Paul Renouard
*Court-Martial at Rennes (Conseil de
Guerre de Rennes)*
L'Affaire Dreyfus, 1899
Lithograph
The Library of the Jewish Theological Seminary of America, New York

This courtroom scene shows Dreyfus standing on platform, his lawyers seated behind him. Hunched over at lower left are the reporters. The witnesses sitting in the first row include General Mercier and the widow of Col. Henry, the forger who conspired against Dreyfus.

The Court-Martial in Rennes

Dreyfus's second court-martial for treason took place in Rennes from August 7 to September 9, 1899. The verdict was guilty, with extenuating circumstances.

Renouard and Couturier were among the artists who attended the trial and sketched their impressions of the leading figures.

226

Plate 133
Charles Paul Renouard
Captain Alfred Dreyfus
L'Affaire Dreyfus, 1899
Lithograph, artist's proof
The Library of the Jewish Theological Seminary of America, New York

Alfred Dreyfus, ruled by discipline and self-control, betrays no emotion.

Plate 134
Charles Paul Renouard
Dreyfus speaks (Dreyfus parle)
L'Affaire Dreyfus, 1899
Lithograph
The Library of the Jewish Theological Seminary of America, New York

The accused, under questioning, testifies to his innocence. His lawyer, Demange, sits behind him at the defense's bench.

Plate 135
Charles Paul Renouard
Exiting the Lycée (Sortie du Lycée)
L'Affaire Dreyfus, 1899
Lithograph
The Library of the Jewish Theological Seminary of America, New York

Leaving the court, Dreyfus is ostracized by soldiers who turn their backs on him in a ritual guard of dishonor.

Le Dossier

Plate 136
Charles Paul Renouard
The Dossier (Le Dossier)
L'Affaire Dreyfus, 1899
Lithograph, artist's proof
The Library of the Jewish Theological Seminary of America, New York

Soldiers cart the prosecution's secret file of nearly 400 documents to the courtroom.

Plate 137
Charles Paul Renouard
Lt. Colonel Picquart
L'Affaire Dreyfus, 1899
Lithograph
The Library of the Jewish Theological Seminary of America, New York

Lt. Colonel Picquart, key witness for the defense, who had suffered dismissal from the army and imprisonment in support of the truth, studies his notes.

Plate 138
Charles Paul Renouard
Studies of de Boisdeffre and Gonse
L'Affaire Dreyfus, 1899
Lithograph
The Library of the Jewish Theological Seminary of America, New York

Heads of Generals de Boisdeffre and Gonse, Army Chiefs of Staff, who were witnesses for the prosecution convinced of Dreyfus's guilt.

Plate 139
Charles Paul Renouard
Dreyfus
L'Affaire Dreyfus, 1899
Lithograph
The Library of the Jewish Theological Seminary of America, New York

Studies of Dreyfus attest to his restraint during the trial.

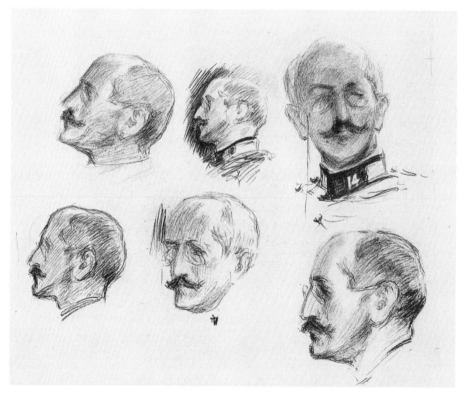

*Plate 140

Charles Paul Renouard

Forzinetti

L'Affaire Dreyfus, 1899

Lithograph

The Library of the Jewish Theological Seminary of America, New York

Forzinetti, the director of the prison of Cherche-Midi, site of Dreyfus's first incarceration in October 1894, believed in Dreyfus's innocence.

Plate 141

Charles Paul Renouard

Verdict

L'Affaire Dreyfus, 1899

Lithograph

The Library of the Jewish Theological Seminary of America, New York

Dreyfus's chief counsel, Demange, overcome with grief, weeps upon hearing the verdict.

Plate 142
Léon-Antoine-Lucien Couturier
Colonel Jouaust, 1899
Graphite on paper
The Israel Museum, Jerusalem

Colonel Albert Jouaust, the presiding
judge of the court-martial, was one
of the two officers who voted for
Dreyfus's acquittal.

Plate 143
Léon-Antoine-Lucien Couturier
Quartet of Officers, 1899
Graphite on paper
The Israel Museum, Jerusalem

Influential witnesses for the prose-
cution include, from left to right,
Generals Mercier, Zurlinden, de
Boisdeffre, and Roget.

* Plate 144
Léon-Antoine-Lucien Couturier
Mercier, 1899
Graphite on paper
The Israel Museum, Jerusalem

The anti-Dreyfusard protagonist,
General Mercier, impresses the court
with his testimony.

* Plate 145
Léon-Antoine-Lucien Couturier
General de Boisdeffre, 1899
Graphite on paper
The Israel Museum, Jerusalem

Appearing for the prosecution, General de Boisdeffre reaffirms his belief that Dreyfus was guilty.

Plate 146
Léon-Antoine-Lucien Couturier
Dreyfus, 1899
Graphite on paper
The Israel Museum, Jerusalem

Composed and dignified, Dreyfus listens to Picquart's testimony. His lawyers sit behind him.

Plate 147
Léon-Antoine-Lucien Couturier
Group of Officers, 1899
Graphite on paper
The Israel Museum, Jerusalem

Two of Dreyfus's accusers, Generals Mercier and Gonse, sit together, engrossed in the proceedings.

Plate 148
Léon-Antoine-Lucien Couturier
Counsel pleading, 1899
Graphite on paper
The Israel Museum, Jerusalem

Portrait of a lawyer, unidentified,
during the proceedings.

Plate 149
Georges Redon
*Attempt against Counselor Labori
(L'Attentat contre Maître Labori)*
La Vie Illustrée, August 1899
Photomechanical print
Bibliothèque Nationale, Paris

An assassination attempt was made
against Dreyfus's lawyer, Fernand
Labori, during the Rennes trial.

Plate 150

Monogrammist OI

Releasing the Pigeons, 1899

Pen and ink on paper

Collection of J. Robert Maguire, Shoreham, VT

Artist-reporters covering the Rennes trial also depicted details of news-gathering and dispatching. Carrier pigeons flew reports and sketches back to OI's paper, *La Patrie,* in Paris.

Plate 151

Monogrammist OI

Guarding the umbrellas, 1899

Pen and ink on paper

Collection of J. Robert Maguire, Shoreham, VT

Mundane activities also caught this artist's attention.

Plate 152

Monogrammist OI

The Caudine Forks: A New Scourge Visited on Rennes (Les fourchés Caudines: Un nouveau fléau abattu sur Rennes), 1899

Pen and ink on paper

Collection of J. Robert Maguire, Shoreham, VT

News photographers, although still a novelty in this period, threatened the livelihood of artist-reporters. OI applies to them the name of a Roman military defeat. Colonel Albert Jouaust, presiding judge of the court-martial, poses for the cameras as he approaches the high school.

Rennes in Photographs

Cameras were not allowed inside the court-room. During breaks in the proceedings, photographers captured the atmosphere in the courtyard of the high school where the proceedings were held and in the streets and cafés of Rennes. Gerschel's series of 200 photographs was published in the volume *The Dreyfus Affair: Five Weeks in Rennes* (*L'Affaire Dreyfus: Cinq Semaines à Rennes*).

Plate 153
Gerschel
Colonel Jouaust, President of the Court
(Le colonel Jouaust président du Conseil)
Photograph
Collection of the Dreyfus family,
Paris

Plate 154
Gerschel
Major Carrière, the Military Prosecutor,
(Le commendant Carrière, commissaire
du gouvernment.)
Photograph
Collection of the Dreyfus family,
Paris

Plate 155
Gerschel
General de Boisdeffre and Maurice Paléologue
Photograph
Collection of the Dreyfus family, Paris

Paléologue acted for the French Ministry of Foreign Affairs throughout the Dreyfus Affair and testified to the Germans' denial of contact with Dreyfus. The two men are pursued by amateur photographers.

Plate 156
Gerschel
Labori and Picquart
Photograph
Collection of the Dreyfus Family, Paris

Fernand Labori served with Demange as counsel for the defense. Georges Picquart, who had been dismissed from the army, took the witness stand in civilian clothes, embarrassed to appear in front of his former uniformed colleagues.

Plate 157
Gerschel
Mathieu Dreyfus and Maître Collenot
Photograph
Collection of the Dreyfus family,
Paris

Mathieu Dreyfus who never lost
his faith in his brother's innocence
conferred with a member of the
legal team during a break in the
proceedings.

Plate 158
Gerschel
*Opening Arguments, 7 August 1899
(Ouverture des débats)*
Photograph
Photo, courtesy of the Bibliothèque
Nationale, Paris

A small camera was smuggled into
the courtroom to take this photograph.

Journalists, Partisans, and Spectators

Witnesses, lawyers, dignitaries, artists, journalists, and spectators mingled in the courtyard of the high school where the court-martial was held.

Plate 159
Gerschel
Alphonse Bertillon After His Testimony
Photograph
Collection of the Dreyfus family, Paris

The criminologist presented a complex argument based on elaborate diagrams in his attempt to prove that Dreyfus was the author of the bordereau.

Plate 160
Gerschel
Madame Dreyfus leaving the prison with her father (Mme. Dreyfus quittant la prison avec son père)
Photograph
Collection of the Dreyfus family, Paris

Constantly pursued by photographers, Lucie Dreyfus finally requested police protection.

Plate 161
Gerschel
At the Court
Photograph
Collection of the Dreyfus family, Paris

The courtroom was crowded every morning as spectators and journalists vied for the few available seats.

Plate 162
Gerschel
The Guard of Dishonor
Photograph
Collection of the Dreyfus family, Paris

Soldiers with their backs turned formed a "guard of dishonor."

Plate 163

Gerschel

Captain Dreyfus Leaving on the Fifth Day (Sortie du Capitaine Dreyfus après le 5me audience)

Photograph

Collection of the Dreyfus family, Paris

A la gloire de Scheurer- Kestner.

H. G. Ibels

After the Pardon

Plate 164
Henri-Gabriel Ibels,
Alfred Dreyfus and his Children (Alfred Dreyfus at ses enfants), 1899
India ink and pen on paper
Musée Carnavalet, Paris

Inscriptions:
On the drawing: "To the glory of Scheurer-Kestner ("A la gloire de Scheurer-Kestner")
On the mount: "Given to Madame Marcellin Pellet, September 20, 1899, as a token of my profound respect for the family of the foremost defender of justice and truth: H. G. Ibels" ("Remis à Madame Marcellin Pellet, le 20 septembre 1899 avec l'hommage de ma profonde considération pour la famille du premier défenseur de la justice et la vérité: H. G. Ibels")

Evoking the prospect of Dreyfus reunited with his children, the artist pays tribute to Scheurer-Kestner, the vice-president of the Senate, whose efforts won Dreyfus a retrial. Dreyfus's pardon and the death of Scheurer-Kestner fell on the same day, just one day before this drawing was dedicated.

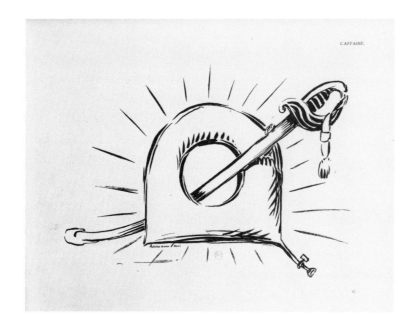

Plate 165

Hermann-Paul (Herman René Georges Paul)

Untitled, no. 37

From the Album, *Guignols,* 1899

Bibliothèque Nationale, Paris

Hermann-Paul, one of the major illustrators advocating the Dreyfusard cause, created sixty images for several journals. The series was finally collected into the album, *Guignols,* published by *La Revue Blanche.*

Plate 166

Hermann-Paul (Herman René Georges Paul)

The Terror (La Terreur), no. 50

From the Album, *Guignols,* 1899

Bibliothèque Nationale, Paris

The caption translated reads, "Is it cholera?" 'No, but it is perhaps 'The Truth'!"

In the wake of revelations of the General Staff's malfeasance, shopkeepers feared riots and shuttered their stores.

243

Plate 167

Hermann-Paul (Herman René Georges Paul)

In the Second Office of the so-called Intelligence Service (after the death of Lieutenant-Colonel Henry). (Au 2me bureau dit des renseignements [après la mort du lieutenant-colonel Henry]), no. 53

From the Album, *Guignols,* 1899

Bibliothèque Nationale, Paris

Hermann-Paul, with an artist's license, projects that after Henry's suicide the officer's colleagues will either follow suit or resign.

Plate 168

Hermann-Paul (Herman René Georges Paul)

Nothing is Accomplished (Rien n'y fait)

From the Album, *Guignols,* 1899

Bibliothèque Nationale, Paris

The Army and anti-Dreyfusard politicians lament that Picquart's imprisonment has done nothing to halt the revision movement.

*Lenepveu: Musée des Horreurs
(Freak Show)*

V. Lenepveu's *Musée des Horreurs,* a series of fifty-one political posters defaming prominent statesmen, journalists, Dreyfusards, and Jews, appeared weekly in Paris, starting in the fall of 1899, after the retrial in Rennes. The series was stopped by an order of the Ministry of the Interior about one year later.

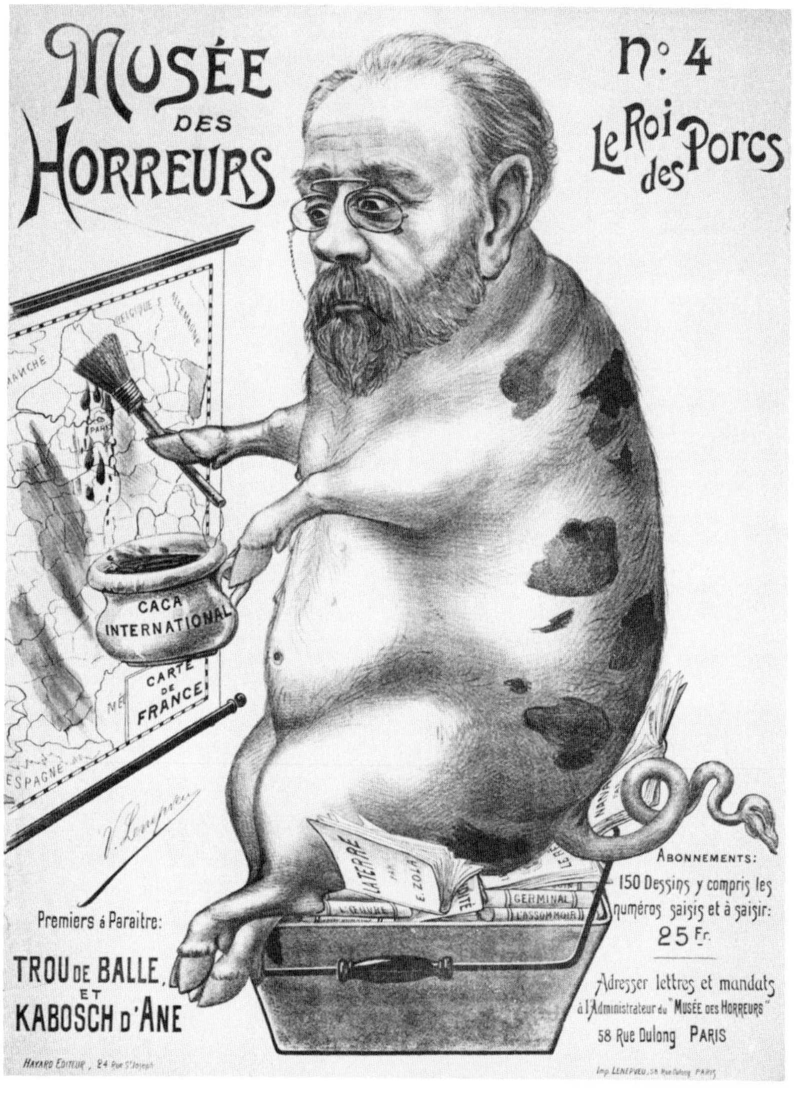

Plate 169

V. Lenepveu

The King of Pigs (Le Roi des porcs)
no. 4

Freak Show (Musée des horreurs), 1900

Lithograph, hand-colored

The Jewish Museum

Emile Zola, archenemy of the anti-Dreyfusards and author of "J'Accuse," is portrayed as a pig, besmirching France with excrement, while sitting atop his own obscene novels.

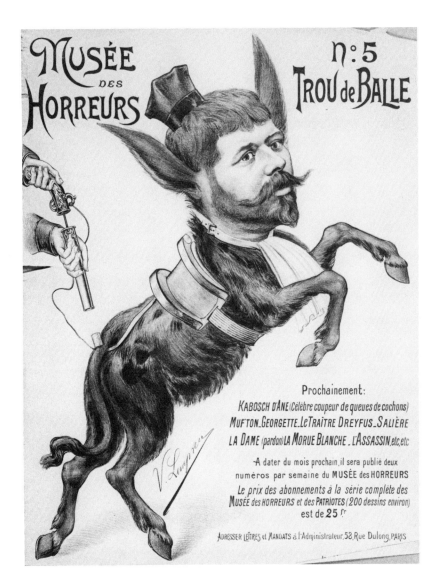

Plate 170
V. Lenepveu
Bullet Hole (Trou de balle) no. 5
Freak Show (Musée des horreurs), 1900
Lithograph, hand-colored
The Jewish Museum

The lawyer Fernand Labori, caricatured as a donkey, defended Picquart, Zola, and Dreyfus at their respective trials. The title refers to the attempt on his life in Rennes when he acted as counsel to Dreyfus.

Plate 171

V. Lenepveu

The Traitor (Le traître) no. 6

Freak Show (Musée des horreurs), 1900

Lithograph, hand-colored

The Jewish Museum

Alfred Dreyfus is represented as the mythological monster, the Hydra, symbolizing an evil that regenerates and which is formidable to overcome.

Plate 172

V. Lenepveu

The White Lady (La Dame blanche), no. 11

Freak Show (Musée des Horreurs), 1900

Lithograph, hand-colored

The Houghton Library, Harvard University

The journalist Caroline Rémy Guebhard used the pseudonym Séverine. She is caricatured as a cow, probably for her well-known charitable works. Lenepveu's appellation, "La Dame blanche," derives from the French reference to an influential woman who remains behind the scenes. Actually Séverine, through her articles in the feminist newspaper *La Fronde* fought passionately for revision.

248

Plate 173

V. Lenepveu

The Elephant from Jordan (L'Elephant du Jourdain) no. 14

Freak Show (Musée des horreurs), 1900

Lithograph, hand-colored

The Houghton Library, Harvard University

The socialist leader Jean Jaurès, depicted as an elephant, sits holding a bottle of Jordan water, whose label carries a recommendation by the government for baptizing cosmopolitans, Freemasons, and other scoundrels. His newspaper *La Petite Dreyfusarde* alludes to the socialist daily *La Petite République,* for which Jaurès wrote pro-Dreyfus articles.

"Jourdain" is a pun on the names Jourdain and the River Jordan.

Plate 174

V. Lenepveu

Ball at the Elysee (Bal à l'Elysee), no. 26

Freak Show (Musée des horreurs), 1900

Lithograph, hand-colored

The Houghton Library, Harvard University

This poster was probably created as a special edition for the opening of the Paris World's Fair on 15 April 1900. The artist cynically postulated a ball at the presidential palace to entertain the mythical "Jewish syndicate" after the amnesty. Laubet's guests include Grand Rabbi Zadoc Kahn, Picquart, Reinach, Dreyfus, and Zola.

Plate 175

V. Lenepveu

Give This to Dreyfus (Porte ça à Dreyfus), no. 29

Freak Show (Musée des horreurs), 1900

Lithograph, hand-colored

The Houghton Library, Harvard University

Yves Guyot, the publisher of *Le Siècle,* is ridiculed as a toad, suggesting that he was in the service of Dreyfus. One of the first journalists to question the matter of Dreyfus's guilt, he played a major role in the campaign for revision by publishing the details of the accusation. He also gained sympathy for the prisoner through his publication of Dreyfus's letters under the title "Letters of an Innocent."

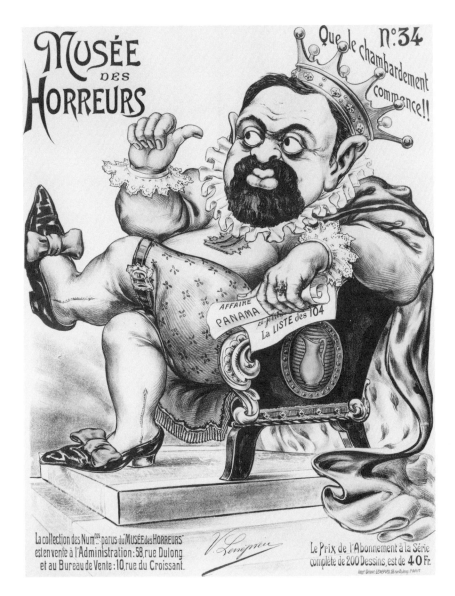

Plate 176

V. Lenepveu

Let the ruckus begin!! (Que le chambardement commence!!) no. 34

Freak Show (Musée des horreurs), 1900

Lithograph, hand-colored

The Houghton Library, Harvard University

To whet the appetites of anti-Semites, Lenepveu resurrects the theme of Jewish involvement in the Panama Canal scandal by invoking the person of Joseph Reinach, nephew of baron Jacques de Reinach, of Panama notoriety. Viewed as the king of bribery, Joseph Reinach clutches his uncle's alleged list, compromising 104 public figures and supposedly granting to him unlimited influence over French politics.

Plate 177

V. Lenepveu

Nathan Mayer, or the origin of billions (Nathan Mayer ou l'origine des milliards) no. 42

Freak Show (Musée des horreurs), 1900

Lithograph, hand-colored

The Houghton Library, Harvard University

Nathan Rothschild (1777–1836) founder of the London branch of the banking dynasty that financed England's war against Napoleon, is caricatured as an avaricious dog—a profiteer who made money on the battlefield of Waterloo over the corpses of patriotic Frenchmen.

The Rehabilitation

In July of 1906, the judgment against Alfred Dreyfus was set aside by the High Court of Appeal; the government voted to restore him to the rank of major; and he was appointed a member of the Legion of Honor. The ceremony, attended by the family and a few close friends, took place in a small courtyard of the Ecole Militaire. A series of postcards records the event.

Plate 178

E. Le Deley, printer

Major Targe explains the proceedings to journalists (Le Commandant Targe expliques aux journalistes comment les choses vont se passer)

La Réhabilitation de Dreyfus no. 3, 1906

Photomechanical print

Collection of J. Robert Maguire, Shoreham, VT

Plate 179

E. Le Deley, printer

After his decorations have been reinstated, Major Dreyfus talks with General Gillain and Major Targe (Après la remise des décorations, le Commandant Dreyfus s'entretient avec le Général Gillain et le Commandant Targe)

La Réhabilitation de Dreyfus no. 4, 1906

Photomechanical print

Collection of J. Robert Maguire, Shoreham, VT

Plate 180

E. Le Deley, printer

General Gillain Confers the Cross of the Legion of Honor on Major Dreyfus (Le Général Gillain confère la Croix de la Légion d'Honneur au Commandant Dreyfus)

La Réhabilitation de Dreyfus no. 5, 1906

Photomechanical print

Collection of J. Robert Maguire, Shoreham, VT

Plate 181

E. Le Deley, printer

Major Dreyfus Resumes his Place in the Ranks (Le Commandant Dreyfus va reprendre sa place dans le rang)

La Réhabilitation de Dreyfus no. 6, 1906

Photomechanical print

Collection of J. Robert Maguire, Shoreham, VT

Aftermath

LA DÉBACLE

Plate 182
Félix Vallotton
The Debacle (La Débâcle), ca. 1905
Wood engraving
The Jewish Museum, Gift of Mr. and Mrs. Herbert D. Schimmel, New York

The Dreyfusard artist Félix Vallotton uses this title to describe the defeat of the army, the Church, and the courts by Justice, in spite of their attempts to suppress it.

L'EXODE

Plate 183
Lyonel Feininger
The Exodus (L'Exode)
Le Temoin, no. 1, 1906
Photomechanical print
Private collection

Between 1901 and 1905, anticlerical sentiment in France resulted in a body of laws culminating in the separation of church and state. Feininger's ironically titled cartoon, *L'Exode,* for the newspaper *Le Temoin,* depicts the expulsion of the Jesuits from Paris.

Painting, Sculpture, Drawing,
Decorative Arts, and Film

Plate 184

Jean-François Raffaëlli

Georges Clemenceau Holding an Electoral Meeting in Paris, at the Circus Fernando in 1883 (Georges Clemenceau tenant une réunion électorale à Paris, au Cirque Fernando en 1883), 1885

Oil on canvas

Musée National du Chateau de Versailles

On the campaign trail, Clemenceau, the charismatic speaker and future Dreyfusard leader, mesmerizes his audience in this painting documenting political expression in the Third Republic.

Plate 185

Alfred-Philippe Roll

The Festival of the Centenary of the Revolution celebrated at Versailles in 1889 (La Fête du centenaire des Etats-Généraux célébrée à Versailles en 1889) 1893

Oil on canvas

Musée National du Chateau de Versailles

United among the celebrants in this sketch for a painting commemorating the centennial of the French Revolution are Zola, Clemenceau, Cavaignac, and Méline, men who, in a few years time, would become avowed foes as a result of the Dreyfus Affair.

Plate 186
Paul Legrand
In Front of 'The Dream' by Detaille (Devant 'Le Rêve' de Detaille), 1897
Oil on canvas
Musée des Beaux-Arts, Nantes

Exhibited at the Salon in 1897, Legrand's painting touched the explosive issues of patriotism and army prestige. As the young boys stand riveted by Detaille's print honoring earlier French military conquests, the old, experienced soldier turns his back on them.

Plate 187
Henri Evenepoel
Fête at the Invalides (Fête aux Invalides), 1898
Oil on canvas
Musées Royaux des Beaux-Arts de Belgique, Brussels

Evenepoel, a young Belgian painter living in Paris, became a passionate Dreyfusard. His genre painting of the Sunday crowd enjoying the grounds of the Invalides (the building housing Napoleon's tomb) was described as an antimilitary taunt in an article in *Le Progrès militaire*. The critic for a military paper would have been highly sensitive, and perhaps defensive, when this work was shown in the Salon of 1899.

Plate 188

Jean-Jacques Henner

Study for *The Levite of Ephraim and His Dead Wife (Le Lévite d'Ephraim et sa femme morte)*, 1898

Oil on canvas

Musée National J. J. Henner, Paris

The Alsatian painter, Henner, based his painting on a biblical narrative of rape and internecine warfare (Judges 19–21). Already bitter and pessimistic over the dismemberment of France following the Franco-Prussian War, he resented the glaring cleavage in French society during the Affair.

Plate 189

Edouard Debat-Ponsan

She Is Not Drowning (Latin: *Nec Mergitur*), also called *Truth Leaving the Well (La Vérité sortant du puits)*, 1898

Oil on canvas

Musée de l'Hôtel-de-Ville, Amboise

Debat-Ponsan, a passionate Dreyfusard, based his Salon entry on the French saying "Truth is hidden at the bottom of the well." As Truth emerges, clerical hypocrisy and military force attempt to restrain her. This pictorial plea for revision with an iconographic reference emblematic of the Affair was later given to Zola by a group of admirers.

* Plate 190

Aimé-Jules Dalou

Study for 'The Triumph of the Republic', ca. 1885

Terra cotta

Photo, courtesy of Australian
National Museum, Canberra

Dalou's monumental sculpture commemorating the centennial of the
French Revolution was unveiled in
November 1899, at a celebration intended to heal some of the rifts of
the Affair. The anti-Semitic press,
however, termed the work *The
Triumph of Dreyfus.*

* Plate 191

Henri-Gabriel Ibels

*The Last Veiled Lady in Place for the
Quadrille (La Dernière Dame voilée,
en place pour le quadrille), ca.* 1899

Pastel on paper

Photo, courtesy of the Musée
Carnavalet, Paris

In this hermetic work Ibels attacks
the military hierarchy responsible
for the conviction of Dreyfus. The
veiled lady of Esterhazy's imagination becomes the skeletal violinist of
a *danse-macabre,* as du Paty de Clam,
Mercier, and de Boisdeffre twist on
their gibbets.

Plate 192

Henri-Gabriel Ibels

The Stroke of the Sponge (Le coup de l'éponge), 1899

Black chalk on paper

Collection of Mr. and Mrs. Herbert D. Schimmel, New York

The founder of *Le Sifflet* reworks the episode recounted in Matthew 27:48. In this sympathetic drawing, Dreyfus replaces the figure of Jesus as a martyr and General Mercier is portrayed as the observer at the crucifixion who commits the ignoble act of giving the dying man a drink of vinegar.

Plate 193

Jean-Louis Forain

The Barman (Le Bardman), 1898

India ink and brush on paper

Metropolitan Museum of Art, New York, Gift of Albert E. Gallatin

The caption reads:

"The Colonel's Drink" (Le Grog du Colonel.)

Forain's title is a pun on the name of Alphonse Bard, a judge on the Criminal Court of Appeal who appeared to the Nationalists as a supporter of the Dreyfus cause. During the court hearings, the judge was accused of having had secret meetings with Colonel Picquart.

This drawing belonged to Edgar Degas who admired the younger artist and collected his work. Both men were ardent anti-Semites and anti-Dreyfusards.

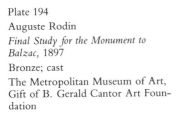

Plate 194

Auguste Rodin

Final Study for the Monument to Balzac, 1897

Bronze; cast

The Metropolitan Museum of Art, Gift of B. Gerald Cantor Art Foundation

In 1898, Rodin refused to accept alternative funds raised by an ad hoc committee after this monument to Balzac was rejected by its original commissioners. Although Rodin later said that he stood apart from politics, at the time he was reported to have been concerned that so many of the subscribers were friends of Zola.

Plate 195

Auguste Rodin

The Thinker (Le Penseur), 1880

Bronze; cast

Collection of B. Gerald Cantor

By 1904 it had become possible to constitute a committee composed of both Dreyfusards and anti-Dreyfusards to raise funds to cast an enlargement of this work. Rodin permitted this project to proceed only because of the apolitical nature of the committee, which included former opponents Joseph Reinach and Henri Rochefort. *The Thinker* was placed in front of the Pantheon in Paris to honor those who established and maintained the French Republic.

Plate 196
Emile Gallé
Sea Horses (Hippocampes), 1901
Blown glass; internal colors; applications; patina; engraved
Musée des Arts Décoratifs, Paris
Inscription:
Joseph Reinach/Emile Gallé/1901
Vitam impendere Vero (Life depends on Truth)

This vase by Gallé was one of several inscribed with poetry or aphorisms expressing the artist's convictions. This work is dedicated to Reinach, one of Dreyfus's earliest defenders.

Plate 197
Emile Gallé
Elms (Des Ormes), ca. 1900
Blown glass; internal colors, hammered; engraved; applications
Musée municipal, Cognac

Elm trees, the ancient symbol of affliction, are the motif of this vase dating from the period of the Affair. Gallé metaphorically comments on the difficulty of obtaining justice for Dreyfus.

* Plate 198
Pablo Picasso
Head of Zola, ca. 1900
Black chalk on paper
Photo, courtesy of Museo Picasso,
Barcelona

In 1900 the youthful Picasso paid his
first visit to Paris, where he encountered Sunyer, the Spanish artist committed to the revision of the Dreyfus
verdict. Picasso had already shown a
sympathy for the victims of social
injustice and this may have influenced his choice of Zola as a subject.

Plate 199
Aimé-Jules Dalou
*Study for 'The Monument to Auguste
Scheurer-Kestner',* 1899–1900
Terra cotta and wire
Ackland Art Museum, Chapel Hill,
NC

A revisionist, Dalou invokes the allegorical figures of Truth and Justice
on this sculptural monument to
Scheurer-Kestner who, as vice-president of the Senate, dedicated himself
to gaining a retrial for Dreyfus.

264

b

a

c

Plate 200a, b, and c
Ferdinand Hodler

200b *Study for Truth I*
Pen and India ink on batiste paper

The Montreal Museum of Fine Arts,
Gift of Mr. and Mrs. Michal
Hornstein

200a *Study for Truth I (La Vérité)*,
1902
Watercolor, pencil and India ink
Private collection, Geneva

200c *Study for Truth I*
Pen and red color on paper

The Montreal Museum of Fine Arts,
Gift of Mr. and Mrs. Michal
Hornstein

Hodler became sympathetic to the
Dreyfus cause under the influence of
the French critic Mathias Morhardt.
His Symbolist allegory depicts Truth
vanquishing the power of falsehood
and malice.

Plate 201

Aristide Maillol

Study for 'The Chained Deed', (L'Action enchainée), third state, 1906–07

Bronze; cast

Collection of Bernard and Josephine Chaus, New York

The revival of political radicalism following the Dreyfus Affair finally made possible a public monument in honor of Louis Blanqui, a major revolutionary figure in the mid-nineteenth century. The artist Maillol, who was not politically active, was close to Clemenceau and perhaps shared his political views.

Plate 202
Georges Méliès
On Devil's Island, 1899
Film still from *L'Affaire Dreyfus*
Photo, the Museum of Modern Art,
Film Stills Archive

The pioneer filmmaker produced an
eleven-reel film on the Affair, re-
staging the events with actors and
sets based on published photographs.
Audiences reacted violently, causing
the government to ban this and other
films dealing with the Affair.

*Plate 203
Tim (Louis Mittelberg)
*Homage to Captain Dreyfus (Hommage
au Capitaine Dreyfus),* 1985
Bronze
Photo, courtesy of the artist

This contemporary statue of Dreyfus, who is shown standing at attention, holding a broken saber, was
proposed and rejected for placement
in the courtyard of the Ecole Militaire, site of his degradation ceremony on 5 January 1895.

Exhibition Checklist

The following checklist is arranged in order of the sections of the exhibition, although the specific works are not always listed in the order in which they are exhibited. In general, works within each section are listed alphabetically by artist, while periodicals and works by unknown artists are listed alphabetically by title. Some works were placed where they seem to make the best visual sense instead of being arranged in accordance with strict rules of chronological organization. All measurements are in centimeters, height preceding width. No measurements are given for periodicals, books, or manuscripts. Plate or figure numbers are given for illustrated works. Unless otherwise indicated, French is the nationality of all artists listed.

Early Films

Late in 1895, the year that began with Dreyfus's degradation, the Lumière brothers demonstrated the first large-screen motion pictures at the Grand Café in Paris. Movies would shortly join the press as a vehicle for feeding a public avid for news of Dreyfus's ordeal. As the trial proceeded in Rennes during the late summer of 1899, Georges Méliès, in Paris, began shooting a twelve-part newsreel "reconstructing" the Affair. A few days later, Charles and Emile Pathé followed with their own six-part docudrama.

Although both films employed actors and obvious sets, the novelty of simulated realism aroused partisan audiences, and the government soon prohibited the filming or exhibition of movies about the Affair. In 1907, the Pathé version was reshot, but because of the French ban, the new film was shown mainly in America.

As government censors recognized, the new technology exemplified by these pioneering films had the potential of becoming a refined tool for manipulating public opinion. The invention of motion pictures during the Dreyfus Affair immediately raised the issues encountered in making films based on actual events—censorship, distortion, and invasion of privacy.

In this exhibition, the Pathé film, shown together with an introductory video presentation, serves as a chronology of the major episodes of the twelve years of the Affair.

1. Georges Méliès (1861–1938),
The Dreyfus Affair, 1899
Film
Rights courtesy of Madeleine
Malthête-Méliès and the heirs of
Georges Méliès. Print courtesy of
Centre Nationale de la Cinématog-
raphie, Bois d'Arcy.
Plate 202

2. Pathé Frères, *The Dreyfus Affair*
1907
Film
Rights courtesy of Pathé Cinéma,
Paris. Print courtesy of Centre
Nationale de la Cinématographie,
Bois d'Arcy.

The Press

The Dreyfus Affair was created in large measure by the Parisian press, then the largest, most
diverse, and most provocative in the world. The
development of the high-speed press, the repeal of
laws governing newspaper censorship, and finally
the invention of new photo printing processes that
allowed an artist's work to be as easily reproduced
as the writer's word led to a new style in journalism—one that was highly sensationalist and
partisan, and frequently irresponsible. Politics and
journalism became inextricably linked as politicians took to journalism and journalists entered
politics.

The press exposed and debated aspects of the
Affair that inflamed public opinion and polarized
French society, creating crises that, not so coinci-
dentally, also increased circulation. While Dru-
mont rejuvenated a failing *La Libre Parole,* with its
exploitation of anti-Semitism, and helped to send
Dreyfus to prison by leaking the news of his arrest,
L'Aurore, with its publication of 300,000 copies of
"J'Accuse," helped to get him out.

The Dreyfus Affair also inspired new illustrated
journals that dealt specifically with this subject. In
these innovative propaganda vehicles, artists manifested their political and social ideology in polemical images. Newspapers were often created in
rival pairs, and frequently benefited as much from
their mutual opposition as from their particular
points of view. Two such journals established at
the time of Zola's trial epitomize this militancy.
Jean-Louis Forain's pungent drawings and subtle,

ironic captions appeared in *Psst. . . !,* an anti-
Dreyfusard four-page weekly, along with those of
its cofounder, cartoonist Caran d'Ache. Dreyfusard artist Henri-Gabriel Ibels reacted immediately
by establishing a counterpart, *Le Sifflet,* employing
the same format and sometimes the same image.

Rival papers competed for attention with their
placards and strident headlines. Many employed
renowned artists to create their posters. In a poster
for the daily *L'Aurore,* Eugene Carrière, a Dreyfusard, focused on the paper's editorial theme—the
dawn of a new day. At the same time, illustrator
Théophile-Alexandre Steinlen's poster for the
anarchist journal *La Feuille* commented on the
press itself with its depiction of reams of blank
paper falling on a confused populace. The vast
outpouring of rhetoric by both sides is reflected in
this work.

Toulouse-Lautrec's poster of 1895 for *La Revue
Blanche* depicted the wife of one of its founders
and expressed the aesthetic aims of the publication.
Later in the Affair, it could be seen as a reflection
of the artist's complete silence, just as it belied the
journal's editorial position on behalf of Dreyfus
and the use of its offices as informal headquarters
for Dreyfusard intellectuals. In sharp contrast,
Henri Rochefort used a vicious cartoon with an
image of Dreyfus and the president who pardoned
him on the 1899 billboard for his daily *L'Intransigeant.* The poster was confiscated by the police.

During the Affair, the visual arts reinforced verbal opinion as the daily press and illustrated journals thrust the issues into the public arena.

3. Louis Anquetin (1860–1932), Poster
for *Endehors*
1898
Lithograph
58 × 76cm
Collection of Mr. and Mrs.
Herbert D. Schimmel
Fig. 6, Kleeblatt

4. Anquetin, Poster for *Le Rire*
1894
Lithograph
152.8 × 110.2cm
Jane Voorhees Zimmerli Art Museum,
Gift of Alvin and Joyce Glasgold

5. Poster for *L'Intransigeant* (illustration by J. Belon)
1899
Photomechanical print
149 × 110cm
Musée de la Presse, Courtesy Christian Bailly
Fig. 4, Kleeblatt

6. Eugene Carrière (1849–1906), Poster for *L'Aurore*
1897
Color lithograph
146.7 × 107cm
Jane Voorhees Zimmerli Art Museum, Gift of Alvin and Joyce Glasgold
Fig. 2, Kleeblatt

7. Jean-Louis Forain (1852–1931), "Let Arms Yield to the Law" (Cedant arma togae) *Psst. . . !*
19 February 1898
Photomechanical print
40 × 28cm
The Jewish Museum, Gift of Charles and Beth Gordon
Plate 42

8. Henri-Gabriel Ibels (1867–1936), "Let's Go" (Allons-y) *Le Sifflet*
24 February 1898
Photomechanical print
40.5 × 26cm
Collection of Mr. and Mrs. Herbert D. Schimmel
Plate 43

9. Théophile-Alexandre Steinlen, Poster for *La Feuille*
1897
Lithograph
136 × 190.5cm
Jane Voorhees Zimmerli Art Museum, Frederick and Lucinda Mezey Purchase Fund
Fig. 3, Kleeblatt

10. Henri Toulouse-Lautrec, Poster for *La Revue Blanche*
1895
Color lithographic poster
130 × 95cm
Collection of Mr. and Mrs. Herbert D. Schimmel
Fig. 1, Kleeblatt

11. *L'Aurore*, "J'Accuse"
13 January 1898
Newspaper
Collection of Mr. and Mrs. Herbert D. Schimmel
Plate 22

12. *La Libre Parole*, "J'Accuse" (Lettre de Drumont)
14 January 1898
Newspaper
Musée de la Presse, Courtesy Christian Bailly
Plate 24

13. Poster for *La Libre Parole*
Color Lithograph
111.6 × 152.4cm
Collection of J. Robert Maguire
Fig. 7, Marrus

14. Poster for *La Lanterne*
c. 1898
Color lithograph
129 × 105cm
Musée de L'Affiche et de la Publicité
Fig. 5, Kleeblatt

The Jewish Community of France

Emancipation and Assimilation. At the time of the French Revolution, the 40,000 Jews in France lived in three distinct communities: several thousand Sephardic merchants in Bordeaux and Bayonne; another small community that had long resided in Provence; and the largest community, consisting of the Yiddish-speaking Jews in Alsace-Lorraine.

As the first Jewish community in Europe to receive civil rights, French Jews occupied a unique place in European history. Their emancipation after the Revolution of 1789 was compared by contemporaries to the liberation from Egypt. The Sephardic Jews of the south were declared free citizens of France by proclamation on 28 January 1790, and finally, on 27 September 1791, the Ashkenazic Jews achieved full equality.

Napoleon approached Jewish assimilation by bringing together an Assembly of Notables from whom he required a statement of political and religious beliefs. The emperor's next step was to convoke the Grand Sanhedrin to further explore these issues. As with Catholicism and Protestantism, he made all religious leaders state employees. He established the Central Consistory and a hierarchical system of Jewish communal units under government jurisdiction. In an engraving of the time, Napoleon is depicted presenting these new laws to a humble and thankful Jewish people, making an adept analogy between his role and that of Moses.

The changing position of the Jewish community is also reflected in the painting *Dedication of a Synagogue in Alsace-Lorraine* (c. 1828), attributed to Georg Emanuel Opitz. This idealized conception shows the pride, interest, and involvement of the entire community—both Christians and Jews—in the creation of a new synagogue by the first generation of emancipated Jews.

Edgar Degas painted a double portrait in 1871 of Rabbi Astruc and General Mellinet, who commissioned this work to celebrate their service together in the ambulance corps during the Franco-Prussian War. Through its reference to French patriotism, the depiction of interfaith friendship, and the choice of a major avant-garde artist, it bears testimony to the possibilities of assimilation of Jews in the later nineteenth century.

Jews also distinguished themselves in both politics and arts, particularly the theater. The actress Rachel, here posthumously portrayed by Gérôme, was a peddler's daughter who became the most famous and influential actress of her generation.

By the 1890s the Jewish population of Paris itself had reached 40,000, many coming from Alsace-Lorraine, which had been severed from France in 1871, or from Russia, refugees from the pogroms that began in 1881. A large number were desperately poor and eked out a living as peddlers, such as this man depicted in an undated Forain lithograph.

The Dreyfus Family. Like many other Jews, the ancestors of Alfred Dreyfus had long been established in Alsace; his father founded a cotton mill that became one of the major textile establishments in southern Alsace. Forced to leave because of the Prussian invasion, the family took refuge in Switzerland. In the fall of 1874, Alfred's father, Raphael Dreyfus, returned to France to register his family as French citizens. Alfred, the youngest, would say later that the foreign occupation of his childhood home led him to choose an army career. He became a lieutenant of the artillery in 1882 and a captain in 1889, when he began to study for entrance into the Ecole de Guerre. His wedding to Lucie Hadamard on 21 April 1890, took place the day after his admission to the Ecole de Guerre. Both events were marked by festive dinners whose decorated menus describe meals that would have been served in a prosperous household of the time.

In these early, happy years of his marriage, after successfully completing his training, Alfred was assigned to the General Staff and his children, Pierre and Jeanne, were born. In 1894, the household was shattered by his conviction for treason and exile to Devil's Island.

Madame Dreyfus made every effort to ensure that the children remained sheltered in a comfortable environment. Their photographs, mounted in a small folding screen, depict them engaged in normal childhood activities, unaware of their father's plight.

15. Decree 30 May 1806
30 May 1806
18 × 23cm (4 pages)
Archives Nationales
Fig. 2, Hyman

16. Edgar-Hilaire-Germaine Degas (1834–1917), *Rabbi Astruc and General Mellinet*
1871
Oil on canvas
14 × 21cm
Mairie de Gerardmer
Fig. 7, Nochlin

17. Jean-Louis Forain (1852–1931), *The Jewish Peddler* (Le Colporteur Juif)
Lithograph on paper
23 × 18.5cm
Boston Public Library
Fig. 8, Hyman

18. Jean-Léon Gérôme (1824–1904), *Rachel*
1859
Oil on canvas
24 × 16cm
Musée Carnavalet

19. Attributed to Georg Emanuel
Opitz (1775–1841), *Dedication of
Synagogue in Alsace*
1828
Oil on canvas
66 × 93cm
The Jewish Museum, Gift of
Mr. and Mrs. Henry Moses
Fig. 5, Hyman

20. Law of 13 November 1791
1791
a) Law Emancipating the Jews of Paris
   21 × 27.5cm (2 pages)
b) Law Emancipating the Jews of
   Alsace
   21.5 × 27.5cm (2 pages)
Printed document
Archives Nationales
Fig. 1, Hyman

21. Formula for Prayer for the
Government
30 August 1809
Collection of Victor Klagsbald

22. *Napoleon Presents the Law Re-
establishing Judaism*
30 May 1806
Hand-colored print
30.5 × 22.5cm
Bibliothèque Nationale
Fig. 3, Hyman

23. Marriage Contract (*Ketubbah*) of
Moise Beaucaire and Esther Abram
1805
Ink on paper
Victor Klagsbald

24. Screen with Family Photographs
(Pierre and Jeanne Dreyfus)
1896
6 photographs in wood-screen frame
27 × 10.5cm
Collection of Simone Perl
Fig. 5, Burns

25. Three Menus for Dreyfus Family
Dinners (including one for the marriage of Alfred and Lucie)
Photomechanical print with ink
additions
15 × 10cm each
Collection of Simone Perl

26. Certificate of Choice of French
Citizenship
30 October 1874
Ink on paper
33 × 18cm
The Dreyfus Family
Fig. 2, Burns

27. Cloth Commemorating Jewish-
Pilgrimage Festivals (formerly Alfred
and Lucie Dreyfus Collection)
Early 19th century
Wool embroidery on cotton
61 × 61cm
Collection of Simone Perl

28. Marriage Contract (*Ketubbah*) of
Alfred and Lucie Dreyfus
21 April 1890
Ink on paper
30.5 × 20cm
The Jewish National and University
Library
Fig. 3, Burns

29. *Class at the Ecole de Guerre*
1891
Photograph
10 × 15cm
The Dreyfus Family
Fig. 4, Burns

30. Nadar, *Portrait of Zadoc Kahn*
Photograph
15 × 11.5cm
Collection of Simone Perl

31. Lucie Dreyfus, Letter to Alfred
1 July 1899
Collection of Mme. S. Perl

32. *At Carpentras*
1900
Photograph
13 × 18cm
The Dreyfus Family
Fig. 7, Burns

34. Calling Card: "Le Commandant
et Mme. A. Dreyfus"
Engraved paper
Collection of J. Robert Maguire

The Third Republic

The Third Republic, established in 1871 after France's defeat in the Franco-Prussian War, accommodated both moderate and extreme political groups on the right (monarchist, militarist) and on the left (socialist, anarchist). Rightist factions often functioned as ideological descendants of the preceding Second Empire, while the leftist factions reflected dissatisfaction with the generally conservative nature of the government. The activities of these groups at every level of participation were reported and satirized by artists and illustrators.

Jean-François Raffaëlli documented this freedom of political expression in his contemporary history painting *Georges Clemenceau en Réunion Publique au Cirque Fernando* (1885), portraying the charismatic leftist leader and future Dreyfusard speaking during an electoral campaign. Painted in the realist style for which the artist is noted, the work exemplifies the focus on contemporary events and settings typical of late nineteenth-century French art. A more violent event, in the rightist camp, was chronicled in *Le Petit Journal* when General Boulanger, a militarist rabble-rouser originally championed by Clemenceau, led an abortive attempt to overthrow the government in 1889, which resulted in his flight from Paris and eventual suicide. This hackneyed and melodramatic image, an aspect of the popular culture of the age, appeared in one of the most sensational of the illustrated papers.

In addition to political reportage, artists questioned and attacked societal inequities such as the exploitation of the workers and the abuse of power by the rich, the church, and the army. Pissarro and Steinlen, who had anarchist ties, treated these themes in their *Turpitudes sociales* (1890) and *Cent Millions,* respectively. Vallotton's woodcuts *L'Anarchiste* (1892) and *A Vingt Ans* (1894) voiced his antiestablishment and antimilitary sentiments.

Vitriolic examples of anti-Semitism in the Third Republic surfaced long before the Dreyfus Affair. And while tied to age-old prejudice, the ideas were now newly concretized into a "modern" ideology. In 1885 Adolphe Willette's illustration "The Jews and the Holy Week" for *Le Courrier Français* branded the Jews as the murderers of Jesus and pleaded for their destruction. One year later, Edouard Drumont published his influential and highly popular anti-Semitic diatribe *La France Juive*; he continued his slandering and propaganda from 1892 on in his illustrated newspaper *La Libre Parole*. With Drumont's backing, Willette ran for office on an anti-Semitic platform in the legislative elections of 1889. The artist and politician now merged as Willette designed a poster to publicize his candidacy in which he denounced the Jews as the enemies of France.

Scurrilous anti-Semitic drawings were also designed by the Comtesse de Martel de Janville (better known by her pseudonyms "Gyp" and "Bob") in collaboration with Drumont and for the newspaper *Le Rire*.

In 1892, anti-Semites were greatly buoyed by the Panama scandal, in which three Jews (Baron Jacques de Reinach, Arton, and Cornelius Herz) were charged with bribing politicians in the course of raising money for the debt-ridden Panama Canal Company. Artists' responses to this crisis ranged from Toulouse-Lautrec's dispassionate lithographs of Arton's trial to Forain's blatantly anti-Semitic illustrations compiled and published in 1893 as the album *Les Temps Difficiles (Panama)*.

These multitudinous political and social undercurrents appear masked in Alfred-Philippe Roll's propagandistic painting commissioned by the state, *Fête du centenaire de la Révolution de 1789* (1893), which portrayed statesmen and literary figures, including Zola, Clemenceau, and Cavaignac, in a seemingly utopian world. One little suspects from this idealistic reportage that many of the participants so charmingly brought together in this moment of national celebration would become archenemies in the wake of the Dreyfus Affair, or that Carnot, the master of ceremonies at this event, would be assassinated by an anarchist the year after Roll completed his commission.

35. Bob (comtesse Sibylle de Martel de Janville, also called Gyp [1850–1932]), "One Thing's for Sure, France Isn't Enjoying Herself" (Sur qu'elle n'est pas à la noce, la France) *Le Rire*
28 December 1895
Photomechanical print
31 × 23.5cm
Jane Voorhees Zimmerli Art Museum
Fig. 37, Cate

36. Bob, "Algerian Jews" *Le Rire*
14 November 1896
Photomechanical print
31 × 23.5cm
Collection of Willa Silverman
Plate 3

37. Bob, "Kike-Rats" *Le Rire*
14 November 1896
Photomechanical print
31 × 23.5cm
Collection of Willa Silverman
Plate 4

38. Bob, "Histoire de la 3ème République" *Le Rire*
14 November 1896
Photomechanical print
31 × 23.5cm
Jane Voorhees Zimmerli Art Museum
Fig. 39, Cate

39. Bob, *It Is the Hope of France* (C'est l'espoir de la France)
Photomechanical print
8.5 × 24cm
Collection of Sibylle Gaudry

40. Bob, *And Do You Sell This?* (Est-ce que fus la fentez [sic])
Photomechanical print
24.5 × 34cm
Collection of Sibylle Gaudry

41. Bob, *And This Mercury, Who Arrived in Paris Only to Steal* (Et Mercure donc, qui est venu à Paris que pour voler)
Photomechanical print
25.5 × 20cm
Collection of Sibylle Gaudry

42. Chanteclair, "Naquet, the Defender of the Poor Youppins [Jews]" (Naquet, Le Défenseur des pauvres youppins) *La Libre Parole Illustrée*
1 June 1895
Photomechanical print
38 × 28.5cm
The Jewish Museum

43. Edouard Drumont, *La France Juive* (illustrated by Frédéric Regency [1849–1925])
Bound book
Centre de Documentation Juive et Contemporaine
Fig. 4, Marrus

44. Jean-Louis Forain (1852–1931), *Sweet Land: A Foreboding* (Doux Pays: Pressentiment)
1894
Drawing
23 × 32cm
Collection of Iris and B. Gerald Cantor

45. Forain, *Les Temps Difficiles*
1893
Book with photomechanically printed illustrations
Collection of J. Robert Maguire

46. Forain, *The Death of France*
Ink, watercolor, and wash on paper
57 × 44cm
Musée Carnavalet

47. Forain, *Artistes et Juifs*
Pen and ink on paper
44.5 × 29cm
Boston Public Library
Fig. 3, Marrus

48. Forain, *La République*
Ink on paper
57 × 44cm
Boston Public Library

49. Hermann-Paul (1874–1940), *Au Ghetto*
Photomechanical print
35.5 × 25.5cm
Jane Voorhees Zimmerli Art Museum

52. Camille Pissarro (1830–1903), *Study for "The Speculators"* (Les Boursicatières)
1890
Ink over pencil on glazed paper
22.5 × 17.5cm
The Ashmolean Museum

53. Pissarro, *The New Idolators* (Illustration for *Turpitudes Sociales*)
1890
Brown ink on glazed paper
30 × 22.5cm
The Denver Art Museum, Edward & Tullah Hanley Memorial Gift
Fig. 4, Nochlin

54. Jean-François Raffaëlli (1850–1924), *Georges Clemenceau Holding an Electoral Meeting in Paris, at the Circus Fernando in 1883* (Georges Clemenceau tenant une réunion électorale à Paris, au Cirque Fernando en 1883)
1885
Oil on canvas
243 × 245cm
Musée National du Chateau de Versailles
Plate 184

55. Henri Rivière (1864–1951), illustrator, *The Wandering Jew* (Le Juif errant)
Book
25.5 × 40.5cm
Collection of Mr. and Mrs. Herbert D. Schimmel

56. Alfred-Philippe Roll (1846–1919), *The Festival of the Centenary of the Revolution, of 1789, Celebrated at Versailles in 1889* (Fête du centenaire de la Révolution de 1789, célébrée à Versailles en 1889)
1893
Oil on canvas
140 × 222cm
Musée National du Chateau de Versailles
Plate 185

57. Théophile-Alexandre Steinlen (1859–1923), *One-hundred Million* (Cent Millions) (published in *Le Chambard Socialiste* of 24 February 1894)
Crayon on paper
35.5 × 17.8cm
New York Public Library Print Collection
Fig. 32, Cate

58. Steinlen, *Today!*
1894
Stencil-colored lithograph
New York Public Library Print Collection
Fig. 33, Cate

59. Steinlen, *Tomorrow!*
1894
Stencil-colored lithograph
32 × 30.5cm
New York Public Library Print Collection
Fig. 34, Cate

60. Henri de Toulouse-Lautrec (1864–1901), *Au Pied du Sinaï* (refused cover illustration for a book by Georges Clemenceau)
1898
Lithograph
26 × 41cm
Collection of Mr. and Mrs. Herbert D. Schimmel
Fig. 19, Cate

61. Georges Clemenceau, *Au Pied du Sinaï* (illustrated by Henri de Toulouse-Lautrec)
Book
26 × 40.5cm
Collection of Mr. and Mrs. Herbert D. Schimmel
Fig. 15, 16, 17, Cate
Fig. 12, Nochlin

62. Henri de Toulouse-Lautrec, *Why Not? Once Is Not a Habit* (for *L'Escarmouche,* 12 November 1893)
Lithograph
33.5 × 26cm
Collection of Mr. and Mrs. Herbert D. Schimmel
Fig. 10, Cate

63. Toulouse-Lautrec, *The Arton Trial (Ribot's Testimony)*
1896
Lithograph
42 × 55.2cm
Collection of Mr. and Mrs. Herbert D. Schimmel
Plate 1

64. Felix Vallotton (1865–1925), *L'Anarchiste*
1892
Ink on paper
17 × 25cm
Musée Cantonal des Beaux-Arts, Lausanne
Fig. 24, Cate

65. Vallotton, *La Charge*
1893
Woodcut on paper
New York Public Library Print Collection
Fig. 26, Cate

66. Vallotton, *The Demonstration*
(La Manifestation)
1893
Woodcut on paper
20.5 × 32cm
The Brooklyn Museum
Fig. 25, Cate

67. Vallotton, "The Revenge of
Panama" (La Revanche de Panama)
Le Courrier Français
1 April 1894
Photomechanical print
35.5 × 25.5cm
Musée de L'Elysée, Lausanne

68. Vallotton, *At Twenty Years of Age*
(A Vingt Ans)
1894
Woodcut on paper
23.5 × 33cm
University of Michigan Museum
of Art
Fig. 27, Cate

69. Adolphe-Léon Willette (1857–
1926), "The Jews and Holy Week"
(Les Juifs et La Semaine Sainte)
Le Courrier Français
5 April 1885
Photomechanical print
Jane Voorhees Zimmerli Art Museum
Fig. 2, Cate

70. Willette, "Edouard Drumont"
Le Courrier Français
16 May 1886
Photomechanical print
35.5 × 25.5cm
Jane Voorhees Zimmerli Art Museum
Fig. 3, Cate

71. Willette, "The Winter Will Be
Hard for the Goyim (the Christians)
This Year" (L'Hiver sera dur pour les
goymes [les chrétiens] cette année)
Le Pierrot
30 August 1889
Photomechanical print
35.5 × 25.5cm
Collection of Mr. and Mrs.
Herbert D. Schimmel
Fig. 4, Cate

72. Willette, *Poster for the Anti-Semitic
Candidate*
1889
Lithograph
138 × 100cm
The Jewish Museum, Anonymous gift
Fig. 6, Marrus

73. *La Libre Parole Illustrée,* "The Jew
is the Friend of the Arts" (Le Juif est
l'ami de l'arts)
26 September 1896
Photomechanical print
38 × 28.5cm
The Jewish Museum

74. "Assassinat du Président de la
République"
Photomechanical print
40 × 30cm
Bibliothèque Nationale

The Affair

First Court-Martial, the Degradation,
and Devil's Island

The press campaign against Alfred Dreyfus
began with the revelation of his arrest. Its themes
were anti-Semitism, fear of Germany, and a
chauvinism focused on the Army. While the mass-
circulated *Le Petit Journal* employed on its cover a
seemingly neutral illustration of the courtroom
and the degradation, its editorial content denounced Dreyfus as "not a Frenchman."

Humorous weeklies such as *Le Pilori* satirized
Dreyfus's degradation in caricature. *Le Rire* and
Le Journal Illustré published drawings of Dreyfus,
comparing him to Judas. Lionel Royer's image for
the latter paper was also widely distributed as an
engraving.

Although dispassionate, a rare photograph of
Dreyfus dwarfed by the architecture and the public
display in the courtyard of the Ecole Militaire
evokes the pathos of what Dreyfus referred to as
"the supreme humiliation," his degradation.
Another photograph taken by the police after
Dreyfus was stripped of his insignia was denounced as "photography as a humiliator" and
raised controversial questions regarding the use of
photographs as an invasion of privacy.

In preparation for his deportation to Devil's Island, Dreyfus requested books so that he could study English and read Shakespeare. He kept a journal in which he described his circumstances and covered pages with repetitious, complex designs while his jailers kept detailed records of his every move. At least one of the guards spent his free time making watercolor renderings of the hut and the guard tower. The bleak setting is reiterated in a photograph of the prison hut and several warders.

75. Bob (comtesse Sibylle Martel de Janville, also called Gyp [1850–1932]), *From Judas to Dreyfus* (De Judas à Dreyfus)
Photomechanical print
38 × 28cm
The Houghton Library, Harvard University

76. J. Chanteclair, "On the Subject of Judas Dreyfus" (A propos de Judas Dreyfus) *La Libre Parole Illustrée*
10 November 1894
Photomechanical print
35.5 × 28.5cm
The Jewish Museum

77. Chanteclair, "Fruitless Cleansing" (Savonnage infructueux) *La Libre Parole Illustrée*
17 November 1894
Photomechanical print
35.5 × 28.5cm
The Jewish Museum
Plate 6

78. Chanteclair, "What Lousy Weather" (Quel Temps de chien. . . !) *La Libre Parole Illustrée*
5 January 1895
Photomechanical print
35.5 × 28.5cm
The Jewish Museum

79. Donville, "En Famille" *La Libre Parole Illustrée*
7 November 1896
Photomechanical print
35.5 × 28.5cm
The Jewish Museum

80. Alfred Dreyfus, Notebook from Devil's Island
26 November–1 December 1898
Ink on paper
Bibliothèque Nationale

81. Alfred Dreyfus, Sketches and Description of Imprisonment
1899
23 × 18cm
Collection of J. Robert Maguire

82. Jean-Louis Forain (1852–1931), *Dreyfus in Prison*
Ink and charcoal on paper
30 × 29cm
Collection of Mr. and Mrs. Bertram H. Bloch

83. Frédéric de Haenen (1853?–1928), *The Degradation of Captain Dreyfus*
1895
Ink wash, crayon, and white gouache on cardboard
31.6 × 50.1cm
Collection of *L'Illustration,* Courtesy of Eric Baschet
Plate 8

83a. Oswald Heidbrinck, "Le Traître," *Le Rire*
5 January 1895
Photomechanical print
31 × 23.5cm
The Jewish Museum

84. Hermann-Paul, *Guignol #46:* "Do you think you are having some thirteen-day affair this year. Ernest, be prudent." (Pense que tu as ton treize jours affaire cette anné Ernest, soi prudent.)
1899
Photomechanical print
29.5 × 37cm
Bibliothèque Nationale

85. Alfred Le Petit (1841–1909), *That Scoundrel D. . .* (Cette Canaille de D)
c. 1899
22 × 17cm
Musée de Bretagne

86. H. Meyer, "The Traitor: Degradation of Alfred Dreyfus" (Le Traître: Dégradation d'Alfred Dreyfus) *Le Petit Journal*
13 January 1895
Photomechanical print
45.5 × 31cm
Collection of Mr. and Mrs. Ronald Bouscher
Plate 9

87. Pépin, "Logique," *Le Grelot*
7 May 1899
Photomechanical print
49 × 34.2cm
Collection of Mr. and Mrs. Ronald Bouscher

88. Charles Paul Renouard (1845–1924), *The 5th of January 1895 at the Ecole Militaire*
1899
Lithograph
35.5 × 27cm
The Library of the Jewish Theological Seminary of America
Plate 12

89. Lionel Royer (1852–1926), "La Dégradation," *Le Journal Illustré*
1895
Newspaper
Musée de Bretagne
Plate 14

90. C. G. Treds (?), "At The Ecole Militaire: The Degradation of the Traitor Dreyfus" (A l'Ecole Militaire: La Dégradation du Traître Dreyfus) *Le Petit Parisien*
13 January 1895
Photomechanical print
45 × 30.5cm
Musée de la Presse, Courtesy of Christian Bailly
Plate 10

91. Tully, "Dreyfus on Devil's Island" (Dreyfus à l'île du diable) *Le Progrès Illustré*
14 November 1897
Photomechanical print
46 × 30.5cm
Musée de Bretagne

92. Gilippo Nereo Vignola (1873–?), "Parade of Execution" (Parade d'exécution) *Le Pilori*
6 January 1895
Photomechanical print
Musée de Bretagne
Plate 13

93. Guards' Record Book (Dreyfus's imprisonment on Devil's Island)
1 January–30 September 1896
Manuscript
28 × 38cm
Private Collection

94. *Le Petit Journal,* "On Devil's Island"
27 September 1896
Photomechanical print
42.5 × 30cm
Musée de la Presse, Courtesy of Christian Bailly

95. *Le Petit Journal,* "Captain Dreyfus before the Court-Martial" (Le Capitaine Dreyfus devant le conseil de guerre)
23 December 1894
42.5 × 30cm
The Jewish Museum

96. *Le Petit Journal,* "Alfred Dreyfus in Prison" (Alfred Dreyfus dans le prison)
20 January 1895
Photomechanical print
42.5 × 23.5cm
The Jewish Museum

97. *A l'école militaire*
5 January 1895
Photograph
15 × 20cm
Collection of J. Robert Maguire
Plate 11

98. *Vue de l'île du diable*
Watercolor
72 × 49.5cm
The Leo Baeck Institute

99. *Vue des îles du salut*
Watercolor
32 × 18cm
The Leo Baeck Institute

100. Unknown, *The Departure Cabin on Devil's Island* (Case du départ à l'île du diable)
Watercolor
21 × 18cm
The Leo Baeck Institute

101. Unknown, *Vue de l'île du diable*
Watercolor
23 × 15cm
The Leo Baeck Institute

102. Unknown, *The Departure Cabin and Yard on Devil's Island* (Case et préau de départe à l'île du diable)
Watercolor
20 × 16cm
The Leo Baeck Institute

103. Unknown, *Guard Tower— Devil's Island*
1899
Ink on paper
18.5 × 11cm
Collection of J. Robert Maguire

104. Alfred Dreyfus's Eyeglasses and Case (used by Dreyfus on Devil's Island)
Glass and Metal
6.5 × 15.5 × 1.8cm
The Dreyfus Family

105. Unknown, *Dreyfus's Prison*
Photograph
16 × 11cm
The Houghton Library, Harvard University
Fig. 6, Burns

106. Police identification photograph of Alfred Dreyfus (after degradation)
1895
Photograph
8.2 × 6.1cm
Collection of Mr. and Mrs. Herbert D. Schimmel
Fig. 2, Martin

The Revision Debate

The largest portion of the visual and verbal polemic surrounding the Dreyfus case came in response to the gradual move to bring about a revision of the first court-martial. Beginning slowly and rather quietly with the publication of Bernard Lazare's *A Judicial Error: The Truth About the Dreyfus Case* in 1896, the debate gradually gained momentum throughout 1897 and finally exploded with Zola's diatribe against the army and government in early 1898. Although Lazare's pamphlet was distributed to the press and members of Parliament in November 1896, the revisionist campaign was not fully launched until almost a year later when public figures such as Senator Scheurer-Kestner, Jean Jaurès, and Emile Zola became convinced of Dreyfus's innocence. When Picquart's allegations against Esterhazy were published, the battle lines were drawn. In *Le Figaro,* Caran d'Ache satirized the effect of the polarization that would take place during the campaign for revision. Caricaturists such as Pépin in *Le Grelot* drew the figure of Truth and the Dreyfusards in their attempts to free her, while the journalists Rochefort and Drumont employed their papers to keep her imprisoned. Pépin's insightful cartoon allegorically predicted the frenzy of the press and the populace during the next two years.

Between Zola's publication of "J'Accuse" and Dreyfus's pardon, the French public would be amused or irritated by cartoons such as Alfred Le Petit's depiction of a laurel branch being devoured by Dreyfusard locusts.

Shortly after the publication of Bernard Lazare's pamphlet, Drumont used a drawing entitled "The Revenge of Dreyfus" on the cover of *La Libre Parole* to express the xenophobic and anti-Semitic program of his journal. It depicts a Jewish businessman carrying bags of money across the border to Germany, while French peasants silently learn of a new tax on bread. During the course of the Affair, an imaginary specter appeared in the anti-Dreyfusard press—the "Syndicate." This supposed brotherhood of Jews, Germans, and later, intellectuals was said to have access to money deposited in Berlin that they used to bribe judges, journalists, and politicians. The Nationalists believed that Dreyfus was the tool of France's enemies and the means for weakening and dividing her.

Two contrasting headlines caught the public's eye on 13 January 1898. As *L'Intransigeant* proclaimed Esterhazy's acquittal, *L'Aurore* published Zola's famous indictment of the army in "J'Accuse." The public's interest in the Dreyfus case and its ramifications is well described in Vallotton's woodcut "The Age of Paper," which shows each patron of a cafe fully engaged in reading one of the numerous dailies available to Paris's information-hungry public.

Zola's trial for libel unleashed a series of vituperative articles and cartoons parodying his bold statement. It led to the establishment of the weeklies *Psst. . . !* and *Le Sifflet,* which would make visual comments on the events and characters involved in the Affair. On the cover of the first issue, Forain set the tenor of the future issues: he portrayed Zola dropping *L'Aurore* into a privy; the caption "Ch'accuse. . . !" is an attempt at a German or Yiddish pronunciation of French. The artists of *Le Sifflet* were usually less caustic in their approach. For his first issue, Ibels depicted Esterhazy, suggesting that he would make a fine emperor.

The trial itself was sympathetically depicted in a series of lithographs by Paul Renouard, a noted draftsman-reporter. His lively portraits of Zola's defense counsel Labori and his sketch of Zola himself would later be included in his album *L'Affaire Dreyfus.*

In the summer of 1898, Picquart and Esterhazy were both arrested as confusion reigned in the offices of the General Staff. The Dreyfusard artist Couturier mocks Esterhazy and his confederate du Paty de Clam in his delineation of their rendezvous behind a public urinal.

The climax of the summer was Major Henry's confession of forgery and his suicide. Alfred Le Petit, whose anti-Dreyfusard cartoons are among the most savage, made a compassionate sketch of the widowed Madame Henry waiting for the judgment of heaven. *La Libre Parole* organized a fund, which it considered her husband's monument, to finance her libel suit against Joseph Reinach. *Le Monument Henry* was sarcastically prefigured in *Le Sifflet* when it announced an imaginary competition for a public monument to the colonel. It portrayed on its cover the study for a sculpture of Henry guarding the secrets of the General Staff.

In an ironic commentary on the summer's events, Caran d'Ache shows Picquart being shaved by spymaster Schwarzkoppen. It postulates a relationship between the two men, while referring to Henry's suicide by his own razor.

107. Abel-Truchet (1857–1918), "J'Accuse" *Les Quat'z'Arts*
23 January 1898
Photomechanical print
32 × 24cm
Collection of Mr. and Mrs. Herbert D. Schimmel
Fig. 44, Cate

108. Christiane Agincourt de Thoury, "The president said, 'I will circumcise the debating parties, and then I'll play yid by ear . . .'" (Le president a dit 'Je veux circoncire les débats, et quand aux conclusions, je passerai youtre. . .' [sic])
Les Quat'z'Arts
27 February 1898
Newspaper
32 × 24cm
The Houghton Library, Harvard University

109. Anquetin, "Drumont et Vacher" *La Feuille*
3 November 1898
Photomechanical print
45 × 32cm
Collection of Mr. and Mrs. Herbert D. Schimmel
Plate 5

110. Raoul Barre, "The Truth Itself" (La Vérité quand même) *Le Sifflet*
17 March 1898
Photomechanical print
40.5 × 26cm
Collection of Mr. and Mrs. Herbert D. Schimmel
Plate 47

111. J. Belon (active 1889–1907), "L'Incident Esterhazy-Labori" *La Patrie*
19 February 1898
Newspaper
91.5 × 71cm
Musée Carnavalet

112. H. Bersonse, "Le Syndicat"
Photomechanical print
51 × 50cm
The Houghton Library, Harvard
University

113. Bob (comtesse Sibylle de Martel
Janville, also called Gyp [1850–
1932]), *Portfolio of Foreign Affairs*
(Portefeuille [sic] des Affaires Etran-
gères)
Photomechanical print
18 × 23.5cm
Collection of Sibylle Gaudry

114. Bob, "Truth Is On the March"
(La Vérité en marche) *Le Rire*
21 May 1898
Photomechanical print
31 × 23.5cm
Jane Voorhees Zimmerli Art
Museum
Plate 65

115. Calot, *Long Live the Army* (Vive
l'armée)
1898
Photomechanical print
55 × 37.5cm
Bibliothèque Nationale
Plate 34

116. Caran d'Ache (1858–1909),
"Let's Go!" (Allons-y!) *Psst. . . !*
10 September 1898
Photomechanical print
40 × 28cm
The Jewish Museum

117. Caran d'Ache, "There He Is"
(Coucou, le voilà) *Psst. . . !*
10 June 1899
Photomechanical print
40 × 28cm
The Jewish Museum
Plate 46

118. Caran d'Ache, "Dinner with
the Family" (Dîner en famille)
Le Figaro
13 February 1898
Graphite on paper
47.5 × 43cm
Bibliothèque Nationale
Plate 54

119. Caran d'Ache, "Intellectual Salons" (Salons intellectuels) *Psst. . . !*
10 December 1898
Photomechanical print
40 × 28cm
The Jewish Museum
Plate 49

120. Caran d'Ache, "The New Religion" (Religion nouvelle) *Psst. . . !*
15 October 1898
Photomechanical print
40 × 28cm
The Jewish Museum

121. Caran d'Ache, "The Revision"
(La Revision) *Psst. . . !*
3 September 1898
Photomechanical print
40 × 28cm
The Jewish Museum

122. Carrey, "The Zola Affair:
Major Esterhazy at the Bar" (L'Affaire Zola: Le Commandant Esterhazy à la barre) *Le Journal Illustré*
27 February 1898
Newspaper
Musée de Bretagne

123. Chevalier, "After the Court of
Assizes, Alone at Last" (Après la
cour d'assises enfin seule) *Le Sifflet*
7 April 1898
Photomechanical print
40.5 × 26cm
Collection of Mr. and Mrs.
Herbert D. Schimmel

124. Clerac, "Truth Is On the
March" (La Vérité en marche)
Le Pilori
29 May 1898
Newspaper
48.5 × 32.5cm
Musée Carnavalet

125. Clerac, "The Punishment of
Zola" (Le Châtiment de Zola)
Le Pilori
6 March 1898
Newspaper
48.5 × 32.5cm
Musée de Bretagne

126. Léon-Antoine-Lucien Couturier (1842–1935), "Le Temple du secret professional," *Le Sifflet*
18 August 1898
Photomechanical print
40.5 × 26cm
Collection of Mr. and Mrs. Herbert D. Schimmel

127. Couturier, *Choral Apotheosis* (Apothéose Orphéonique)
1898
Pencil on brown paper
49 × 32.5cm
Bibliothèque Nationale
Fig. 8, Kleeblatt

128. Couturier, *The Temple of Professional Secrecy* (Le Temple du secret professionnel)
Watercolor on paper
Musée de Bretagne
Plate 21

129. Delfosse et Dousvinel, "I prove" (Je prouve) *La Patrie*
16 January 1898
Newspaper
Musée Carnavalet
Plate 23

130. Donville, "Judas Defended by His Brothers" (Judas défendu par ses frères) *La Libre Parole Illustrée*
14 November 1896
Photomechanical print
38 × 28.5cm
The Jewish Museum

131. Charles Walsin-Esterhazy, Letter to Daily Chronicle (from London)
28 February 1899
Manuscript
Collection of J. Robert Maguire

132. Fertom, "The Crowning of a Career" (Couronnement d'une carrière) *Le Pilori*
23 January 1898
Newspaper
48.5 × 32.5cm
Musée de Bretagne

133. Fertom, "La Débâcle" *Le Pilori*
27 February 1898
Photomechanical print
Musée de Bretagne
Plate 37

134. Jean-Louis Forain (1852–1931), "Cassation" *Psst. . . !*
9 April 1898
Photomechanical print
40 × 28cm
The Jewish Museum, Gift of Charles and Beth Gordon

135. Forain, "The Epaulettes of Joseph" (Les Epaulettes de Joseph) *Psst. . . !*
23 June 1898
Photomechanical print
40 × 28cm
The Jewish Museum, Gift of Charles and Beth Gordon
Plate 50

136. Forain, "Un Succès" *Psst. . . !*
2 April 1898
Photomechanical print
40 × 28cm
The Jewish Museum, Gift of Charles and Beth Gordon
Plate 56

137. Forain, "La Détente" *Psst. . . !*
8 October 1898
Photomechanical print
40 × 28cm
The Jewish Museum, Gift of Charles and Beth Gordon

138. Forain, "The Dreyfus Affair: Very well, Father Salomon, where were we?" (L'Affaire Dreyfus: Eh bien père Salomon, où en sommes nous) *Psst. . . !*
6 August 1898
Photomechanical print
40 × 28cm
The Jewish Museum, Gift of Charles and Beth Gordon

139. Forain, "The Hour of the Courier" (L'Heure de courrier) *Psst. . . !*
9 July 1898
Photomechanical print
40 × 28cm
The Jewish Museum, Gift of Charles and Beth Gordon

140. Forain, "Au secours" *Psst. . . !*
23 April 1898
Photomechanical print
40 × 28cm
The Jewish Museum, Gift of Charles and Beth Gordon

141. Forain, "Allégorie: L'Affaire Dreyfus" *Psst. . . !*
23 July 1898
Photomechanical print
40 × 28cm
The Jewish Museum, Gift of Charles and Beth Gordon

142. Forain, "A Versailles" *Psst. . . !*
28 May 1898
Photomechanical print
40 × 28cm
The Jewish Museum, Gift of Charles and Beth Gordon

143. Forain, "I Accuse" (Ch'Accuse) *Psst. . . !*
5 February 1898
Photomechanical print
40 × 28cm
The Jewish Museum, Gift of Charles and Beth Gordon
Fig. 50, Cate

144. Forain, "Another house we won't be dining in again" (Encore une maison où nous ne dînerons plus) *Le Rire*
24 December 1898
Photomechanical print
31 × 23.5cm
The Jewish Museum
Plate 57

145. Forain, "Neighborhood Drudgery" (Le Corvée de quartier) *Psst. . . !*
26 February 1898
Photomechanical print
40 × 28cm
The Jewish Museum, Gift of Charles and Beth Gordon
Plate 44

146. Georges et Rodolphe, "Dedicated to Clemenceau" (Dedié à Clemenceau) *Le Père Peinard*
6 February 1898
Photomechanical print
33.5 × 24cm
The University of Michigan Library, Labadie Collection

147. Frédéric de Haenen (1853?–1928), *Crisis in Algeria* (Affaire d'Algérie)
1898
Photomechanical print
38 × 26cm
Bibliothèque Nationale
Plate 40

148. Halrymple, "Will She Be Rescued" *Puck*
18 January 1899
Photomechanical print
The Houghton Library, Harvard University

149. Hermann-Paul (1874–1940), *Guignol #37:* "Untitled"
1899
Photomechanical print
29.5 × 37cm
Bibliothèque Nationale
Plate 165

150. Hermann-Paul, *Guignol #50:* "The Terror" (La Terreur)
1899
Photomechanical print
29.5 × 37cm
Bibliothèque Nationale
Plate 166

151. Hermann-Paul, *Guignol #60:* "Nothing Is Accomplished" (Rien n'y fait)
1899
Photomechanical print
29.5 × 37cm
Bibliothèque Nationale
Plate 168

152. Hermann-Paul, *Guignol #53:* "In the second office of the so-called information service. After the death of Lt. Colonel Henry" (Au deuxième bureau dit de rensignements. Après le mort du Lt. Colonel Henry)
1899
Photomechanical print
29.5 × 37cm
Bibliothèque Nationale
Plate 167

153. Hermann-Paul, *Guignol #43:* "Beautiful Youth, Down with Zola" (Belle Jeunesse à bas Zola)
1899
Photomechanical print
29.5 × 37cm
Bibliothèque Nationale
Fig. 47, Cate

154. Huard (1874–1965), "The State of the Dreyfus Affair" (L'Etat de l'affaire Dreyfus) *Le Rire*
22 January 1898
Photomechanical print
31 × 23.5cm
Jane Voorhees Zimmerli Art Museum

155. Henri-Gabriel Ibels (1867–
1936), "Caught Again. Drawing
Without Title" (Ressaisissement.
Dessin sans légende) *Le Sifflet*
2 April 1899
Photomechanical print
40.5 × 26cm
Collection of Mr. and Mrs.
Herbert D. Schimmel

156. Ibels, "Musée National:
L'Armée de Condé" *Le Sifflet*
7 July 1898
Photomechanical print
40.5 × 26cm
Collection of Mr. and Mrs.
Herbert D. Schimmel

157. Ibels, "The Truth" (La Vérité)
Illustration for *Le Sifflet,* 14 July 1898
Ink and crayon on paper
31 × 26cm
Musée de Bretagne
Fig. 54, Cate

158. Ibels, "Esterhazy the First! Why
Not?" (Esterhazy 1er! Pourquoi pas?)
Le Sifflet
17 February 1898
Photomechanical print
40.5 × 26cm
Collection of Mr. and Mrs.
Herbert D. Schimmel

159. Ibels, "The League of Patriots
1870–1898, All the Same" (LDP
1870–1898, quand-même) *Le Sifflet*
14 April 1898
40.5 × 26cm
Collection of Mr. and Mrs.
Herbert D. Schimmel

160. Ibels, "Of Gold, of Mud, of
Blood" (De l'or, de la boue, du sang)
Le Sifflet
16 June 1898
40.5 × 26cm
Collection of Mr. and Mrs.
Herbert D. Schimmel

161. Ibels, "Following the Famous
Revelations of M. Cavaignac"
(Après les fameuses révélations de
M. Cavaignac) *Le Sifflet*
14 July 1898
Photomechanical print
40.5 × 26cm
Collection of Mr. and Mrs.
Herbert D. Schimmel

162. Ibels, "Colonel Henry Keeps
the Secret of the General Staff" (Le
Colonel Henry gardant le secret de
l'état major) *Le Sifflet*
21 October 1898
40.5 × 26cm
Collection of Mr. and Mrs.
Herbert D. Schimmel

163. Ibels, "He Sings! They'll Pay!"
(Il chante! Ils paieront!)
Ink, wash, crayon, gouache on paper
28 × 20cm
Musée Carnavalet

164. Ibels, "Rapier Wit" (L'Esprit du
sabre) *Le Sifflet*
3 March 1898
Photomechanical print
40.5 × 26cm
Collection of Mr. and Mrs.
Herbert D. Schimmel
Plate 48

165. Ibels, "The Secret File: The
Light" (Le Dossier secret: La
Lumière) *Le Sifflet*
1 November 1898
Photomechanical print
40.5 × 26cm
Collection of Mr. and Mrs.
Herbert D. Schimmel

166. F. G. Keronan, "Les Nouveaux
frères Siamois" *Le Père Peinard*
30 October 1898
Photomechanical print
34 × 24cm
The University of Michigan Library,
Labadie Collection

167. *La Libre Parole Illustrée,* "The
Monopolies at the Stock Exchange"
(Les Accaprements à la bourse de
commerce)
28 November 1896
Photomechanical print
38 × 28.5cm
The Jewish Museum

168. Bernard Lazare, *A Judicial Error:
The Truth Concerning the Dreyfus
Affair* (Une Erreur judiciaire:
La Vérité sur l'affaire Dreyfus)
1896
Book
Collection of J. Robert Maguire

169. Charles-Lucien Léandre (1862–1930), *Mr. Scheurer-Kestner Consults the Clairvoyant* (M. Scheurer-Kestner consulte la voyant)
1897
Crayon, charcoal, and gouache on paper
44 × 31cm
Musée Carnavalet
Fig. 43, Cate

170. Léandre, "General Boisdeffre" *Le Rire*
17 September 1898
Ink on paper
31 × 23.5cm
Jane Voorhees Zimmerli Art Museum

171. Léandre, "Three Heads Under the Same Hat: Barrès, Coppée, Lemaître" (Trois Têtes sous un meme bonnet: Barrès, Coppée, Lemaître) *Le Rire*
25 March 1899
Photomechanical print
31 × 23.5cm
Jane Voorhees Zimmerli Art Museum

172. Léandre, "J. Reinach" *Le Rire*
16 September 1899
Photomechanical print
31 × 23.5cm
Jane Voorhees Zimmerli Art Museum

173. Léandre, "Arthur Meyer" *Le Rire*
10 June 1899
Photomechanical print
31 × 23.5cm
The Jewish Museum
Fig. 40, Cate

174. Léandre, "The Actors in the Great Dreyfusian Comedy (Picquart Affair)" (Les Acteurs de la grande comédie dreyfusienne [Affaire Picquart]) *Le Rire*
30 July 1898
Photomechanical print
31 × 23.5cm
Jane Voorhees Zimmerli Art Museum

175. Léandre, "General Zurlinden" *Le Rire*
24 September 1898
Photomechanical print
31 × 23.5cm
Jane Voorhees Zimmerli Art Museum

176. Léandre, "Alphonse de Rothschild" *Le Rire*
16 April 1898
Photomechanical print
31 × 23.5cm
Jane Voorhees Zimmerli Art Museum

177. Léandre, "Drumont" *Le Rire*
5 March 1898
Photomechanical print
31 × 23.5cm
Jane Voorhees Zimmerli Art Museum

178. Alfred Le Petit (1841–1909), *Défense de la République: Affaire Dreyfus* (Méline à Remiremont)
c. 1898–1899
Ink on paper
21.7 × 16.5cm
Musée de Bretagne

179. Le Petit, *Mme. Widow Henry Still Awaits the Judges!* (Mme. Veuve Henry attend toujours des juges!)
c. 1898
Ink on paper
22 × 17cm
Musée de Bretagne

180. Le Petit, *A Laurel Branch* (Une branche de laurier)
c. 1898–1899
Ink on paper
21.5 × 16.7cm
Musée de Bretagne

181. Le Petit, *The Affair* (L'Affaire)
c. 1898–1899
Ink on paper
25.5 × 16.5cm
Artine Artinian Collection
Plate 58

182. Le Petit, *The Return of Zola to the Good City of Paris* (Le retour de Zola dans sa bonne ville de Paris)
c. 1898–1899
Ink on paper
25.5 × 16.5cm
Artine Artinian Collection

183. Le Petit, "La Débâcle (in
L'Etrille)"
27 February 1898
Photomechanical print
42 × 39cm
Musée Carnavalet
Plate 38

184. Le Petit, *Zola hydrophobe*
c. 1898–1899
Ink on paper
25.5 × 16.5cm
Artine Artinian Collection
Plate 62

185. Le Petit, *Counting the Votes*
(Le depouillement)
Ink on paper
25 × 16.5cm
Musée de Bretagne
Fig. 2, Suleiman

186. Le Petit, *Masks for Shrove Tuesday* (Masques pour le mardi-gras)
c. 1898–1899
25.4 × 16.5cm
Artine Artinian Collection

187. Le Petit, *Apotheosis: Honor and Money* (Apothéose: L'Honneur et l'argent)
c. 1898–1899
Ink on paper
22 × 16.8cm
Musée de Bretagne

188. Maximilien Luce (1858–1941),
"The Revenge of the Doctor (Bertulus)" (La Revanche du médecin"
[Bertulus]) *Le Père Peinard*
31 October 1897
Photomechanical print
The University of Michigan Library,
Labadie Collection

189. Luce, "M. Forain, ex-
communard, actuellement chevalier
de la légion d'honneur" *Le Père
Peinard*
27 February 1898
Photomechanical print
33.5 × 24cm
The University of Michigan Library,
Labadie Collection

190. Luce, "Soldiers' Girls" (Filles à
soldat) *Le Père Peinard*
2 October 1898
Photomechanical print
34 × 24cm
The University of Michigan Library,
Labadie Collection
Plate 52

191. B. Moloch (1849–1909), "Zola
the Reckless" (Zola le téméraire)
L'Image Pour Rire
1898
Photomechanical print
30 × 22cm
Bibliothèque Nationale
Plate 25

192. Monogrammist L. G., "Verdict
de l'affaire Dreyfus"
Photomechanical print
26 × 34cm
Bibliothèque Nationale
Plate 18

193. Pépin, "The Truth" (La Vérité)
Le Grelot
19 December 1897
Photomechanical print
45.5 × 30cm
Bibliothèque Nationale
Fig. 3, Martin

194. Pépin, "The Affair
Dreyfus-Esterhazy—The Picture of
Marital Love" (L'Affaire Dreyfus-
Esterhazy—Tableau de l'amour con-
jugal) *Le Grelot*
30 January 1898
Photomechanical print
47 × 32cm
Bibliothèque Nationale
Plate 53

195. Maximilien Radiquet (1816–
1899), "The Procession of the
Leagues" (La Procession des ligues)
Le Rire
28 January 1899
Photomechanical print
31 × 48cm
Jane Voorhees Zimmerli Art
Museum

196. Charles Paul Renouard (1845–
1924), *Don't Ever Confess* (N'avouez
jamais)
Crayon on paper
54 × 34cm
Musée Carnavalet
Plate 19

197. Renouard, *Yves Guyot*
1899
Lithograph
35.5 × 26.5cm
The Library of the Jewish Theological
Seminary of America

198. Renouard, *La Fronde*
1899
Lithograph
26.5 × 34cm
The Library of the Jewish Theological
Seminary of America
Plate 17

199. Renouard, *Joseph Reinach*
1899
Lithograph
35.5 × 26.5cm
The Library of the Jewish Theological
Seminary of America

200. Renouard, *Octave Mirbeau*
1899
Lithograph
25.5 × 28cm
The Library of the Jewish Theological
Seminary of America
Plate 112

201. Renouard, *Labori–Closing
Arguments*
1899
Wood engraving
4 (each 15 × 13cm)
The Library of the Jewish Theological
Seminary of America
Plate 30 a, b

202. Renouard, (a) *Clemenceau,*
(b) *Demange as a Witness*
1899
Lithographs
14 × 12.5cm; 35.5 × 26.6cm
The Library of the Jewish Theological
Seminary of America

203. Renouard, *Confidences*
1899
Lithograph
19 × 26cm
The Library of the Jewish Theological
Seminary of America

204. Renouard, *Emile Zola*
(Zola Trial)
1899
Lithograph
35.5 × 26.5cm
The Library of the Jewish Theological
Seminary of America

205. Renouard, *Jean Jaurès*
1899
Lithograph
32 × 26.5cm
The Library of the Jewish Theological
Seminary of America

206. Renouard, *Esterhazy (Têtes
d'expression)*
1899
Lithographs
4 (each 15 × 13cm)
The Library of the Jewish Theological
Seminary of America
Plate 29, a–d

207. Renouard, *Rochefort, Déroulède,
Barrès and Quesnay de Beaurepaire*
1899
Lithographs
13 × 10cm; 13 × 10cm; 18 × 10cm;
18 × 10cm; 18 × 10cm
The Library of the Jewish Theological
Seminary of America

208. Renouard, *Lawyers for Both
Sides*
1899
Lithograph
23 × 21.5cm
The Library of the Jewish Theological
Seminary of America
Plate 26

209. Renouard, *Bernard Lazare*
1899
Lithograph
34 × 25cm
The Library of the Jewish Theological
Seminary of America

210. Renouard, *40 Upper Gloucester
Road, London* (Esterhazy)
1899
Lithograph
31.5 × 23.5cm
The Library of the Jewish Theological
Seminary of America
Plate 20

211. Antonin Reschal, *Open Letter to
M. Zola* (Lettre ouverte à M. Zola)
January 1898 (?)
Broadside
33 × 50cm
The Houghton Library, Harvard
University

212. Lucien Guirand de Scevola (1871–1950), "You Won't Carry That One Away Cheap" (Celui la, tu ne l'emporteras la-luxe) *Les Quat'z'Arts*
10 April 1898
Photomechanical print
Collection of Mr. and Mrs. Herbert D. Schimmel

213. Théophile-Alexandre Steinlen (1859–1923), "Boisdeffre's Sheep" (Les Moutons de Boisdeffre) *La Feuille*
28 February 1898
Photomechanical print
46 × 32cm
Collection of Mr. and Mrs. Herbert D. Schimmel
Fig. 41, Cate

214. Steinlen, "Let's Salute Them" (Saluons-les) *La Feuille*
18 January 1899
Photomechanical print
46 × 22cm
Collection of Mr. and Mrs. Herbert D. Schimmel
Plate 111

215. Steinlen, "Striking Arguments" (Arguments Frappants) *La Feuille*
21 January 1898
Photomechanical print
46 × 32cm
Collection of Mr. and Mrs. Herbert D. Schimmel
Fig. 45, Cate

216. Steinlen, "Rochefort Is Dying! Rochefort Is Dead" *La Feuille*
16 June 1898
Photomechanical print
46 × 32cm
Collection of Mr. and Mrs. Herbert D. Schimmel
Plate 32

217. Felix Vallotton (1865–1925), "There Is No Dreyfus Affair" (Il n'y a pas d'affaire Dreyfus) *Le Cri de Paris*
20 November 1898
Photomechanical print
28.5 × 19.5cm
Musée de L'Elysée, Lausanne

218. Vallotton, "The Age of Paper" (L'age du Papier) *Le Cri de Paris*
23 January 1898
Photomechanical print
28.5 × 19.5cm
Bibliothèque Nationale
Fig. 46, Cate

219. Vallotton, "At Home" (En Famille) *Le Cri de Paris*
13 February 1898
Photomechanical print
28.5 × 19.5cm
Bibliothèque Nationale
Plate 55

220. Vallotton, "The Statue of the Major" (La Statue du commandant) *Le Cri de Paris*
29 January 1899
Photomechanical print
28.5 × 19.5cm
Bibliothèque Nationale

221. *The Esterhazy Affair—Conclusive Identification of the Handwriting* (Affaire Esterhazy—identité absolute des écritures)
Newspaper clipping
Bibliothèque Nationale

222. *The Proof of Dreyfus's Treason* (La Preuve de la Trahison de Dreyfus)
Photomechanical print
57 × 37cm
Boston Public Library

223. *The Question of the Day* (La Question du jour)
Photomechanical print
Boston Public Library
Plate 35

224. *The Zola Trial: The Verdict* (Le Procès Zola: Le Verdict)
1898
Newspaper clipping
Bibliothèque Nationale

225. *Zola and His Intellectuals* (Zola et ses intellectuels)
Photomechanical print
31 × 22cm
Bibliothèque Nationale
Plate 36

226. "La Cuisine de l'état-major"
Le Père Peinard
25 September 1898
Photomechanical print
34 × 24cm
The University of Michigan Library,
Labadie Collection
Plate 75

227. "Anti-Semitic Pastime in Algiers," illustrated by Louis Chevalier, *Le Sifflet*
14 April 1898
Photomechanical print
40.5 × 26cm
Collection of Mr. and Mrs.
Herbert D. Schimmel

228. "Arrest of Picquart" *La Libre
Parole*
14 July 1898
Newspaper
91.5 × 71cm
Musée de la Presse, Courtesy
Christian Bailly

229. "Identity of the Handwriting"
(Identité des ecritures) *Le Siècle*
6 January 1898
Newspaper
Musée de la Presse, Courtesy
Christian Bailly

230. "Letter to the President of the
Republic by Emile Zola" (Lettre au
president de la République par Emile
Zola) *L'Aurore*
22 December 1900
Newspaper
Collection of Mr. and Mrs.
Herbert D. Schimmel

231. "Long Live Zola" (Vive Zola)
Les Droits de l'homme
25 February 1898
Newspaper
Musée de la Presse, Courtesy
Christian Bailly

232. "Major Esterhazy Is Acquitted"
(Le Commandant Esterhazy acquitter)
L'Intransigeant
13 January 1898
Newspaper
Musée de la Presse, Courtesy
Christian Bailly

233. "Our Trial" (Notre Procès)
L'Aurore
3 April 1898
Newspaper
Musée de la Presse, Courtesy
Christian Bailly

234. "Response to the Summons by
Zola" (Réponse à l'assignation par
Zola) *L'Aurore*
13 February 1898
Newspaper
Musée de la Presse, Courtesy
Christian Bailly

235. "The Real Traitor by Jean
Jaurès" (Le veritable traître par Jean
Jaurès) *La Petite République*
18 August 1898
Newspaper clipping
Bibliothèque Nationale

236. "The Anti-Semitic Clique" (La
Clique antisémite) *La Grande Bataille*
21 August 1898
Newspaper
91.5 × 71cm
Musée de la Presse, Courtesy
Christian Bailly

237. "The Henry Subscription"
(Subscription Henry) *La Libre Parole*
28 December 1898
Newspaper
91.5 × 71cm
Musée de la Presse, Courtesy
Christian Bailly

238. "The History of the Dreyfus-
Esterhazy Affair" (L'Historique
de l'Affair Dreyfus-Esterhazy)
Le Gaulois
10 January 1898
Newspaper
Musée de la Presse, Courtesy
Christian Bailly

239. "The Trial of l'Aurore" (Le
Procès de l'Aurore) *L'Aurore*
19 July 1898
Newspaper
Musée de la Presse, Courtesy
Christian Bailly

240. "The Saber and the Holy
Water" (Le Sabre et le benitier)
L'Aurore
13 February 1898
Newspaper
Musée de la Presse, Courtesy
Christian Bailly

241. "The Evidence of Colonel Picquart" (Les Aveux de Colonel Picquart) *Le Jour*
12 February 1898
Newspaper
91.4 × 71.12cm
Musée de la Presse, Courtesy Christian Bailly

242. "To Each His Own Share" (Chacun à son lot), illustrated by A. Lemot *Le Pèlerin*
18 December 1898
Photomechanical print
38 × 30.5cm
Musée de la Presse, Courtesy Christian Bailly
Fig. 5, Marrus

243. "Zola in the Court of Assizes" (Zola en cour d'assises) *L'Aurore*
20 February 1898
Newspaper
Collection of Mr. and Mrs. Herbert D. Schimmel

The High Court of Appeals

Between September 1898 and June 1899, a judicial battle raged over Dreyfus's conviction. The High Court finally ordered a retrial based on the secret communication of evidence during the court-martial and conflict over the authorship of the major piece of evidence—the bordereau. In the press, Le Petit published a gruesome fetus named "Revision," while Ibels's drawing in *Le Sifflet* referred to the evidence that a secret file had been shown to the military judges. Renouard made numerous prints of the proceedings of the High Court of Appeals, chronicling rather straightforwardly the pomp witnessed in those chambers.

244. Bob (comtesse Sibylle de Martel de Janville, also called Gyp [1850–1932]), *They Are Displaying Great Zeal Toward the Trial of This Pink Carnation* (Lors du procès de l'oeillet rouge, ils deployerent un grand zèle . . .)
Photomechanical print
19 × 24.5cm
Collection of Sibylle Gaudry

245. Léon-Antoine-Lucien Couturier (1842–1935), "For the King" (Pour le Roy!) *Le Sifflet*
3 March 1899
Photomechanical print
40.5 × 26cm
Collection of Mr. and Mrs. Herbert D. Schimmel
Plate 45

246. Couturier, "Bad Year, Good Year?" (Mal an, bon an?) *Le Sifflet*
6 January 1899
Photomechanical print
40.6 × 26cm
Collection of Mr. and Mrs. Herbert D. Schimmel

247. Jean-Louis Forain (1852–1931), "Pantomime" *Psst . . . !*
28 January 1899
Photomechanical print
40 × 28cm
The Jewish Museum, Gift of Charles and Beth Gordon

248. Forain, "Take These to the Grand Rabbi" (Portez-ça au grand rabbin) *Psst . . . !*
11 February 1899
Ink on paper
40 × 28cm
The Jewish Museum, Gift of Charles and Beth Gordon

249. Forain, "The Civil Power" (Le Pouvoir Civil) *Psst . . . !*
24 June 1899
Photomechanical print
40 × 28cm
The Jewish Museum, Gift of Charles and Beth Gordon

250. Forain, "For the Criminal" (A la criminelle) *Psst . . . !*
8 April 1899
Photomechanical print
40 × 28cm
The Jewish Museum, Gift of Charles and Beth Gordon

251. Forain, "Between Allies" (Entre Allies) *Psst . . . !*
14 January 1899
Photomechanical print
40 × 28cm
The Jewish Museum, Gift of Charles and Beth Gordon

252. Mono H. A., "Les Bourreau-crates" *Le Père Peinard*
13 November 1898
Ink on paper
34 × 24cm
The University of Michigan Library, Labadie Collection

253. Henri-Gabriel Ibels (1867–1936), "It Was Bound to Happen! There'll Be Repercussions" (C'était écrit! Il y a une suite) *Le Sifflet*
April 1899
Photomechanical print
40.5 × 26cm
Collection of Mr. and Mrs. Herbert D. Schimmel

254. Charles-Lucien Léandre (1862–1930), "Waldeck-Rousseau, Galliffet, and Millerand" *Le Rire*
8 July 1899
Photomechanical print
31 × 23.5cm
Jane Voorhees Zimmerli Art Museum

255. Léandre, "Acceptance of the Case by the Court of Appeals" (Comment on tue) *Le Rire*
8 October 1898
Photomechanical print
31 × 23.5cm
Jane Voorhees Zimmerli Art Museum

256. Alfred Le Petit (1841–1909), *Poor Revision* (Pauvre Revision)
c. 1898–1899
Ink on paper
25.5 × 16.5cm
Artine Artinian Collection

257. Le Petit, "*Le Figaro: The Secret File*" (Le Figaro: Le Dossier Secret)
c. 1899
Ink on paper
20 × 17cm
Musée de Bretagne
Plate 60

258. Le Petit, *The High Court: Rights of Man* (Haute Cour: Droits de l'homme)
Ink on paper
20.5 × 17cm
Musée de Bretagne

259. Le Petit, *Incident in the Audience* (Incident d'audience)
c. 1898–1899
Ink on paper
25.5 × 16.5cm
Artine Artinian Collection

260. Le Petit, *The Balances of the Year 1898* (Les balances de l'année 1898)
c. 1898–1899
Ink on paper
25.5 × 16.5cm
Artine Artinian Collection

261. Le Petit, *Do Not Touch . . . Picard [sic]* (Ne touche pas . . . Picard)
c. 1898–1899
Ink on paper
25.5 × 16.5cm
Artine Artinian Collection

262. Le Petit, *They Had to Use Forceps* (Il a fallu les forceps)
c. 1898–1899
Ink on paper
25.5 × 17cm
Artine Artinian Collection
Plate 59

263. Georges Manzana Pissarro (1871–1961), "Miss Liberty Being Tortured on the Rack" *Le Père Peinard*
8 and 15 January 1899
Photomechanical print
34.3 × 24.1cm
The University of Michigan Library, Labadie Collection
Plate 77

264. Charles Paul Renouard (1845–1924), *The Combined Chambers*
1899
Lithograph
30 × 42.5cm
The Library of the Jewish Theological Seminary of America
Plate 109

265. Renouard, *The President of the Court*
1899
Lithograph
33 × 26cm
The Library of the Jewish Theological Seminary of America

266. Renouard, *Entry of the Magistrates*
1899
Lithograph
34.5 × 22.5cm
The Library of the Jewish Theological
Seminary of America
Plate 108

267. Renouard, *A Glance from the
President*
1899
Lithograph
19 × 27cm
The Library of the Jewish Theological
Seminary of America

268. Renouard, *M. Bard Reading
His Report*
1899
Lithograph
15 × 20cm
The Library of the Jewish Theological
Seminary of America
Plate 110

269. Renouard, *Mme. Dreyfus and
Her Children*
1899
Lithograph
26.5 × 40.5cm
The Library of the Jewish Theological
Seminary of America

270. Félix Vallotton (1865–1925),
"This Way, General" (Par ici mon
general) *Le Cri de Paris*
25 June 1899
Photomechanical print
25.5 × 18cm
Musée de L'Elysée, Lausanne

The Second Court-Martial in Rennes

From the time when Dreyfus's return to France during a downpour was observed by illustrator George Redon until he was reconvicted, the press maintained its heated coverage.

In the weeks before the trial *Psst . . . !* continued its anti-Dreyfusard campaign, commenting on the involvement of the prince of Monaco, a supporter of Dreyfus, in a drawing by Forain. The artist depicts the presentation of a new pair of epaulettes as a gift to Dreyfus from the prince. Numerous illustrations, either photographic or hand-drawn, of Madame Dreyfus as she made her daily visit to the prison were published. She was so pursued by photographers that she finally requested police protection.

Interest in the proceedings was so intense that the authorities severely limited the number of reporters and artists allowed into the courtroom. Photographers were completely excluded, although Gerschel managed to photograph most of the luminaries, including Dreyfus himself.

Renouard completed his extensive series of prints, of which the most poignant are Demange, Dreyfus's lawyer, despondent after the verdict, and Dreyfus as he walked between the two rows of soldiers, their backs turned in a guard of dishonor. Other artists in the courtroom included Monogrammist OI, whose drawings were published in *La Patrie,* and Couturier for *Le Petit Bleu.* In sharp contrast to these reporters, the anarchist artist Maximilien Luce viewed the court-martial in allegorical terms in his lithograph *Truth at the Court-Martial.*

The headline of 10 September 1899, in *La Libre Parole* announced once again: "The Traitor is Condemned." Ten days later, Dreyfus accepted a pardon with the proviso that he could continue his efforts to vindicate himself.

271. Albert Bettenger (1846–1919),
"Le Retour du Capitaine Dreyfus"
L'Illustration
8 July 1899
39 × 28.5cm
Collection of Mr. and Mrs. Ronald
Bouscher

272. Caran d'Ache, "The Joys of the Return" (Les Joies du retour)
Psst . . . !
1 July 1899
Photomechanical print
40 × 28cm
The Jewish Museum

273. Georges Clarin, *Labori and Dreyfus at Rennes*
c. 1899
Etching on paper
50 × 33cm
Collection of Simone Perl

274. Léon-Antoine-Lucien Couturier (1842–1935), *Carrière, Military Prosecutor*
1899
Pencil on brown paper
31.3 × 22cm
The Israel Museum

275. Couturier, *Generals Mercier, Zurlinden, Boisdeffre and Roget*
1899
Pencil on paper
31 × 24cm
The Israel Museum
Plate 143

276. Couturier, *Generals Mercier, Gonse, Jannet*
1899
Pencil on paper
31.5 × 24cm
The Israel Museum

277. Couturier, *Counsel Pleading at Rennes*
1899
Pencil on cream paper
30.5 × 24cm
The Israel Museum
Plate 148

278. Couturier, *Colonel Jouaust*
1899
Pencil on cream paper
12.5 × 14.5cm
The Israel Museum
Plate 142

279. Couturier, *Dreyfus*
1899
Pencil on cream paper
31.3 × 23.7cm
The Israel Museum
Plate 146

280. Lucie Dreyfus, Letter to Alfred Dreyfus
1 July 1899
Collection of Simone Perl

281. Jean-Louis Forain (1852–1931), "Sweet Country: Friends of Power" (Doux Pays: Amis du Pouvoir)
L'Echo de Paris
5 September 1899
Photomechanical print
Musée de la Presse, Courtesy Christian Bailly

282. Forain, "The Court Will Appreciate It." (Le Conseil appréciera)
Psst . . . !
9 September 1899
Photomechanical print
40 × 28cm
The Jewish Museum, Gift of Charles and Beth Gordon

283. Forain, "At Rennes" (A Rennes) *Psst . . . !*
26 August 1899
Photomechanical print
40 × 28cm
The Jewish Museum, Gift of Charles and Beth Gordon

284. Forain, "For Dreyfus" (Pour Dreyfus) *Psst . . . !*
8 July 1899
Photomechanical print
40 × 28cm
The Jewish Museum, Gift of Charles and Beth Gordon
Plate 51

285. Gerschel, *Photograph Album: Rennes Trial*
1899
Album of 48 photographs
The Dreyfus family
Plates 153–163

286. Gravelle, *The Return from Devil's Island* (Le Retour de l'île du diable)
1899
Photomechanical print
55 × 37cm
The Houghton Library, Harvard University

287. Henri-Gabriel Ibels (1867–1936), "Basile's Reason—Slander Away! There will always be something left!" (La Raison de Basile—Calomniez! Il en restera toujours quelque-chose) *Le Sifflet*
20 January 1899
42.5 × 26cm
Collection of Mr. and Mrs. Herbert D. Schimmel

288. G. Julio, "The Catastrophe" (Le denouement) illustration for *La Reforme*
11 September 1899
Ink on paper
25 × 50cm
Musée de Bretagne

289. G. Julio, "Nobel Mission!" illustration for *La Reforme*
6 August 1899
Ink on paper
25 × 48.5cm
Musée de Bretagne
Plate 88

290. Charles-Lucien Léandre (1862–1930), "Demange, Defender of Dreyfus" (Maître Demange, Défenseur de Dreyfus) *Le Rire*
12 August 1899
Photomechanical print
31 × 23.5cm
The Jewish Museum

291. Léandre, "Arma (Billot, Cavaignac, Mercier) Toga (Manau, Loew, Bard)" *Le Rire*
4 February 1899
Photomechanical print
31 × 23.5cm
Jane Voorhees Zimmerli Art Museum

292. Léandre, "Clemenceau" *Le Rire*
30 July 1899
Photomechanical print
31 × 23.5cm
Jane Voorhees Zimmerli Art Museum

293. Alfred Le Petit (1841–1909), *The Boat That Brings Back Dreyfus* (Bâteau qui ramene Dreyfus)
c. 1899
Ink on paper
20 × 15.5cm
Musée de Bretagne

294. Maximilien Luce (1858–1941), *Truth at the Court-Martial* (La Vérité au conseil de guerre)
Lithograph on paper
57 × 45.5cm
Archer M. Huntington Art Gallery, The University of Texas at Austin, Gift of Alvin and Ethel Romansky, 1978
Fig. 53, Cate

295. M. Makul, *Mme. Dreyfus Entering the School*
Ink on paper
16 × 20cm
Collection of J. Robert Maguire

296. Georges Redon (1869–1943), *At the Port of Haliguen—The Departure* (A Porte Haliguen—Le Débarquement)
Photomechanical print
31 × 48cm
Bibliothèque Nationale

297. Redon, "The Attempt on M. Labori's Life" (L'Attentat contre M. Labori) *La Vie Illustrée*
August 1899
Photomechanical print
34 × 24.5cm
Bibliothèque Nationale
Plate 149

298. Charles Paul Renouard (1845–1924), *Sketches of Dreyfus* (Têtes d'expression)
1899
Lithograph
25.5 × 32cm
The Library of the Jewish Theological Seminary of America
Plate 139

299. Renouard, *Dreyfus in Profile*
1899
Lithograph
33 × 25cm
The Library of the Jewish Theological Seminary of America
Plate 133

300. Renouard, *Georges Picquart*
1899
Lithograph
35.5 × 26cm
The Library of the Jewish Theological Seminary of America
Plate 137

301. Renouard, *Sketches of Generals
Boisdeffre and Gonse*
1899
Lithograph
26 × 25cm each
The Library of the Jewish Theological
Seminary of America
Plate 138

302. Renouard, *The Dossier*
1899
Lithograph
26 × 32cm
The Library of the Jewish Theological
Seminary of America
Plate 136

303. Renouard, *Court-Martial
at Rennes*
1899
Lithograph
27 × 42cm
The Library of the Jewish Theological
Seminary of America
Plate 132

304. Renouard, *Dreyfus Speaks*
1899
Lithograph
35.5 × 25.5cm
The Library of the Jewish Theological
Seminary of America
Plate 134

305. Renouard, *Exiting the Lycée*
1899
Lithograph
26 × 35cm
The Library of the Jewish Theological
Seminary of America
Plate 135

306. Renouard, *The Verdict*
1899
Lithograph
30 × 26.5cm
The Library of the Jewish Theological
Seminary of America
Plate 141

307. Sabattier, "The Dreyfus Affair
at Rennes: The Accused During Cross-
examination" (L'Affaire Dreyfus à
Rennes: l'accusé pendant l'interrogation) *L'Illustration*
12 August 1899
Photomechanical print
39 × 28.5cm
Collection of Mr. and Mrs.
Ronald Bouscher

308. Louis Sabattier, "The Dreyfus
Affair at Rennes: The Accused During
the Interrogation" (L'Affaire Dreyfus
à Rennes: l'accusé pendant l'interrog-
atoire) *L'Illustration*
16 September 1899
Collection of Mr. and Mrs.
Ronald Bouscher

309. Monogrammist MAS, *Innocence!
(Dreyfus on the Witness Stand)*
August 1899
Ink on paper
21.5 × 14cm
Collection of J. Robert Maguire

310. Monogrammist OI, *Dreyfus
Answering the Witnesses*
August/September 1899
Ink on paper
38 × 51cm
Collection of J. Robert Maguire

311. Monogrammist OI, *Guarding the
Umbrellas*
August/September 1899
Ink on paper
8.5 × 19.5cm
Collection of J. Robert Maguire
Plate 151

312. Monogrammist OI, *Dreyfus with
Police Leaving Military Station*
10 August 1899
Ink on paper
16 × 23cm
Collection of J. Robert Maguire

313. Monogrammist OI, *Women
Expelled from the Courtroom*
9 August 1899
Ink on paper
24 × 19.5cm
Collection of J. Robert Maguire

314. Monogrammist OI, *The
Caudine Forks: A New Scourge Visited
on Rennes*
August 1899
Ink on paper
14.5 × 24.5cm
Collection of J. Robert Maguire
Plate 152

315. Monogrammist OI,
Mme. Labori with Her Husband
13 August 1899
Ink on paper
15 × 19cm
Collection of J. Robert Maguire

316. Monogrammist OI, *Releasing the Pigeons*
1899
Ink on paper
12.5 × 17cm
Collection of J. Robert Maguire
Plate 150

317. Monogrammist OI, *Journalists at Their Table During a Pause*
18 August 1899
Ink on paper
13 × 16cm
Collection of J. Robert Maguire

318. *L'Aurore,* "Lettre à Mme. Dreyfus"
22 September 1899
Newspaper
Musée de la Presse, Courtesy Christian Bailly

319. *L'Eclair,* "The Rennes Trial—Dreyfus is Condemned" (Le Procès de Rennes—Dreyfus Condamné)
11 September 1899
Newspaper
Musée de la Presse, Courtesy Christian Bailly

320. *L'Intransigeant,* "The Two Traitors. Dreyfus Condemned! Déroulède in Prison" (Les Deux Traitres. Dreyfus Condamné! Déroulède en Prison)
21 September 1899
Newspaper
Musée de la Presse, Courtesy Christian Bailly

321. *La Libre Parole,* "Le Traître Condamné"
10 September 1899
Newspaper
Musée de la Presse, Courtesy Christian Bailly

322. *Le Patriote Illustré,* "Mme. Dreyfus on Her Way to the Prison at Rennes" (Mme. Dreyfus se rendant à la prison de Rennes)
23 July 1899
Newspaper
Musée de la Presse, Courtesy Christian Bailly

323. *Le Petit Bleu,* "Generals Mercier, Zurlinden, Boisdeffre and Roget" (illustrations by Couturier)
7 September 1899
Newspaper
Musée de la Presse, Courtesy Christian Bailly

324. *Le Petit Journal,* "The Court-Martial at Rennes: The Condemnation of Dreyfus" (Conseil de Guerre de Rennes: Condamnation de Dreyfus)
10 September 1899
Newspaper
Musée de la Presse, Courtesy Christian Bailly

325. *Le Petit Parisien,* "The Arrival of Dreyfus at Quiberon" (Arrivée de Dreyfus à Quiberon)
16 July 1899
Newspaper
Collection of Mr. and Mrs. Ronald Bouscher

326. *Le Reveil de Nord,* "The Revision of the Dreyfus Trial" (La Revision du Procès Dreyfus)
3 May 1899
Newspaper
Musée de la Presse, Courtesy Christian Bailly

327. *Le Siècle,* "The Lies of Photography" (Les Mensonges de la photographie)
12 January 1899
Newspaper
Musée de la Presse, Courtesy Christian Bailly

Aftermath

After the pardon Dreyfus was reunited with his family at his sister's home in Carpentras. Ibels, who had consistently supported the cause, gave a drawing of Dreyfus with his children as a gift to the family of Senator Scheurer-Kestner, who died the day of the pardon. He inscribed his drawing, "To the glory of Scheurer-Kestner." Another Dreyfusard artist, Félix Vallotton, summarized the Affair in his wood engraving *The Debacle,* a rout in which the church, the army, and the courts are defeated by justice.

Alfred Dreyfus continued his efforts to find new grounds on which to base an appeal. The Dreyfusards, never a homogeneous group, fragmented even further as many opposed the defense tactics in Rennes, Dreyfus's acceptance of a pardon, and later, the passage of the amnesty law. In 1904, when the Criminal Chamber of Appeals agreed to review the verdict, Forain, still an anti-Dreyfusard, published a vicious courtroom scene captioned: "Joseph [Reinach] to Dreyfus—Get out of here, you'll give us away. . . ."

Lyonel Feininger's print of 1906 entitled "The Exodus," depicting a file of priests, abstracts one of the political outcomes of the Affair. The ancient conflict between social reformers and the Church was renewed during the Affair, particularly in the newspaper published by the Assumptionists, *La Croix,* which reflected a point of view similar to that of *La Libre Parole.* Prime Minister Waldeck-Rousseau began a reform of the Church to secure his Republican government. Religious orders were dissolved, religious schools were closed, and finally in 1905 a law was passed separating church and state.

328. L. Berteault, "The Monumental Arch of the Universal Exposition"
L'Illustration
14 April 1900
Photomechanical print
48 × 40cm
L'Illustration, Courtesy Eric Baschet

329. Robert-Adrien Deletang (1874–1951), *The Dream of Joseph Reinach* (Le Rêve de M. Joseph Reinach)
28 December 1902
Photomechanical print
31.5 × 42cm
Bibliothèque Nationale

330. Lyonel Feininger (b. New York, 1871–1956), "The Exodus" *Le Temoin, No. 1*
1906
Photomechanical print
36 × 63cm
Anonymous Lender
Plate 183

331. Jean-Louis Forain (1852–1931), *Joseph to Dreyfus—Get out of here, you'll give us away* (Joseph à Dreyfus: fous le camp, tu nous trahirais)
Graphite on paper
30 × 41cm
The Houghton Library, Harvard University
Fig. 6, Martin

332. Forain, *Joseph to Dreyfus, Get out of here, you'll give us away* (Joseph à Dreyfus, fous le camp, tu nous trahirais)
Le Rire, 12 March 1904
Photomechanical print
25 × 43cm
Boston Public Library

333. Forain, *Soldier and Priest*
Lithograph
28 × 44cm
Boston Public Library

334. Henri-Gabriel Ibels (1867–1936), *A la gloire de Scheurer-Kestner*
20 September 1899 (inscription date)
India ink and gouache on ocher paper
25 × 20cm
Musée Carnavalet
Plate 164

335. E. Le Deley, *The Rehabilitation of Dreyfus* (La Réhabilitation de Dreyfus)
Six postcards
Heleotype
Collection of J. Robert Maguire
Plates 178–181

336. Alfred Le Petit (1841–1909), *Bourse de Paris*
c. 1900
Ink on paper
21.5 × 16.5cm
Musée de Bretagne

336a. Le Petit, *Justice: The Amnesty According to Waldeck* (Justice: l'amnestie selon Waldeck)
c. 1900
Ink on paper
20.3 × 17cm
Musée de Bretagne

337. Louis Sabattier (1863–1935), *The Closing of the Congregational Schools. "Mothers of Families," Sunday, July 27, at the Place de la Concorde* (La fermeture des écoles congréganistes. Manifestation des «mères de famille», le dimanche 27 juillet, sur la place de la Concorde)
21 August 1902
Photography highlighted with ink and gouache
37.6 × 60cm
L'Illustration, Courtesy of Eric Baschet

338. Théophile-Alexandre Steinlen (1859–1923), "The Pope as a Spider" *L'Assiette au beurre*
26 February 1902
Photomechanical print
38 × 48cm
Jane Voorhees Zimmerli Art Museum

339. Steinlen (1859–1923), *Small Penny*
1900
Color lithograph
135 × 95cm
Jane Voorhees Zimmerli Art Museum, Gift of David and Mildred Morse
Fig. 52, Cate

340. Steinlen, *Paris, par Zola*
1898
Color lithograph
140 × 200cm
Jane Voorhees Zimmerli Art Museum, Gift of Norma Bartman
Fig. 1, Suleiman

341. Félix Vallotton (1865–1925), "Father, a Story" (Père, une histoire) *Le Cri de Paris*
1 October 1899
Photomechanical print
25.5 × 18cm
Bibliothèque des Arts, Lausanne

342. Vallotton, *The Debacle* (La Débâcle)
Wood engraving
32 × 50cm
The Jewish Museum, Gift of Mr. and Mrs. Herbert D. Schimmel
Plate 182

343. Vallotton, *Boy, It's Heavy* (Ce qu'elle est lourde)
1899
Ink on paper
Jane Voorhees Zimmerli Art Museum

Posters, Souvenirs, Games, Ephemera

The pervasiveness of the Dreyfus Affair in French society was demonstrated by the commercial ventures it fostered in the form of games, souvenirs, postcards, and posters. Expressing both pro- and anti-Dreyfus sentiments, these objects served the dual goals of propaganda and profit.

Two board games for adults, which caricatured the protagonists of the Affair, were "The Game of the Dreyfus Affair and Truth," geared to Dreyfusards, and its anti-Semitic counterpart, "The Game of 36 Heads." Novelties included the "Zola-Mouquette," a pull-toy revealing the writer's buttocks inscribed with the message "My heart belongs to Dreyfus." The "The Secret Veiled Lady" souvenir showed Dreyfus luxuriating on Devil's Island and used a rotating wheel and apertures to uncover additional images. In comic-strip fashion the prints "Histoire d'un Innocent" and "Histoire d'un Traître" disseminated their partisan versions of the Affair to children. Illustrated covers of books of cigarette papers, such as "The Bordereau Paper," ironically named after the document that convicted Dreyfus, reached a general audience.

Postcards, a new and appealing means of communication, proliferated and even became collectors' items. Images relating to the Affair were supplied by illustrators and photographers. The caricaturist Orens designed many cards, including "The Thermometer of Truth" and "The Jaurès-Dreyfus Cakewalk." Couturier, a Dreyfusard, created the highly successful series "History of a Crime," a group of eighteen postcards retelling the events with original drawings and text. In addition, thousands of personal greeting cards were sent to Dreyfus on Devil's Island and later to Rennes, and to his wife, Lucie, from supporters and well-wishers throughout Europe.

The development of photographic techniques resulted in the expansion of the camera's political and propagandistic roles. Images could now be reproduced easily and cheaply in the media. The photographer Gerschel took more than two hundred pictures of the Rennes trial that appeared in various publications; he also did portraits of Bernard Lazare and Colonel Picquart.

Photography was effectively used in the poster "Dreyfus is a Traitor," which linked an anti-Dreyfus text to images of five ministers of war. The Dreyfusards responded immediately with their poster "Dreyfus is Innocent," featuring photographs of eleven prominent men affirming, in the accompanying text, Dreyfus's innocence. Testifying to the tremendous influence and potential of the camera, the Dreyfusard newspaper, *Le Siècle,* published in 1899 "The Lies of Photography," displaying fictive composite portraits, in order to warn the public of the danger and ease of falsifying photographs.

Perhaps the most ambitious posters constituted V. Lenepveu's "Musée des Horreurs," a series of fifty-one political hand-colored lithographs defaming prominent statesmen, journalists, Dreyfusards, and Jews. The prints appeared weekly in Paris starting in the fall of 1899, after the retrial in Rennes, and were stopped by an order of the Ministry of the Interior about one year later. Lenepveu succeeded in these visual character assassinations by attaching peculiar animal bodies to naturalistically rendered faces.

(Note: Objects in this section are arranged by type, rather than by artist.)

344. E. Charaire *Dreyfus is a Traitor*
(Dreyfus est un traître)
1898
Photomechanical print
61 × 35cm
Archives Nationales
Plate 105

345. E. Charaire, *Dreyfus is Innocent*
(Dreyfus est innocent)
1898
Photographic poster
61 × 35cm
Boston Public Library
Plate 106

346. "The Lies of Photography"
(Les Mensonges de la photographie)
Le Siècle
11 January 1899
Photomechanical print
73 × 41.5cm
Robert Maguire
Plate 107

347. *The History of an Innocent*
(Histoire d'un innocent)
Photomechanical print
Boston Public Library Print Department
Plate 73

348. *The History of a Traitor*
(Histoire d'un traître)
Photomechanical print
59.5 × 44cm
Philadelphia Museum of Judaica at Congregation Rodeph Shalom
Plate 74

349. Clerac, *The Life of Zola* (La Vie de Zola)
13 February 1898
Photomechanical print
38 × 28cm
Musée Carnavalet

350. C. Storel, *International Picture Alphabet* (Internationales Bildes A-B-C)
16 April (?)
Photomechanical print
Musée Carnavalet

351. V. Lenepveu, *Museum of Horrors: 1.* "Jew-ball" [Joseph Reinach] (*Musée des Horreurs: 1.* "Boule de Juif")
Poster
Hand-colored lithographic poster
64.5 × 49cm
The Houghton Library, Harvard University

352. V. Lenepveu, *Museum of Horrors: 2,* "Only One-eye. The Blackmailing Banker" [Baron Alphonse de Rothschild] (Musée des Horreurs: 2. "N'a qu'un oeil. Banquier brocanteur")
Hand-colored lithographic poster
65 × 49cm
The Houghton Library, Harvard University

353. V. Lenepveu, *Museum of Horrors*: 3. "Into the Kennel" [Louis Lépine] (Musée des Horreurs: 3. "A la Niche")
Hand-colored lithographic poster
64.5 × 49cm
The Jewish Museum

354. V. Lenepveu, *Museum of Horrors*: 4. "The King of Pigs" [Zola] (Musée des Horreurs: 4. "Le Roi des Porcs")
Hand-colored lithographic poster
64.5 × 49cm
The Jewish Museum
Plate 169

355. V. Lenepveu, *Museum of Horrors*: 5. "Bullet Hole" [Labori] (Musée des Horreurs: 5. "Trou de Balle")
Hand-colored lithographic poster
64.5 × 49cm
The Jewish Museum
Plate 170

356. V. Lenepveu, *Museum of Horrors*: 6. "The Traitor" [Dreyfus] (Musée des Horreurs: 6. "Le Traître")
Hand-colored lithographic poster
64.5 × 49cm
The Jewish Museum
Plate 171

357. V. Lenepveu, *Museum of Horrors*: 7. "Donkey Head" [Zadoc-Kahn] (Musée des Horreurs: 7. "Kabosch d'Ane")
Hand-colored lithographic poster
64.5 × 49.5cm
The Houghton Library, Harvard University

358. V. Lenepveu, *Museum of Horrors*: 8. "Georgette" [Picquart] (Musée des Horreurs: 8. "Georgette")
Hand-colored lithographic poster
64.5 × 49.5cm
The Houghton Library, Harvard University

359. V. Lenepveu, *Museum of Horrors*: 10. "Cornelius Herz's Old Chum" [Georges Clemenceau] (Musée des Horreurs: 10. "L'ex-copain de Cornelius Herz")
Hand-colored lithographic poster
64.5 × 49.5cm
The Houghton Library, Harvard University

360. V. Lenepveu, *Museum of Horrors*: 11. "The White Lady" [Séverine] (Musée des Horreurs: 11. "La Dame blanche")
Hand-colored lithographic poster
65 × 50cm
The Houghton Library, Harvard University
Plate 172

361. V. Lenepveu, *Museum of Horrors*: 12. "His Filthiness" [Henri Moret] (Musée des Horreurs: 12. "Crassus")
Hand-colored lithographic poster
64.5 × 49cm
The Jewish Museum

362. V. Lenepveu, *Museum of Horrors*: 14. "The Elephant of Jordan" [Jean Jaurès] (Musée des Horreurs: 14. "L'Eléphant du Jourdain")
Hand-colored lithographic poster
64.5 × 49.5cm
The Houghton Library, Harvard University
Plate 173

363. V. Lenepveu, *Museum of Horrors*: 17. "How One Succeeds" [Gaston Auguste Marquis de Galliffet"] (Musée des Horreurs: 17. "Comment on arrive")
Hand-colored lithographic poster
65 × 49cm
The Houghton Library, Harvard University

364. V. Lenepveu, *Museum of Horrors*: 20. [Emile Loubet] (Musée des Horreurs: 20. "Boum boum! madame!!")
Hand-colored lithographic poster
65 × 50cm
The Houghton Library, Harvard University

365. V. Lenepveu, *Museum of Horrors*: *26*. "A Ball at the Elysée" [Emile Loubet, Dreyfus, Zola, Reinach, Picquart, Zadoc Kahn] (Musée des Horreurs: 26. "Un Bal à l'Elysée")
Hand-colored lithographic poster
65 × 49cm
The Houghton Library, Harvard University
Plate 174

366. V. Lenepveu, *Museum of Horrors*: *29*. "Give This to Dreyfus" [Yves Guyot] (Musée des Horreurs: 29. "Porte ça à Dreyfus!")
Hand-colored lithographic poster
65 × 49cm
The Houghton Library, Harvard University
Plate 175

367. V. Lenepveu, *Museum of Horrors*: *30*. "The Punishment" [Emile Loubet] (Musée des Horreurs: 30. "Le Châtiment")
Hand-colored lithographic poster
64 × 49cm
The Houghton Library, Harvard University

368. V. Lenepveu, *Museum of Horrors*: *33*. "Going to Break" [Pierre Waldeck-Rousseau] (Musée des Horreurs: 33. "En train de crever")
Hand-colored lithographic poster
65 × 49cm
The Houghton Library, Harvard University

369. V. Lenepveu, *Museum of Horrors*: *34*. "Let the Ruckus Begin" [Joseph Reinach] (Musée des Horreurs: 34. "Que le chambardement commence!!")
Hand-colored lithographic poster
64.5 × 49cm
The Houghton Library, Harvard University
Plate 176

370. V. Lenepveu, *Museum of Horrors*: *35*. "The People's Amnesty" [Dreyfus] (Musée des Horreurs: 35. "Amnistie populaire!")
Hand-colored lithographic poster
65 × 50cm
The Houghton Library, Harvard University

371. V. Lenepveu, *Museum of Horrors*: *42*. "Nathan Mayer or the Origin of Billions" [Nathan Mayer Rothschild] (Musée des Horreurs: 42. "Nathan Mayer ou l'origine des milliards")
Hand-colored lithographic poster
65 × 49.5cm
The Houghton Library, Harvard University
Plate 177

372. V. Lenepveu, *Museum of Horrors*: *51*. "The Breton Clown" (Musée des Horreurs: 51. "Le Polichinelle Breton")
Hand-colored lithographic poster
64 × 49cm
The Houghton Library, Harvard University

373. Adrien Barrère (1877–1931), *Paul Déroulède* (as fetus in biological specimen container)
Terra cotta figurine in mold-blown glass
32 × 6.5cm
Musée Municipal René Sordes, Suresnes

374. Barrère, *Salomon Reinach* (as fetus in biological specimen container)
Terra cotta figurine in mold-blown glass
18 × 9cm
Musée Municipal René Sordes, Suresnes

375. Barrère, *Henri Rochefort* (as fetus in biological specimen container)
Terra cotta figurine in mold-blown glass
25 × 8cm
Musée Municipal René Sourdes, Suresnes

376. Barrère, *Waldeck-Rousseau* (as fetus in biological specimen container)
Terra cotta figurine in mold-blown glass
25 × 11cm
Musée Municipal René Sourdes, Suresnes

377. *The Secret of the Veiled Lady*
(Le Secret de la dame voilée)
Photomechanically printed novelty
14 × 9.7cm
Boston Public Library
Plate 67

377a. *Poor Joseph*
(Pauvre Chausef)
Photomechanically printed novelty
Boston Public Library

378. *Zola-Mouquette,* "My Heart for
Dreyfus" (Zola-Mouquette, "Mon
Coeur à Dreyfus")
Photomechanically printed novelty
20 × 9cm
Musée Carnavalet
Plate 66

379. *Zola-Mouquette*
January 1898
Photomechanically printed novelty
20 × 9cm
Collection of J. Robert Maguire
Plate 66

380. *The Last Judgment—Dreyfus
Hanged "Ah! The dirty beast!"* (Le
Jugement dernier—Dreyfus pendu
"Ah! La sale bête!")
Novelty
Photomechanical print on paper
with metal
15 × 8cm
Musée Carnavalet

381. Léon Hayard, *Jugement dernier
du syndicat*
Photomechanically printed novelty
21 × 10cm
Collection of J. Robert Maguire

382. *Zola Dropped in the Shit* (Zola
dans la me . . . lasse)
Paper novelty
17.2 × 12.2cm
Collection of J. Robert Maguire

383. *The Game of the Return of
Dreyfus* (Jeu de Bolles)
Novelty
25.5 × 16.5 × 1.5cm
Musée Municipal René Sordes,
Suresnes

384. A. Lambot, "*The Game of 36
Heads*" (Jeu de 36 têtes)
Published in *L'Antijuif,* 12 February
1899
Photomechanically printed novelty
44 × 61cm
The Houghton Library, Harvard
University
Plate 72

385. *Rules of the Game of the Dreyfus
Affair and of Truth* (Règle du Jeu de
l'Affaire Dreyfus et de la Vérité)
Novelty
43.2 × 59.4cm
Collection of Mr. and Mrs.
Ronald Bouscher
Plate 71

386. Souvenir Buttons, Dreyfus &
Picquart
1.5cm each
Musée Municipal René Sordes,
Suresnes

387. *The Zola Affair: Portrait of the
Principal Witnesses* (L'Affaire Zola:
Portrait des principaux temoins)
Pleated fan
Printed paper, collage
40 × 75cm
Musée Carnavalet
Fig. 10, Kleeblatt

388. *The Dreyfus Affair: Pictures from
France and Abroad* (L'Affaire Dreyfus:
L'image en France et à l'étranger)
Pleated fan
Printed paper, collage
40 × 75cm
Musée Carnavalet

389. *The Dreyfus Affair: At Rennes*
(L'Affaire Dreyfus: A Rennes)
Pleated fan
Printed paper, collage
40 × 75cm
Musée Carnavalet
Fig. 11, Kleeblatt

390. *The Dreyfus Affair: The Proscrip-
tion; Reading of the Sentence* (L'Affaire
Dreyfus: La dictée; lecture de la sen-
tence)
Pleated fan
Printed paper, collage
40 × 75cm
Musée Carnavalet

391. *The Dreyfus Affair: The Rennes Trial* (L'Affaire Dreyfus: Le procès de Rennes)
Pleated fan
Printed paper, collage
40 × 75cm
Musée Carnavalet

392. Embroidered Mat with depictions of Dreyfus, Zola, Picquart
Embroidered cotton
38 × 50cm
Collection of Ben Apfelbaum

393. *Box of Cigarettes* (Boîte des Cigarettes russe)
Paper box
8.5 × 4 × .5cm
Musée Municipal René Sordes, Suresnes

394. *The Bordereau Paper—"At the Cherche-midi"* [prison] (Le Papier du bordereau—"Au cherche midi")
Cigarette paper
7.5 × 4.5cm
Musée Carnavalet
Plate 68

395. *The Bordereau Paper—"On Devil's Island"* (Le Papier du bordereau—"A l'île du diable")
Cigarette paper
7.5 × 4.5cm
Musée Carnavalet
Plate 70

396. *The Bordereau Paper—"At the Court of Appeals"* (Le Papier du bordereau—"A la cour de cassation")
Cigarette paper
7.5 × 4.5cm
Musée Carnavalet
Plate 69

397. Charles Huard (1874–1965), *ch Dreyfus, Reinach et cie.* (Dreyfus, Reinach and co.)
Photomechanically, printed songsheet
28 × 35.5cm
Boston Public Library
Fig. 8, Marrus

398. *La Sans Patrie*
Photomechanically printed songsheet
28 × 36cm
The Houghton Library, Harvard University

399. *L'Affaire*
Photomechanically printed songsheet
The Houghton Library, Harvard University

400. *Emile Courtet, "The Qualities of a Jew after Gall's Method"* (Les Qualités de Juif, d'après Gall)
La Libre Parole Illustré
23 December 1893
Photomechanical print
38 × 28.5cm
The Jewish Museum

401. Alfred Le Petit, *Dreyfus Assessed According to his Skull and Physiognomy* (Dreyfus juge par son crâne et par sa physiognomie)
c. 1898–1899
Ink on paper
25.5 × 16.5cm
Artine Artinian Collection

402. Emile Courtet, *Free Gift from La Libre Parole* (Prime Gratuite offerte par *La Libre Parole*)
Poster
45 × 30cm
The Houghton Library, Harvard University

403. Couturier, *You Want Some Confessions?* (En voulez-vous des aveux?)
1899
Photomechanical print
34 × 24.5cm
Bibliothèque Nationale
Plate 41

404. *France Stirs* (La France bouge)
Photomechanical print
28 × 38cm
The Houghton Library, Harvard University

405. *The Reply of All the French People to Emile Zola* (Le Réponse de tous les Français à Emile Zola)
1898
Printed pamphlet
28 × 19.5cm
Collection of J. Robert Maguire

406. *The Circumcision of Rochefort* (Le Circoncision de Rochefort)
Photomechanical print
40 × 28cm
The Jewish Museum, Gift of Mr. and Mrs. Herbert D. Schimmel
Plate 33

407. *Long Live the Army* (Vive l'armée)
Photomechanical print
40 × 29cm
Boston Public Library

408. Léon Hayard, publisher, *The Ramparts of Israel* (or the Twelve Apostles of Dreyfus) (Les Ramparts d'Israel [ou Les Douze Apôtres de Dreyfus])
Hand-colored lithographic poster
66 × 48cm
Collection of J. Robert Maguire

409. *Manifestation-National*
17 January 189(?)
Broadside
21 × 13cm
The Houghton Library, Harvard University

Postcards

One hundred and five postcards with photographs or caricatures of the protagonists; Couturier's series of eighteen cards, *Histoire d'un crime*; and expressions of support or Jewish New Year's greetings from France and foreign countries. Musée de Bretagne, Rennes, Plates 78–104 and 126–130

Orens, Album of twenty-six satirical postcards
The Dreyfus family, Paris
Bob, Album of twenty-five satirical postcards
The Dreyfus family, Paris
Orens, Five crayon studies for postcards
J. Robert Maguire
Anniversary card with notation regarding Alfred Dreyfus
Ben Apfelbaum
Truth Emerging from the Well
Suite of postcards
Mr. and Mrs. Ronald Bouscher, Amsterdam
Jewish New Year's card depicting Alfred Dreyfus
The Houghton Library, Harvard University

The Protagonists

410. Bary, *Reinach*
Photograph
16 × 11cm
The Houghton Library, Harvard University

411. Bary, *Drumont*
Photograph
16 × 11cm
The Houghton Library, Harvard University

412. Buizard, *Esterhazy*
Photograph
16 × 11cm
The Houghton Library, Harvard University

413. Ladrey Disderi, *Méline*
Photograph
16 × 11cm
The Houghton Library, Harvard University

414. Gerschel, *Picquart*
Photograph
16 × 11cm
The Houghton Library, Harvard University

415. Gerschel, *Lazare*
Photograph
16 × 11cm
The Houghton Library, Harvard University

416. Gerschel-Paris, *Dreyfus*
Photograph
16 × 11cm
The Houghton Library, Harvard University

417. Nadar, *Zola*
Photograph
16 × 11cm
The Houghton Library, Harvard University

418. Nadar, *Bertillon*
Photograph
16 × 11cm
The Houghton Library, Harvard University

419. A. Naviel, *Labori*
Photograph
16 × 11cm
The Houghton Library, Harvard
University

420. Neyroud, *Mme. Henry*
Photograph
13 × 18cm
The Houghton Library, Harvard
University

421. Paris-Neyroud, *Henry*
Photograph
16 × 11cm
The Houghton Library, Harvard
University

422. Eugène Pirou, *Demange*
Photograph
16 × 11cm
The Houghton Library, Harvard
University

423. Pirou, *Clemenceau*
Photograph
16 × 11cm
The Houghton Library, Harvard
University

424. Pirou, *Boisdeffre*
Photograph
16 × 11cm
The Houghton Library, Harvard
University

425. Pirou, *Scheurer-Kestner*
Photograph
16 × 11cm
The Houghton Library, Harvard
University

426. Satorny, *Rochefort*
Photograph
16 × 11cm
The Houghton Library, Harvard
University

427. Vierne Vetel, *Mercier*
Photograph
16 × 11cm
The Houghton Library, Harvard
University

The Expression of World Support

428. *Testimonial of the Highest Esteem
to Capt. and Mme. Dreyfus*
(Temoignage de haute estime au
Capt. and Mme. Dreyfus)
August 1899
Delft, tin-glazed earthenware
39 × 57cm
Collection of Simone Perl

429. Dreyfus Family Thank You
Card
Engraved paper
7.5 × 11.5cm
Musée de Bretagne
Plate 131

430. Prince Constantin S. Karadja
Letter, 10 August 1906
Collection of Simone Perl

431. Prince of Monaco
Letter, July 1906
The Dreyfus Family

432. Lady Stanley, Letter to Capt.
Dreyfus
22 September 1899
The Dreyfus Family

433. Twelve Letters to Capt. and
Mme. Dreyfus from supporters in
Rome, New York, Copenhagen,
Geneva, etc.
Autumn 1899
Musée de Bretagne

434. Marseille, "Hommages à Alfred
Dreyfus"
20 September 1900
Bound book with ink inscription
30 × 20cm
Collection of Simone Perl

435. Antwerp, *Autograph Album*
10 September 1899
Silver, tooled leather, ink on paper
The Dreyfus Family

436. "Hommage à Capt. et Mme.
Dreyfus"
Engraved paper
35.5 × 25.5cm
Musée de Bretagne

The Expression of Personal Conviction: "The Salon of the Intellectual"

Artistic Response. Although much of the polemical battle inspired by the Dreyfus Affair was made manifest in the periodicals, broadsides, posters, and ephemera hawked on the streets of Paris, artists, writers, and intellectuals expressed themselves in their own media. Works were created not to sway popular opinion but to declare a position—to make a personal statement about either the Affair itself or the ideological issues underlying it.

In the Salon des Artistes Français of 1898, Evenepoel's *Fête at the Invalides* was seen as a disparagement of the military. In the same salon, an allegorical reference to the Affair was made by Debat-Ponsan in his painting of Truth restrained by the Church and the Army. This work would have serious effects on the artist's friendships and career.

A different issue arose that year at the Salon de la Société Nationale, where Rodin's monument to Balzac had been rejected by its commissioners. Rodin, in turn, withdrew the work and refused funds raised by a group of avant-garde artists and intellectuals. Not wanting to politicize the work, he commented that too many friends of Zola had contributed.

The ideological warfare of the Dreyfus Affair was largely conducted by pen rather than by sword, as is demonstrated in Evenepoel's drawing of Clemenceau at his desk and Vallotton's painting of activist-critic Félix Fénéon in his office at the *Revue Blanche.*

Some artistic works focused on Joseph Reinach, who was, together with Zola, the major target of the caricaturists. A vase of 1901, *Sea Horses,* by the decorative artist Emile Gallé is dedicated to Joseph Reinach. It is one of several works by this artist in glass and in wood bearing inscriptions that express his strong support of revision. Lucien Lévy-Dhurmer also inscribed a sensitive pastel portrait of Reinach to his sitter, a personal friend. Anti-Dreyfusard Forain, who for many years treated the world of the dancer as a subject for social satire, included a plump, semiticized Reinach, in the unflattering guise of a debaucher, in a backstage scene at the ballet.

Artists offered their creations as tribute to the champions of their cause. The last work of Dreyfusard sculptor Dalou was his monument to Scheurer-Kestner for the Luxembourg Gardens. Conventional allegorical figures of Truth and Justice flank an obelisk that surmounts the Senator's portrait medallion. Samuel Hirszenberg, who would emigrate to Palestine in 1907, found his theme in the nascent Zionist movement, considered by many to stem from Herzl's coverage of Dreyfus's degradation in 1895. Hirszenberg's prize-winning work in the 1900 Paris World's Fair, *The Wandering Jew,* was hung inconspicuously in the Russian Pavilion.

The intense passions aroused by the Affair are visualized in the twelve lithographs entitled *Hommage des Artistes à Picquart,* published as a protest against the persecution of the officer who endangered himself in attempting to gain justice for Dreyfus. The artists who contributed to this album were members of a social radical group that included Bernard Lazare, the first of the intellectuals to propose revision. The images include traditional representations of Truth and Justice as well as the radical icon, the stonebreaker. The album contains over 30,000 signatures collected by six newspapers in late 1898 and early 1899. Among the signatories are Paul Signac, Claude Monet, Edouard Vuillard, Anatole France, and Victorien Sardou.

437. Jacques-Emile Blanche (1861–1942), *Portrait of Marcel Proust*
1892
Graphite on paper
26.5 × 18.5cm
Bibliothèque Nationale

438. Aimé-Jules Dalou (1838–1902), *Study for the Monument to Auguste Scheurer-Kestner*
1899–1900
Terra cotta and wire
20 × 11.5 × 10cm
The Ackland Art Museum
Plate 199

439. Dalou, *Truth Denied* (Vérité
méconnue)
c. 1895
Bronze
22 × 19 × 11cm
Allen Memorial Art Museum
Fig. 17, Kleeblatt

440. Edgar-Germaine-Hilaire Degas
(1834–1917), Sketches of Ludovic
Halévy
Crayon and charcoal
32 × 27cm
The Baltimore Museum of Art,
Nelson and Juanita Grief Gutman
Collection

441. Henri Evenepoel (1872–1899),
Fête aux Invalides
1898
Oil on canvas
80 × 120cm
Musées Royaux des Beaux-Arts de
Belgique
Plate 187

442. Evenepoel, *Portrait of
Clemenceau Writing*
1899
Chalk on paper
20 × 22cm
Musée Clemenceau
Fig. 14, Kleeblatt

443. Jean-Louis Forain (1852–1931),
In the Wings (Dans les coulisses)
1899
Oil on canvas
60.5 × 73.8cm
The Art Institute of Chicago,
Mr. and Mrs. Martin A. Ryerson
Collection
Plate 2

444. Forain, *The Barman* [Bard]: *The
Colonel's Drink* [Le Bardman: Le
Grog du Colonel)
Ink and wash on paper
28.5 × 36.5cm
Metropolitan Museum of Art, Gift
of A. E. Gallatin, 1922
Plate 193

445. Emile Gallé (1846–1904), *Elms*
(Des Ormes)
c. 1900
Blown glass; internal colors;
hammered; engraved; applications
24 × 15 × 10cm
Musée Municipal de Cognac, Gift of
James Boucher
Plate 197

446. Gallé, *Sea-Horses* (Les Hippocampes) [Dedicated to Joseph
Reinach]
1901
Blown glass; internal colors; applications; engraved
19cm
Musée des Arts Decoratifs, Bequest
of Joseph Reinach
Plate 196

447. Gallé, *Two-Tiered Table* (inscribed: "Sicut hortus semen germinat, sic Deus germinabit Justitiam" [Just as the garden brings
forth its seed, so God will bring
forth Justice])
Various woods, inlaid
81 × 90 × 64cm
Musée de l'Ecole de Nancy
Fig. 15, Kleeblatt

448. Jean-Jacques Henner (1829–
1905), *Study for The Levite of Ephraim
and his Dead Wife*
1895–1898
Oil on canvas
31 × 54cm
Musée Nationale Jean-Jacques
Henner
Plate 188

449. Henner, *Study for Truth*
c. 1898
Oil on cardboard
29 × 38cm
Musée Nationale Jean-Jacques
Henner

450. Samuel Hirszenberg (Polish,
1865–1908), *The Wandering Jew*
1899
Oil on canvas
343 × 292cm
The Israel Museum
Fig. 18, Kleeblatt

451. Ferdinand Hodler (Swiss, 1853–1918), *Study for Truth I*
1903
Watercolor, pencil, and india ink on paper
33.5 × 48cm
Private Collection, Geneva
Plate 200a

452. Hodler, *Study for Truth 1*
c. 1902
Pen and india ink on batiste paper
42.3 × 9.3cm
The Montreal Museum of Fine Arts, Gift of Mr. and Mrs. Michal Hornstein
Plate 200b

453. Hodler, *Study for Truth I*
c. 1902
Pen and red color on paper
34.6 × 6.9cm
The Montreal Museum of Fine Arts, Gift of Mr. and Mrs. Michal Hornstein
Plate 200c

454. Henri-Gabriel Ibels (1867–1936), *The Stroke of the Sponge* (Le Coup de l'Eponge)
Graphite and gouache on paper
31 × 24cm
Bibliothèque Nationale

455. Ibels, *The Stroke of the Sponge* (Le Coup de l'Eponge)
1900
Black chalk on tan transfer paper lined with mulberry paper
32 × 25cm
Collection of Mr. and Mrs. Herbert D. Schimmel
Plate 192

456. Scheurer-Kestner, Letter to Jean-Jacques Henner about *The Levite of Ephraim*
29 May 1898
Musée Nationale Jean-Jacques Henner

457. Paul Legrand (1860–?), "In Front of *The Dream* by Detaille"
1897
Oil on canvas
1.34 × 1.05cm
Musée des Beaux-Arts, Nantes
Plate 186

458. Lucien Lévy-Dhurmer (1865–1953), *Joseph Reinach*
1899
Pastel on paper
35.5 × 28cm
Bibliothèque Nationale

459. Aristide Maillol (1861–1944), *Movement Enchained* (Monument au Auguste Blanqui: l'Action enchainée), 3d state
1906–1907
Bronze
218.5 × 81 × 81cm
Collection of Bernard and Josephine Chaus
Plate 201

460. Edouard Debat-Ponsan (1847–1913), *Nec mergitur*
1898
Oil on canvas
240 × 155cm
Musée Municipal d'Amboise
Plate 189

461. Charles Paul Renouard (1845–1924), *The Court-Martial at Rennes* (Conseil de guerre de Rennes)
1899 (?)
Oil on canvas
61 × 51cm
Ordre des Avocats à la Cour de Paris

462. Auguste Rodin (1840–1917), *Monument to Balzac*
1897
Bronze
106 × 44.5 × 42cm
Metropolitan Museum of Art, Gift of B. Gerald Cantor Art Foundation
Plate 194

463. Rodin, *The Thinker*
1880
Bronze
37.5 × 20 × 28.9cm
Collection of B. Gerald Cantor
Plate 195

464. Félix Vallotton (1865–1925), *Félix Fénéon at the Revue Blanche*
1898
Oil on cardboard
52.5 × 106.5cm
Josefowitz Collection
Fig. 13, Kleeblatt

465. *The Artists' Homage to Picquart*
(Hommage des Artistes à Picquart)
Preface by Octave Mirbeau.

Louis Anquetin, *To Colonel
Picquart, 1 January 1899* (Au Colonel
Piquart, 1er janvier 1899)
Pierre-Emile Corneiller, *Homage
to Colonel Piquart* (Hommage au Col-
onel Piquart)
Adolphe Ernest Gumery, *To
Picquart, Awakener of Souls* (A
Picquart éveiller d'armes)
Hermann-Paul, *Untitled*
Maximilien Luce, *Don't Think of
your Sword; Take this Pickaxe* (Ne
regrettes pas ton épée; prends cette
pioche)
Lucien Perroudon, *Untitled*
Hippolyte Petitjean, *Untitled*
Georges Manzana Pissarro, *Untitled*
Louis Armond Rault, *Untitled*
Theo van Rysselberghe, *Untitled*
Joaquin Sunyer, *Untitled*
Félix Vallotton, *He is Innocent* (Il
est innocent)
1899
Portfolio of 12 lithographs
Each 35.6 × 25cm

Collection of Mr. and Mrs.
Herbert D. Schimmel
Plates 113–124

Degas-Halévy Schism

Among the former Impressionists, many of whom became Dreyfusards in the late 1890s, Degas stands as the paradigmatic anti-Dreyfusard and anti-Semite. Degas's friendship of many years with the librettist Ludovic Halévy ended abruptly in November 1897. In happier times, as an intimate of the household, Degas had depicted Ludovic Halévy and his sons (Elie and Daniel) numerous times, and he photographed himself with Madame Halévy, an informal assistant, during experiments with photography. By an odd coincidence, Alfred Dreyfus, in 1900, found himself in the same Swiss hotel as Degas. Knowing of Degas's antipathy, Dreyfus wrote to a friend: "if he comes to speak to me, I shall turn my back on him."

Degas had also had a close relationship with Ludovic's cousin, Geneviève Bizet Straus, the widow of Georges Bizet. He also broke with her because her salon had become the rallying point for Dreyfusard intellectuals. Her son, Jacques Bizet, joined with his friend Marcel Proust and his cousins Elie and Daniel Halévy to collect the signatures published as the "Manifesto of the Intellectuals."

466. Edgar-Germaine-Hilaire Degas
(1834–1917), *Ludovic Halévy Finds
Mme. Cardinal in the Dressing Room*
c. 1880–1883
Monotype, second of two
impressions
21.5 × 16cm
Smith College Museum of Art, Gift
of Selma Erving, 1927.

467. Degas, *Degas et Louise Halévy
sous la lampe*
Photograph
Collection of Henriette Guy-Loé and
Geneviève Noufflard

468. Elie Halévy, Letter to Bouglé
16 November 1897
Collection of Henriette Guy-Loé and
Geneviève Noufflard

469. *Madeleine Bizet, Paul Hervieu
and Mme. Straus Reading Journals*
1898
Photograph
9 × 12cm
Collection of Henriette Guy-Loé and
Geneviève Noufflard
Fig. 7, Kleeblatt

470. *Charles Haas, Mme. Straus,
Cavé, Ganderax*
Photograph
18 × 13cm
Collection of Henriette Guy-Loé and
Geneviève Noufflard

471. *Mme. Straus, Proust, and Friends*
Photograph
Collection of Henriette Guy-Loé and
Geneviève Noufflard
Fig. 3, Suleiman

472. *Mme. Straus, Mme. de Pier-
rebourg, Mme. André de Rothschild, et
al in a Drawing Room*
Photograph
18 × 24cm
Collection of Henriette Guy-Loé and
Geneviève Noufflard

473. *At Dieppe. Members of the Halévy, Lemoine and Blanche families with Edgar Degas*
Photograph
Collection of Henriette Guy-Loé and Geneviève Noufflard

474. *Degas, Mme. Straus, Cave, Ganderax*
Photograph
18 × 13cm
Collection of Henriette Guy-Loé and Geneviève Noufflard

475. *Reading the Newspapers at Sucy* (Halévy Family)
Photograph
Collection of Henriette Guy-Loé and Geneviève Noufflard

476. *Mme. Bizet-Straus*
Photograph
Collection of Henriette Guy-Loé and Geneviève Noufflard

477. Alfred Dreyfus, Letter
c. 1900
Collection of J. Robert Maguire

478. *Ludovic, Elie and Daniel Halévy at Zola's Funeral*
(Les trois messieurs Halévy a l'enterrement de Zola)
1902
Photograph
Collection of Henriette Guy-Loé and Geneviève Noufflard
Fig. 4, Suleiman

Men of Letters: Literature and Correspondence

In addition to artists who expressed their opinions on this *cause célèbre* in their art, others did so in literature and personal correspondence. During the course of the Affair, Monet wrote several letters to Zola praising his courage. Pissarro commented in his well-known letters to his son and in a congratulatory card sent to Zola the day after publication of "J'Accuse." Writers and musicians from other countries also spoke out during the Affair: Henry James wrote to his brother William of his distaste for France "*en décadence,*" and Edvard Grieg refused to tour France after Dreyfus's second conviction.

Senator Scheurer-Kestner wrote to his fellow Alsatian, Jean-Jacques Henner, complimenting him on his symbolic painting in the salon, *The Levite of Ephraim and His Dead Wife,* while lamenting over the course of events in the crucial spring of 1898.

The Dreyfus family had been sent thousands of letters by ordinary people, as well as by well-known artists and intellectuals, during the trial at Rennes. When rehabilitation finally came to Alfred Dreyfus in 1906, he also received congratulations from long-time supporters such as Anatole France, Sarah Bernhardt, poet Lugné-Poë, and the prince of Monaco.

The Affair permeated even fiction. Writers from Zola to Anatole France, as is so frequently the case in that medium, portrayed in their works the issues and events that were prominent in their personal lives. Proust's *Remembrance of Things Past* is the best-known literary expression of the power of the Affair in polarizing Parisian society. Roger Martin du Gard's novel *Jean Barois* actually stages some of the major occurrences of the Dreyfus Affair in its scenes, while Anatole France's *Penguin Island* uses allegory to satirically "veil" the Affair. Even though Romain Rolland's play *The Wolves* transposed the events of the Dreyfus Affair into the revolutionary era of the previous century, few Frenchmen failed to see the similarities to current events.

479. Sarah Bernhardt, Letter to Alfred Dreyfus
July 1906
The Dreyfus Family

480. Henri-Edmond Cross, Letter to Theo van Rysselberghe
Autumn 1899
Collection of Mr. and Mrs. Herbert D. Schimmel

482. Anatole France, Letter to Dreyfus
14 July 1906
18 × 13cm
The Dreyfus Family

483. Emile Gallé, Letter to unknown recipient
19 March 1898
Collection of Mr. and Mrs. Herbert D. Schimmel

484. Edvard Grieg, Letter: Refusal
to tour France during the Dreyfus
trial
12 September 1899
Collection of J. Robert Maguire

485. Henry James, Letter to
William James
2 April 1899
Houghton Library, Harvard
University

486. Joseph Joachim, Letter to
Mme. Labori
22 August 1899
Collection of J. Robert Maguire

487. Lugné-Poë, Letter to
Alfred Dreyfus
14 July 1906
Collection of Simone Perl

488. Octave Mirbeau, Letter to
Mme. Zola during Zola's exile
1898/1899
Collection of J. Robert Maguire

489. Claude Monet, Letter to Zola
24 February 1898
Bibliothèque Nationale

490. Monet, Letter to Zola
14 January 1898
Bibliothèque Nationale

491. Monet, Letter to Mme. Zola
3 March 1898
Collection of J. Robert Maguire

492. Monet, Letter to Mme. Zola
4 October 1902
Collection of J. Robert Maguire

493. Nadar, *Emile Zola*
Photograph with inscription to
Alfred Dreyfus
11 × 16cm
The Dreyfus Family

494. Camille Pissarro
14 January 1898
Bibliothèque Nationale

495. Marcel Proust, Telegram to
Labori
18 August 1899
The Houghton Library, Harvard
University

496. Vuillard, Letter to Vallotton
25 July 1898
15 × 25.5cm
Fonds Félix Vallotton

497. Maurice Barrès (1862–1923),
Ce que j'ai vu à Rennes
Paris: E. Sansot, 1904
The New York Public Library

498. Anatole France (1844–1924),
L'Anneau d'améthyste
Paris, 1898
The New York Public Library

499. France, *Funerailles d'Emile Zola;
discours prononce au cimetière
montmartre le cinq octobre 1902*
Paris: E. Pelletan, 1902
The New York Public Library

500. France, *L'Ile des pingouins*
Paris: Calmann-Levy, 1908
The New York Public Library

501. France, *Monsieur Bergeret à Paris*
Paris, 1900
The New York Public Library

502. Roger Martin du Gard (1881–
1958), *Jean Barois*
Paris: Gallimard, 1926
The New York Public Library

Bibliography

The literary production generated by the case of Alfred Dreyfus has been immense. Two bibliographic studies have already been devoted to the Affair (see Desachy and Lipschutz), and these, together with many of the works included below, under the heading *Affair,* contain a vast amount of material pertaining to the case and its ramifications in French and European society. The recent work of Jean-Denis Bredin (ibid.) is noteworthy as an essential reference for all future studies of the legal and wider aspects of the Affair and also for its detailed and lucid guide to sources and bibliography. The aim of the following list is to provide reference to further bodies of material and, more especially, to indicate those works that have been most useful to the editor and the research staff in their preparation of the present exhibition. The several essays contributed to the catalogue each cite sources relevant to the specializations of the respective scholars, but these are not necessarily duplicated in the bibliography following.

General

"Album Jaurès." Tome 11, *Musée Jaurès,* Castres, 1965.

Arendt, Hannah. *Antisemitism.* New York: Harcourt Brace and World, (1951) 1968.

Bernard, Marc, ed., et al. *Emile Zola in selbstzeugnissen und bilddokumenten.* Trans. Hansgeorg Maier. Hamburg: Rowohlt, 1959.

Byrnes, Robert Francis. *Antisemitism in Modern France.* New Brunswick, N.J.: Rutgers University Press, 1950.

Debray, Régis. *Teachers, Writers, Celebrities: The Intellectuals of Modern France.* Trans. David Macey. London: Verso, 1981. (First published as *Le Pouvoir intellectuel en France.* Paris: Editions Ramsay, 1979.)

Encyclopaedia Universalis. Paris, 1970.

Farmer, Paul. *France Reviews its Revolutionary Origins: Social Politics and Historical Opinion in the Third Republic.* New York: Octagon, 1963.

Feldman, Egal. *The Dreyfus Affair and the American Conscience, 1895–1906.* Detroit: Wayne State University Press, 1981.

Grande Dictionnaire encyclopaedique larousse. Paris, 1984.

Héritier, Jean. *Histoire de la troisième république.* 2 vols. Paris: Librairie de France, 1932–1933.

Hyman, Paula. *From Dreyfus to Vichy: The Remaking of French Jewry, 1906–1939.* New York: Columbia University Press, 1979.

Jackson, J. Hampden. *Clemenceau and the Third Republic.* London: English Universities Press, 1946.

Mannheim, Karl. *Ideology and Utopia: An Introduction to the Sociology of Knowledge.* Trans. Louis Wirth and Edward Shils. San Diego: Harcourt Brace Jovanovich, 1985. (Originally published in German as *Ideologie und Utopie,* 1929.)

Marrus, Michael R. *The Politics of Assimilation: The French Jewish Community at the Time of the Dreyfus Affair.* Oxford: Clarendon Press, (1971) 1980.

Martin, Benjamin F. *The Hypocrisy of Justice in the Belle Epoque.* Baton Rouge, La., 1984.

Mayeur, Jean-Marie, and Rebérioux, Madeleine. *The Third Republic from its Origins to the Great War, 1871–1914.* Trans. J. R. Foster. Cambridge: Cambridge University Press, 1984. (Originally published in French as *Les Débuts de la troisième république, 1871–1898* and *La République radicale? 1898–1914,* Paris, 1973, 1975.)

Painter, George D. *Marcel Proust: A Biography.* New York: Random House, (1959) 1978.

Palais des beaux-arts de la ville de Paris. Paris. "Georges Clemenceau, 1841–1929: Exposition du cinquantenaire," exh. cat. 15 November 1979–6 January 1980.

Marcel Proust: Selected Letters, 1880–1903. Garden City, N.Y.: Doubleday, 1983.

Richardson, Joanna. *Zola.* London: Weidenfeld and Nicolson, 1978.

Rutkoff, Peter M. *Revanche and Revision: The Ligue des Patriotes and the Origins of the Radical Right in France, 1881–1900.* Athens, Ohio, and London: Ohio University Press, 1981.

Siegel, Jerrold E. *Bohemian Paris: Culture, Politics, and the Boundaries of Bourgeois Life, 1830–1930.* New York: Viking Penguin, (1986) 1987.

Soucy, Robert. *Fascism in France: The Case of Maurice Barrès.* Berkeley, Los Angeles, London: University of California Press, 1972.

Thompson, Kenneth. *Beliefs and Ideology.* Chichester and London: Ellis Horwood and Tavistock Publications, 1986.

Thomson, David. *Democracy in France: The Third and Fourth Republics.* 3d ed. London: Oxford University Press, (1946) 1958.

Tilly, Charles. *The Contentious French.* Cambridge, Mass.: Belknap, 1986.

Tuchman, Barbara W. *The Proud Tower: A Portrait of the World before the War, 1890–1914.* New York: Macmillan, 1966.

Vizetelly, Ernest Alfred. *Emile Zola, Novelist and Reformer, An Account of His Life and Work* (1904). Reprinted Freeport, N.Y.: Books for Libraries Press, 1971.

Weber, Eugen. *France: Fin de siècle.* Cambridge, Mass., and London: Belknap, 1986.

Wilson, Stephen. *Ideology and Experience: Anti-semitism in France at the Time of the Dreyfus Affair.* London and Toronto: Associated University Presses, 1982.

Winock, Michel. *Edouard Drumont et cie.: Anti-sémitisme et fascisme en France.* Paris: Editions du Seuil, 1982.

Zeldin, Theodore. *France, 1848–1945.* 2 vols. Oxford: Oxford University Press, 1977.

Zola, Emile. *Oeuvres complètes.* Vol. 14. Ed. Henri Mitterand. Paris: Cercle du livre précieux, 1970.

The Affair

Bredin, Jean-Denis. *The Affair: The Case of Alfred Dreyfus.* Trans. Jeffrey Mehlman. New York: Braziller, 1986. (First published as *L'Affaire,* 1983.)

Chapman, Guy. *The Dreyfus Case: A Reassessment.* New York, 1955.

Cherasse, Jean A., and Boussel, Patrice. *Dreyfus, ou l'intolérable vérité.* Paris: Editions Pygmalion, 1975.

Delhorbe, Cécile. *L'Affaire Dreyfus et les écrivains français.* Neuchâtel and Paris: Editions Victor Attinger, 1932.

Desachy, Paul. *Bibliographie de l'affaire Dreyfus.* Paris: Edouard Cornély, 1905.

Dreyfus, Alfred. *Cinq Années de ma vie.* Paris: Maspero, 1982.

Dreyfus, Pierre. *Dreyfus: His Life and Letters.* Trans. Betty Morgan. London: Hutchinson, 1937.

Halasz, Nicholas. *Captain Dreyfus: The Story of a Mass-Hysteria.* New York: Simon and Schuster, 1955.

Herzog, Wilhelm. *Der Kampf einer Republik: Die Affäre Dreyfus, Dokumente und Tatsachen.* Zürich: Europa Verlag, 1932.

Hoffman, Robert Louis. *More than a Trial: The Struggle over Captain Dreyfus.* New York: The Free Press, 1980.

Johnson, Douglas. *France and the Dreyfus Affair.* London: Blandford Press, 1966.

Kedward, H. R. *The Dreyfus Affair: Catalyst for Tensions in French Society.* London: Longmans, Green and Co., 1965.

Knobel, Marc. *La Réhabilitation du Capitaine Alfred Dreyfus?* (*1898–1945*). Mémoire de Maîtrise, Université de Paris, Institut d'histoire des relationes internationales contemporaines, 1982–1983.

La France de l'affaire à nos jours. Paris: Bibliothèque du Centre de documentation juive contemporaine, 1964.

Lewis, David L. *Prisoners of Honor: The Dreyfus Affair.* New York: William Morrow and Company, 1973.

Lipschutz, Léon. *Une Bibliothèque Dreyfusienne, essai de bibliographie thématique et analytique de l'affaire Dreyfus.* Paris: Editions Fasquelle, 1970.

Miquel, Pierre. *L'Affaire Dreyfus*. Paris: Presses Universitaires de France, 1959.

Paléologue, Maurice. *An Intimate Journal of the Dreyfus Case*. Trans. Eric Mosbacher. New York: Criterion Books, 1957.

Reinach, Joseph. *Histoire de l'Affaire Dreyfus*. 7 vols. Paris: La Revue Blanche, 1901–1911. Reprinted Paris: Fasquelle, 1929.

Snyder, Louis L. *The Dreyfus Case: A Documentary History*. New Brunswick: Rutgers University Press, 1973.

Zola, Emile. *L'Affaire Dreyfus: La Vérité en marche*. Paris: Charpentier, 1901.

Print Media, Photography, the Press and Caricature

Bellanger, Claude, et al., eds. *Histoire générale de la presse française, vol. 3. de 1871 à 1940*. Paris: Presses Universitaires de France, 1972.

Beraldi, Henri. *Les Graveurs du dix-neuvième siècle*. Paris, 1886.

Bottomore, Stephen. "Dreyfus and Documentary." *Sight and Sound,* Autumn 1984: 290–293.

Bibliothèque Nationale, Paris. "Le Dessin d'humour du quinzième siècle à nos jours," exh. cat., 1971.

Boussel, Patrice. *L'Affaire Dreyfus et la presse*. Paris: A. Colin, 1960.

Brisson, Adolphe. *Nos Humoristes*. Paris: Librairie Georges Baranger, 1900.

Deberdt, Raoul. *La Caricature et l'humour français au neuvième siècle*. Paris: Librairie Larousse, 1898.

Dreyfus-Bilderbuch, Karikaturen Aller Völker über die Dreyfus-affaire. Berlin: Dr. Eysler and Co., 1899.

Duché, Jean. *1760–1960: Deux Siècles d'histoire de France par la caricature*. Paris: Editions du Pont-Royal, 1961.

English, Donald E. *Political Uses of Photography in the Third French Republic, 1871–1914*. Ann Arbor, Mich.: UMI Research Press, 1984. (Revised edition of Ph.D. thesis, University of Washington, 1981.)

Feaver, William, and Gould, Ann. *Masters of Caricature, from Hogarth and Gillray to Scarfe and Levine*. New York: Knopf, 1981.

Fuchs, Eduard. *Die Juden in der Karikatur: Ein Beitrag zur Kulturgeschichte*. Munich: Albert Langen, 1921.

Gaultier, Paul. *Le Rire et la caricature*. 2d ed. Paris: Librairie Hachette, 1906.

Grand-Carteret, John. *Zola en images*. Paris: Felix Juven, 1908.

———. *L'Affaire Dreyfus et l'image*. Paris: Flammarion, [n.d.].

Granoux, Xavier, and Fontane, Charles. *"L'Affaire Dreyfus": Catalogue descriptif des cartes postales illustrées, françaises et étrangères, parues depuis 1894*. Paris: Daragon, 1903.

Lambert, Susan. "The Franco-Prussian War and the Commune in Caricature, 1870–1871," exh. cat. *Victoria and Albert Museum*. London, 1971.

Lethève, Jacques. *La Caricature et la presse sous la troisième république*. Paris: Armand Colin, 1961.

Luckhardt, Ulrich; Sonnabend, Martin; and Timm, Regine. "Lyonel Feininger: Karikaturen, Comic Strips, Illustrationen, 1888–1915," exh. cat. *Museum für Kunst und Gewerbe*. Hamburg, 1981.

McCauley, Elizabeth Anne. *A. A. E. Disderi and the Carte de Visite Portrait Photograph*. New Haven and London: Yale University Press, 1985.

Malhotra, Ruth. *Horror-Galerie: Ein Bestiarium der dritten französischen Republik*. Dortmund: Harenberg, 1980.

Musée Carnavalet, Paris. "Journal Universel, L'Illustration: un siècle de vie française," exh. cat. 27 January–26 April 1987.

Rogès, Louis. *L'Affaire Dreyfus: Cinq Semaines à Rennes*. Paris: F. Juven, [n.d., 1899?].

Scheyer, Ernst. *Lyonel Feininger: Caricatures and Fantasy*. Detroit: Wayne State University Press, 1964.

Shikes, Ralph E., and Heller, Steven. *The Art of Satire. Painters as Caricaturists and Cartoonists from Delacroix to Picasso*. New York: Pratt Graphics Center and Horizon Press, 1984.

Terrasse, Antoine. *Degas et la Photographie*. Paris: Denoël, 1983.

Veyrat, Georges. *La Caricature à travers les siècles*. Paris: Charles Mendel, 1895.

Art and Artists

Alexandre, Arsène. *Jean-François Raffaëlli: Peintre, Graveur et sculpteur.* Paris: H. Floury, 1909.

Allentown Art Museum, Allentown, Pa. "Eugenè Carrière, 1849–1906: Seer of the Real," exh. cat. 2 November 1968–26 January 1969. Introduction by Richard Teller Hirsch.

Argencourt, Louise d', and Druick, Douglas, eds. *The Other Nineteenth Century: Paintings and Sculpture in the Collection of Mr. and Mrs. Joseph M. Tannenbaum.* Ottawa: The National Gallery of Canada, 1978.

Bantens, Robert James. *Eugenè Carrière: His Work and his Influence.* Ann Arbor, Mich.: UMI Research Press, 1983. (Revised edition of Ph.D. thesis, Penn State University, Pa., 1975.)

Bénézit, Emmanuel. *Dictionnaire critique et documentaire des peintres, sculpteurs, dessinateurs et graveurs de tous les temps et de tous les pays par un groupe d'écrivains spécialistes français et étrangers.* 10 vols. (1911). Revised ed. Paris: Librairie Gründ, 1976.

Blanche, Jacques-Emile. *Portraits of a Lifetime, 1870–1914.* New York: Coward-McCann, 1938.

Boggs, Jean Sutherland. *Portraits by Degas.* Berkeley and Los Angeles: University of California Press, 1962.

Bourgeois, Léon. *L'Oeuvre de Roll.* Paris: J.-E. Bulloz, 1908.

Brettell, Richard, and Lloyd, Christopher. *A Catalogue of the Drawings by Camille Pissarro in the Ashmolean Museum, Oxford.* Oxford: Clarendon Press, 1980.

Brüschweiler, Jura. *Eine unbekannte Hodlersammlung aus Sarajevo.* Bern: Benteli, 1978.

Cate, Phillip Dennis, and Gill, Susan. *Théophile-Alexandre Steinlen.* Salt Lake City: Gibbs M. Smith, Inc., 1982.

Cate, Phillip Dennis, and Boyer, Patricia Eckert. "The Circle of Toulouse-Lautrec: An Exhibition of the Work of the Artist and of His Close Associates," exh. cat. *The Jane Voorhees Zimmerli Art Museum,* Rutgers University, New Brunswick, N.J., 17 November–2 February 1986.

Clark, T. J. *The Painting of Modern Life: Paris in the Art of Manet and his Followers.* New York: Knopf, 1985.

Dauberville, Jean, and Dauberville, Henry. *Bonnard: Catalogue raisonné de l'oeuvre peint.* Paris: Editions J. et H. Bernheim Jeune, 1965.

Delteil, Löys. *Le Peintre-graveur illustré.* 31 vols. Paris: Delteil, 1906–1930.

Fourcaud, Louis Boussef de. *L'Oeuvre de Alfred Philippe Roll.* Paris: Armand Gureinet for the Musées Nationaux, 1896.

Halévy, Daniel. *My Friend Degas.* Middletown, Conn.: Wesleyan University Press, 1964. Trans. and ed. Mina Curtiss. (First published as *Degas parle. . . .* Paris: La Palatine, 1960.)

Hayward Gallery, London. "Pissarro," exh. cat. 1980–1981.

Herbert, Eugenia W. *The Artist and Social Reform: France and Belgium 1885–1898.* New Haven: Yale University Press, 1961.

Herbert, Robert L., and Herbert, Eugenia. "Artists and Anarchism: Unpublished Letters of Pissarro, Signac and others." *Burlington Magazine* 102 (November 1960): 472–482.

Hess, Hans. *Lyonel Feininger.* New York: Harry N. Abrams, 1961.

Janis, Eugenia Parry. *Degas Monotypes.* Cambridge, Mass.: Fogg Art Museum, Harvard University, 1968.

Lambotte, Paul. *Henri Evenepoel.* Brussels: G. Van Oest, 1908.

Levin, Miriam R. *Republican Art and Ideology in Late Nineteenth-Century France.* Ann Arbor, Mich.: UMI Research Press, 1986. (Revised edition of Ph.D. thesis, University of Massachusetts, 1981.)

Mâlthète-Méliès, Madeleine, and Quevrain, Marie. "Georges Méliès et les arts. Etude sur les rapports avec les courants artistiques." *Artibus et historiae* 1 (1980): 133–144.

Memorial Art Gallery, University of Rochester. "Artists of La Revue Blanche: Bonnard, Toulouse-Lautrec, Vallotton, Vuillard," exh. cat. 1984.

Minervino, Fiorella. *Tout l'oeuvre peint de Degas.* Paris: Flammarion, 1974.

Musée du Luxembourg, Paris. "Gallé," exh. cat. 29 November 1985–2 February 1986. Catalogue by Françoise-Thérèse Charpentier and Philippe Thiebaut.

Musée du Petit Palais, Paris. "Ferdinand Hodler, 1853–1918," exh. cat. 11 May–24 July 1983. (Exhibition traveled from Berlin to Zurich.)

McMullen, Roy. *Degas: His Life, Times and Work.* Boston: Houghton Mifflin Company, 1984.

Pissarro, Camille. *Letters to his Son Lucien.* 4th ed. Ed. John Rewald. London and Henley: Routledge and Kegan Paul (1944), 1980.

Reff, Theodore. *Degas, The Artist's Mind.* New York: Metropolitan Museum of Art, 1976.

Ritchie, Andrew Carnduff. *Edouard Vuillard.* New York: The Museum of Modern Art, 1954.

Roger-Marx, Claude. *Vuillard: His Life and Work.* London: Elek, 1946.

Roger-Miles, L. *Alfred Roll.* Paris: A. Lahure, 1904.

Rosenblum, Robert, and Janson, H. W. *19th Century Art.* New York: Abrams, 1984.

Royal Academy of Arts, London. "Post-Impressionism: Cross-Currents in European Painting," exh. cat. 17 November 1979–16 March 1980.

Russell, John. *Edouard Vuillard, 1868–1940.* Toronto: Art Gallery of Ontario, 1971.

Seailles, Gabriel. *Eugene Carrière: Essai de biographie psychologique.* Paris: Librairie Armand Colin, 1922.

Seltzer, Alexander. *Anarchism, Anti-Semitism and the Press: A Critical Evaluation of Three Artists' Response to the Dreyfus Affair.* M.A. thesis, University of Cincinnati, 1972.

Shikes, Ralph E., and Harper, Paula. *Pissarro: His Life and Work.* New York: Horizon Press, 1980.

Terrasse, Antoine. *Pierre Bonnard.* Paris: Gallimard, 1967.

Thieme, Ulrich, and Becker, Felix, eds. *Allgemeines Lexikon der bildenden künstler von der antike bis zur gegenwart.* 37 vols. Leipzig: Seemann, 1912. Reprinted Zwickau: Ullmann, 1960.

Thomson, Richard. "Camille Pissarro, *Turpitudes Sociales* and the Universal Exhibition of 1889." *Arts* 56 (April 1982).

Weisberg, Gabriel P. "The Realist Tradition: French Painting and Drawing, 1830–1900," exh. cat. *The Cleveland Museum of Art,* Cleveland, Ohio, 1980.

White, Barbara Ehrlich. *Renoir: His Life, Art and Letters.* New York: Abrams, 1984.

Photo Credits

All illustrations other than those listed below are courtesy of the lender. References are to photographers, followed by essayist and figure number, or plate number.

Australian National Gallery, Canberra: pl. 190

Bibliothèque Nationale, Paris: Cate, fig. 6, 49; Nochlin, figs. 10, 11, pls. 61, 63, 64, 158

Beinecke Rare Book and Manuscript Library, Yale University: pl. 22

Foundation Calouste Gulbenkian, Lisbon: Nochlin, fig. 6

Harvard University Press: Nochlin, fig. 9

Susan Eve Jahoda: Burns, figs. 2, 4, 5, 7; Marrus, fig. 7, pls. 58, 59, 62, 73, 74, 153–157, 159–163, 178–181

Suzanne Kaufman: Hyman, figs. 4, 6, 7

Metropolitan Museum of Art: Cate, fig. 11

Musée Carnavalet, Paris: pl. 191

Musée d'Orsay, Paris: Nochlin, figs. 1, 5

Museo Picasso, Barcelona: pl. 198

Museum of Art, Rhode Island School of Design: Nochlin, fig. 8

Museum of Modern Art, Film Stills Archive: pl. 202

John Parnell: Cate, figs. 22, 37, 39–41, 44, 45, 50; Hyman, fig. 5; Kleeblatt, figs. 4, 6; Marrus, figs. 2, 5, 6; Martin, figs. 1, 2, 5, pls. 3–7, 9–12, 15–17, 20, 24, 26–30, 32, 33, 42–51, 56, 57, 108–125, 132–141, 150–152, 169–171, 182, 192

Jean-Luc Planté, Geneva: pl. 200a

Nathan Rabin: Cate, figs. 4, 5, 9, 10, 15–20; Kleeblatt, fig. 1; Nochlin, fig. 12, pl. 1

Réunion des Musées Nationaux: pls. 184–185

Erika Sanger: pl. 106

Studio Image, Nancy: figs. 15, 16

Victor's Photography: Cate, figs. 1–3, 7, 8, 12–14, 21, 23, 29, 31, 35, 36, 38, 42, 48, 51, 52; Kleeblatt, figs. 2, 3; Suleiman, fig. 1

Courtesy of Dina Vierny, Paris: pl. 201